On Reason

DUKE UNIVERSITY PRESS   Durham and London   2008

On Reason

RATIONALITY IN A WORLD OF

CULTURAL CONFLICT AND RACISM

EMMANUEL CHUKWUDI EZE

© 2008 Duke University Press

All rights reserved.

Printed in the United States of America

on acid-free paper ∞

Designed by C. H. Westmoreland

Typeset in Warnock Pro by Keystone

Typesetting, Inc.

Library of Congress Cataloging-in-

Publication Data appear on the last

printed page of this book.

PUBLISHER'S NOTE

On December 31, 2007, while this book was in production at Duke University Press, Emmanuel Chukwudi Eze died after a brief illness. Emmanuel was born in Agbokete in northern Nigeria, received his early education at Jesuit schools in the Congo, and earned his Ph.D. from Fordham University in 1993. He taught at Bucknell University from 1993 to 2000, when he joined the philosophy department at DePaul University. He was the founding editor of *Philosophia Africana* and published influential postcolonial histories of philosophy in Africa, Europe, and the Americas. He was a brilliant and provocative thinker as well as a compassionate human being. Duke University Press joins his family, friends, and colleagues in the academy in mourning his untimely loss.

Reynolds Smith
FOR THE PUBLISHER

FOR NNAMDI

our coming was expected

Contents

Preface:

What Is Rationality?

My intention in this book is quite modest. I would like to provide some descriptions and arguments in support of various conceptions of the nature of reason. Displaying a variety of points of view is necessary because whatever anyone may think of it, what we mean when we refer to a person as being rational in general, or having a reason for doing or believing something in particular, is not only complex but also, in more than the surface features, elusive, enigmatic, and mysterious. The processes of reasoning, like all processes of reflection or modes of consciousness, are not neatly laid out in a linear and determined way, as if the processes were highways or railroad tracks.

Arguments that reason is a substance perceived clearly and distinctly were popularized at the beginning of modern philosophy by René Descartes. But the intervening centuries—especially the last two—have not been particularly Cartesian. Many today consider most of Descartes's views on rationality excessively dogmatic. What I intend to do here, however, is beyond pointing out the errors of others or adjudicating centuries of argument. My goal is to assume the standpoint of twenty-first-century philosophical interests, then try to find the most viable and accessible languages in which to describe—as well as contribute some answers to—the questions: What is reason? What do we mean when we ascribe rational qualities to others, for example when John says that Jill has a reason for acting such and such? What does it mean to say about yourself that, when you did such and such, you were acting rationally?

These questions have been proposed and addressed by disciplines as diverse as artificial intelligence, logic, cognitive science, game and decision theory, law, psychology, medicine, and neurobiology.[1] Indeed, current publications on rationality, and research prospects in the related fields, are so extensive that it is doubtful that any single effort could adequately capture everything in the field. For this reason, instead of attempting a quantitative and exhaustive treatment of my questions, I will focus on the qualitative and exploratory.

This choice of method is, I believe, a virtue. The virtue derives from the nature of the subject matter: the characteristics of rationality itself. The nature of human rationality seems to require that the best way to define reason philosophically is by demonstration. The demonstration will require amassing empirical or scientific evidence for the rational, and reflecting on this concept of evidentiality. It is only from such demonstrative acts that we can explore what is at stake in the activity itself. It is my task therefore to render explicit—by reflective, exploratory analysis—that which is already implicitly comprehended in rational action. I will discuss what it means to have a reason to act, and will carry out the discussion from various levels of abstraction. First, I describe reasoning intuitively, in language that reveals rationality as a practical disposition; then I interpret and explain this disposition. I then provide a theoretical overview of the description, interpretation, and explanation of the disposition considered rational. This third and final theoretical standpoint is a discursive justification of my method as well as a justification for the structuring of the substantive issues in the previous levels of analysis. Each chapter of the book therefore follows—sometimes very elaborately, sometimes less so—this tripartite organization: description, interpretation and explanation, and justification.

To adequately comprehend what we are thinking when we say that someone is behaving rationally, and arrive at such comprehension from the legacies of multiple traditions in philosophy and from insights available in the nearby disciplines, requires complex levels of exploration.

PAIN

But, above all, it is my hope that, taken together, the various practical intuitions, interpretations and explanations, and justifications will constitute different examples of reasoning-in-action. These exemplars of rationality-in-act reveal the grounds of reason's abstract principles as well as the relations of these principles to practical interests of individuals, institutions, and cultures. I thereby hope to discover how to test not just the claims of individuals to rationality but also the rationality of cultural practices and other kinds of events that claim to be productive of reason. My methodology, indeed, provides proof of the truth of the statement *Anaghi akwu ofu èbé ènéné manwu*: Rationality, like a work of art, is best appreciated from multiple points of view.

If this outline of the questions and my method sound not only sketchy but also formal—in other words, abstract—that is because it is only at the most general levels that one best explores the answers to the question What is rationality? As evident in the beginning considerations, I take it that the key problems in explaining rationality are located in the empirical-descriptive tasks. But it is also true that it is only under some kind of generality that I can hope to shed light on the subsequent stages in the development of the many aspects of the question. To fail to recognize and address this uniquely multivalent character of the problem would amount to locking up my inquiry within a domain of the most narrowly empirical and applied. In the introduction, I explain in detail why such a narrow perspective is not a sound option. I also explain what we can expect from the methodological requirement of generalization.

NOT A THING

For now, it suffices to note this guiding idea: reason is not a thing—whether the notion of a thing is thought materially or nonmaterially. For although reasoning has empirical and objective groundings in the world of things, the idea of reason itself cannot be reduced to the same world of objects or events. One cannot locate the activity of reasoning as a point on a continuum between the objective practicality of worldly objects and the autonomous, generalizable character of subjectivity. In fact, this is the classic insight available to us not just from the philosophic traditions but also from the traditions of the empirical and the social sciences, some of which I discuss later on. It is also precisely the choice of the point of the rational, a choice on a continuum between concrete empiricities and general abstractness, that makes us characterize a methodological location of the concept of rationality as either positivistic or idealist. Nat-

PAIN

urally, each methodological position associates itself with substantive philosophical arguments. The arguments, in turn, are known to divide philosophers into camps, often pitting the members of one camp against the members of its neighbors. Thus, you might have the naturalist against the historicist, the empiricist against the idealist, the realist against the antirealist, the nominalist against the antinominalist, and so on.

From any philosophical position, however, it is very difficult not to think about rationality as a thing. For example, whether you consider yourself an empiricist or an idealist, an objectivist or a subjectivist, it is difficult to abstain from the temptation to believe that reason must somehow have a base—a base which, itself, must be founded upon something naturally, historically, or transcendentally immutable. Descartes's and Plato's negotiations of this well-known temptation are the most memorable. Plato and Descartes were, of course, different kinds of idealists. But both Platonism and Cartesianism share important cooperative as well as antagonistic historical relationships.

This book's arguments about rationality are neither Platonic nor Cartesian. In some ways, however, the positions advocated or displayed in my arguments, as approaches to descriptions of rationality, may echo both Plato's and Descartes's tendencies to abstraction and to generality. These similarities, however, cannot be stretched any further: they are echoes. For example, I will not argue for the existence of any of the doctrinal essences Plato or Descartes ascribed to rationality. Yes, I ascribe content-related normative structures—call these *figures* of thought—to my descriptions of practical, substantive contents of rationality. But these structures do not fall under the traditional conception of substance; they are thoroughly historical.

Similarly, the non-Platonic and non-Cartesian theories of rationality I propose may be capable of supporting the attribution of formal foundations to the procedures we call reasoning (as a content of experience) and judgment (as the framework of logical justification of experience). But this understanding of foundation and form is entirely historical; it is subject to experience, and therefore subject to culture and to society. The language of justification of these modes of experience and judgment—once we start to think of this language as a theory of rationality—can accurately be called a theory of the *conceptual everyday* or of the *conceptual vernacular.*

I arrived at these conclusions and the terminology after examining the works of many experimental psychologists who, since 1900, have tried to identify measurements of intelligence or identify where intelligence is located, but who have not made any more progress than their counterparts in philosophy.[2] In 1904 Charles Edward Spearman proposed a psychometric analytic for what he called the *g* factor. But even at that time, this supposedly general factor of intelligence was explicitly recognized by Spearman, as well as by his peers who reviewed the work, as a psychological construct.[3] Since these beginnings, significant progress has been made on the research questions in the cognitive sciences, including the works of Jean Piaget, Lawrence Kohlberg, and Carol Gilligan.[4] In recent decades, too, discoveries in genetic biology as well as in computing and artificial intelligence have shed much-needed light on the nature of human intelligence. But no one is surprised that continued talk about either the *g* factor or, more recently, the genetic aspects of intelligence have not provided experimentally reliable evidence that human reasoning is located in isolatable chemical elements in the human body.[5] The most promising approaches to the question of intelligence in the experimental sciences—like the parallel approaches to questions about logic, reasoning, and the mind in linguistics and philosophy— have remained not just empirically observational or technologically manipulative but also, phenomenologically speaking, experientially composed. They are the forms of everyday historical experience, at the most intuitive and reconstructive levels, which I attempt to capture as a field of philosophical investigation. In this book my conception of experience as the everyday or vernacular is more philosophically modest than anything you will find in classic phenomenology, especially with regard to phenomenology's transcendental posturings, and the resultant derogation of everyday cultures of the peoples of the world. By engaging but ultimately renouncing transcendental phenomenology, what I hope to gain is, literally, the world. When I spoke earlier about the possibility of investigating both the implicitly and explicitly conceptual vernaculars of rationality, I was speaking in reference to the task of philosophical analysis of experience in everyday cultures of everyday peoples.

In justifying my critical vernacular standpoint from the perspectives of other theories, there is no quicker way to proceed than to point out the difference it makes. I can start with an appeal to a recent statement by

Joseph Margolis. Speaking about his own views on the relationship between biology, society, and rationality, Margolis argues that "our culturally formed powers are 'potentiated'—no more than that—by our biology."[6] However, in speaking about "how and in what specific normative
regard" biology or other forms of life and nature constraints may be
attributed to "the range of our reflexive competence," we merely think—
we pretend, as Margolis puts it—to "judge from the vantage of biology."[7]
But what is wrong with this biological judgment? Not much, you might
say, except for the important fact that this is a *judgment*. I agree with
Margolis that biology-potentiated cultural powers are rationally subaltern to the capacity for judgment. Biology, conceptually speaking, sub-
tends language, society, tradition, and history.

It is within these larger and more extensive categories of experience,
what I have called the vernacular, that one is able to conceptually judge
not just right and wrong but also the characters of truth and untruth
with regard to claims of reason. This affirmation of experience in the
vernacular does not, in itself, deny the bodily constraints (physical, biological, and symbolic) to which humans are also subjected. But the affirmation is important as a moment of recognition, as Margolis writes
about biology, that "no reasonably imposed biological constraints are
ever so strictly defined that alternative, even irreconcilable, proposals
can be convincingly ruled out at the level of legitimating critique."[8]

In the chapters that follow, when I speak about the *rational*, I speak
both literally and metaphorically. I use the term to describe occurrences
or actions that might be observed in either natural or social worlds, but
always within reflectively legitimated—not merely naturalistic—frameworks. Likewise, because we enact *reasoning* in cognitive dispositions to
the world, in this book I use the word *reason* to stand for normatively
reconstructed descriptions of the complex processes of that cognitive
act. Furthermore, when I use the word *rationality*, I intend to capture
those ideal reconstructions of reason which are necessarily internally
and historically differentiated. I may speak, for example, about conceptions of rationality derived from observations of specifically embedded
human interactions with the natural world. I may speak about rationality
from the standpoint of observations of everyday demands for, and offer-
ings of, accounts of the self in intersubjective human relations. I may
speak about the rational in regard to judgments of qualities of my per-

ceptions of internal thoughts or external objects I consider beautiful, ugly, or awful in aesthetic evaluations of experience. Finally, I may speak of rationality in regard to assumed or projected moral norms and ideals (whether religious or secular in origin). I will, in short, speak about rationality in diversity. It is within these very diverse forms of the idea of the rational that I explore the roles of inherited intellectual traditions and transmitted patterns of cultural and social formations in the constitutions of what I characterize as vernacular representations of reason. I aim to clarify the similarities within, as well as the differences across, the various forms of conceptions of rationality.

I start with the justifiable premise that reason is not a thing—that is, it is not a self-subsisting object, substance, or essence among other self-subsisting objects, substances, and essences—but rather a field of mental acts in perception, understanding, and explanation, including the frameworks of comprehension and justification of the horizons of the field itself. I then attempt to characterize my ordinary intuitions into the everyday cultural characteristics and histories of rationality. In these admittedly passive observations, the reader can observe, reflectively, not just one level but many levels of activities that may go by the name *reason*. These considerations about the idea of the rational allow us to see how it is the case that not every productive characteristic of experience which is not subjective is thereby representative of a "thing." In fact, not everything which is not subjective is an object. If this characteristic, which I ascribe to rationality, appears to some readers as enigmatic, it is because it is. I hope, however, that in what follows one can come, on one's own, to the intuitive recognition that though rationality is not a thing, it does not lack objectivity. I will guide the reader to see in one's own mind's eye what the formal contours of the productive work of reasoning looks like; to observe the emergences of competing individual and social conceptions of rationality; and to reconstitute in one's own mind what one rationally believes must be the criteria for determining what should count and should not count as adequate or ideal grounds for a claim that one has a reason for doing or thinking something.

Reasoning is indeed productive work. Both the productivity and the product can be seen most clearly in areas of reflective self- and collective identity formations. But it can also be seen in the brutally instrumental relations we adopt toward the rest of nature. The productivity of reason is, moreover, obvious in the moral and aesthetic norm-orientations in which a sense of the rational beauty of the world and of nature acquires, for humans at least, specific social, cultural, and historical forms. Because of this variety of levels of productive activities and their descriptions, the reflective and dialogical method is one way the reader can come to recognize rationality not as a thing but yet in its objectivity. In other words, rationality is a quality we can only notice by, and ascribe to, other things. For example, we notice and ascribe it to what I said, what you did, the event of yesterday, and so forth. Rationality, in this argument from the vernacular in experience, culture, and history, is never something standing or floating somewhere all by itself.

My goal and procedures may be summed up as follows: What types of reconstructions will display to us the core of what we judge as the rational? Having indicated that the question can be approached with either an emphasis on the descriptive-analytic method or with an emphasis on substantively postulating claims about how a specific proposition is or is not rational, I have chosen the former approach. Therefore, starting from a basis in favor of methodological description and analysis of rationality, instead of debating the rationality or irrationality of specific contents of specific rational propositions, I have therefore located the best historical and cultural manifestations of the rational in the following dominant categorical reconstructions:

1. the calculative or mechanical and materialistic,
2. the formal or logical,
3. the hermeneutic or interpretive, and
4. the phenomenological models.

To these—durable and fairly uncontested—models I added three more:

5. the empirical-probabilistic,
6. the skeptical, and
7. the political.

The goal is to explain and critique each of these models of rationality in order to determine the contours of the rational in its theoretically vernacular, ordinarily contemplative and ethical, morally pragmatic, and technically humanistic objectivities.

Acknowledgments

Parts of some chapters of this book were presented, in earlier drafts, at various fora. By order of gestation of the ideas, the materials in chapter 4 are the oldest. The first two sections of that chapter were presented under the title "The Idea of History in Postcolonial Discourse" at the John Hope Franklin Center at Duke University on 12 April 2003. I would like to thank Walter Mignolo, who hosted the presentation as part of the center's seminar on Dialogical Ethics and Critical Cosmopolitanism. In addition to Mignolo, Wahneema Lubiano and George Lamming were in the audience during my talk. They offered helpful comments that led to appreciable revisions to what was, at that time, a project in a draft form.

The subsection of chapter 5 titled "Rationality and the Politics of Memory" is the result of a presentation to a humanities faculty seminar at the University of Cape Town on 17 October 2003. I wish to thank those responsible for inviting me to the university: Ramphele Mamphele (at that time the vice chancellor) and Robin Cohen (at that time dean of the graduate faculty of the humanities). André du Toit, who was head of the department of political studies, was responsible for the organization of the seminar at which my paper was delivered. I am immensely grateful to André and fellow participants for their questions and insights both during the seminar and throughout my six months' work at the university.

Last but not least, the UNESCO conference on the "Encounter of Rationalities," co-organized by the International Council of Philosophy and Humanistic Studies and the African Center for Advanced Studies in Porto Novo, Benin, on 18–22 September 2002, provided in particular ways some of the thematic organizations that have guided my current uses of the concept "rationality" and my effort to trace its historical contours in selected literature. Although I had completed my doctoral thesis, "Rationality and the Debates about African Philosophy," in 1993, the quality and quantity of the interventions at the 2002 UNESCO conference confirmed for me to what extent the "rationality" debate transcended the debate's origins in the incipient traditions of postcolonial anthropology of the early 1960s. I hope that this book best approximates what the UNESCO conference had in mind when it spoke about internal and external rational encounters within and across cultures.

Reports by anonymous readers for Duke University Press guided my revisions of the manuscript. The readers' comments particularly helped me in avoiding a cryptic style of argumentation. In addition to the readers, I thank J. Reynolds Smith, executive editor at the press, and his assistants; they are the best editors you could imagine.

Introduction:

Diversity and the Social

Questions of Reason

IDENTITY

How can we find the best model of a philosophical method to conceptualize the diversity of reason in experience? This is a unique problem
because diversity as such can be thought about only through the idea of
identity.[1] Similarly, we can understand identity, but only in the thought
of what it is not: diversity. It is, therefore, all the more difficult to *think*
diversity when the diversity in question is diversity in reason itself.

We can attempt to bypass this difficulty by projecting the idea of
diversity into surrogate practical concepts, such as multiplicity, pluralism, or multiculturalism. But all of these concepts are elusive. Let us
take, for example, the most current of them, multiculturalism. It is believed, on the one hand, that multiculturalism is about heterogeneity
and therefore about the problem of multiple identities.[2] From the point
of view of the currently fashionable uses of the concept, Adorno was one
of the first to theorize this idea of identity as a form of multiplicity. In his
Hegelian book on aesthetics, Adorno argued that "matters of true philo-

sophical interest at this point in history are those in which Hegel, agreeing with the tradition, expressed his disinterest," namely, "nonconceptuality, individuality, and particularity—things which ever since Plato used to be dismissed as transitory and insignificant."[3] In our time, the exemplars of the contested insignificant form the trinity of contemporary criticism: gender, race, and class, a trinity whose inner forms and affinities are far from conceptually articulate.[4] It is probably because of the difficulties involved in coherently thinking this trinity that some critics have come to believe, in the extreme, that diversity is no more than an ideology: an idée fixe that has been used by intellectuals and in the general culture to license the degradation of common values. Some advocates of this perspective on the identity of diversity rarely hide their distaste not only for academic discourses of multiculturalism but also for any practices of multicultural politics.[5]

But there is another meaning to diversity, a meaning somewhat removed from the present cultural and political contestations of the term, through which we can understand identity. Diversity, from this point of departure, takes as its focus the *act* of thought. In this thoughtful act the diversity in reason poses a particular problem for any identity that legitimately wishes to constitute itself as a historical singularity. In reflecting on such an act of thought, as I do here, I will not be concerned with the specific social and political interests that drive some of the intellectual arguments: monoculturalism versus multiculturalism, racialism versus nonracialism, genderism versus gender-blindness, social democratic ideals versus raw capitalist class values, and so on. I would rather pursue an understanding of the conditions that generate these and other positions in conflicted civil and political societies. My overall goal is to shed light on the general but implicit grounds on which the overtly antagonistic social and political contests over the idea of diversity are currently negotiated. The reader ought to bear in mind, then, that what follows is a series of interrogations of the logical conditions that allow one to hold the thought of a social concept—in this case, the concept of identity or diversity.

The two-part thesis I wish to defend can be plainly stated: The modern mind cannot but think diversely. Diversity is not as local or practical a matter as some would like to think. My project, accordingly, is to investigate the nature of the thought of diversity in the cultural and postcolonial histories of modernity and postmodernity. From this investigation I draw what some might consider a startling conclusion: diversity constitutes a necessary condition of thinking in general. Without diversity there is no thought. And without thought there is no mind. Of course, one can imagine having sensation without thought, a brain but no mind, body but no spirit, nature without culture. But one actually makes an identity only in relations of diversity, in dialogic and agonistic interaction with objects considered nonidentical.

It is to focus on this these that I said we would not be concerned with accounting for the practical, and especially the social and political, contestations that currently frame both reflective and unreflective understandings of ideologies and counterideologies of diversity-as-multiculturalism. I suggest we bracket the politics, not because the concept of cultural diversity that animates multiculturalism is in opposition to a theory of *experience* of diversity, as practice may be said to be in opposition to theory . Rather, we can leave politics out of immediate consideration because analysis of concepts may be all one can expect of philosophy *as philosophy*. What sorts of political activism one may choose to engage in with the help of an analytical concept is, of course, supremely important. But, out of respect for the work of thought itself, it is only fair to recognize that, at least on some occasions, thinking can be work enough.

DIVERSITY

The reader who has come so far may be tempted to accuse me of what some consider an old vice. A yearning to transcend partisanship, or, at least, to live between camps but intellectually remain above the factions, is a desire as old as philosophy itself. From Plato through Soyinka to Rawls this tendency is usually, and correctly, associated with philosophical idealism. In the American tradition before Rawls (we'll return to Plato and Soyinka at another point), Emerson speaks from the perennial intention of romantic philosophical idealism when he boasts, "Some great decorum, some fetish of a government, some ephemeral trade, or war, or man, is cried up by half mankind and cried down by the other half, as if all depends on this particular up or down." But, he adds, "The odds are that the whole question is not worth the poorest thought which the scholar has lost in listening to the controversy." To the scholar in such a situation of controversies, in danger of losing precious time in contemplating the universal, Emerson advises, "Let him not quit his belief that a popgun is a popgun, though the ancient and honourable of the earth affirm it to be the crack of doom."[6]

Prior to the transcendentalist American tradition represented by Emerson and others, and in fact from the earliest days of Platonism in Western philosophy to our contemporaries in the postcolonial traditions, the problem of the relation between the universal perspective of the scholar and the immediate necessities of particular social, political, and historical debates is a constant theme. If we consider the issues from, as suggested, the point of view of thought as such, the problem of the universal and the particular stems from conflicts arising between two antagonistic tendencies *in* reason. The antagonism is at the root of thought itself. Moreover, it is the sort of antagonism that *enables* thought. Because this antagonism is rooted in thought and productive of thought, therefore, it is appropriate to characterize the problem of the universal and the particular—from the point of view of the scholar who takes thinking seriously—as a problem of mind and world. Or better: a problem of mind-in-world.

Because of its rootedness in the nature of mind, and on account of its dialectical productivity, the problem of diversity makes it impossible for thought to conceptualize in a transparent way its own constitutive relations: the relations between thought and mind, concept and object, or word and thing. At the beginning of the *Critique of Pure Reason*, Kant describes the intellectual problems which may lead to questions about these relations. As if to point out that the relationship between mind and world is fundamentally, metaphysically speaking, corrupt, Kant argues that reason has a peculiar trajectory in at least "one kind of its cognitions."[7] I shall shortly enumerate the specific elements of this kind of cognition. In general, they are the ones in which, as in the concept of diversity, thought is troubled by questions which it cannot dismiss, because they are posed by the nature of reason itself, but which it also cannot, all round, satisfactorily answer.

One would think that, under such circumstances, thought would desist from trying to build a secure, foundational, and comprehensive metaphysical picture of *that* aspect of the world—but it doesn't. Before Kant, Francis Bacon had clearly pointed out this tragic fact. "The human understanding," Bacon writes in the *Organon*, "is unquiet." He then lists themes on which thinking "cannot stop or rest, and still presses onward, but in vain." The following are some prominent examples: "We cannot conceive of any end or limit to the world, but always as of necessity it occurs to us that there is something beyond. Neither, again, can it be conceived how eternity has flowed down to the present day, for that distinction which is commonly perceived of infinity in time past and in time to come can by no means hold; for it would thence follow that one infinity is greater than another, and that infinity is wasting away and tending to become finite." Moreover, similar "subtlety arises touching the infinite divisibility of lines, from the same inability of thought to stop."

Another area of epistemic problems, which Bacon also considered troublesome, though more mischievous, is the idea of ultimate causality. "In the discovery of causes," he notes, "although the most general principles in nature ought to be held merely positive, as they are discovered, and cannot with truth be referred to a cause, nevertheless the human understanding being unable to rest still seeks something prior in the order of nature." To Bacon's already long list, I add: thought would most certainly like to have the concept of a complete picture of our own mental capacities; an indubitable grasp of the transcendental conditions of the thing—the object—we claim to be the target when we say we know something; and a complete metatheory of the relations between our known subjective mental landscape and the objective landscape of the external world. But the uncertainties and the errors—the potentially serious damage to knowledge—to which some of these different movements of thought could lead are patently obvious. For example, as Bacon was aware, "in struggling toward that which is further off," thought "falls back upon that which is nearer at hand ... which [has] relation clearly to the nature of man rather than to the nature of the universe, and from this source [has] strangely defiled philosophy."

This defilement, as we saw in relation to Kant, is the outcome of widely held epistemic desires and their metaphysical aporias. In this light, the problems of thought appear as a perversion of reason. David Hume, famously, nearly dismissed most metaphysical questions, and more, in just such terms. The questions, he suggested, are "strained" and "ridiculous."[8] At the end of the part "Skeptical and Other Systems of Philosophy" in the *Treatise* (Section vii, "Conclusion of This Book"), Hume complains, "The intense view of these manifold contradictions and imperfections in human reason has so wrought upon me, and heated my brain, that I am ready to reject all belief and reasoning, and can look upon no opinion even as more probable or likely than another."[9] Normal questions take on skeptically frightening proportions: "Where am I, or what? From what causes do I derive my existence, and to what condition shall I return? Whose favour shall I court, and whose anger must I dread? What beings surround me? and on whom have I any influence, or who have any influence on me? I am confounded with all these questions, and begin to fancy myself in the most deplorable condition imaginable, invironed with the deepest darkness, and utterly deprived of the use of every member and faculty."[10] Hume's final solution to his strained and ridiculous musings is to take flight into an idea of nature. "Most fortunately," he declares, "it happens that since reason is incapable of dispelling these clouds, nature herself suffices to that purpose, and cures me of this philosophical melancholy and delirium, either by relaxing this bent of mind, or by some avocation, and lively impression of my senses, which obliterate all these chimeras."[11] In other words, to relieve the mind of its thoughtful burdens, nature itself gently distracts thought from some of its extraordinary epistemic responsibilities. "I dine, I play a game of backgammon, I converse, and am merry with my friends; and when after three or four hours' amusement, I would return to these speculations, they appear so cold, and strained, and ridiculous, that I cannot find in my heart to enter into them any farther."[12] Following Hume, let us colloquially characterize this solution as the triumph of the heart over the head.

In technical terms, however, this Humean naturalistic solution can hardly be characterized as theoretically adequate. Kant certainly—and rightly—found it inadequate. In more recent works, such as John McDowell's *Mind and World*, we can see fairly clearly why empirical naturalism, combined with philosophical skepticism, has provided a persistently inadequate response to what Hume colorfully diagnosed as clouds and darkness in human reason.[13] The contradictions and imperfections of reason exist because, in knowing a thing, the mind starts, as Kant writes, "from principles that it cannot avoid using in the course of experience, and that this experience at the same time sufficiently justifies it in using." But these same principles, curiously, misguide reasoning to go ever deeper, in pursuit of never-ending questions. Because such transcendental questions lack closure, the questions leave the deeper interests of thought open-ended, and throw into permanent doubt the hope that the dream of complete rationality could ever be realized.

The picture, as it emerges from Hume's and Kant's critiques, is that thought, blinded by its hopes and dreams, surreptitiously serves itself with empirical principles that it is not entitled to use (something we can see in plainer light). The questionable use of empirical principles occurs because reasoning finds itself *compelled* to resort to principles that go beyond all possible use in experience; yet because of "cloud" and "darkness," this unwarranted use of principles of experience seems beyond suspicion—so much so that even common sense appears to agree with it. By succumbing to this blindness, human reason, as Kant puts it, plunges itself into contradictions. Curiously, Kant also suggests that reason, by itself, can gather from this last development that its pseudo-epistemic procedures are the product of errors "hidden somewhere," even though reason may be incapable of discovering the errors.[14]

If—in addition to those of Bacon, Hume, and Kant—our own cultural and historical observations are accurate, we ought to ask: What could be the truest meaning of these necessary "errors" in thought? Where is the "somewhere" that the causes of the errors might be hidden? Why, and how, specifically, do the epistemic blindnesses and errors in thought necessarily plunge the mind into clouds, darkness, and contradictions? Moreover, how well does the mind appreciate its dilemma; its own self-deconstruction?

Although Kant claims that one could gather from the consequences that something must be wrong with the infrastructure of a metaphysically oriented reason, it is far from clear how deep is the mind's proper recollection of these errors. Beyond Plato's mythological programs, we are not even clear about the mind's capacity for recollection.[15] (For example, do not acts of remembering frequently confuse memory with history?) Working from these hesitations, in the chapters that follow, I lead us to see how modern philosophers underestimated the extent of the problematic conditions under which thought may risk its claims of autonomy beyond the empirical, beyond memory, and beyond history.

For example, the mind's metaphysical quandary extends right into Kant's own characterizations of the same quandary. What if the so-called error, darkness, and contradiction into which reason plunges itself constitute the indices of what I referred to earlier as the radical and productive antagonism in thought? What if the supposed cloud and the darkness, noted by Hume, are the negative roots of thought? What if contradiction is the intellectually generative power of this negativity? Whereas Hume saw clouds and contradictions and imperfections, and Kant pointed to unknown errors of the mind responsible for the darkness and contradictions in thought, I suggest that we re-describe these putative clouds, errors, and darkness as themselves constitutive of a necessary historical—rather than skeptical or transcendental—fate: the epistemic and moral fates of reason in history.

This suggestion is fundamental to the defense of our stated thesis, though not as radical as it sounds. Some philosophers, borrowing religious metaphors, believe that humans are subject to an original Fall: a mythical fall into, and then reemergence of consciousness from, a primordial state of Paradise into states of reason. Or these philosophers speak about humankind's emergence from the innocence of unknowing to the mortality of knowing.[16] Some Continental philosophers translate these mythological schemas—and the questions the schemas bring into view about the nature of mind, self, and world—into yet more esoteric languages of Being-in-Difference.[17] But outside of these mythically proportioned metaphors and concepts, the idea of ordinary, vernacular, historical fates of reason can stand out—and should be able to stand out—on its own terms.

It is in the hope of the recovery of the ordinary, therefore, that I have preferred to talk about the problems of thought as the problem of diversity in thought, and of the problems of diversity in the world as also a problem in the thought of diversity. To talk this way is already to speak in the languages of history and of the everyday. Unlike the idealist or excessively romantic approaches, where the everyday is derogated, respectively, to the realm of mass ignorance or to the realm of the boringly bourgeois, I suggest a different approach to what should be seen as the ordinary problem of reason: How do you articulate diverse historical forms of rationality?

Specifically, the vernacular language of the ordinary in experience reveals the roots of the complexities in thought that some modern, and some postmodern, philosophers prefer to attribute to real and invented metaphysical worlds. For us, analyses of language—any language—in relation to ordinary experience indicate what you could call a gap in thought, *a breach in tongue*. This breach indicates not some inherent ignorance of ordinary minds compared to the metaphysical insights of professional philosophers. Rather, it points to a general distance between thought and mind, discourse and reason, concept and object, the universal and the particular, or the typical and the unique. A breach in tongue is therefore an indication of moments of an epistemic gap in everyday linguistic perception. But this is a productive gap. It is a generative absence absolutely necessary for the autonomous (that is, not causally determined) emergence of thought. This emergence can be called freedom of thought or the freedom of mind. To speak of a breach in tongue, therefore, is to think of this breach only as the space of a generative absence from which the mind constitutes its own figures as acts of thought, as acts of speech. Obviously, an absence is *not* a thing; it is a gap. Thought is that which composes itself—because of nothing and so to speak out of nothing—as a need: the need of tongue; the need for speech; the need for voice. Thought is the need for language. We can therefore establish an intimate and absolute conceptual relation not simply between thought, word, and world but also between language and freedom of thought. The breach in tongue is therefore the origins of freedom, whereas freedom is the work of—the working-out of—the need for tongue, the need speech, and the coming to voice. For all this, the best definition of thought is: That which spontaneously composes itself as, in itself, an object of work: the work of freedom of "mind," namely, the freedom of a voice, the freedom self, the freedoms of cultures, and the freedom of the world. As we called the spontaneity of this work freedom, then, we can say that it is only in the history of the work that thought becomes manifest as universal language—the language of freedom as expression of mind. It is because language is thus thoroughly historical that thinking, too, is historically fated. And inasmuch as thinking is both worldly and historically fated, there cannot be just one way or one kind of expression of thought. There are many forms of expressions of thought. There are many universal languages of reason.

The vernacular language I deploy in the upcoming chapters to describe both the breach in tongue and its various forms of gap in the rationality of experience suggests how one might go about thinking the ethics of freedom and the morality of experience in general, but also the ethics and morality of variously rooted social and cultural experiences of freedom. Ethics and morality are necessary consequences of freedom; they flow from the breach in tongue without which freedom neither exists nor makes any epistemological sense. It is therefore in the relations within thought in experience (between concept and object, word and thing) that we make plausible not just the rationality of the negative in thought but also the positive reality of rationality and its freedom: they are bound as well as bounded to history in the ethics of care for self and the moral concern for the other. On the one hand, you could consider this an application of the epistemological principle derived from our original thesis to the domain of social problems. This option would be available in the language of applied science: the philosophy of morals; ethics of identity; or social and cultural ethics. On the other hand, instead of the language of application of a science to a separate domain of experience, one could consider morality and ethics not as separate domains in society to which one applies a theory of an ordinary rationality. In fact, in my particular choice of the concept of the ordinary to qualify the theory of rationality that I have proposed, it was my intention to attenuate the problems associated with traditional philosophy, where it is presupposed that rationality is something you could abstractly derive from outside of social or everyday experience, and then apply the abstractions to that experience. In contrast to the traditional language of a high science of thought applied to, as it were, a low domain of experience of life, I have shown that, in the origins of thought, there is to be found, both coincidentally and non-coincidentally, the experiences of concepts of the morally high and concepts of the morally low, the ethically sublime and the ethically ridiculous, just as we found the absence of, or a breach in tongue coincidentally with the need for speech, and in the same ways one would think about necessity and freedom. I hope to also show that the deeper epistemic and moral significance of these various distinctions, themselves, are best grasped by inquiries into the spontaneous and reflective origins of thought in ordinary experience.

I conclude now, therefore, that the obviousness of the relations between rationality and freedom, and ethics and morality, is already there when, for example, we try to explain the relations between mind and thought, concept and object, and language and things. Because of the non-coincidence between the two poles (I address this in full in chapter 2), one intuitively apprehends in the idea of freedom all the potential of a world composed of not just the existential realities of the self and its other but also the moral necessity of mutual respect and justice toward the identities of self and other. It is as if, in the very desire to explain how we come to knowledge of objects, we can also already perceive, in embryonic forms, all the range of paradoxes—epistemological as well as moral—that are implicated in, and across, human subjectivities.

This tri-aspected (epistemic, ethical, and moral) reality of what I call *reason in experience*, or *vernacular rationality*, can be encountered by directly addressing questions such as: Why do we experience the self as transcendent, on the one hand, and recognize the desire of the self for material and social rootedness, on the other? In general, questions like this evoke the issues we already suspect as potential occasions for error. But we have also re-described the questions. In the redescription, the old question in a new form acquires a new meaning. For example, a problem which was previously understood as an epistemic problem regarding the limits of what can be known, has become an important marker of a different kind of act of recognition: it marks the points of origin of moral and ethical experience of freedom of thought. Before, in the idea of limit, we were led to speak about epistemic "failures" of reason as a limitation in thought; now, in the acts of our own redescription, I have invited ourselves to recognize, in the same limitations, sites of productions of language and of historical insights. In what I have called a breach in tongue, for example, there is that idea of the limit or of gap precisely because of the non-coincidence of rationality with itself in ordinary experience. But there is also, in and because of the non-coincidence, a relation of productivity inherent to the facts, as well as to the intuitive logic we have, of experience. It is out of this productivity that speech and freedom co-constitute their origins and their tasks as, respectively, the works of language and time. Language and time are the origins of the world and of history.

But how do we, today, best confess freedom as a historical task? How do we confess—and convert—the epistemic limits in experience into morally significant insights? In this book I offer some suggestions by tracking the historical vicissitudes of ordinary reason across a range of ideas and concepts currently deployed in debates not only about identity and difference but also about culture, tradition, and history; philosophy and science; literature and the arts; and politics, war, morality, and the law. I do not pursue a comprehensive philosophical worldview, however; this is more modestly one man's effort to practice philosophy as a critique of concepts.

My methodological circumspection derives from an Afro-modern postcolonial vernacular tradition of thought, where philosophy is best understood as an evolving critique of abstractions common in one's society. As we shall see when we study Du Bois in chapter 5, prior works on the critical legitimation of consciousness and the ethical and moral concerns I have sketched are best referred to as vernacular theories of rationality. In my discipline, philosophy, this designation is helpful if we keep in mind the fact that it is Kant's legacy that dominates the landscape of twentieth-century philosophy, at least in the Western worlds. From Kant, academic philosophy has inherited the quandary of explaining how it is that the mind can spontaneously authorize its self-constitution and self-governance; how it can, when necessary, correct the errors in its own cognition of objects; and how it can restrain itself from the extravagance —the overreach beyond the boundary of all experience—to which the force of reason's own spontaneity drives it. If the mind's exuberance is cause for the metaphysician and the dogmatic transcendentalist to celebrate, for the vernacular or critical philosopher of concepts, it is a moment of hope in the triumphant emergence of the subject's consciousness in the midst of nature, and a source of efforts to explain the work of cognition in general, the critical sciences in particular, and the idea of history in experience. If there is no science of things without the touchstone reference to nature in the order of experience, then Kant is right: one must put dogmatic metaphysical idealism on the critical block. But the transcendental problematic of rationality looks different when we disclose the original terms of the underlying assumptions about reason. This disclosure must also constitute the grounds of a normative dislocation: What if the metaphysical error in reason is also the root condition of the problem of diversity of being? What if diversity in existence makes epistemic sense in relation not just to reason but also to an ethics of memory and of history?

Taking these questions seriously requires, at a minimum, that difference or diversity in a post-Kantian and postcolonial sense be seen as resulting from the perceived gap in the dynamic relation between objective conditions of truth (things, values, interests, or means-and-ends relations) and subjective cognitive predispositions (concept, idea, formal procedures of explanation and justification) found in a post-Kantian and postcolonizing world. If experience is always mediately situated within these objectivities and subjectivities, then the clouds, darkness, and contradictions between the two poles account in part for the perceptual gap—the breach in tongue—we think must exist, or have difficulty explaining why it shouldn't exist, within the thought of post-Kantian and postcolonial experience and history.

Experience—and by this I mean not the relation of a transcendental apperception with itself, but ordinary, vernacular, everyday experience— is the epistemic locus and the moral index of both the fateful mark of freedom of thought and of diversity of identities in being. There is historical grandeur, a grandeur both tragic and heroic, in thinking that even the Kantian tribunal of the so-called Transcendental Reason must submit to this sort of fate in experience and culture. Experiences of race, class, and gender, and the cultural and political liberations from the conquests of colonialist reason enable these ruptures. These are absolute —because irreversible—ruptures in history. My task in this book is to show how, in fact, it is reason as such—not its transcendental glorifications—which must re-invest history with meaning and continuity in everyday life.

When I use the word *experience*, then, I have in mind merely the meaningful fates of reason in the ordinary historical encounters of diversity in thought, culture, and society. Experience in this regard is the reflective composition of the memories of the ruins of Reason; it is a series of histories of hopes and accumulated wisdom in the actions of worldly subjects of reason. But experience is also worldly reason in search of greater freedom and liberty, in each culture and in all cultures, for all humankind. Experience is the openness of the particular to the diversely universal.

INDIVIDUALITY AND TYPE

What is the best way to comprehend in experience, and explain out of experience, the concept of reason? Consider the problem in this way. In ordinary speech we tend to subsume diverse events under the singular term *experience*. But this idea of experience is only a formality—a conceptual structuring of empiricities and overcoming of diversity among them. The concept of experience—and likewise the idea of difference between self and other—derives not just from nature or the world (the things we believe cause the events we perceive) but also from the formal activities of thought. In acts of thought we cognitively bring multiple activities of perception or interactions with nature and the social world into unities of concepts such as *reason*, *idea*, or *experience*. But each of these terms is no more than a successful patchwork of insightful *relations* across gaps in perceptual aspects of experience. These are gaps in dimensions of thought, the dimensions which Hume called clouds, and Kant sources of error. Though it is a marker of blindsight, the conceptual breach produced in and by thought by the self-constitution of its own figures is the very basis of insight in perception. This insight is, in turn, the basis of judgment in experience.

This description presupposes a recognition that even in the innermost moments of insightful perception, insight is possible only because of the noncoincidence of reason with the transcendental conditions of the concept of its object. That we know what we know in perception, or grasp what can be grasped in judgment, is a result of that failure of coincidence. We succeed in knowing only because the transcendental ambition posited by thought in its own negative origin escapes at the very moment of insight. What is left as light in thought, what is left of thought as enlightening, is the trace—the figure—of that which forever excuses itself from reason by sloughing itself in the secret night of thought as reason's enabler. It is as if we are left holding the slough of an absence, but a slough which illuminates: it is the light we call reason.

But we can go further. We should also recognize in the nonidentity of thought with itself the conditions of the conceptual limitations required not just by the diversity in thought (marking experience as open) but also in the diversity of the world (reason is not only of thought but also of the worldliness of things). Diversity is also a condition of the objectivity of objects, and of the susceptibility to rationality of the worldliness of the world. The noncoincidence of the conditions of rationality of both thought and world with neither thought's own thoughtful grounds nor the things of the world is thus evidence of diversity in thought as well as of multiplicity in extrasubjective natural facts and social worlds. The noncoincidence, finally, contaminates and marks the points of uncertainty about adequate relations between concept and object, perception and reason, and judgment and thought in experience. This last observation, as we shall see in chapter 3, has implications for theories of relations between language and things, between language and memory, and between language and history.

We can make the above abstractions—and their consequences for theories of rationality—clearer. When you think or say that you know your way around, in reference to the activity of studying, you mean precisely that if you wanted to study, for example, at home, you know where to find the things you need, how to walk up to the things, and how to use them to accomplish the activity we call studying. You can see right now, in your mind's eye, that your knowledge—the substance of what you meant when you said you know—is a patchwork of presuppositions and judgments. What you claim to know is nothing other than a conclusion reached by putting together diverse units of information about different things, things that in themselves may or may not already be unities priorly, rightly or wrongly, conceptually assembled by you or by others (a shelf, a book, a table, a chair, a lamp, the idea of reading, and so forth).

To effectively demonstrate having knowledge of your study in view of engaging in the activity of reading, which we call studying, means that you can mentally organize spatial and temporal relations between diverse units of reality (objects, ideas, values, desires, means and ends, and so on). It also means that you know how to use this mental map to intervene in—that is, reorganize according to your active or passive needs and intentions—the existence of the realities which constitute your study environment. This knowledge of parts of your existence— your capacities for intellectual insight, willing, and acting—involves at a particular time exploiting not just existing or potential relations between your intention and one or another objects of the world but also exploiting the relations or potential relations among objects that, without your thoughtfully enlightened—rational—intervention, may or may not be otherwise related, or at least not meaningfully related in the way that this meaning could have been attributed to you because of your intention, judgment, and decisions.

You can also do a similar demonstration by reversing the formulation. If I am lying in bed in the dark of the night and feel a general desire to read, and intend to satisfy the desire now, and if I know my way around my study, I will switch on the bedside lamp, get out of bed, and shuffle to a room and to the shelf that I think has the kind of books that I think I desire to read. I will select one among these options, walk to the reading desk and chair, sit, turn on the desk lamp, open the book, and read. I will organize and practically execute similar knowledge if I desire to write. Or wish to eat and know my way around the kitchen. Or go to the cinema if I know my way around the neighborhood. My experience of reading, writing, or going to the cinema, though we may speak about experience in the singular, is in truth a result of intellectual and practical cobbling together of desires, ideas, and objects over abysses in thought— abysses whose subjective existence are externally signaled in our worldly sense of time in our actions, and in the existence of worldly objects or values which are the focus of insight. What we call experience, in the singular, thus appears to be a form of a conditional: it is riddled with presuppositions and implicit knowledge, yet practically adequate as the triumph of desire, will, reason, and behavior over realities otherwise different one from another.

I might even narratively use words to communicate to others, or record in memory or on paper, this idea of experience as the contingent intellectual and practical organizational triumph of this part of my existence over the diversity in the realities of thought and of the world. I could report to my friends that I made possible for my consciousness the enjoyment or appreciation of a specific ordering of ideas and things: I created a world that I found aesthetically pleasing, intellectually satisfying, and morally sound. I read Achebe, Kant, and Bacon; ate egusi and wild salmon; and saw a Kurosawa film at the Egungu Theatre. I might extend my intentions further in the reporting if I volunteered the above information in implicit invitation that the audience, too, might similarly appreciate these events should they choose, as I did, to organize one for themselves, or participate when next I organize one. If they joined me in the adventures—say, a weekend of reading and discussion, dinner, and a movie—I could, afterward, speak about *our* experience of *the* weekend.

But even at that level, though I am entitled to speak about experience or about "my" or "our" weekend in the singular, upon reflection on the details of the objective conditions of the things and ideas involved in the making of the singularities of *the* experience of a world, it is undeniable to my senses and in thought itself that such a world is a rough composition. The composition is absolutely necessary because one is not a spirit or ghost who, as such, could supposedly be anywhere at any time. One orders reality because one must devise ways of identifying or categorizing one's interactions with objects, values, ideas, and so on; we order our experiences of things, including the relations among the orders of experiences. These multilayered experiential organizations and reorganizations of objects allow one the very apprehension of events—events being occurrences meaningfully constituted in space and time, as geography and in history.

Events are our culture- and tradition-sensitive systematizations of disparate interactions with aspects of natural and social realities. We can even further enhance the systematization of the interactions with the natural world by *extending* predictively the relations we see or think exist in past or current events. But whether directly or by intuitive extension, systematization—or at least *this* sort of rational systematization of things and events which become experience—is not possible without what I have been doing here: generalization. Generalization is a process whereby I select features of one thing and then of another, which is otherwise different from the first, in order to arrive at a class, type, or mental picture. This picture, when held in the mind, allows one, with intention (in view of a course of action such as late-night reading, brunch, or a movie), to think of different things as naturally or socially, cognitively or affectively (in any case, in one way or another, depending on what I intend to do and what I know) related in a meaningful way. This is the only possible condition—the one and the same condition of possibilities of willing and acting, passively (contemplatively) or actively (productively)—for the formation of general concepts about experience, or about the diverse units of things and values that constitute the worldly insight into the empiricities of experience.

A vernacular or ordinary critique of both experience and rationality therefore takes as its point of departure the claim that what we call perception, as well as the object of perception, is internally diverse. The language of the vernacular is opposed to the esoteric as the ordinary is opposed to the metaphysical, transcendental, or quasi-transcendental. Because this critique assumes that humans are confronted with the radically temporal nature of subjectivity in experience, the *concept* of a thing, as well as the *type* of thing we objectify in conception, must itself be internally temporally differentiated.

My claims here become more evident when you consider the possible answers to this question: If required to do so, on the basis of what can you justify your conceptual classification of objects? The answer seems easy: On the bases of the *things*, the objective nature of the very things conceptually generalized about. But you could also answer: The subjective and intuitive impressions of the effects these things have on your feelings— your affects and moods. Or, you could choose to combine the two answers: You conceptually make classes or types *for* otherwise diverse entities on the grounds *of* your differentiated but related apprehensions of the objective qualities of the individual entities. In this last answer you admit to consciousness the subjective considerations (thoughts, feelings, sympathies and antipathies) intuitively developed about entities in their natural or social state. A transcription of your logical procedure would be: "Though *d* and *t* and *y* each *look* different to me, I *say* (judge, suppose, and so forth) that they are all letters." Or: "Though these objects feel by touch (look, sight, etc.) different from one another, they are all cola nuts." How are you able to produce these and similar kinds of judgments? If called upon to do so, how would you describe the rational procedures one must follow to justify the generalization in your judgment?

In the case of the letters, you might make an appeal to their use. Each letter is successfully employed in writing the English language (among others). Though each may be different from the other, every one of them is recognizable to you, right now, as a building block for communicating thoughts and ideas in the language. Since the building blocks of written Igbo, Twi, and Czech also include the same letters, and letters are called alphabets, *d*, *t*, and *y* each look to you like known letters, and so you generally consider them, together, alphabets. In the case of the cola nuts, the principle of classification—and therefore the justification of the generalization—is again primarily practical, not theoretical. One might recognize or remember, and therefore be interested in pointing out, sources of caffeine. We think: Though each of these nuts looks, feels, and tastes different, they all, when pressed, yield liquid caffeine. But note that one could remember or recognize other generalities than alphabets or caffeine-things in *d*, *t*, and *y* or in the different-looking objects called cola nuts. Likewise, "letters" and "cola" or "nuts" could be applied to groupings of objects other than the objects we put together in each example. One could therefore not only possibly reclassify the different entities we have now generally called letters and cola nuts, but also reclassify the general names while choosing to keep the underlying objects generalized about. "Cola nuts," along with, say, coffee beans, could become "caffenuts." With this last label, and once again with an eye on purpose, if a doctor required a person to have an intake of some unit of caffeine per day, the person need not worry whether she eats the green or the red kola nut, the soft or the hard one, or simply drinks a sufficiently caffeinated cup of coffee.

If your circumstances changed further, you could produce yet another class or type for the cola nuts and the coffee beans. Perhaps now you wish to decorate a kitchen. You are interested in the aesthetic and specifically the *visual*: the appeals of the multicolored cola nuts or the dark brown coffee beans at this time and in this place provide a different classificatory motive. In the mind, with the emphasis of attention on the aesthetic, one could imagine the beauty of transparent jars of cola nuts and coffee beans placed with fresh flowers on top of an armoire. Together, we could call this new assembly of decorations "biocolors." In yet another situation, in search of the most general, complete, and descriptive classification possible, we could emphasize more than just one specific aspect of the objects of generalization. This occasion might require that we communicate all we know about the objects. We would search for a type that would conceptually encompass the objective and subjective qualities of the entities, the similarities and differences between them, their actual or potential subclass status in relation to other classes of objects, and so forth. Yet once again even in this—the most general attempt to produce the most general type or class—we must rely on what we think is the motive to generalize. If we think the paramount intention is beyond immediate technical need of use, we will produce a suitable kind of type. If, for example, we think the overriding motives for generalization by a new concept are passive, contemplative, completeness of *description*, then we provide specificities and generalities that we hope would satisfy. Likewise, if we simply wish to see, purely as an intellectual challenge, the most general type of *concepts*, we combine all we know about the objects of generalization with all we know about every prior rigorous general concept about the objects in order to produce an all-around intellectually, technically, and aesthetically satisfactory idea of a type. Classification and reclassification are always practical and theoretical possibilities.

UNIVERSALITY

What translates classification from the realm of the possible to that of the actual is, as we have seen, generalization. Generalization is the necessary logical link between the possible and the actual, the most universal and the most particular. Because of this, we can reaffirm a truth in my earlier theses: The missing link between the universal and the particular is necessarily *in* the concept, and specifically *within* the processes of conceptual generalization. After all, what are grounds for generalization if not the will to systematize? First, there is the need to systematize in the necessity to act and therefore, as in my beginning thesis, in the need to think. To think in this sense is to reason with purpose: passive, introspective, contemplative, or active. In fact, there will be nothing to call *experience of mind, will, things, values, ideas,* or *the world* without thought.

Whether or not one prefers to capture these processes from my own examples or from other demonstrations, the argument at stake is that everyday reasoning requires the individual to engage in processes of subsuming diversity and difference under actual and possible unities of general experience. Rationality cannot be distinguished from these processes. And that is why we must say that reason is very ordinary. It is also why we should wonder at the ingenuity of some philosophies which deliberately or inadvertently complicate what is already in plain view.

Though disagreements may be naturally expected over the portions of my theses which argue that the primary motive for the processes of reasoning is practical (since these processes are always introspectively, reflectively, purposeful, even when the purpose is merely abstract generalization), the disagreements are largely about words. Others may call this practicality *utility* (Mill), *instinct* (Dewey, Wiredu), *interest* (Habermas), *the democratic* (Rorty), *the aesthetic* (Nietzsche), *use* (Wittgenstein), or *biopower* (Foucault). Whatever you think it should be called, I have merely suggested that the practical is what traps, like a net, the negative impulse in thought. These traps are the mind's nets over the negative origins of thought which, as figures of thought, both compose and illuminate the mind. The light of reason is the trace of the figure of the negative in perception. Judgment is possible in experience because the conceptual nature of perception is evidence not just of memory but also of the history of a world.

In short, rationality is a bridge over a breach; it is a practical response to the difficult condition of thought in the world, and of experience in history. The positive origin of reason in the negativity of the world is negative only because, though functionally subject to the rational as ideal, the reasons for the power of experience ultimately remain, for themselves, without known or knowable reason; they must remain so by virtue of what I called the epistemic, ethical, and moral requirements of ordinary reason. While some may choose to call my analytic abstemiousness "negativity" or, worse, a position for or against the Other of Reason, none of these appellations are, for me, ordinarily necessary.[18] For one, from any thinkable point of view and not just the ordinary and vernacular, the proposed Other of Reason cannot be entirely Other. Nor could reason be any longer Hegel's reason. Alexandre Kojève took care to dispose of this brand of high Hegelianism. The language of a supposed Other of Reason must itself be entirely ordinary because, as we saw in the discussion of experience, concern with the practical in the everyday (I wish to read a book, eat, see a movie, have a quiet conversation with a friend, write, or say a prayer to God) is the hypothetical origin of rationality itself. The locution *Other of Reason*, if it is to have any meaning, must therefore itself be defined within the bounds of the fates of reason in experience. Even then, the extraordinary and surreptitious languages of the Other of Reason cannot be confused with the ordinary and vernacular languages of reason in experience.

Unlike in the hyperbolic and rationally inflated claims usually made on behalf of the Other of Reason, we *know* the fateful history of reason in experience because we understand the fatality of its origins in thought. In fact, what lends experience—and therefore history—its hope and grandeur, even in tragic circumstances, is precisely *that* ethical and moral potential in reason: the knowledge that as negation of negation, reason in the ordinary is the reflective and hopeful affirmation of autonomy of will. But *will*, here, is just another term for the innumerable, morally thoughtful, small purposes we make out of the world in the forms of self, objects, and their histories. My insistence on the ordinary is thus a manner of highlighting the point of view that high theoretical depth is a secondary, and ethically and morally ambiguous, dependent function of thinking. The primary question, "To think or not to think?": that is the essence of the vernacular and of the practical universal.

AUTONOMY OF THE WORLD

While it would be flamboyant to claim that the most general picture of the rationally universal must be discerned in these, admittedly imperfect, pages, I try in the subsequent chapters to provide glimpses of the reasons for the suspicions I have stated as a two-part thesis. The main argument is that it is not just the world but also our concepts of the world that are historically fated to diversity. In fact, when we analyze the judgments we make about the world by the most rigorous theoretically stipulated criteria, there is little doubt that the bases of the general and universal judgments we make about worlds of experience appear to provide us with higher levels of emotional and practical satisfaction than we may be conceptually entitled to at any time.

Whereas some prefer to see this as a cognitive condition of error, darkness, and contradiction, I have aimed to theorize it as fateful conditions of diversity *in* reason. Whereas some think that this is a condition humans could overcome through a critical transcendental reduction of the projects of reason, I have chosen to celebrate the diversity in reason as the primary, generative condition of autonomy: the autonomy of the ethical and moral will. For the individual, autonomy constitutes the grounds of the ambiguous sense that experience is a site of fate, and for this reason a site of ethical struggle and of moral concern. This is a struggle and a work necessary not only to know the truths about natural and social worlds but also to morally achieve authenticity in identity—to become more nearly what one truly knows oneself as—in the contexts of, respectively, the natural constraints and the general morality that governs our relationships to nature and with others who, similarly, have embarked on the works of world- and self-making. For a people—a tradition, a culture, a community, a nation, and the world—autonomy is the will to fashion in freedom a collective identity and a shared historical sense of purpose from which alone individuals or groups can creatively derive a sense of at-home-in-the-world, however fleeting. For humanity, as totality, autonomy is our conflicted will for a historically dependent liberation from a seemingly faceless and anonymous nature. With these general considerations as background, the ordinary and the vernacular perspectives on reason that I seek to articulate can be interpreted as an insistence that *experience* and *history* are our only reliable indices of the universal.

1

Varieties of Rational Experience

In this chapter I discuss six varieties of theories of reason. These theories implicitly or explicitly advocate different ideals—models—of rationality. When I speak about the *theories of reason* and their corresponding *rational ideals* I call them *conceptions of rationality*. It will be obvious that whereas some of the conceptions of rationality are internally consistent as well as compatible with other conceptions of rationality, others are not. That is why I have preferred to speak about all of them as varieties of conceptions of rational experience. From my point of view, reason—on account of these theories and the forms of rationalities they collectively advocate—can be accurately characterized as internally diverse and externally pluralistic. Without arguing for a particular hierarchical ranking—only for their diversity and their compatibility or incompatibility—I will explain and critique the *calculative, formal, hermeneutical, empiricist, phenomenological,* and *ordinary* conceptions of rationality.

CALCULATIVE REASON

Calculative rationality is the model most familiar in the periods and places we characterize as modern. The historical identification of this form of rationality with modernity is due largely to the dominance of empirical science and its technologies in the modern processes of acquisition, organization and archiving, and practical uses of experimental knowledge. A modern culture's idea of knowledge is inescapably embedded in the rational self-image and in the historical teleology of the natural and the social sciences. This historical teleology is most explicit in the philosophical thought emerging out of the European Enlightenment, notably in the works of Thomas Hobbes, René Descartes, and Francis Bacon.

Hobbes gave the modern idea of rationality its clearest formulation. It is his terminology that justifies describing this theory of reason as *calculative*. Hobbes thinks that when we "reasoneth," all we do is calculation. Thinking is the act in which we conceive "a sum total from addition of parcels; or conceive a remainder, from subtraction of one sum from another: which, if it be done by words, is conceiving of the consequence of the names of all the parts, to the name of the whole; or from the names of the whole and one part, to the name of the other part. And though in some things, as in numbers, besides adding and subtracting, men name other operations, as multiplying and dividing; yet they are the same: for multiplication is but adding together of things equal; and division, but subtracting of one thing, as often as we can."[1] If all reasoning is reducible to calculation—specifically addition and subtraction—then the best model of acts of reasoning may be found in the mathematical sciences.

But beyond the field of mathematics, one could also translate the basic mathematical requirements of Hobbes's model of rationality into the metaphorical languages of positivity (addition or multiplication) and negativity (subtraction or division). In this translation, any domain of experience, including the realm of language, could be subjected to the mathematically and instrumentally quantifiable. By the same token, the task of any valid philosophy or science must consist in discovering, through verifiable and replicable experimental procedures, the rationality of nature and of the world in just this way that rationality has been

defined. In modeling rationality on this logical and technical presupposition, this notion of reason and the underlying rationality of the world are
considered directly or indirectly regulated by logical processes represented, or potentially representable, as usable information. All information would be, in turn, actually or potentially numerically quantifiable.

An intuitive appreciation of Hobbes's picture of thinking, however, reveals a number of problems—notably, its reductionism. After all, one
could easily think of occasions when reasoning has little or nothing to do
with addition and subtraction. When we take pleasures or displeasures
(e.g., in poetry), or speak in order to rationally stipulate the permissible
and impermissible in morality, it is difficult to see exactly how the
thought in this kind of experience is merely a process of addition or
subtraction. How is it possible to reduce aesthetic experience or moral
feelings to a mathematical calculation? Hobbes, however, insisted that
just as we learn in mathematics to add and subtract numbers, or in
geometry to add and subtract angles and proportions, we also add and
subtract "in consequences of words" when we make aesthetic and moral
judgments. In logic, Hobbes believed, we generally learn to "add . . .
together two names to make an affirmation, and two affirmations to make
a syllogism, and many syllogisms to make a demonstration." This logical
principle, he believed, is the same in acts of linguistic reasoning, such as
poetic grammar and moral rhetoric, as in mathematical or geometric
demonstrations. Similarly, in domains such as politics and law, the logic
of addition and subtraction is also the rule. For example, politicians
follow the principle of calculation because they "add together pactions to
find men's duties." Lawyers, too, merely add and subtract "laws and facts
to find what is right and wrong in the actions of private men."[2]

In its strongest terms, Hobbes's claim means that any natural facts or
human actions that can be quantified are rational, whereas those facts or
actions that are not quantifiable, not calculable, cannot be deemed rational. This is a quantitative-formalistic conception of reason, in which
quantifiability and calculability are isomorphic with rationality. An intended consequence of this doctrine is new conceptions of science and
philosophy: whatever is not intelligible through calculation is simply
unscientific, and a philosophical proposition is practically irrelevant as
well as meaningless if it does not conform to the principle of addition
and subtraction. Reason, under this theory of science and philosophy, is

nothing more than a natural logical machine good only for material computation. This model of rationality simultaneously bears on what may be considered meaningful and meaningless, true and false, and useful and useless. That is why, for Hobbes, all meaningful, truthful, and useful words are proper names. For example, a truthful statement "consisteth in the right ordering of *names* in our affirmations," and a proposition is meaningful only if in it "a man that seeketh precise truth had need to remember what every *name* he uses stands for, and to place it accordingly."[3] A useful statement is one that contains nothing but truthful and meaningful names in an order that accurately reflects the quantifiable logical relations of addition and subtraction among the names.

In light of this theory of names, we can say that Hobbes's is a mechanistic and materialist model of the rational. This model embodies a radical naturalism that had its origins in scientific Renaissance movements. The rise of natural philosophy during the Renaissance suggests a rejection of medieval scholasticism in favor of introducing more empirical approaches into philosophical inquiry. Philosophers sought models of reasoning that allowed better classifications of objects in the natural world. This was one motivation behind the origins and growth of the field of natural history, for natural history was predicated on the belief that a correct taxonomy of beings reflected an order believed embedded in nature by its creator. Classifiability itself became evidence of the existence of this order and a reflection of the providential intelligence. Human reason and its capacity to classify was thus understood as a direct instrument to uncover God's own intelligent design in nature and perfect the moral ends of humanity. Hobbes saw in mathematics and technology a combination of humankind's divinely endowed intelligence and the earthly power of this intelligence. The purpose of this power was scientific comprehension of the material world and the technological application of this knowledge to ends intended by God and humans: dominion and guardianship over human destiny and the rest of God's creation. Hobbes explains that "in geometry—which is the only science that it hath pleased God hitherto to bestow on mankind—men begin at settling the significations of their words; which settling of significations, they call definitions, and place them in the beginning of their reckoning." Then, to highlight the systematic natural design of the mathematical and technological model of reasoning, he adds that the "light of human minds is perspicuous words, but by exact definitions first snuffed, and purged from ambiguity. Reason is the pace; increase of science, the way; and the benefit of mankind, the end."[4]

Hobbes's view of rationality and science has a deeper anthropological and historical structure . I call this an articulation of necessary relations between identity and reason. This is evident in Hobbes's conjunction of the imperative to produce useful knowledge with the need to expand the structures of the rational in the spheres of language, culture, society, and politics. Furthermore, this view of reason requires that the rationality, function, values, and ends of aesthetic experience, and the fields of the arts in general, must remain marginal in relation to idea reason, because aesthetics is without obvious "meaning." (The meaningful relates to the meaningless in just the same way the useful relates to the useless and order to disorder.) For Hobbes, the meaning of any proposition can only be instrumentally determined. And since, for him, instrumentality and function define not just the core but also the whole of rationality, the rationality of art is not self-evident as long as art is considered primarily subjective and to be judged only by the non-instrumental or non-objective idea of individual or cultural taste. If one asked about poetry or painting, "Is it true or false?" Hobbes would reply that the arts potentially belong, ontologically, to a realm of ambiguity in which truth and untruth, order and disorder, and reason and unreason compete for reality. Hobbes condemns poetry as "senseless and ambiguous words." Poetic use of metaphorical language is nothing but an *ignes fatui* "wandering amongst innumerable absurdities." Hobbes was convinced that poetry and the arts in general lead in only one direction: toward the debasement of language, the corruption of culture and of morality, social strife, and, ultimately, seditious behavior.[5]

We can confirm that Hobbes worked within an emerging modern consensus about the nature of rationality when we consider the writings of one of his mentors, Francis Bacon. In writing *The New Organon*, Bacon hoped to undertake the first study of modern scientific consciousness. Whereas Galileo wished to extend scientific knowledge to the objective bodies of the planets, Bacon saw himself as mapping out the subjective order of reason. But both thinkers are united in the belief that causal laws regulated both the objective and subjective dimensions of nature. The *Organon* is a systematic, naturalistic, and materialistic account of the conditions of rationality. It claims to establish the best principles and methods of knowledge. The word "new" in the title suggests an intention to supplant the Aristotelian organon, or logic, that dominated the works of medieval thinkers such as Thomas Aquinas.[6]

Prior to the publication of the *New Organon* in 1620, Bacon had already made a name for himself with *A Treatise on the Advancement of Learning*, a shorter book published in 1605. The main thesis of the *Treatise* is that only the natural sciences can provide dependable knowledge. "Invention," Bacon writes in that book, "is of two kinds: the one of arts and science." In line with what we see in Hobbes, however, the arts are devalued in favor of the sciences. The arts, Bacon writes, are "absolutely deficient." The reason for this deficiency, again consistent with what was advanced by Hobbes, is that the arts have little or no instrumental, that is, applied technological function. In quite crude terms, Bacon argues that "the immense regions of the West Indies [would have] never been discovered" had the explorers relied on poetry, painting, or music. Instead, it was their knowledge of mathematics and geometry, and their application to shipbuilding and navigation, that allowed the political and economic expansion of the British Isles into what eventually became the British Empire.[7]

Hobbes's and Bacon's ideas about science are inseparable from their advocacy of technology. For them, the truth of reason is science and the truth of science is technology, hence Hobbes's definition of reasoning as calculation and Bacon's dictum that knowledge is power.[8] By reducing rationality to quantitative scientific reasoning, and all scientific thinking to useful calculation, Bacon placed himself in a position to lament the wastefulness of time spent pursuing artistic achievements. For Bacon, as for Hobbes, the pursuit of the arts actively threatened both the growth of scientific knowledge and the economic and cultural cohesion of the social and political order. Yet Bacon was harsher than Hobbes in his warnings about the corrupting effects of nonscientific activities. Bacon's critique of epistemic and moral decadence manifesting itself as artistic and literary activity was entirely radical: "The advancement of arts," he warned, "hath made no . . . progress" in production of useful knowledge about any aspects of nature.[9] The project and promise of his *Organon* was to redirect the course of science away from nonproductive and misleading beliefs about the supposed harmlessness of the arts.

If, as Bacon argues, reasoning outside the rules of mathematics, geometry, and closely related sciences is no reasoning at all, then arts are manifestations of irrationality and must be not only culturally degraded but also, when possible, banned. Similarly, academic study of the arts is unnecessary because whatever legitimate objectives such courses of study might have could be better accomplished and realized in the methods of the *New Organon*. Whatever moral or technical worth or authority lay in artistic works could and must, Bacon and Hobbes hoped, be reduced to a combined system of meaning, truth, and logic that conformed to the mechanical and instrumental model of reason. This combined system, however, cannot reveal in its own methods any appropriation of the subjectivity or outright irrationality associated with the arts. The scientific method can advance only by overcoming competing methods—a competition resulting from, in the first place, a confusing plurality in which the scientific method is tempted by the diversions of the nonscientific spirit of the arts. "Let men," Bacon advised, "cease to wonder if the whole course of science be not run, when all have wandered from the path, quitting it entirely, and deserting experience, or involving themselves in mazes, and wandering about, whilst a regularly combined system would lead them in a sure track, through its wilds to the day of axioms."[10] The expectation was that a newer form of rationality would emerge by a reordering of the plurality of methods. But this reordering is possible only if science assumes as its sole mission the will to truth in the formalistic-quantitative principle of science-as-technology.

Hobbes's and Bacon's emphasis on general, universal method in the sciences was familiar in the philosophical cultures of the modern Age of Reason. They were not the only ones to notice the practical—even culturally and politically imperial—potential of the evidence-based conception of science and its technologies. The goal of the scientific method is to establish a mechanical rational process that generates certain, reliable, and usable knowledge. This form of ideal knowledge, to which Descartes also aspires in his writings on science and logic, would be free of subjective interpretations—free of what Bacon more derisively referred to as "argument and discourse." For Bacon, only facts (not arguments or interpretations) and technology (not magical or theological beliefs) could drive the enlightened development of the scientific method. Science, thus understood, is the process of directly rendering naked, brute facts about the nature of the material world. Evidence-based science unveils the logic of matter and reveals the deepest secrets of nature.

The causal law of nature is also the law of reason. And it is this reason that grounds—or should ground—whatever may be considered rational in subjective experience itself. In an analogy suggesting the expected directness of the relationship between the causal law of nature and the law of reason, Bacon compared methods of acquiring knowledge to three ways of walking: one could feel one's way in the dark; one could be led, even in the daylight, as if one were blind; or one could direct one's own steps with the benefit of daylight. These images of light and darkness, of the self-determination to walk with one's own agency rather than being led by the will of another, suggest the direct availability of the power of both the objective and subjective natural light of reason. To systematize the scope and the power of this light was the project of the Enlightenment, the Age of Reason. Compared to the dark paths in caves and mazes presented by "argument and discourse," the true method of the experimental science is rather a solid, straight, open-eyed—in short, guaranteed—walk to truth, an epistemological slam dunk. Whereas in arguments and discourse "a man tries all kinds of experiments . . . as if . . . led by the hand," true experimentation by scientific method is based only on "learned experience,"[11] on brute empirical facts learned from observation and on replicable calculation. By these means alone can one establish in the simplest form a general method "that could be applied with certainty and across the board."[12]

The *New Organon* claims its newness by presenting itself as a ground-clearing exercise. Since one must get rid of bad habits of thinking before one can discover the new and better ways, Bacon classifies the false habits that stand in the way of true science. In biblical language, he lists four "idols": the Idol of the Tribe, the Idol of the Den, the Idol of the Market, and the Idol of the Theater.[13] A science under the influence of one of these Idols is therefore an idolatry, a worship of falsehood. Each kind of falsehood has unique qualities and threatens in its own way the knowledge of truth. Under the sway of the Idol of the Tribe, for example, human reason is threatened by attachment to a tribal fog, capable of enveloping the entire history of the human race and casting a spell on humanity's scientific and moral sense. This fog is a naïve and uncritical attitude that humans can adopt toward nature. It casts a sensual spell on perception, so that reason becomes aesthetically enchanted. A mind overcome by this first and most common of the idols is both enthralled and stupefied by the natural, sensual world. However, the real danger—apart from its essential uselessness—of the state of sensual enthrallment and stupefaction is not in the aesthetic enchantment itself. It is rather in the imaginative magnification of subjective mood and affect, which results in an incapacity for objectivity, an incapacity that imposes upon reason. A mind that is thus incapacitated will have difficulty determining how nature actually is to a nonenchanted, instrumental consciousness. Without an objective end toward which the natural or subjective expressive experience is instrumentalized, the aesthetically enchanted mind has a capacity only for poetic and artistic exhibitionism. As we saw earlier, for Hobbes and Bacon, only the technical and instrumental quantification and uses of nature by reason may be considered reasoning at all.

Although Bacon admits the possibility of distortion in thought when he writes "all . . . perceptions both of the senses and the mind bear reference to man and not to the universe" and accepts that "the human mind resembles those uneven mirrors which impart their own properties to different objects, from which rays are emitted and distort and disfigure them,"[14] he nevertheless held that humans are, in the final analysis, accountable for the errors in what we assume either about the nature of the world or about our own ways of coming to knowledge of that world. When we make rational judgments, then, we alone are responsible for our cognitive errors. For example, when from a first sensual or mental impression we draw conclusions that suppose "a greater degree of order and equality in things, than [a more objective consciousness] really finds,"[15] we cannot blame nature but rather our enthrallment to the fog of the Idol of the Tribe. Likewise, the culprit could not be the senses, for the senses neither lie nor deceive: they simply feel. The culprit, the idolater, is the agent-owner of the senses, the mind or mental faculty whose job is to calculate objectivity from distorted sensation to undistorted principles and axioms.

Similarly, if human "understanding," instead of measuring and calculating facts to establish the truth of nature, gives way to subjective impressions, and spins abstract theories to suit this subjectivism, then the fault for the lack of reason is not in the facts or in the subjective sensation of facts but in the incapacity of the understanding to use objective methods of evaluation to discover the truth about the empirical laws governing the facts. This materialistic and positivistic epistemological empiricism therefore considers abstraction and theory, on their own, as "idol" speculations. Like poetry and the arts, theory building is not merely harmless recreation but rather a positive obstacle to the advancement of true and reliable science.

In line with certain tenets of materialism and positivism that, philosophers and historians of science generally believe, go back to the ancient Egyptian geometricians and the ancient Greek atomic philosophers, Bacon's modern embrace of empiricism was a polemical act. Whereas key modern rationalists closer to the Platonic idealist tradition accept that errors in reasoning are attributable to the passion of the senses, they also believed that it is abstraction—*theory*—that could correct the errors of passion and the senses. To Bacon, however, error in reasoning cannot be attributed to sensation as such: an error in reasoning or judgment is a failure to take accurate measure and report accurately what had been given by nature as facts, as data, in *sensation*. One discovers the causal laws governing the facts not by "thinking" (arguing, for example) but by measuring. Theory cannot correct an error of fact. When it claims to be able to do this, theory itself is in error. The only thing that can remedy error is calculation. Error, therefore, is the fault of a reason that has *either* been enchanted by the senses and passion *or* become lost in the fogs of its own idealistic, theoretical abstractions. A healthy reason, on the other hand, is one that generates knowledge by observing, measuring, calculating, and reporting information about nature as given directly in sense data.

The observational, calculative, and reportorial functions of thought are thus indeed incompatible with either misidentification of understanding with aesthetic sensuality or theoretical abstraction. For example, unlike abstractions in theory and in theoretical discourse, the modern empiricist believes that observation and measurement are not arguments about facts: they are objective reports of facts. What is reported—fact—is the necessary and predictable information about nature transmitted to reason through observable sense perception. To empirically cure the mind of its errant abstractions and especially the necessarily misguided theoretical sophistry, Bacon offers this recommendation: "It is better to dissect than abstract nature." Aware that this experimental and materialistic outlook on method has a history—a history in opposition to what he considered the "traditional" idealist philosophies of Platonism, and of course having chosen the partisan company of the physical philosophers and practical geometricians of pre-Socratic Egypt and Iona—Bacon polemically stood against the "argumentation and discourse" he claimed to be the essence of medieval Scholasticism. Against Scholasticism, he proposed an explicit return to "the method employed by the school of Democritus." The atomists and the materialistic method, he promised, will lead to "greater progress in penetrating nature."[16]

Ironically, it was this bold return to philosophical naturalism and the empirical method of reasoning that Bacon had in mind when he spoke about new grounds for founding a new science. Unlike Descartes, a contemporary who advocated *clear and distinct* ideas, Bacon championed *clear and demonstrable* ideas. Against both Scholasticism and Cartesianism, the Baconian path to science leads not through theory and speculation, but through the collection of data, measurements, and calculation, for the truths of nature are revealed not by discourse and arguments but by the experimental method. To reject this method is to succumb to the Idol of the Tribe.

Similar to the Idol of the Tribe, the Idol of the Den is a threat to all minds. But unlike the Idol of the Tribe, the Idol of the Den is idiosyncratic in its manifestation. It is peculiar to "each individual's mind and body." It is also peculiar to accidents of "education" and "habit."[17] These peculiarities make it harder to produce a uniform or general account of the characteristics of the Idol of the Den. So I shall try to capture the Idol's essential qualities by contrasting it with next Idol, the Idol of the Market.

Because habit, custom, and tradition play key roles in the miseducation of individuals, conventional opinions develop and govern individual minds as well as social relations, and miseducation and conventional opinion make both individuals and social relations sources of errors: they affect a person's or a society's capacity to think and behave in rational ways. In language, for example, both long-standing traditions of usage as well as ephemeral conventions are capable of creating climates of minds in which communication and social intercourse are distorted and opaque. These corruptions in language, no matter the sources, lead to intellectual confusions and errors whereby, as Bacon put it, "men imagine that their reason governs words, whilst, in fact, the words react upon the understanding."[18] Whereas reason-governed uses of words are rational, the abstract deployment of words for rhetorical effect is irresponsible sophistry, a show of cleverness with words without regard to soundness of reason and to factual truth. Decoupled from facts and the empirical quest for truth through measurement and calculation, sophisticated abstractions do not reveal any facts about the world. Abstract uses of words in ways that conform to mere theoretical understanding rather than fact-based natural reasoning both obscure and positively harm prospects of knowledge of the natural and the social worlds. The Idol of the Den and the Idol of the Market stand for, respectively, smaller and larger scale corruptions of public lives by the use and abuse of language. In small social units and even a larger group such as a nation, intentional or unintentional corruption of language may be observed. For example, instead of its use as means of communicating information, language could also be sophistically used to hide information, to spread false information, and to mislead by all sorts of indirection.[19]

Bacon, as natural philosopher, believed that words must reflect the material essence of the thing the word is used to describe. He considered terms that had no reference to elements of the natural or social word as either superfluous or as assistants to other words that *do* factually describe the world. When he noted the seemingly arbitrary ways in which conventions rather than naturalistic realism governed individual and public speech, he consistently characterized these conventions as forms of Idols. Because the nonscientific uses of language are learned from the cradle (Den) and in social commerce (Market), even the names chosen for these idols must be materially transparent. Presumably, if the Idols did not corrupt human language, both everyday and technical uses of language would be able to reflect facts of nature and of sense data in the most objective and transparent fashion. Every word would function like a proper name: a direct material referent to measurable qualities of objects *and* their causal laws as established in empirical reason.

Thus, what is at stake for Bacon in the problems of the Idols of the Den and of the Market is wider than the issue of accurately or inaccurately naming a thing. More generally, his concern is the metaphysical question of the relation between concept and object, or word and thing. The two Idols corrupt this relation. The underlying metaphysical belief is that nature—like a book of grammar, the grammar of reason—needs to have each of its letters in the right place. Words should reflect the rightness of the position of the things they refer to in the chain of beings that constitute nature. But they should also reflect materially the essential qualities of the objects. Measurement and calculation demonstrate the causal necessity regulating the relations among objects. Language, if it is language of reason rather than sophistry, ought to reflect meaningfully the logical position of each object in nature, the intrinsic qualities of the object, and the causal network that binds one object to another under a causal chain of natural law.

For language and sociality to be governed by the Idols of the Den and of the Market is the same as to enthrone universally the governments of prejudice and sophistry. The Idols, at a minimum, prevent growth of knowledge of the material world as well as development of rational transparency in social communication. The lack of transparency, in turn, encourages disregard for objectivity, the growth of untruth, and the immoral and harmful acts of lies and deception. Against these Idols, their conventions, and the confusion of words they promote in social intercourse, Bacon searched for a purer vocabulary for factual truths and information exchange—purer because it would communicate only the essential nature of material objects or social relations as shown by quantifiable methods of measurement.[20] To corrupt a language is literally to misplace its letters, words, sentences, or paragraphs in such a way that the natural and objective conditions of nature which language is meant to communicate become lost. Such a de-natured language, having lost the world, becomes subjective chains of signs to which the speakers—in flights of abstractions or fancy, in situations of social competition—willfully assign whatever meanings they consider suitable. "Man," Bacon cautioned, "always believes more readily that which he prefers."[21]

The fourth and final Idol, the Idol of the Theater, can be considered a version of the third—with the exception that the Idol of the Theater afflicts only the highly educated individual or group because it is a kind of ignorance specific to the professional or the expert. The ignorance occurs when the learned becomes too attached to his "method" or "school of thought." This emotional or otherwise epistemically inordinate attachment makes the promoters of the method or school rigid, complacent, and incapable of change in light of new knowledge. As with the Idol of the Den—only this time afflicting the class of experts who are rooted in an existing intellectual orthodoxy—the savant suffering from the Idol of the Theater holds, Bacon says, "dogmas of peculiar systems of philosophy."[22] The error here, obviously, is not in the courage to hold fast to one's system of knowledge production, but in the wrongheadedness of holding fast to a system that requires change—the sort of system of philosophy that Bacon also calls "impractical" science. The impractical, in this unique sense, is, of course, a fatal flaw to materialistic reason. Tellingly, however, with the exception of Democritus's empirical materialism, Bacon regarded "all systems of philosophy hitherto received or imagined, as so many plays brought out and performed, creating fictitious and theatrical worlds."[23] If *all* known philosophical systems since Socrates are the abstract inventions of the scholars rather than patient empirical observation and mastery of objective nature or societies, it is, of course, only because Bacon was working from a peculiar conception of rationality, a conception tied to a particular metaphysics of nature and of language. But he hoped that humanity would conquer all its idols, and that philosophy would become, at last, a rigorous science of nature and society. This hope is sustained by the thought that the errors in reason do not "introduce themselves secretly into the understanding." Instead, they are routinely propagated by those who should know better, since the idols are "manifestly instilled and cherished into the memory by the fictions of theories and depraved rules of demonstration."[24] As Bacon also noted, the cure for this intellectual depravity cannot be found in more *philosophical* arguments (the Idol of the Theater). What is required is observation and experiment. Instead of argument and discourse, measurement and application will determine whether an idea is true or false, sound or unsound, scientific or merely philosophical. As Leibniz memorably put this way of thinking: Let us calculate, Sir.

FORMAL REASON

We get the best picture of this conception of rationality if we compare it to the ideal of calculative reason promoted by Hobbes and Bacon. It is obvious that their ideal of calculation was driven by the needs of modern, even culturally imperial-minded, science-and-technology. "Reasoning" for Hobbes and Bacon, was immediately interpreted to mean advancement of science in service of the modern—albeit somewhat less critically conceived historical—"progress of man." This modern practical commitment and, frankly, partisan polemics against everything but quantitative science can be easily seen from this chart:

	POSITIVE USE	CONSEQUENCE	ABUSE
COGNITION	Reason	Rationality	Misconception
NAME	Reference	Determinate meaning	Misnomination
PREDICATION	Representation	Accuracy in representation	Misrepresentation
SIGNIFICATION	Communication	Social transparency	Miscommunication
CRITICISM	Government	Sociality	Quarrelsomeness
ARTS	Frivolity	Entertainment	Silliness

This matrix accurately portrays the naturalistic and positivistic philosophies of Hobbes and Bacon, including their shared disdain for aesthetics and the arts and the compensatory idealization of cogitation as quantitative objectification. In this representational scheme of calculative rationality, literature and the arts, in general, come to stand as symbols for either the irrational, the useless, or the meaninglessly silly.[25]

But we can see that, while exaggeratedly claiming to abhor abstraction and the abstract, both Hobbes and Bacon were not immune from them. Not only are their conceptions of rationality formally rigid, monolithic, and intolerant of difference, but their ideas about the work of reasoning seems, in places at least and from a more hermeneutically historical point of view, hypostatic. In what follows I isolate the formal character of rationality as such by using the robustly materialistic and positivistic ideas of Hobbes and Bacon as a starting point. In doing so we can highlight Hobbes's and Bacon's achievements as well as explore the magnitude of the contradictions—not to mention some outright errors—hidden in their theories of reason and in the bold models of rationality.

The basis of all formalism is the appeal to the independence of the abstract and the logical domains of reason in relation to the contexts of experience. Ironically, in addition to our counterintuitive reliance on the works of the materialists and positivists Hobbes and Bacon, in the ancient word it is in Aristotle rather than in Plato that we can best see the historical power of the most technical concept of "form." In many ways, Aristotle's *Organon*, a collection of six pieces of work on logic (λογίσμός),[26] is a partial but adequate point of exploration to guide our inquiry on the nature of rational formalism. Though an epistemological realist, Aristotle in his "Prior Analytics" and "Posterior Analytics"—the third and fourth parts of the *Organon*—shows how one can map universal laws intrinsic to beings, thought, and language. Because nature itself is law-like in constitution, natural beings naturally fall into, and manifest, different categories (κατηγορία) of reality. In scientific classification, for example, these categories are revealed as law-like in objects and in the concepts of the objects. For example, when we speak about substance and accident, or of genera, species, and individuals, we do not merely "abstract" subjectively. In the mind's representations—representations that are logically formalizable—we capture actual modes of either the external world or the internal constitutions of the mind itself. The categorical division of names and words into their simplest units of meaning, the formal analytical study of relationships within and across such units or terms of meaning, and the dialectical articulation of the forms of meaning with the objects of sense, the formal outlines of which the categories and the analysis were intended to reveal—these are the contents and the outline of Aristotle's program in the *Organon*. Categorical, logical, representations are meant not only to show us how things are but also to explain how we necessarily think about them: in kind and properties; subject and predicate; substance and accidents (of quantity, quality, relation, place, date, posture, possession, action, and passivity). It is in the logical representations of these relations across the categories that science must find its task and method, namely, to establish universal laws of beings and to do so in a language. This language, of course, must be the language of reason itself: logic. This is why logic, for Aristotle, is the ideal form of human language, for it most accurately frames and mirrors the truths of the various states of what is objectively or subjectively real: the scientific categories of thought *are* the categories of beings.

These insights were best captured in the standard chain of reasoning of the syllogism. The syllogistic method of thinking guides language away from mere sophistry and onto the paths of logic, reason's own internal requirements of formal coherence as well coherence of form with the state or states of being of which it is a form. In the syllogism is thus fulfilled several levels of human expectations about universal intelligibility: the intelligibility of *existence*, of the *thinking* of the existence, and of the mutually *relational transformation*—a kind of deep, dialectical translation—of the thought of being (the thing that exists) into meaningful words, signs, or images of the existent. Words, signs, or images may be oral or graphic but, in any case, must be expressions of truths in nature (object), mind (subject), and objective and subjective relations.

The simplest representational version of this relation is the standard form of deductive logic. The classic definition of deductive reasoning is a "discourse in which certain things being stated, something other than what is stated follows of necessity from their being so."[27] To deductively generate knowledge, one only needs to proceed in order from one true statement to another in a process of necessary implication, such as:

All animals are mortal ($P \rightarrow Q$).
All men are animals ($S \rightarrow P$).
All men are mortal ($S \rightarrow Q$).

The middle term, "animals" (P), necessarily implicates the predicative "mortal" (Q), and therefore the first premise "All animals are mortal" ($P \rightarrow Q$), to the conclusion, "All men are mortal" ($S \rightarrow Q$). The necessity in the implications can also be thus formally stated:

A is a predicate of B.
But B is a predicate of C.
Therefore A is a predicate of C.

These demonstrations are usually called *a priori* truths because they are acquired by a priori reasoning, *deductive* logic.

Induction, by contrast, is the process in which, by observing certain empirical facts repeatedly, "the universal that is there," as Aristotle says, "becomes plain."[28] Unlike deduction, where the movement is from "first principles" to particular cases, the general to the concrete, in induction the procedure is reversed. When a mind observes a particular thing, say, a house, the memory stores the forms of the sense data activated in the perception and, after observing other similar objects, the mind generates from the particular experiences of houses a general concept with a general meaning. The inductive process and the universal concept thus yielded offer greater knowledge both about what is observed and about the experience of observation. Thus, though sense-perception as such cannot attain the universal, the process of induction, on the basis of repeated experiences of particulars, introduces to the mind a formal structure of otherwise dispersed empirical experiences. The logic of induction is thus the rite of passage from the particular to the universal, from subjective experience to objective.

Inductive logic contains an empiricist element in a way entirely unique to it. In fact, it marks the place of the dividing line between philosophical empiricism and idealism. Whereas the idealist maintains, for example, that mathematics is a superior science dealing with real essences of numbers, the empiricist's attempt to formalize modes of thinking as deductive and inductive points to the need for greater accountability of thought in relation to the experience of demonstrable sense—not just mental—data. Yet, unlike the proponents of calculative rationality who would reduce all knowledge to the demonstrable, the rational formalist, in a tradition perhaps best understood in our invocations of Aristotle, must accept that "not all knowledge is demonstrative." On the contrary, says Aristotle, "knowledge of the immediate premises is independent of demonstrations."[29] In other words, if we assume every principle needs syllogistic or demonstrable proof, there would be need for proofs ad infinitum—and nothing would be proven.

Is Aristotle suggesting that certain principles of reason are known immediately, without *any* demonstration?[30] Or does he mean to say that the truth or untruth of certain principles may never be known? If there were such a principle or principles of reason, the best candidate in Aristotle's writings must be the principle of contradiction. In its logical form, the principle, as variously stated in the *Metaphysics*, says: "Of two propositions, one of which affirms something and the other denies the same thing, one must be true and the other false." Or in another version: "The same thing cannot be an attribute and not an attribute of the same subject at the same time and in the same way."[31] The truth of this and similar propositions of principles, according to Aristotle, are beyond philosophical and empirical interrogation, for they are what make interrogation at all possible. (One could argue that Wittgenstein has "dissolved" this Aristotelian question. Works by Wittgenstein as well as American pragmatists like Rorty allow one to explain how—in a kind of partition of perception and thought—a reasonable person might come to hold the belief that *p* and the belief that *not-p* without believing that (*p and not-p*). An epistemic condition like this raises questions about what is meant by "alternative" rationalities.)[32] But if we stayed with Aristotle's examples, and if we designed an Aristotelian hierarchy in reasoning, it might look something like this: first principles which are perceived intuitively; that which is derived necessarily (syllogistically, from first principles); and contingent "observation" or mere experience (a matter of opinion, convention, habit, and tradition), which may or may not cash out as rational by the inductive method.

If, however, we ask why the first item is a law (e.g., that something cannot be said to be true and not true at the same time), it is not clear that there is an answer beyond the restatement of the law. We restate by pointing out that *that* is the formal requirement of conditions of reason as such. We therefore call it a law because it expresses, in the abstract, an ideal that reason *both* idealistically stipulates for itself *and* aspires to respect. The law-likeness derives from the internal force of reason. This force—the force of argument—can also be given a formal representation. For example, if "*A* is the case," and it is irrational to affirm that "*A* is the case and *A* is not the case" (if *A* means the same thing in both instances and the word "same" is taken in its ordinary meaning in the English language), logicians would be able to demonstrate the rightness of the reasoning:

1. If P:

$P(\text{TRUE})$

$\sim P(\text{FALSE})$

2. If $\sim P$:

$P[\sim \sim P]\ (\text{FALSE})$

$\sim P\ (\text{TRUE})$

3. If P:

$(P \vee \sim P)\ (\text{TRUE})$

$\sim(P \vee \sim P)\ (\text{FALSE})$

That is the basic formula for testing logical proofs: TF, FT, and TF. We can also test the law in other variations of the proof:

4. Socrates is a man or Socrates is not a man [P v $\sim$$P$]

    4.a. Socrates is a man (P) [TRUE]

    4.b. Socrates is not a man ($\sim$$P$) [FALSE, $\sim$($\sim$P)]

    (Or: 4.1.a. Socrates is not a man ($\sim$$P$) [TRUE]

    4.1.b. Socrates is a man (P) [FALSE, $\sim$(P)])

5.a. Socrates is male and dead or Socrates is not male and not dead ((P & Q) v $\sim$(P & Q))

    5.a.i. (P & Q) TRUE

    5.a.ii. ($\sim$$P$ & $\sim$$Q$) FALSE

    5.a.iii. (P & $\sim$$Q$) FALSE

    5.a.iv. ($\sim$$P$ & Q) FALSE

where 4 and 5 are, respectively, TF, FT, and TFFF. Either of the proofs can be varied to generate other conforming standards.[33]

But if this logic of these demonstrations is so self-evident, why did Aristotle (and many since) suspect that the rational grounds of the forms themselves could not be independently—without infinite regress—demonstrated? If this remarkable suspicion is true, why is the question of the truth or untruth status of the forms of proof beyond the demonstrably thinkable?

I will explore this question more seriously in the next sections, under the hermeneutical and phenomenological theories of rationality. There we will be in a position to ask: If the rationality of grounds of demonstrated conditions of logical truth cannot themselves be logically *directly* demonstrated, can the same grounds be *indirectly* elaborated? If formal-demonstrative logic cannot justify—beyond the analytical or tautological—its own logical rules, then the conditions of the possibility the rules themselves must be subjected to hermeneutical explorations or phenomenological investigations. In such a hermeneutics or phenomenology, rather than seeking an explanation of what is already an explanandum, we would be concerned to produce narratively representational examples and counterexamples of the law presupposed in the explanandum.

HERMENEUTICAL REASON

Can hermeneutical exploration offer elaborate truths about the supposedly hidden grounds of reason? To be equal to this task, a hermeneutical elaboration and narration would have to show what it would be like to think and act *as if* it is not irrational to believe *p* and *not-p* and not believe that. On what grounds is it absurd to say, for example, "It is the case that it is raining and it is not raining" or "It is not true that 'It is raining' and 'It is not raining' is false"? For a start, an effective hermeneutical account cannot be yet another layer of logical proofs per se. It has to be a contextual *exemplification* of the necessary general grounds or universal principles of rationality as such.

Hermeneutical procedures can indeed offer interpretive insights into otherwise problematic beliefs about what it means to be rational or act rationally. Such beliefs include the everyday understanding that in the normal run of affairs, the mutual expectation is that people do not speak or act in ways that violently ignore the grounds of rules assumed in the use of such terms as "is," "and," and "or." To ignore the necessary rationality of these or similar grammatically foundational terms—on the grounds that, as we saw in Aristotle, their own grounds cannot be independently (independent of grammatical demonstration) proven—is to deny the very conditions of possibility of communication as well as of any proof-making. But what would be a reason that grounds other reasons but whose rationality could not itself be directly logically demonstrated?

If I am presented with the numbers 2, 4, 6, 8. . . . and 3, 6, 9, 12 . . . and I consider myself rational because I can go on, what is the reason of the rules on the basis of which I am able to go on? What makes following a rule rational? What are the grounds of the order, logic, or reason I must assume in going on with a numerical series? One could answer that, in this case, a "reason" for rules is reducible to the simple, most basic building blocks of thought: identity (*P*) and nonidentity (*not-P*), multitude (P *and* Q), equality ("*P* = *Q*"), and so on. If I understand these basic building blocks (as I understand 2, 4, 6, 8 . . .), I can put together larger units or series. To reason is therefore to grasp what is required in the cognitive organization and application of units and series in varieties of practically similar or conceptually related circumstances.

Suppose I know that Mr. Ugwu lives at #2 Assorock Street, but I do not know anyone else who lives on the same street. If, however, I learn that Mr. Equebe will hand-deliver a letter to Mr. Usman, whose address happens to be #10 Assorock Street, I can reasonably go on to believe that, if the same Assorock Street is in a town where street houses are

numbered odd and even, there cannot be more than three houses between the Ugwu and the Usman residences. In this simple operation of
reasoning, however, there are vast presuppositions or conditions of pre-
understandings. Without these presuppositions or pre-understandings,
the coherent chain of reasoning would be entirely impossible.

But if every belief-in-support of a reason requires its own sets of presuppositions or environmental pre-understandings in order to be rational, we can say that every reason is already a work of interpretation—a
web of both implicit and explicit elaborations on prior, ongoing, and
open-ended, related beliefs. We call these elaborations—the making explicit of the implicit in potentially rational beliefs—a "hermeneutical" exercise. Against the tendency to reduce reasoning to logical systems or calculation (addition and subtraction, positive and negative, and so on), there
appears to be a need to show why and how any fuller conception of *any*
form of reason must require a hermeneutical component or dimension.

For example, is it possible to find in the presuppositions behind prima
facie good reasoning or a system of logic the relation of some of its
presuppositions to unreason as well as to reason? Can a condition of
truth have a relation to untruth or conditions of untruth? Is it possible to
find, as grounds of a prima facie rational belief, relations of the belief's
rationality to implicit or explicit systems of unbelief? In at least one
sense, hermeneutical caution suggests that some of the answers to these
questions must be in the affirmative. After all, to take our most recent
example, there could be nowhere called Assorock Street. Our characters
could have been invented. It would therefore be in a different context—
the context of fiction, for example—that the truth of my story about the
residences of Assorock Street may be more appropriately evaluated.
Since the nature of any pre(sup)position is such that its truth shifts with
the contexts of the propositions announced from the positions, we
should accept that, at a deeper level, well beyond the gap between what is
real and what is imagined (the *ontological* question), the same affirmative answer should be extended to the same question if posed in regard
to the order of reason as such (i.e., within the context of reason's *logical*
formality).

What I have in mind in these last claims requires further illumination.
Bertrand Russell is credited with the gem: "An inconsistent system may
well contain less falsehood than a consistent one."[34] A similar saying is

attributed to Emerson: "A foolish consistency is the hobgoblin of little minds."[35] Why must we read these aphorisms as other than what they seem: witticism against excessive, pedantic, rationalism? Can we stretch them into the domain of philosophical or principled polemics against rationality as such? I say we can't because, first, the bodies of works of these writers are not known for their polemics against reason in favor of irrationalism. Second, we have already detected that in the course of ordinary logical procedures, and when the starting point of such pro- cedure is purely formal, it is easy to consider reasoning as "abstract," "rigid," or "artificial." By each of these terms I mean to suggest that that form of reason (sometimes unnecessarily) constrains or distorts what one could consider the emotional or affective timbre of our experience. In everyday language, we regularly hear complaints about "cold" logic or a "cold" heart. This suggests a conflict in experience between the "head" (reason) and the "heart" (feeling; mood or affect). When an existentialist or materialist thinker therefore makes appeal to the category "concrete experience" or "material conditions of life," it is usually a critique of abstract reasoning in the sense of cold or historically disembodied logic as just defined.

Bacon, for example, ridiculed abstract reasoning as a disembodied impediment to the experience of "reality" or "truth," just as an existen- tialist today might deride what she considers empty logical abstractions from the richness of "life," "death," and "meaning." The materialist and the existentialist can even logically demonstrate the silliness or the moral danger they claim to be implicit in abstract and disincarnate rea- son. They could formally propose:

A. All men are mortal ($P \rightarrow Q$).
Socrates is a man ($S \rightarrow P$).
Socrates is mortal ($S \rightarrow Q$).
B. Men are not mortal ($P \rightarrow \sim Q$).
Socrates is a man ($S \rightarrow P$).
Socrates is not mortal ($S \rightarrow \sim Q$).

While A is existentially and logically true, B is existentially false though logically correct. What can save us, the materialist or the existentialist might ask, from similar but more complex errors in either unverified or unverifiable presuppositions in abstract rationality? What is the remedy for the rational excesses of formalistic reason? Is there a logical rule by which one can systematically and a priori preclude oneself from affirming, wrongly, the nature of the real on the basis of a formally correct reasoning about what reason *thinks* to be the real?[36] Like a computer, the syllogisms should give us the result of whatever data we put into it. Although we can guarantee to the highest levels the reliability of the computation (because, for example, no law of contradiction is violated: the how of the computation is correct and certainly correct), there is no equivalent law guaranteeing that what we choose to compute is not itself in a condition of error and of untruth.

Heidegger and Gadamer, among others, think they have found a way around these problems of abstract reason. They demand that all studies of rationality include the hermeneutical analysis of the ontological— the existential—status of reason as such. If we can think logically but wrongly about things that exist, should we not ask if the logical form of reason is an imperfect form in regard to knowledge? If it is an imperfection, logical or moral, what kind of cultivated virtue of mind is required for its remedy? The hermeneuticist insists not only that a truth-claim must demonstrate that its computation is correct, but also that the computation and its rational or potentially irrational presuppositions are, respectively, ontologically justified or accounted for. This justification must proceed in ways existentially deeper than the procedures of a general logic. The idea of the existential also calls for a way to get beyond the merely logical-representational problems of reason in order to address the moral presuppositions of the freedom of reason. How do truth-sentences (*t*-sentences) arrive at their truth contents? How does a word come to mean what it does? What is the law in the grammatical law? Even before one proposes answers to these questions, what would it mean to give an adequate account of the reasons for these kinds of questions?

In technical concepts like *saying* and *rendering*, Heidegger develops the argument that in reason thought *gathers* the world meaningfully. To "gather," he awkwardly writes (though this is my translation), is to allow "what comes to presence to lie present in the presencing." If an expression claims to be reasonable and to have truth-value, then "that-which-has-been-said" ought to also mean "that-which-has-been-shown." The reasonable or truthful is therefore "what lies-present as such."[37]

But what does it mean to be present as such, to be shown, or rendered? Does this mean a kind of truth whose truth is revealed without argument? What does such an idea of "presence" amount to in relation to terms like "reason," "being," or "world"? What is the existential truth of objects without the arguments—the reasons—for that truth? Heidegger does not pursue these questions by grammatical analysis, perhaps because of antipathy to what he often derogatorily refers to as "representational" thinking. While he considers positive analyses of structures of grammar to be superficial and insufficiently philosophical, he asks how it is possible that being and *ratio*, existence and logic, or things and words "belong-together." But if calculative and logico-representational thinking can never enlighten the ground of this belonging-together, what is the alternative to calculation and logical representation?

Heidegger's work indicates that the superficiality of what he calls representational thinking can be escaped or transcended through a return to reason's *Geschick*—the return of thought to its ontological and historical configurations. It is in the histories of reason—the destinies of *Dasein*, the histories of individuals and nations; in the lives of societies, cultures, and civilizations—that one must return in order to fruitfully ponder reason's universal "ground" as well as meditate on the multiplicity of reason's social, cultural, and historical forms. In the ideas of *ground* of reason and *histories* (or destinies) of reason, Heidegger suggests larger frameworks within which studies of rationality might expand beyond what is obvious in calculative or representational thought. In the suggestion that, for example, a history of thinking should be part of any fuller analytical study of thought, or that a history of reason must be part of any serious study of logic, is the recognition that thought or reason and logic might be more than meets the calculative and instrumental eye in the narrowly conceived, immediate, applicatory needs of science-as-technology. Heidegger indeed suggests that the *reason* of modern science and technology harbors more than it positively reveals. Like the Christian theologian who was prepared to grant to the Jew the status of a "hidden" Christian, Heidegger is convinced that modern *ratio*, dominated as it is by calculative and formal conceptions of reason, hiddenly remembers what properly, if now only implicitly and as an echo, is a transcendental horizon which belongs to the origins and history of reason. In *ratio*, we are told, "the representation of beings with respect to the fact that they are, and are in this and that way, is a representation that has being in sight and hence, although without knowing it, has something like ground/reason in sight."[38] The ground and histories which are in sight—the being or existence of things which reason is supposed to render conceptual—echo, in modernity, a distant, primal past of reason as well as reason's far-off, future destinies. But modernity, claims Heidegger, has forgotten not only this ground of reason but also the meaning of the loss of the ground, and therefore jeopardizes its own future. It is not only that modern humanity has forgotten the histories of its own reason; we have also forgotten the meaning of the forgetting. Yet the state of forgetfulness is an active one. This is so because it is also "natural" for representational reason to raise questions about the grounds of its own existence. Heidegger refers to this sort of questioning as the Question of the Principle of Reason.

In *What Is Thinking*, for example, he makes a suggestive distinction between "thinking" and "reasoning." He denies the terms' synonymity in part because correct reasoning usually requires only that its procedure be rationally proper. A proper reasoning is thus one governed and justified according to the dictates of the rules of reason itself. Furthermore, the justification can be empirically inductive or logically deductive—the kind of demonstration we see, for example, in Descartes's "Rules for Properly Conducting the Reason and Seeking Truth in the Sciences." But there should also be a distinction between satisfying conditions of rational demonstration, as in good evidence of reasoning, and satisfying existentially the historical grounds of reason's spontaneous self-production. In thinking, for example, one is faced with broader dimensions of exercises of reason; the question is not only what a demonstration of reasoning is about, but the conditions of productions of the reason. In *The Principle of Reason*, accordingly, Heidegger takes issue with the idea that truth in thinking is *propositio vera*. If thinking were merely about producing true propositional judgments, "reason" would be nothing beyond *connexio praedicati cum subjecto*, the connection of what is stated with that about which the statement is made. Truth in the scenario would be no more than the thing in judgment that gives justification (reason) for the connecting of a subject and a predicate.[39] To "give reason," in this narrowest sense, is to render an account of the truth of judgments, and the rational ground of the truth of such judgments would be provided as a formal representational accounting. Heidegger partially accepts, though challenges, these conceptions of reason, judgment, and truth.

Heidegger's work on these issues is more immediately motivated by Kant than by Descartes. Heidegger takes it that the Question of the Principle of Reason is at the heart of the problems Kant raised in the *Critique of Pure Reason* concerning the transcendental grounds of subjectivity. From this Kantian point of view, a specific meaning of reasoning as representational accounting emerges in Heidegger's appropriations of the German vernacular *rechnen*, reckoning. To reckon, Heidegger says, is "to represent something *as* something," "to orient something *in terms* of something," or "putting something *in order for* something." He then argues that reasoning as *rechnen* amounts to "[taking] one's bearing from something"[40] or taking something into account.

When one reckons with something, one keeps an eye on what is reckoned, orients oneself by it, and acts according to this orientation. To reckon or count on something, therefore, means to *expect* it: to figure or anticipate what is counted on as something upon which to build a reason for an orientation. This meaning of reckoning—and therefore of reason as a mode of reckoning, a figure of orientation—cannot be subsumed under calculation, if by this term we mean numbering by addition and subtraction. Reasoning as figuring-out an orientation, *reckoning with*, is not guidance by calculus. Or, if it is a kind of calculus, then *calculus* must mean more than mere procedural counting. "Calculus" henceforth could be that which is counted upon, what thus functions to orient the counter, as that around which something is elaborated. In the elaboration the word "calculation," surprisingly, suggests that there is more to counting than the processes of addition and subtraction. This is because in counting one also *counts on*. To count on something is to figure it into a deliberation. What is counted on thus also becomes a basis of the reason for the deliberation. This becomes a way to say that when one counts, the counting is not primarily an abstract mechanical procedure of addition and subtraction, but rather an opening of a path into questions about why and how one counts on. And counting on is not about numbers, but is a deliberation about grounds of reason for an orientation:

about a *choice* of orientation in thought and action. It is an understanding of *why* one counts.

Heidegger's argument, I think, is that even in what is prima facie a mechanical act of reckoning with, there is more going on than passively procedural interactions with facts. Because it is also an act of cognitive orientation, counting as a counting-on also involves the question of the freedom of the subject in need of the numerical orientation. If to reckon with also means to choose—to deliberate—in order to bring what one reckons with into the open, then, we should ask, What is brought about in the open when one reckons, since counting is also a process of *production* of a cognitive value? What is so produced must include not just quantification of objects counted but also the conditions of the possibility of any act of quantification. In a way, in Heidegger's account of the reckoning act, the fact of freedom of thought comes about: a worldly *event* occurs, or, as Heidegger preferred to put it, there appears "an *efficere* belonging in the realm of *ratio*."[41]

In summary, in contrast to the writings of Hobbes and Bacon, in Heidegger's work, to count is to count on, so that the thought of counting is no longer only objective quantification. Instead, the emphasis is dislocated and placed on productive deliberation—the free exercise of reason—involved in the activities. Far from passive receptivity, in deliberative reckoning, Heidegger believes, beings are "forced" to appear in particular ways, by a certain orientation or rules. Beyond dispassionate quantification, then, accounting also means qualitatively *figuring* out the meaning of beings that are calculatively forced to appear in the calculator and to the objective observer. This process of appearance of beings and the objectifications are processes involving, at least implicitly, transcendental production of reason. Likewise, what appears to us as nature calls into view problematic histories of beings—including the history of humans in the world. This, I think, is why Heidegger seems convinced that all forms of rational appearance—what we call events—produced as rational by *Dasein's* deliberative self-orientation in the world ought to be attributed to reason's *efficere*, or historical effectivity. This is the hermeneutical dimension of the rational, as opened up and presented within elaborations of ontological and historical "destinies" of humans as objects of thought as well as thinking subjects.

EMPIRICAL REASON

The tension between instrumentalist and hermeneuticist conceptions of rationality is the more interesting because it derives from notable every-day experiences. We usually take for granted that, while computers may be programmed to (logically) calculate values they cannot (historically) reason. Computers, by mechanical procedures, are programmed to re-produce virtually predictable results of calculable variables. Thinking, on the other hand, is an organically, bodily embedded, reflective human activity; at least that much one learns from, among other places, the works of the anthropologist Hubert L. Dreyfus.[42] Thinking is organic because it is embedded life and its defining processes are *spontaneous* activities. When one speaks about the spontaneity of human reasoning, therefore, the word "reason" is a reference to the creative emergence of mind in the world across vast areas that include the emotional aspects of perception (empathy, imagination, willing, etc.). Books like *What Computers Still Can't Do* show that the exercise of rational autonomy in humans does not yet have, and perhaps could never have, an exact parallel in mechanically calculative machines. Machines, of course, can be said to operate "autonomously." But by this we usually mean that the machine is mechanical: automated, programmed, or robotic. Human autonomy, by contrast, presupposes a clearer gap between antecedence and precedence, suspended in time, between past and future. It is obviously this gap which makes intelligible all debates about the human will ("Is there such a thing?") or, if there is such a thing, additional debates about the necessity or legitimate scope of its freedoms ("What is the morality of freedom?"). Unlike questions we ask about, or pose to, computers, what is usually defended in these and similar questions about human reason in relation to the will is, in the final analysis, the significance of our capacity for *experience*.

As we saw earlier, those who offer a nonreductive defense of the ra-tional autonomy of the human will must reference the concept "abstrac-tion" as a bridge term over the gap motivated by reason in experience, the gap we know must exist only because of the freedom of reason in the world. This oldest, richest, and most complex concept of abstraction functions as follows. On the one hand, to say that something, for example, a painting, is abstract is to be alert to the fact that the painter, with little or no reference to real-world objects, made up figures on a canvas. The abstractness of the painting derives from the self-sufficiency of meaning or meanings of the work in the work itself. Rather than a claim to direct representation of the world, abstract paintings are abstract because their meanings are figuratively open: they are subject to interpretation at a level higher than they would have been had they been tightly bound, representationally speaking, to an object external to the painting. To appreciate an abstract work of art, therefore, the observer need not search for the aesthetic experience in objects outside the painting itself: the painting does not claim to stand for a meaning external to the painting, and if it does, the relation to the world of objects figured in the painting is not primarily an imitation. What makes an abstract work of art abstract is thus the carrying within itself of a nonimitative meaning, since the work of art announces itself as having acquired a logic as well as inhabiting and exhibiting a world of figuration all its own. To require that an abstract painting represent something other than its own necessary aesthetic principles of figuration is to misunderstand the meaning of the abstract in abstract painting.

On the other hand, one also uses the word "abstract" to suggest, more technically, that a figure of art is an abstraction *from* something beyond or even other than its own figurative rules of aesthetic production. Even abstract *figures* are not necessarily hermetic. Ambivalently, the abstract in this sense could be a peculiar, figurative, translation of a worldly claim, an event, or an idea. The abstract here is a nonliteral sketch *of* something. The sketched figure is considered an abstraction—say, the caricature of a historical figure—especially when the artistic genre can also claim to be satiric, ironic, or parodic. In these genres, the aesthetic value is often precisely in the oblique or hinted reference to the historical object of the satire, irony, or parody. An abstract work of art could thus also be a caricature: a stylized distortion of an object having existence external to the work of art. In this instance, the meaning of the abstracted work of art cannot therefore claim to be absolutely independent of all and any cultural, social, and historical references. After all, even an artwork might be referentially limited by the materiality of the modes of its aesthetic composition, production, and reproduction.

The aesthetic capacity of the abstract genre often capitalizes on the audience's response in a particular way: it is funny, beautiful, or scary because we recognize *both* the independence of the artwork as aesthetic object *and* the immediate emotional, social, and historical dependences of the meanings that the viewer projects onto the artwork. Aesthetic appreciation of even the abstract is predicated on the fact that the abstraction takes on an aesthetic life of its own while reminding the audience of its relations to—for example, an imagined or actual *hint* at—an object or wider context of material experience. This hinting intrusion or extension to something-other-than-itself, no matter how faintly the other is formally echoed or re-echoed, and whether well known or only superficially apprehended and remembered by an audience, becomes a codeterminant of the reception of the artistic, figurative abstraction. Abstraction here takes on the life of an object: a kind of formal *re*-presentation.

Retaining these ambivalent meanings of abstraction will help us grasp what I propose as the concept of reason in empirical experience. This ambivalence productively points to the richness in form—as in the form of experience. When I argued, over Aristotle, about the rational status and meaning of form in the logical processes of deduction and induction, I considered the formal qualities in both kinds of logic as evidence of a universal law intrinsic to both the subjectivity of human thought and the objectivity of the natural world. Form, Aristotle believes in his own Platonic moments, is a quality in Being. Objects or natural events accordingly have, for example, formal and material causes. The form of a thing therefore belongs to the logic of its existence, for a form is that in an object or event which makes it intelligible to reason. Form, in other words, is that on account of which human experience of the world can reflectively acquire the character of intelligibility. When Aristotle uses the phrase "like knows like," it is to explain how human reason (the soul) is capable of re-cognizing order in nature as a productive grasp of rationality in experience. Reason in experience is affirmation of an ontological familiarity of the mind with the form of the world. It is on the grounds of this familiarity or likeness that a subject may be capable of spontaneously expressing freedom as law by constituting the world as *its* own: a world of experience.

Ambivalence in the concept of abstraction allows us to reflectively affirm the conditions of possibility of freedom in experience. The ambivalent nature of the processes of abstraction retains, in the concept of abstraction, the idea of reason's certain openness to the world. This openness is constituted as form, or figure. It is the figuration of the "abstract" in experience that, paradoxically, introduces openness and freedom into the course of human encounters with otherwise entirely natural worlds. In the form of experience, both reason and world are intimately, mutually, and ambivalently mediated. The metareality of this formal ambivalence, which I also characterize as the ambivalence of formality, can be variously described.

Considered in one way, this ambivalence of formality is a description of mind that can be elaborated by way of Kant's critique of the antinomies of pure reason, and I have partially offered such an elaboration in the introduction to this book. Considered another way, the idea of ambivalence of form in experience can also be thought in relation to time. I do this in chapter 4, in my discussion of experience in relation to memory as well as the writing of history. What I can do here is show why, when the great empiricists sought to explain the nature of reason—or unreason—they started and ended the discussion with experience. In its earliest edition, David Hume's *A Treatise of Human Nature* had the subtitle "Being an Attempt to Introduce the Experimental Method of Reasoning into Moral Subjects." The first part of Book 1 ("On Understanding") also had a prominent section, called "Of Ideas, their Origin, Composition, Connexion, Abstraction." These titles indicate that for Hume, the surest marker of the empiricist theories of origins of reason is experience (in Hume's English, "experiment" or the "experimental"). Experience, in turn, was decomposed into four key theses: (a) Perception is nothing but impression (sensation) and the ideas we form of sensation; (b) ideas are the formal imprint of sensation on structures of feeling (emotion) and memory; (c) thinking is no more than the passive reception and active reproduction of ideas in the form of abstract images of perception; and (d) in light of all the preceding observations, the principle of reason consists in nothing other than the simple or complex formal structures of law-like relations of objects and ideas, what Hume called "constant connexion." For Hume, it is merely constant connexion *in* experience that governs both the comparative relations and the discursive representability of ideas. There could be no deeper metaphysical source of reason—or at least, his empirical kind of reason.

What strikes some as the apparent "superficiality" of the structure of

Hume's empiricism masks, I am sure, empiricism's radicalism. Because so much in this older tradition of empiricism echoes the insights I seek to capture in the idea of an ordinary reason or vernacular rationality, it is worth making the effort to retrace some of Hume's most obvious—though some say, obscure—steps. He argues, for example, that all "the perceptions of the human mind resolve themselves into two distinct kinds, which I shall call impression and ideas." As to the difference between impression and ideas, it is essentially nonexistent, since it consists merely "in the degrees of force and liveliness, with which they strike upon the mind, and make their way into our thought or consciousness." Specifically, "those perceptions, which enter with most force and violence, we may name impressions: and under this name I comprehend all our sensations, passions and emotions, as they make their first appearance in the soul. By ideas I mean the faint images of these in thinking and reasoning; such as, for instance, are all the perceptions excited by the present discourse, excepting only those which arise from the sight and touch, and excepting the immediate pleasure or uneasiness it may occasion."[43] But if all reasoning is a work *of* experience and work *in* experience (specifically in the simple or complex traces of sensation and the ideas formed of sense data), the empiricist's challenge is to produce an account of the rationality presumed given in, and as, "experience." Our question to the empiricist may be phrased like this: What, pray, is the relation between sensation and abstraction in thought?

On the one hand, when Hume speaks of the "resemblance betwixt our impressions and ideas in every other particular, except their degree of force and vivacity," it is not clear how one gets from the former (impression) to the latter (ideas). What, really, is a resemblance? Hume probably thought he dispatched this question when he says: "When I shut my eyes and think of my chamber, the ideas I form are *exact* representations of the impressions I felt." But what *exact* representation? In what sense is the representation just so? Which picture or theory of representability shall we presuppose here? In fact, for Hume, a thing is successfully represented when there is no "circumstance of the one [the represented], which is not to be found in the other [the representee]." But as we saw in the discussions of the concept of abstraction—as an indirect means of representation, as translation, or as *re*-presentation—the relationship between the represented and the representee is never, simply, that of exactness. Rather, it is a relation or relations fraught with intentional and unintentional figurative openness, productive ambiguity, and, ultimately, ambivalence.

When Hume switches to other theories of representation, he believes that "ideas and impressions appear always to correspond to each other."[44] But like the earlier concepts (resemblance, exact representation), "correspondence" is not without its own histories of difficulties in epistemology. In fact, Richard Rorty has tried to entirely dispatch from epistemology this idea of correspondence between mind and object. I am therefore going to conclude that Hume's basic intuitions on these subjects—despite his skeptical assertion of the rule of "constant connexion"—is a legacy fraught with as many resilient insights as unanswered questions. Though he seemed aware of what I characterized as ambivalence in the nature of form (after all, he wrote: "I observe that many of our complex ideas never had impressions that corresponded to them, and that many of our complex impressions never are exactly copied in ideas"),[45] the implications of this and similar qualifications require addressing—beyond the confines of the relations between simple and complex ideas—what I have also called the problems of the ordinary in reason and in experience.

Some of Hume's thought experiments therefore bring out questions we must now consider decisive. The questions ought to be examined beyond the merely rhetorical because, beyond what we see in Hume's equivocations, I suspect that in the final analysis Hume's radical skepticism derives its strength in large measure from his refusal to address the full implications of the question he barely raises about the nature and rational status of representation or, better, representability.

One should note that Hume has a better theory of correspondence when he writes: "I venture to affirm, that the rule here holds without any exception, and that every simple idea has a simple impression, which resembles it, and every simple impression a *correspondent* idea." Moreover, in regard to the comparative relations across ideas, Hume also says: "Thus we find, that all simple ideas and impressions resemble each other; and as the complex are formed from them, we may affirm in general, that these two species of perception are exactly *correspondent*."[46] It is equally important to note that "correspondence" in this context is no more than the production of forms that, somehow, successfully bear perceptual resemblance to that which the formation (or "representation") is a form of. Thus whether one speaks in the language of "participation" (Plato) or "correspondence" (Hume), the idea is the same: an epistemic relation has been posited. But even this generous reading of Hume substantially revises, I believe, the skepticism that should rightly be regarded as Hume's dominant legacy. After all, he explicitly says that once the sort of epistemic relation mentioned has been "discovered," there is no need to ask further questions about the meanings of "correspondence" since the concept "require[s] no farther examination."[47] But if there is no need for such further examination, how are we to account for the logic—the rationality—in the acts of representation? What is representability?

Within the empiricist framework, that which is representable as well as the conditions of the possibility of representation as such appear to remain occult. Hume makes the problems both apparent and obscure when he summarized the *Treatise* in these words: "That all our simple ideas in their first appearance are deriv'd from simple impressions, which are correspondent to them, and which they exactly represent."[48] If this is the empiricist's conception of rationality, the conception cannot resolve the questions it raises simply by ignoring its own terms of debate. If, for example, we reformulated the empiricist conceptual problems in matters concerning the possibility of "exact representation," we ought to start with a more basic problem: What is conception? Is there an exact— or immaculate—conception of the forms of objects in experience? The relation between form and content of worldly objects indeed poses for the empiricist a problem similar to the one faced by the Platonist in matters of the distinction between form and matter, or essence and accident. The power of what I called ambivalent openness of reason in experience is such that it seems to lead straight either to empirical skepticism or metaphysical dogmatism. Can this ambivalence be conceptually overcome?

Some shy away from this question because they think that what can be positively salvaged in the dream of empirical reason remains, today, alive primarily in the languages of contingency and probabilism—the model of rationality associated in its origins with the mathematical work of Thomas Bayes, notably his *Essay towards Solving a Problem in the Doctrine of Chances*.[49] The Bayesian theorem, or Bayesianism for short, has become so popular in the humanities that not only analytical epistemologists but also philosophers of religion have sought to make the model useful in discussions of issues from the meanings of "truth" to calibrating the degrees of rationality of proofs of God's existence. Ethicists, too, currently use Bayes to analyze how good a judgment about "the good" can be in various professional contexts. In *Bayesian Epistemology*, a full-length study and critique of these developments, Luc Bovens and Stephan Hartman argue that the science of probability is indeed suitable to address the problems of reason in experience. The suitability, the authors claim, resides precisely in the fact that Bayesianism circumvents the non-self-evident metaphysical questions about the epistemic status of *fact*. How do we come to form, Bovens and Hartman ask, a belief about anything in experience? How does one reason correctly not just about the exactness of the form of our thinking about an object of fact, but also about the truths of the "fact" of the object in the supporting, thoughtful justification of our reasoning? Using Bayesianism, they answer that we accept a fact as fact based on a number of probabilistic procedures, such as How *expected* is the information we assume (preconception or background beliefs) about the fact? and How *reliable* are the sources of available information about the fact? Our reasoning between these first and second conditions, expectedness and reliability, Bovens and Hartman show, are driven by the logic of *plausibility*. This logic—much like Hume's "constant connnexion"—a priori disposes the subject to accept information as plausible according to the greater or lesser reliability of the given source(s).

Yet the assessment of the reliability of the sources, as greater or lesser, depends in turn on the plausibility of the available information. Since we cannot have *all* potentially relevant information at our disposal, good "reasoning," on the basis of these and similar conditions of inferential processes, is achieved when there appears to be a cognitive coherence between the plausible and the reliable. For Boven and Hartman, therefore, plausibility and reliability of presuppositions are the first hallmarks of conditions of validity in empirical or probabilistic reasoning. Probabilistic reasoning, however good it is, thus remains a logic of contingency: it can never present itself as error-proof, since it has no in-built guarantee of its own epistemic success.

To illustrate this contingency in reason, Bovens and Hartman appropriate the following story from the Old Testament:

When Isaac is an old man and has lost his vision, he asks the elder son Esau to fetch and prepare him some venison, and he promises that he will bless him. God has told Isaac's wife Rebecca that Esau would serve his younger brother Jacob. Hence, Rebecca favours Jacob and urges him to pretend that he is Esau so that he and not Esau will receive their father's blessing. Jacob expresses his concern that his sham will never work since he is less hairy than Esau and his father will recognize him. Rebecca then clothes Jacob in Esau's clothes and covers his hands and neck with goatskin. When Isaac receives Jacob, he is faced with incoherent information. He remarks that the voice is the voice of Jacob, but the hands are the hands of Esau. To form an opinion about who is standing in front of him, he asks his son to come closer. It is the smell of Esau's clothes that leads him to conclude incorrectly that it is Esau. The information provided by his hearing and his touch is too incoherent to form any beliefs about the identity of the person before him. It is only when he acquires an item of information from his sense of smell that coheres with a previous item of information that he is willing to believe that it is Esau whom he is dealing with.[50]

Because this tale has an unsatisfactory end from Isaac's point of view, Bovens and Hartman acknowledge that not even their own Bayesian-plus requirement of coherence is full-proof against error. Coherence of information is no guarantee that a judgment based on the information could not be wrong.

The possible conditions of a desirable cognitive guarantee of truth cannot be possibly probabilistically fulfilled for a number of reasons, a few of which can be briefly enumerated. Coherence, like correspondence, is a problem because, first, the *degrees* of coherence within the various parts of the reasoning process may vary. Second, the pieces of basic units of information that form a given coherence may be reliable, but only more or less. And third, the subjective disposition of the agent —Bovens and Hartman's "expectedness" which we bring to the information that forms the basis of assessment of coherence and incoherence— may or may not be objectively valid to any reasonable degree. There seems to be only one conclusion available to us: The form of reason in experience is fated to its own empirical conditions. Because of this fatality in the prior conditions in which the work of empirical reasoning must operate, many of the essential philosophical challenges in the idea of a universally empirical reason remain, as I see it, to be satisfied.[51]

It is of interest to note that when they considered some of the above challenges, Bovens and Hartman drew an equally startling conclusion. While recognizing that, for greater credibility, the "probabilistic framework" needs "to give a precise account of the relevant notion of coherence, so that we can order various information sets according to their relative degree of coherence," they quickly add that this expectation "has *never* been met." They therefore conclude, just as dramatically, that the expectation, in principle, "cannot be met."[52] If these assertions are true, are we left with the choice of accepting that there is only one task left for the epistemologist: to pity Isaac—and learn from his fate, his "mistake"? Is there a guarantee that such lessons learned are always better than the sources of errors at the root of the occasion of the learning? Is the empirical ideal forever condemned not only to the possibility of subjective errors but also to objective threats of worldly contingency, incompleteness, and indeterminacy?[53]

Of course, to insist that the world must be the way a desire for closed logical systems dictates it should be is no different from—is only the flip side of—an insistence, as we saw in some aspects of Hume, that thought must *exactly* represent what we think an impression is. But what if we cannot exactly represent existence in thought? My suspicion is that if this failure at representation is not necessarily on account of any known irrationality of existence, then it must be primarily because of reason's own reflectively ambivalent relation to itself, an ambivalence I argued is at the core of what we call "experience." I have also signaled—and marked—the possible sites of this lack of self-coincidence of reason with itself in experience. I have tried to call this the "gap," "spontaneity," or "autonomy" of the rational. But in the final analysis, and by whatever name, the open-ended character of rationality in experience suggests the need for recognition that there can be no immaculate, nondialectical conception of existence or its representation. For example, if, as I showed in the last section of the introduction, we cannot expect logic to introduce a permanent closure to either memory or to history, the enduring and viable task of empirical reason must remain how to discern the contours of *historical forms* of conditions of reason and of truth in experience. And as I will show in chapters 3 and 4, no one culture or philosophic tradition can convincingly claim, exclusively, to be equal to this very primordial task.

PHENOMENOLOGICAL REASON

Any phenomenological account of rationality is invariably embedded in discussions of a larger theme: the question of consciousness. The success of the phenomenological movement is predicated on the demise of the modernist myth that consciousness is something in the mind, where "mind" is understood as a mental entity functioning like a machine inside the brain.[54] Research programs in neurology, empirical programs in cognitive psychology and medicine, and anthropological fieldwork done on what were once suspected to be primitive cultures have supplanted much of the modernist mechanical conception of mind. The interdisciplinary pictures emerging from these newer research programs show that philosophy of consciousness has taken some radical postmodernist turns.[55] From the works of Husserl and Sartre to Ricoeur, phenomenology can be credited with major contributions in the revolution in post-Cartesian philosophical studies of consciousness. This section is devoted to a critique of the complex theories and the historical consequences of this post-Cartesian development.

Writing about some of these consequences, George Lakoff and Mark Johnson, in *Philosophy in the Flesh*, argue that fundamental changes in the understanding of mind necessarily lead to changes in our understanding of cultural and social identities. Because questions of mentality and identity are conceptually interconnected, it is to be expected that where it is discovered through empirical research that, for example, human rationality is not at all what the Western philosophical tradition has held it to be, then, those who bear the self-understandings and social identities dependent on the disputed conceptual tradition might feel that they had been "misled about their identities."[56] Lakoff and Johnson go further, writing that "it is shocking" for people to "discover that we are very different from what our philosophical tradition has told us we are."[57] Yet, of course, the shock of new discoveries can also be liberating. It can even exhilarate because creative developments of newer forms of self-understanding, with accompanying newer ethical, moral, and aesthetic dispositions, can lead to progressive revisions of cultural and social identities informed by the philosophical consciousness. Although this progressivist argument remains implicit in Lakoff and Johnson, it is a natural consequence of their postmodern scientific discoveries. It is this focus on the postmodern that lends *Philosophy in the Flesh* its most deconstructive taste. Their sustained critique of Cartesianism is so obviously announced right in the title of the polemical text.

The discipline of phenomenology is itself at the forefront of the progressive revision and transitions of conceptions of identities, from the modern to the postmodern. Although it may be true that thinkers like Herder, Fichte, Dilthey, and Senghor pioneered the phenomenological methods, the greatest systematizer of the movement as a subfield in philosophy—and across the social and human sciences—was Edmund Husserl.[58] The key task of phenomenology, as Husserl explains, is to understand at a fundamental level the nature of perceptual consciousness. What kinds of insight can rigorous analysis of the multilayered constitution of appearance of consciousness provide into the universality of experiences of self in the humanities and the social sciences, particularly psychology? What insights does the same phenomenon provide into the "subjective" foundation of knowledge in the natural sciences? In Husserl's work these two aspects of phenomenology point to different but related methodological approaches to the study of consciousness.

The psychological dimensions of the phenomenological experience concern analyses of the appearance of mind. According to this aspect of phenomenology, one can define consciousness as the existential state of any perceptually oriented awareness. I say "oriented" to mean focused, as in a gaze. But phenomenologically speaking, a gaze is a gaze whether or not that at which it is directed is considered real or unreal, true or false, particular or general. From this perspective, what determines the essential character of consciousness is neither the reality nor the unreality of its object of perception. Nor is it the validity or invalidity of a judgment made on the basis of the perception, the focus of its gaze. One can be right or wrong about a conclusion drawn about what one thinks one perceives, but the error does not make the consciousness any less a consciousness. A consciousness whose object of perception is true is no more a consciousness than the one whose objective perception is false. In its simplest form, then, consciousness is best described as *pure* perception—without regard to the conditions of appearance or the claims of truth or validity that may be made on behalf of the object of consciousness. Husserl calls the science that studies pure consciousness *pure psychology.*

Though it does not matter whether the conditions of the appearance of pure consciousness are real or unreal, there would be no consciousness at all without a constitutive "object"—that toward which consciousness is oriented and which therefore accounts, in a fundamental way, for the very possibility of the appearance of consciousness. There are therefore two formal-categorical preconditions for the appearance of *any* consciousness: the subject of perception (*ego*) and its object (*thema*). The ego is the main subjective psychological pole of the perception, whereas the thema is the more objective end of the perception, as the object of consciousness. Since there can be no consciousness without its being consciousness of something, the categorical position of the thema in the constitution or "rise" of consciousness is absolute. But it is useful to remember that the thema is merely a *categorical* point of focus: the content may be true or false, right or wrong, rightly judged or misjudged, and so on. No matter, the function of the thema is merely to serve as an anchor for simple consciousness to emerge *as* the relation of an ego to a thema.

An object of consciousness must indeed be thema-tic, the thema being the necessary other in perception that gives, appropriately, the-matic unity to the perceptual consciousness. As categorical rather than specific in its function, moreover, consciousness's thema may be empirical (e.g., a physical thing), but it need not be. It may be a memorial (as in remembered matters), an idea or concept (as in thinking), a value (as in judgment), means and ends (as in willing), aesthetic (imaginative sensibilities), or passions (e.g., love, hate, etc.).[59] Two examples from Husserl clarify these claims. First, Husserl suggests that if we "try to grasp and describe any kind of external perception—say, the perception of this tree—as a purely psychic datum" (i.e., a tree, which stands there in the garden, outside my perception), I will notice that my perception "is what it is—namely, something psychic—[only] insofar as it is a perception 'of this tree.'" Husserl argues that without this "of this" or "of that," the perception "cannot be described in its own essential psychic make-up." This is the case because "the inseparability of this element is shown by the fact that it remains with the perception even when the perception is shown to be an illusion."[60] That consciousness cannot emerge absent a thematic object is thus a given, and a shorthand to capture this first of two related truths is the saying Consciousness is always already consciousness-*of*.

In the second example, however, additional and more complex meanings emerge from what, in the first example, appeared to be a uniquely simple idea (i.e., the fact of consciousness-of). The complexity of the thematic articulations of consciousness unfolds when one pauses to closely analyze its supposedly simple and pure makeup. On closer examination, instead of being simple, perceptual consciousness is a complex of multiple relations organized by the ego. As already noted, this organization includes the thematization of the perceptual *object* (even as a categorical formality). But the thema, in turn, is implicated in a perceptual *sense*, that is, as a sense-content of a perceptual belief, a belief arising from what it is presumed the appearance of consciousness perceptually *means*. For example, if, in order to hold in view the purity of the psychological makeup of the ego's consciousness, I mentally bracket out from the ego's perception the content of its thema (say, the fact that I am looking at *this* tree), the bracketed content can still be seen to have belonged, constitutively, to my perception. Husserl recognizes this, and therefore recommends that phenomenological analysis be accompanied by a provisional bracketing of the content of consciousness only *so that the formality of consciousness itself may appear as an object of perception*. He used the Greek term *epoché* to describe this methodological requirement. The moment of epoché allows one to see that the content of a thema is not a rigid, lifeless element in consciousness; rather, the content of a thema appears *in* (not only *to*) consciousness—and does so, in Husserl's formulation, "as a vitally self-constituting unity in the fluctuating multiplicities of modes of appearance."[61]

Embedded therefore in the apparent, simple unity of consciousness are complex, multiple, dynamic, and mutually self-constituting perceptual relations. Yet the multiplicities, no matter how fluctuating and dynamic, if they are to appear as consciousness-of, must also assume the "appearance of . . ." This conceptual demand for appearance as unity is such that, no matter the internal distinctions of its objects, in order for consciousness to perceptually appear to itself, the multiple dimensions of the perception must be synthetically constituted merely as the consciousness of *an* appearance. This is why Husserl calls any phenomenal appearance "the consciousness of one and the same thing."[62] To illustrate this, he noted how, ordinarily, seeing something like "a fixed and unchanged brass cube" means to "run through its form as a cube: the individual surfaces, edges, corners, as well as its color, luster and other determinations as a spatial thing."[63] But we know that instead of bringing the cube to cognizance in this direct way, we could focus the gaze on how, and in what kinds of changing perspectives, the cube presents itself. Though the multiplying of perspectives changes nothing about the actual weight and size of the cube, we do come to appreciate the experiences of it differently. And under yet more complex attention to perception, we might bring more to notice: for example, how the very same cube appears differently as 'something nearby' than as 'something far off'; which modes of appearance it offers when we change our orientation; or how each individual determination within the process of perception presents itself as a determination in the multiple modes of appearance belonging to a particular point of view. In phenomenological perception, there is, not one possibility, but many possibilities of modes of appearance of the object of perception as the object of consciousness.

For this reason the talk of *modes* of appearance of the cube is apt because, like the consciousness it is meant to illustrate, it captures the diversity in the phenomenological experience. If I remember the cube I saw or imagine a cube I have not seen, my memory or imagination may formally remain one and the same throughout as I remember or imagine the cube's various modes of appearance. Though I remember or imagine the varied appearances differently and differentially *I* remain the same as the subject of the memory or imagination. The difference is important since it suggests that, no matter how much unity the phenomenological gaze (remembering, imagining, willing, desiring, etc.) might have, it cannot permanently obliterate the fact that in any act of perception there is what Husserl called the "functioning processes of lived experience." The processes are the implicit or explicit thematics, real or illusory, of an act of perception that, as we saw above, always remains—albeit latently[64]—in any consciousness of . . .

In light of what my analysis established in the section regarding empirical reason, the phenomenologically latent, ungraspable, and implicit aspects of any act of perception can be explanatorily proposed as the internal source of multiplicity, instability, and indeterminacy in what might otherwise have been a naïve or dogmatic consciousness. In acknowledging this dimension of conditions of perception, phenomenological description (like its object: phenomenological perception) must be at least dual or multilayered. On one level, the level of appearance, perception can be described as merely formal, cognitive, and conceptually grasping at a perceived object. On another level, a qualitatively different level of evaluation, the phenomenological perception reveals itself (because of the implicits in its conditions of possibility) *as* the unbounded in actual experience. In this second-level perceptual perspective, what is phenomenologically "seen" is subjective appearances. They are subjective because, though present to cognition as synthetic or unified in the act of consciousness, the appearances are nevertheless known in the consciousness to be also existing (think again of the cube) as *self-same now in this way as in that way.*

This last observation holds true not just for some class of external or instrumental perceptions (the cube, tree, or house) but also for any kind of subjective perception that can be described, interioristically, as "I experiences." For example, "I think," "I will," "I desire," "I feel," "I love." Because of this dual dimension of consciousness, we must conclude that there is no ego or perceptual mind without a thema—whether this thema is objective or subjective. It is the thema that offers to the psyche the required conditions of a point, or points, of self-articulation as a unity. Implied here, too, however, is an acknowledgment that the unity of appearance is such that its object is not defined simply by real or illusory content but by category: the thema is an element of *form* in experience. Though not possible without the intentionality of the ego, this form of appearance in experience is nevertheless a crucial part of the mind's own world. In the notion of intentionality, thus, Husserl sought to capture the subjective dimension of a rational, worldly mind.

Phenomenological Reduction

"Phenomenology" derives its name from its claim to be a science of the mind. Rather than study an object of perception, it takes, according to Husserl, "as its primary thema the act of perception itself." Perception thus focused on itself uncovers, among other objects of pure consciousness, "the manifoldly changing 'subjective ways' in which its worlds 'appear," and the ways these worlds are consciously known."[65] The goal of phenomenological analysis is therefore to enlighten the fields of the ego. It does this by a process of "reduction," a four-step procedure that achieves the said enlightenment by increments. The first step is the intuitive recognition that perception is fundamentally intentional. Second, there is the *epoché*—the methodological bracketing of the object of this intentionality, so that the pure structure of intentionality can be isolated in its purity. Third, the reconstruction of that which is now the isolated "object" of perception, that is, the structure of "empty" intentionality of perception. Fourth and finally, the procedural, "quality control" to ensure that steps 1 through 3 have been faithfully followed. Fidelity to this four-step method, Husserl believed, guarantees that what is comprehended in thought is indeed the pure psychological structure of the act of perception. Though he was not quite as economical in the formulation of these procedures as I have made them, Husserl nevertheless believed that when successful, the phenomenological decomposition of intentional perception reveals the difference between knowledge-of (psycho-phenomenological) and knowledge-that (philosophico-phenomenological). Once the reduction is successful, the next step is to translate the picture of the phenomenological knowledge-of and knowledge-that thereby generated as a difference between, respectively, the general science of pure psychology and the metascience of transcendental philosophy.

Notice that the difference between the disciplines was nearly obvious in the very technique of reduction. In fact, it seems that Husserl designed the technique in order to show how, in what is thought to be a simple reflective return of consciousness to itself in experience, "there is no progressively perceived thing, nor any element perceived as a determination within it, that does not appear, during perception, in multiplicities of different appearances."[66] Yet despite this difference in the rationalities of the ontology of appearances, all appearances are said to be "given" and "grasped" by the ego *as* a formal unity.

But if—from the point of view of the grasping and self-grasping cogito —appearances are "as continuously one and the same thing,"[67] these useful questions arise: How is nature (passively) *given* to the mind? How does the mind (actively) *grasp* what is given? These questions, in Husserl's divisions, are in a unique sense essentially psychological: they are problems in general psychology, which in turn is distinct from though supposing anthropo-zoology. In the essay "Phenomenology," when Husserl asks, "What is the general theme of psychology?" he answers, "Psychical being and psychical life that exist concretely in the world as human and, more generally, as animal." Since the realities of the human animal present themselves in two levels, the difference between these levels are reflected within the methodology of psychology. In one aspect of this method, the scientific approaches necessary to study anthropological and zoological life, the orientation is toward a physical reality. And "like all realities," Husserl notes, "animal realities are spatio-temporal, and . . . admit of a systematically abstractive focus of experience upon that factor in them that is purely *res extensa*."[68] In the other aspect, however, anthropological realities are recognized as unlike pure physical objects. At this level the "animal" in question does not exist simply as nature: it exists as 'subjects' of a 'mental life.' "[69] Based on this recognition, Husserl argues, the psychologist must adopt a "systematic purity and a differently focused abstractive attitude," an attitude that manifests itself methodologically as an orientation toward a "completely new kind of psychic experience." General psychology is the discipline that studies psyche life "from the purely psychic to the purely psychic"[70] and can thus produce a comprehensive science of mental life. But it is only phenomenological psychology that is capable of bridging the methodological difference between anthropo-zoology and general psychology, because its focus of study is the psychophysical experience. Husserl hoped that phenomenological psychology would make "the real form of the relatedness of the psychic to physical corporeality . . . thematic."[71]

Yet Husserl pushes these methodological arguments further. He decouples the general prospect of general psychology (i.e., the cognition of psychic life) from not only its basis in anthropo-zoology but also from itself. He asserts yet a different, third-level domain of research, namely, the domain of transcendental science. The subject matter of this "higher" science is essentially logical: it studies the justificatory grounds on the basis of which all the other, lower level sciences, empirical or general, exist.[72] Yet the method of this last and final basis of science—any science—must obey the requirements of the phenomenological method. In that case, its method will be a transcendental phenomenology.

Transcendental Reason

Transcendental phenomenology is therefore a kind of philosophy of logic. Beyond the psychological, its goal is to provide entirely a priori justifications of the reason claimed to be the foundation of any kind of science. It is here that Husserl believes he has found a way to dissolve or reorganize traditional problems in transcendental philosophy into new programs of research in a better science, transcendental phenomenology. But first, this new transcendental science would have to justify its own scientificity.

For example, how it is possible to move from a general psychological analysis of intentionality to a foundational science of general psychology? Husserl asks himself "Is there—corresponding to the idea of a universal experience directed exclusively to 'subjective phenomena'—a self-contained field of experience that stands over against universal experience of the world, and thus a basis for a self-contained science?" He answers with an appeal to what he calls the domain of "rationality proper." He writes, "At first, one may object that a new science is not required, since all merely subjective phenomena, all modes of appearance of what appears, belong naturally within psychology as the science of the psychic."[73] If one takes this "first" impression as the basis of judgment, it is clear that it is not only the nature of the project of transcendental philosophy that is brought under question but also the rational status of general psychology. For unlike physics and mechanics, truths in the science of psychology cannot claim to depend on "natural" laws (e.g., causality) in the same way that, say, the truths of force or motion can make such a claim. Thus, in addition to showing why both empirical and pure psychology are rational, transcendental phenomenology intends to show how this "why" question is itself answered by a legitimate (though transcendental) science.

In the most immediate way, to reveal such transcendental grounds of the rationality of the social as well as the psychological sciences is to reconsider the foundational relations between "pure" (a priori) and "impure" (a posteriori) dimensions of the sciences in regard to their post-Kantian subjectivity. Husserl took this path, and framed the issues in this way:

> [Here is] the idea of a universal task: instead of living in "the" world directly in the "natural attitude" and, so to speak, like "children of this world," that is,

instead of living within the latently functioning life of consciousness and thereby having the world, and it alone, as our field of being—as now-existing for us (from out of perception), as past (from out of memory), as coming in the future (from out of expectation)—instead of judging and valuing this world of experience and making it the field of theoretical or practical projects—instead of all that, we attempt a universal phenomenological reflection on this entire life-process, be it pre-theoretical, theoretical or whatever. We attempt to disclose it systematically and thereby to understand the "how" of its achieving of unities. Thus we seek to understand in what manifold typical forms this life is a "consciousness-of"; how it constitutes synthetically conscious unities; how and in which forms these syntheses, as syntheses of passivity and spontaneous activity, run their course and thereby in particular how their unities are constituted as objectively existing or not existing, and the like; and thus finally how a unified world of experience and knowledge is there, operative and valid for us, in a completely familiar set of ontic types.[74]

This is, by any measure, a tall task for a tall science. If transcendental phenomenology's first major hurdle is to explain its own scientificity so that it can explain the scientificity of all social and human sciences, it is not surprising that Husserl would choose to strive to formulate this level of phenomenology as a method to unveil the "universal" in reflection. Nor is it surprising that he would require that the scope of this reflection be anything less than the "entire life-process" of humanity.

But how *can* transcendental phenomenology claim to know and to provide the grounds not just of all possible unities of experience in the mind (e.g., a version of the classic Kantian project) but also of the logical grounds of the rationalities of all historical institutions of science? On the one hand, and at a minimum, an adequate method for such an unusual science would require as a precondition a grasp of the purely psychic element of the *cogito* in any type of perception. We can easily see how this project would be attractive to phenomenological psychology, and how the method of *epoché* may be the self-constituting subjectivity of the ego *as it appears in its worldly appearance* and not as a positive psychologist might seek to reify it in perception. What adequate—and universal—account can Husserl give about this *world*, or what he preferred to call the "entire life-process"? Husserl's transcendental project can and should be evaluated separately, or at least with different criteria, on each of these dual aspects of its scientific aspiration.

Regarding the first aspect of this aspiration, Husserl hoped that any future psychology (the task of psychology "in the next hundred years," he wrote in 1945) must be to carry through a phenomenological reform of the discipline. He also hoped that philosophy would follow psychology in the same direction. The idea was that, together, psychology and philosophy held the key to reform that would lead to a phenomenological foundation—or refoundation—of the rest of the humanities.

In 1945 Husserl was also clear about the problems that needed reform; he even warned of the danger that could result if the reform did not occur. In philosophy, for example, he complained about naturalism. While praising Hume, in whose work, he notes, "one could see . . . the first projection of a pure psychology carried through in almost perfect [*reiner*] consistency," he nevertheless faults Hume's work because the consistency was maintained only within an egocentric *psychology*. Locke's epistemology, too, is found wanting. While recognizing Locke's "first attempt at a phenomenological transcendental philosophy,"[75] Husserl puts the emphasis on the *attempt*. Though he believes Locke was guided by a "great insight," he however "fell into the error of psychologism." Regarding empiricism generally, Husserl argues that "in spite of its many deep premonitions and its rich promise," the movement fell short in both positive-psychological and transcendental-philosophical areas, a two-sided error attributable to the fact that empiricism lacked "any radical reflection on the goal and possibilities of a pure psychology" as well as "the basic method of [transcendental] phenomenological reduction." Being thus blind to "intentionality" as such means also being blind to the tasks and special methods that flow from this view of consciousness. This leads not only to a false psychology of man but also to a false philosophy of psychology. Empiricism, Husserl implies, was the origin of the "crisis" he diagnoses at the heart of the traditions of modern European sciences.[76]

The more encouraging, earlier steps on the path to phenomenology, by Husserl's own version of the movement, took shape in the work of Franz Brentano, for it was Brentano who in a "great discovery" realized that both Locke's psychologism and Kant's transcendentalism could be reconciled through a "revaluation of the scholastic concept of intention-ality."[77] This conceptual reconciliation of the systems of Kant and Locke with scholasticism led Brentano to a radical reconception of mental phenomena. But even in Brentano some empiricist inhibitions remained in the form of a bias in favor of naturalism. The inhibition and bias prevented Brentano from taking any radical advantage of Kant's tran-scendental idealism. Saddled with the empiricist baggage from Locke, it seems Brentano could walk only so far, as far as pure psychology. But since psychology of any sort requires its own absolute foundation in transcendental philosophy, what was needed but lacking in Brentano was a concept of transcendence not just of naturalism but of general psychology's scientific positivism—its psychologism. Husserl saw his own work as the overcoming of this last problem.

Yet transcendental phenomenology would seek to do more. In order to establish the transcendental subjectivity of science—any science—both psychologism and positivism would have to be replaced by a pro-gram of universal transcendental phenomenology.

This program requires, according to Husserl, "a broadened and fully universal phenomenological reduction (the transcendental reduction) that does justice to the universality of the problem and practices of 'epoché' regarding *the whole world of experience and regarding all the positive cognition and sciences that rest on it.*"[78] In short, the contribu-tions of empiricism and positive psychology along the path leading up to this phenomenological transformation highlight for philosophy the need to problematize the concept of "understanding." How is under-standing at all possible? (As I phrased the question after reading Hume in the section on Empirical Reason, "What is representability?") Husserl thinks that the question cannot be answered without a proper transcen-dental reduction of humanity's universal "intentionality."

If Locke's *Essay* and Hume's *Treatise* thus represent the problems identified by Husserl as much as they contain the beginning explorations of the answers to the problems, transcendental philosophy is a new and clear departure from empiricism and naturalism. For Husserl, "the thrust of the transcendental problem is to interrogate the sense and the legitimacy of an objectivity that becomes consciously known in the im-manence of pure subjectivity and that presumably is demonstrated *within* the subjective grounding-processes."[79] This is radical subjective idealism. From this idealist's point of view, the true philosophical question is a question about "anything and everything objective."[80]

Of course, there is already in Descartes a formulation of a different version of idealism. In the intention of the *ego cogito*, one can already detect some elements of Husserl's preferred turning point: in the *Meditations*, for example, as Husserl himself did not fail to notice, the insight was already there that, "as far as the knowing ego is concerned, everything we declare to really be and to be-thus and-so . . . is only as something believed-in within subjective beliefs." Included in this "everything" is, indeed, anything. Similarly for Husserl, "everything" means *absolutely* everything we know. Thus, whatever we say is-thus-and-so is only something *as* represented, thought, felt, valued: in other words, something phenomenologically given in consciousness. Husserl formulates this as "The subjective conscious life in pure immanence is the place where all sense is bestowed and all being is posited and confirmed."[81]

But where, assuming there is one, is an Archimedean point for such a universal, nonpsychologistic, subjectivity? Husserl gives the affirmative answer to the question of existence of such a subjectivity, and he seems to say *Look* at the world. Think about how *you* can know anything about the world. It is this subjectivity that requires objective analysis. But "objectivity" does not mean objectivizing and objectivistic. The procedure and aim of transcendental analysis of the phenomenon of subjectivity is "to clarify what subjectivity can and does accomplish . . . in its hidden immanence." When successful, the body or bodies of such analyses would constitute an event, namely, "a systematic and pure self-understanding of the knower," any knower. This self-understanding—when not only its phenomenological existence but also its universality is rendered logico-transcendentally evident—is nothing less than "a disclosure of the life of thinking, exclusively by means of 'inner experience.' "[82]

The value of this "subjective" science—the science of phenomenological idealism—to the positive disciplines of the sciences is, for Husserl, self-evident, and for several reasons. First of all, if everything about the world is-thus-and-so only because of our "inner experience," we can see that knowledge of the transcendental grounds of the same inner experience is absolutely crucial to any fuller appreciation of the humanistic and universal dimensions of the foundation of the knowledge in the empirical sciences. For example, we can hardly say we have fully understood the truth of the judgments we make about entities in the world if we lack a fuller understanding of the ultimate grounds of the basis of the judgments. Second, while the phenomenological perspective makes the transcendental reasons an absolute necessity for humanistically grounding the positive sciences, the reverse, Husserl claims, cannot be claimed as necessarily true. This is due to the fact that, already as we saw in Descartes's *Meditations*, the ego cogito in itself was able to "put out of play" the beings of the entities of experience. Having conceptually removed from being not only the realities of the things of the world but the reality of the empirical world as such, Descartes was left with "what remains in play," namely, the ego cogito as the *universum* of pure subjectivity. In short, the things and the world needed Descartes to know them, but the thinking thing of Descartes which was not of the world does not need the world—in fact, had to leave the world out of conceptual play—in order to know itself *as* the universal. This pure knowledge of a pure subjectivity—which cannot be confused with the empirical I, "this man," for example, René Descartes—is a qualitatively different kind of entity. Its immanence, which is where it authorizes its own validity, is, as Husserl adds, "presupposed by, and therefore has intrinsic priority over, all positive cognition."[83]

In the end, however, Husserl's Cartesian meditations draw a line between himself and Descartes insofar as he does not elaborate, as Descartes tried to do, a quasi-theological basis as justification of the ultimate foundation of the cogito. Although history or humanity plays for Husserl a categorical role similar to God in Descartes, his appropriations of Descartes's idealistic epistemology—much like his equally deep, though less convivial dialogic readings of the epistemologies of Hume and Locke—were for a purpose other than mere idealism. The purpose was to validate the project of transcendental phenomenology as a necessary scientific program. Hence, when the time came to name the newer territories on which this newer scientific program intended to make its mark, Husserl seemed to echo the earliest Platonism as much as the modern thinkers. About the goal of the phenomenological method he writes, "Instead of a reduction merely to purely psychic subjectivity (the pure minds of human beings in the world), we get a reduction to transcendental subjectivity by means of a methodical epoché regarding the real world as such and even regarding all ideal objectivities as well (the 'world' of number and such like)." At the end of this reductive process, it is hoped that what remains in validity is exclusively the *universum* of "transcendentally pure" subjectivity and, enclosed within it, all the actual and possible "phenomena" of objectivities, and all modes of appearance and modes of consciousness that pertain to such objectivities.[84]

In summary, transcendental phenomenology must be a result of total and pure universal *epoché* or it is not a science. But it has to be *epoché* because Husserl wanted no less than "a completely new kind of experience that can be systematically pursued: transcendental experience." This new quest for absolute experience deriving from an equally new idea of science is, moreover, attainable because human subjectivity—the "subject" matter—is also transcendentally absolute or "complete" because it functions everywhere, though Husserl also presumed that the completeness functions only in hiddenness. But what is hidden can be brought to light through phenomenological exploration of its "whole transcendental life." This kind of program of phenomenological exploration is what Husserl means by opening up "the thematic field of an absolute phenomenological science." It is a different—absolute and universal—kind of science because it encompasses within itself "all transcendental or rational-theoretical inquiries."[85]

CRITIQUE OF TRANSCENDENTAL REASON

Husserl's phenomenology is indeed *post-Cartesian*—and not just because it is *after* Descartes in a historical sequence. It is so also because it assumes Cartesianism only to claim to scientifically perfect it. My appraisal of the strength and weaknesses of this neo-Cartesianism therefore naturally presupposes the already large bodies of established critiques, particularly postcolonial and feminist critiques, of the Cartesian project.

Transcendental phenomenology indeed sought to bring out and radicalize what was the most philosophical about Descartes's work. Though it openly lays claim to studying experience as a form of life and world, its covert task is to elaborate an understanding of the universally "hidden" aspect of this life—what Husserl called the "whole transcendental life."

Husserl's pure new science thus remains relevant to the life of outer worldly experience and of the positive sciences only because he hopes transcendental phenomenology will be able to account for the "real," subjectively ideal, conditions of the universality of both unreflective and reflective experiences of the world, including the world of the sciences. We can see in this the seeds of developments in post–World War II philosophy in Europe. Existentialists like Jean-Paul Sartre and Albert Camus built upon this phenomenologic analytical distinction between the hidden and the revealed to describe the subjective experiences of "nothingness," the emotionally resonant kinds of experience variously characterized as "nausea," the "absurd," the "hole," or the "magical." Writers like Maurice Merleau-Ponty and Paul Ricoeur continued in various ways the phenomenological program by extending it to analysis of the relationship between body and mind, instinct and rationality, and nature and history. Last but not least, one of Husserl's students, Martin Heidegger, would exploit Husserl's evocation of a hidden ground of both world and truth in his own more historical diagnoses of what for Heidegger became the "ontological question." The seeds of this question, including their blossoming into Heidegger's critiques of the ontotheological traditions in the history of Western metaphysics, can be said to be already announced not just in Husserl's phenomenological reductions but also in his more overt descriptions of an apparently epistemological problem in modern science as really being about historical crises of the Western world.

These influences are hardly surprising since Husserl wanted transcendental phenomenology to show, in the most universal terms, who humans must be like *as* knowers—knowers of anything at all. What can be known on account of the human condition, and what are the various ways subjectivity and knowability must authentically appear in order, respectively, to be the sort of being that knows and the sort of appearances about which meaningful things could be said? The practice of phenomenology from the standpoint of analysis of intentionality invariably opens this method to questions about the nature of reason, truth, knowledge, and reality. Phenomenology thus moves these questions beyond the merely empirical or materially positivistic into a transcendental complex. Speaking about this seamless transition, Husserl notes how a "transcendental theory of reason is distinguished from [phenomenological deduction] only in the starting point of its inquiries, since carrying out such a theory presupposes the universal *studium* of the whole of transcendental subjectivity: it is one and the same a priori science."[86] But this statement also serves a kind of warning, namely, that the origins of rationality can never be deduced empirically—it can be pursued only transcendentally. And it is this particular aspect of phenomenological approach to rationality that has guided my own reading of Husserl. As can be seen from my preface, Husserl's approach to the problem of rationality shares with my conception of ordinary reason this conviction: that not even the most empirical reason can fully justify all the grounds of even its own empiricities by a reductive appeal to the empirical and positivistic in experience. In chapter 3 we shall see that no new developments in post-Husserlian genetics or psychology have been able to show that this truth about natural reason, as well as the historical institutions of rationality, could not any longer hold.

But then we must also ask the question: How can phenomenology show that even in that most transcendental realm of reason its own scientific status derives from accordance with some objectively universal procedures? How would phenomenology noncircularly prove that its own procedures are capable of redeeming phenomenology's claims to truth not just in ideally absolute subjectivity of experience but also in the practices of historical scientific institutions? After all, Husserl himself argued against any naïve metaphysical postulates when he noted that phenomenology should be considered "anti-metaphysical." Additionally, he urged phenomenology to "reject . . . every metaphysics concerned with the construction of purely formal hypotheses." Whether we consider these statements good or bad definitions of the idea of the metaphysical, we can still see the essential point: phenomenology cannot appeal to metaphysics to justify its scientific status. Moreover, where there are well-founded metaphysical questions to be addressed, Husserl is of the opinion that, "like all genuine philosophical problems, all metaphysical problems *must return to a phenomenological base*."[87] Because of all that, and in light of Husserl's quarrels with empiricism, naturalism, and positivism, we are left with the suggestion that Husserl found fault in these isms not on pragmatic grounds but on account of their insufficient historical consciousness. It may sound paradoxical, but it is true that, for example, historicism can easily turn itself into an ahistorical science.

When he directly addresses the question, Husserl thinks that up until his time "the a priori sciences that have developed historically do not at all bring to realization the full idea of a positive ontology." This is because the a priori sciences dealt only, and thus incompletely, "with the logical form of every possible world . . . and the eidetic form of a possible physical nature," and were thus "stuck in transcendental naivety and consequently are burdened with those shortcomings in foundation-building that necessarily follow from it."[88] Husserl believed that he had opened a new horizon for these sciences themselves to become more conscious of and, by the grace of phenomenology, better enlightened about: the necessity to establish a method to account for any and all possible sciences of *experience*. Such self-conscious sciences are *ontological*: they address questions that arise "on the basis of a free *ideal* variation of factual experience in relation to its world of experience." Far from being antiscientific, phenomenology presents itself as the truest science because it completes all the other sciences by bringing to view the hidden subjective and the most humanistic grounds of every science. "On the one hand," Husserl explained, "there is an a priori ontology that systematically explores the structures that essentially and necessarily belong to a possible world, i.e., everything without which a world as such could not be ontically thought. But on the other hand there is phenomenological correlation-research, which explores the possible world and its ontic structures (as a world of possible experience) with regard to the possible bestowal of sense and the establishment of being, without which that world equally could not be thought."[89] To neglect the a priori science of transcendental philosophy is not only to deform philosophy but to mispractice any and all kinds of science. When he surveyed the history of modern science in the Western world, Husserl believed that "all positive sciences . . . [function] in transcendental naivety" because, "without realizing it, they do their research with a one-sided orientation in which the entire life that transcendentally constitutes the real unities of experience and knowledge remains hidden to these sciences."[90]

Because of its radical claim to absolute consciousness, transcendental phenomenology appears to escape all the problems we ordinarily associate with "pure" logical deductions that seek to present themselves as the reasons of the empirical sciences. For example, in Husserl's hands, transcendental philosophy, as if by magic—after all, he suggested we needed only to *look* at the world—protects itself from accusations of creating a vicious epistemic circle while at the same time displaying the way out of psychologism, positivism, and scientism. It seems that we cannot raise any protests by charging either metaphysical naïveté or empty idealism. Nor can we charge reductionism, for what is reduced in phenomenology is in itself the ideal subjective condition of the possibility of truth in experience.

In the end, transcendental philosophy claims that the empirical sciences must come to depend on subjective idealism. The idealism is said to be the only true objectively universal condition of the possibility of a world—including the worlds of the sciences. For if it is indeed the case that the positivistic sciences do not understand, and do not wish to account for (they repress) the true grounds of the scientificity of their own practices, then a new science may be required to uncover and justify both the sciences and their naïve states of existence. The new science will also be required to analytically justify its own transcendental claims. Yet it seems that any true transcendental reduction is ultimately driven by its own internal needs (rather than the shortcomings claimed to exist in the positive sciences), namely, its own subjective idealism. It is this idealism—a quest to isolate the a priori conditions of an absolute consciousness—that, after all, leads to *both* claims of a universal transcendence of the sciences *and* to subjective grounding of the transcendental phenomenological *epoché*.

But recall that the movement that started the idealistic impetus was the question, How do the multiplicities of appearance of the world unify themselves in consciousness? Husserl certainly thinks that first-order scientific practices cannot themselves answer this question. The question, if it is to make any sense at all, requires a different kind of science, a science at another level of consciousness—the ideally transcendental level—in order to account for the grounds on which the universal character of any possible science can be shown to derive the rational conditions of its possibility. The grounds of the possible unities of the various appearances of scientific experiences or traditions may be seen, after the universal transcendental reduction and "according to their own cognitional senses," to be what they are: "unities of transcendentally constituting multiplicities." So we get a situation where, paradoxically, it is argued that only idealism allows the empirical sciences to "thoroughly understand and justify themselves."[91]

Husserl believed that modern European sciences were in crisis for two related reasons: philosophical *ignorance* of the absolute science of the sciences and, consequently, a *mal-practice* of the particular positive sciences because of this ignorance. He notes, "If there is any lack of clarity as regards their origins, and consequently any failure regarding knowing their genuine and necessary sense, this lack of clarity gets transmitted to the whole theoretical make-up of the positive sciences." It is just on account of such a transmission that "in most recent times the defectiveness of all positive sciences has been disclosed by the crisis of foundations into which all positive, empirical and a priori sciences have fallen."[92] This religious metaphor of a Fall is significant both in itself as well as in the further and quite productive uses to which Husserl's post–World War II European disciples, particularly Heidegger, would put it. Yet we can show that while the basis of its first claim to truth (the problem of positivism, for example) may be explained, the second universal conclusion reached beyond the diagnosis is hardly similarly obvious.

As with Hegel's work, one can reasonably insist that Husserl's uses of the word "science"—particularly the idea of a science of logic—require disambiguation. In what sense does transcendental philosophy share a meaning of "science" with, say, the sciences of artificial intelligence and robotics? In what sense might economics as social science share more than metaphorical or analogical "transcendental" self-understanding with, say, psychoanalysis? While it inspired a legitimate critical movement against scientism, it remains difficult to imagine that those who actually practice (not just critique) the sciences across the disciplines will someday reach scientific agreement not only about the how (the question of method) but also about the ultimate why (the ontological question) that arises or could arise from the various scientific disciplines. This is what makes so contentious the claims—successive and dazzling in the choice of vocabulary—that phenomenology is the only "pure," "absolute," "full," "complete," "genuine," "comprehensive," "originary," "free of unclarity" science.[93] If one were not already convinced, it is difficult to imagine that the repetitiveness of these sweeping descriptions contributes to make their claims more convincing.

ORDINARY REASON

In *Philosophy in the Flesh* Lakoff and Johnson write, "[Ours] is not the innocuous and obvious claim that we need a body to reason; rather, it is the striking claim that the very structure of reason itself comes from the details of our embodiment."[94] This argument and others like it advocate what might appear to some as a crass Darwinism in conception of rationality because it seems to define reason by use rather than transcendence. "Rationality," say Lakoff and Johnson, "is the way we make use of, *rather than transcend*, our animal nature . . . the same neural and cognitive mechanisms that allow us to perceive and move around also create our conceptual systems and modes of reason."[95] Contrary to what we saw in phenomenology, this is a robustly anthropological conception of reason held together by an equally robust if implicit naturalistic biology.

Rather than Husserl or phenomenology, it was Descartes and his Cartesian idea represented in the "I think" that were at the immediate receiving end of Lakoff and Johnson's critiques. Their version of philosophical naturalism lines up behind Nietzsche, Freud, Marx, and Foucault against Descartes and generally the modern rationalistic tradition he inaugurated. But to fight Descartes in this way is to reject both metaphysical foundationalism and transcendental idealism.

A theory of reason as ordinary resists the temptation to choose sides for or against Darwinism or Cartesianism. This resistance is based on the principled idea that there are more important basic and vernacular domains of research on reason and rationality which philosophy would do better to focus upon. My theory of the ordinary nature of reason and the linguistically vernacular history of rationality find support in recent but well-founded efforts to overcome the aporias that necessarily arise from purely materialistic or idealistic conceptions of the "essence" of rationality. In *The Mind's Provisions*, for example, the historian of philosophy Vincent Descombes asks, "Where do we locate the mind?"[96] His answer, on the surface, is deceptively simple: we must thoroughly question the question before we can understand it in order to arrive at the answer that there is not one "where" but multiple natural and social complexes through which the mind can be said to have and express its existence.

If one is a subjectivist one would like to think that the mind exists within the body of a person or persons. If one is an objectivist one would like to think that the mind exists in nature and imposes its law-like character on individuals. Descombes refers to these groups as the "internalist" and "externalist" camps, the former represented by Descartes, Locke, Hume, and Husserl and the latter by Feuerbach, Marx, and the early Foucault. Whereas internalists want to transcendentally deduce or phenomenologically reduce the mind or consciousness, the externalists believe that the mind is something to be universally explained by reference to either objective nature or the objectively historical and social institutions of society.

Whereas metaphysics and ontology are primary areas of inquiry about consciousness for the internalist, the externalist argues that grounds for objectivity cannot be attributed to the subjectivity of an individual's mentality, for the mental processes active within the subjectivity of the individual are said to have been externally preconditioned. From the externalist's point of view, the mental processes of the mind are no more than individually mediated representations of objective forms of social life—forms of life whose "regimes of reason" constitute and justify the rationalities of the disciplines within, and out of which, the individual and society must construct their identities. Where the internalist seeks absolute grounds for a priori truths about the self and other, the historical materialist, for example, thinks that all searches for such grounds are themselves enabled and ultimately constrained by the social and institutional histories of the discipline that engages in the quests. The externalist believes that not even philosophical consciousness itself can be adequately explained without reference to social relations and cultural institutions such as family, religion, and schools; race, gender, and sexuality; or class, economic, and political positions.

We can avoid getting caught in the middle of the crossfire between internalism and externalism if we refocus the question inherited from Descombes. To the question "*Where* is the mind?," Descombes responds, "The condition of mind is neither interiority, nor subjectivity, nor calculating power, but rather, autonomy in determining the goals it undertakes."[97] Let us assume that this idea of autonomy—the autonomy of the rational will—is a fruitful starting point for our inquiry into the nature of what is the most ordinary about reason. What would be a concept of reason, a theory of rationality, based on this presumptive historical au-

tonomy of mind? If we colloquially called this an anthropological definition of *intellectual freedom*, the task still remains to characterize the
ordinarily cultural, social, and historical reason or modes of reason of this
freedom. I start, then, with the claim that humans *make* their own minds.

In fact, we make up our minds all the time. This is an everyday task
revolving around any number of individual psychological or socially
collective purposes, so that the concept of "making" a mind is plain
though not facilely deployed. The philosophical significance of the vernacular can be seen when we think of the depth in the very idea of making.
For example, we do not make anything out of nothing. Nor does it follow
that a maker is always aware or even clear about the why and the how
one's mind is in the making. Similarly, even when the *what* to be made is
known, the consequences of the making or the made may not always
result in, or as, what might have been intended by the making. To ask
"What is a mind?"—or, more accurately, in light of our inquiry: What are
the reasons of the mind?—is to transcend the problematic formulated as
internalist or externalist anthropologic accounts of rationality. Instead, I
assume that culture, society, and history are constructed, made by individuals or groups of individuals acting—making up their minds in freedom—within and out of relationships to nature, to self, and to others.

However one chooses to think of it, therefore, the subjective work of
making an objective world must remain seminal to the very idea of
autonomy of mind. This conception of autonomy as freedom of action—
the freedom-to-make—must be seen as preeminently *natural*, as required of a concept of nature.[98] To make-up (one's) mind, objectively
speaking, is to do what individuals or societies do when they creatively
fashion or refashion states of existence by subjective requirements ex-
erted upon a conception of reality that presupposes as background an
idea of nature. The sense of "purpose" or meaning in personal or social
psychology therefore requires historical institutions or cultural horizons
for which a meaning or a worldly reason is *made* out of an implicit or
explicit background of general nature.

This is what is meant when we are told *Please make up your mind.* Or
when we tell others, *You have to make up your own mind.* What else
could be meant when we hear these things? In fact, in everyday language,
we also expect the speaker to mean something like "Please make a *decision*"—such as in "Please choose between *x* and *y*." "Choosing" in this

sense presupposes judging: the weighing of facts or information, and then making up one's mind about what is or what should be the case on the basis of the fact and one's subjective relations to the fact and the contexts of the facts. What we perceive and say (judge) we perceive is or ought to be the case becomes the stories we (rationally will to) tell about the facts. Making-up one's mind in these contexts means no more than the periphrases "Please tell me what you *think* about such and such." Whether in the former or latter formulation, the central theme is the ordinary expectation of rationality, namely, a demand on us for a cognitive or affective production of acts of freedoms defined as "giving" a reason or reasons.

Analysis of any everyday uses of language in any culture reveals that we routinely assume that there exists, somewhere, a mind.[99] The demand routinely placed on this mind ($M1$) is the presupposition that it can and should "think" about (i.e., examine, decide) an objective item or a subjective issue (T_1, T_2, T_3, etc.) and report, when asked or as otherwise necessary, to another mind or other minds ($M2$) what it is $M1$ thinks about T. These trinitarian relations hold whether or not T is a physical existent, a concept of an object, a belief about value, an imaginary quantity, or the thought of means to an end. The logical framework in the relations also holds whether or not either of the Ms is an actually existing person or an imagined interlocutor. A necessary fact evident in the exhortation *Make up your mind* is thus the host of presuppositions naturally available and which we make explicit within cultures when we believe that one is capable of making up a mind. We presuppose an *interaction* among and across relatively independent, autonomous units of meanings. For example, we believe that there are minds already made up and capable of communicatively sharing cogitative contents. We also presume that there are subject matters, objective and subjective states of the worlds relatively independent of minds and about which a mind is thought to have, or to be able to develop, a perspective or opinion. We also at least implicitly take for granted that we can intelligibly exchange points of view with individuals holding possibly different opinions. Finally, we presume that social and cultural environments are such that it is acceptable and even desirable to have an opinion of one's own—and speak publicly and ethically from an opinion. We take for granted, we expect, differences of opinion.

Together, these presuppositions constitute evidence of a culture of what I defined earlier as intellectual freedom. It is a culture—a culture of mind-making—in which the natural cognitive developments of mind are nurtured and generally valued. Such a culture gives us a general picture of the location of mind in the sociality of self. This is the context in which it makes sense to explain Lakoff and Johnson's claim that "the very structure of reason itself comes from the details of our embodiment." What is the body—and therefore embodiment—but the social self? In *Existentialism and Human Emotions* Sartre shows just how what we usually consider mere bodily matter is neither plain not just, well, mere flesh and bones. Judith Butler, from a Hegelian background, also gives the idea of body stunningly symbolic reconfigurations.[100] The body is discursively both matter and idea: a bundle of surplus perceptions. The perceptions may be natural and passionate, medico-technological, political, but in any case always the locus of social relations. To speak of freedom of thought as a process of mind-making is to raise questions about the social locations and autonomy of the self. In Kant, for example, to speak of autonomy of mind is synonymous with affirmation of the self's subjective, intentional spontaneity as rational. As an uncaused dynamic act, the mind's spontaneity is ipso facto the subjective power of its own self-determination. The power to self-determination is achieved through an intentional self-regulation in which the mind simultaneously gives itself self-definition or self-reflective organization. Both subjective and social, the mind's intrinsically constitutive openness to self and others makes the descriptive language of inside/outside of the mind entirely relative.[101]

With this as background, we are now in a better position to answer the question: Where can we locate the mind? If I could not know that *this* is a tree if there were no tree in existence, neither could I cognitively recognize the existing object for what it is without my capacity to form its concept, such as *tree*. In parallel to the relation between empirical intuition and concept, we can say that it is in the interplay of nature and language where at least one line of the investigation into the historicity of the mind's spontaneity needs to be located; in the nexus of the dynamics involved in perception and the use of language and other forms of symbolization lies a fruitful terrain in which to explore the practical meanings of a freedom of thought as well as thought's historical sources of freedom. If an empirical object appears in acts of cognition according to conceptual rules imposed upon experience by the mind, then at least one meaning of the phrase *Make up your mind* must be interpreted to reflect the act of conceptually insightful or judgmentally experiential world-making in conformity with rules—rules spontaneously legislated by otherwise "empty" categories of intentional subjectivity in open relation to an objectively natural and social world.

Finally, because it posits no noumenal *Ding an Sich* as found in Kant, Husserl's work leaves open the prospect of thinking that in his theory of an absolute and universal subjective foundation of intentionality is a form of a third—a medium—in the relations between perception and the ego on the one hand, and perception and its thema on the other. Husserl generically used the word "transcendental" for this third, emphasizing instead the central role of the rational will in the phenomenologic and worldly constitution of subjectivity's absolute transcendence. The intentionality of consciousness, accordingly, locates between the existence of the ego and of the object that appears to such an ego a subjective horizon of normative values and transcendental logical laws of thought philosophically (instead of psychologically) phenomenologically reduced and hermeneutically interpreted. This horizon and its phenomenal requirements as law are both universal and historically distinct from the constituting transcendental conditions because, though the two levels of phenomenological analysis are inseparable, they are nonetheless analytically distinguished. As a state constituting the ego and the object yet differing from them, the law of the third is a state of mind: at once passive and active; a transcendentally ecstatic, absolutely universalizing subjectivity. This spontaneity and its universality is, for Descartes as for Husserl, the very condition of the possibility of the I think.

I have suggested that the Cartesian and Husserlian pictures of a state of mind need to be thought differently, and thought also differently than in the flamboyant terms we encounter in Kant's transcendental critiques. But we should go further. We should speak about the mind in the language of merely *figures* of reason. We can define a figure of reason as insightful representation of experience in thought. Representability in this sense is entirely defined as the capacity to weave out of, and over, the cloud, the darkness, and the negatively productive contradictions within thought of the practical and everyday concepts in and through which subjectivity emerges as such. To represent is to objectively fashion a concept of an insight; it is a production of the history of experience.

This characterization is compatible with Husserlianism insofar as it encodes the insight that what Husserl preferred to call intentionality is neither ego nor its object: both are required conditions, but intentionality remains in itself the pure space of Kantian-type apperception exhibiting only the distinguishable relatedness of subject and object. But I have proposed that we escape the world of idealism, absolute or merely transcendental. Speaking about figuring the mind is my way of insisting on the vernacular-induced conviction that there is an irrevocable mark of a gap within thought and language on account of which subjectivity can only indirectly and diversely figure, as nonidentity, its own historical (re)presentations. This gap exists not just in the noncoincidence of the ego and its thema but also within the subjectivity of the ego and on account of time: the time-ous nature of all that is perceptual.

A vernacular conception of rationality must therefore present itself as empirically ordinary rather than absolutely speculative or speculatively transcendental. Rather than a transcendental philosophy, a reflective account of experience in the vernacular—a vernacular phenomenology, if you wish—seeks to uncover neither the idea nor the grounds above or below experience. Nor is it interested in asking whether such an idea is pure or impure. A vernacular theory of rationality aims to recover the ordinary laws in the everyday experience of things and of the subjectivity of other subjects. It derives its epistemic power from learned practical principles on the basis of which a self constitutes simultaneously its own autonomy as well as the autonomy of the objectivity of the world.

In the final analysis, what does it mean to say that the mind is made up? From whichever angle one looks at it, a mind (M)—that which we say forms opinions and judgments about self and objects, events, or values (T)—constitutes itself in the very acts of such opinion-formation. Because these acts are the thoughtful work we call reasoning, they are inherently cognitive: they are conceptual and representational. The processes of opinion-formation and judgment-making therefore automatically entail the very composition of the site of insight: they entail a thoughtful composition of self, the other, the world, and nature. It is in the midst of this composition that a mind can appear to be "holding" a rational point of view: an idea, a concept, an intention, a judgment, an interest, an index of pleasure or displeasure, and so forth.

Because it is constituted in acts of thought (cognizing, deliberating, valuing, judging, etc.), a mind is not only always already made but is also always making up itself. Similarly, self- and collective identities and social institutions, because they are mindfully cultural and historically fashioned, are objectively dynamic forms of consciousness and formations of mind. Identities, whether of individuals or institutions, are thus mindfully fashioned, in conformity to subjective ideals, as worldly artifacts of thought. Identities, like any subjective or objective worldly artifact, are symbolically constituted bodies (icons) as well as bodies of symbols (artifactually traditional compositions of things, ideas, values). Social symbols are therefore artifacts of mind; they are representational expressions of objects as figures—figurative artifacts—of mind.

A determination of the ordinary grounds of rationality can therefore hardly be achieved without taking into account the self-constituting power of the mind in relation to its factual representations of the world. Similarly, what I say is *my* mind achieves self-consistency only in the processes of a dynamic composition of its objects of representations. Consequently, what we ordinarily regard as production of reasons for a belief about an aspect of a world is not more and not less than possession of adequate grounds—that is, references—in experience to justify formation of the belief in the first place. We might even produce reasons for production of *this* rather than *that* reason as support for this or that judgment already grounded or susceptible to being grounded in experience. At whatever level the discursive practice, however, it qualifies as a reasoned belief: a belief with actually or potentially intersubjective and objective rational support. Reasoned evidence of any such support is not, however, external to the structure of belief. Nor is belief something we add to the law of reason. Rational grounds for belief *are* the law of reason.

2

Ordinary Historical Reason

To slightly complicate a question posed by Virginia Woolf: How is it possible to connect the thing with the meaning of the thing? If Woolf assigned to fiction writing the task of carrying the mind "across the chasm which divides the two without spilling a single drop of its belief,"[1] what in everyday experience allows one to form this belief in the first place? Unlike literary fiction, academic philosophy gets around the problem of grounds for everyday beliefs about things by saying, in the language of the moderns, that one's concept "mirrors," "represents," or "corresponds" to the object. Today, particularly in postmodern social sciences, others say that discourses "construct," "deconstruct," and "reconstruct" the social and cultural worlds that are objects of study. I intend in this chapter to first highlight and then reconfigure the problems involved in these modern and postmodern ways of talking about things and how we come to beliefs about what things mean. Since there is a large body of literature on the subject, I examine only the most recent discussions and the outstanding debates. Over all, I hope to show how—contrary to the sense one might get when eavesdropping on philosophers arguing—the positions assumed in these discussions, as well as the resolutions offered to the problems, are inherently tied to vernacular but unstated ethical and aesthetic assumptions.

THOUGHT AND THINGS

In a series of books, *Descartes: The Project of Pure Inquiry, Ethics and the Limits of Philosophy, Moral Luck,* and *Truth and Truthfulness,* Bernard Williams developed at least three kinds of related languages that humans employ in the making of concepts. There is, first, the language of science (e.g., physics) that seeks to present an absolute description of natural states of the world. The absolute character of this language derives from the fact that physics, like other natural sciences, aims to describe with predictable certainty the universal and nonrelativistic laws that govern the natural relations of its objects. This language of science is different from the language of morality and ethics. This second type of language seeks to provide—in general ethics, for example—a "thin" description of ethical truths (e.g., the concepts of rightness, goodness, justice). When ethical language is contextual rather than general, we speak of the third kind of moral and ethical discourse: a "thick" language in which one makes culturally relativistic moral judgments (e.g., Was it right for the company driver, on her way to the office, to refuse to give a lift to an unacquainted old lady who had asked for a ride?). While the first type of language allows the physical scientist to explain and predict the behavior of nature under causal laws (e.g., gravity, planes, optics), the second allows a thinker in one language to make either cross-cultural or intra-cultural moral judgments. Whereas the language of intercultural moral-ity is suitable for evaluating behaviors of peoples who live in another culture, or peoples who lived in a past which the speaker could never experientially recapture from an internal point of view, the thick lan-guage of intracultural moral judgment is suitable for evaluating social experiences in which one can easily imagine oneself a participant.

The problems with these distinctions in language present themselves when we imagine that most human ways of talking do not fit into these absolute poles. In everyday life, most individuals do not use language in the ways a physicist or an ethicist does. And even within the expert community, the languages of a majority of the sciences—especially in the fields of historical, social, and literary sciences, not to mention the yet more ambiguous areas of interdisciplinary studies—do not easily starkly present themselves under the umbrellas of the physical versus the moral.

If Williams's position on the first type of language (the ideal language of causality in science) is inspired by the early Wittgenstein, the Wittgenstein of the *Tractatus*, his position on the second type of language, regarding the possibility of a distinction between general and situational or thin and thick statements in ethics, keeps in view the implications of the arguments of the later Wittgenstein, the Wittgenstein of the *Investigations*. For this Wittgenstein, cultures and societies are embedded in forms of life within which the internal participants play language games. Language games are intrinsically evaluative: they encode not only cognitive dispositions but also aesthetic and moral arguments or demonstrations about the speaker's motives, actions, and purposes. Within this background, to say that cross-cultural moral judgment can only be "thin" (e.g., we can say that we know that some things are good and others are bad, certain things are just and others unjust, or some things are beautiful and others ugly) is to admit that one does not inhabit all possible forms of life, and therefore can speak only as a situated mind. As situated, one's general language cannot be, a priori, presumed to penetrate the particulars of all possible human experiences. One can therefore speak thickly only where one concretely shares a worldview rather than abstract concepts alone. To make moral concepts thick and useful at the levels of everyday social interactions requires a shared way of life: linguistic, religious, political, commercial, and so forth.[2]

But there is also a strong current of relativism in Williams's thinking that may not permit—or does permit, but not to the degree I have just indicated—the optimistic outlook on cross-cultural communication. The relativism suggests that any cross-cultural judgment, no matter how reflexive and thorough its critical processes, might not be decontextually objective. It admits that cross-cultural dialogue may enlarge the rules of each interlocutor's language game, so that in the development of capacities for newer linguistic rules and norms the participants may acquire newer cultures. But then this newer, larger language would also be seen to possess its own cognitive conceptual as well as practical contextual limitations. There is, in short, no hope for the possibility of a *general mind*—a mind decontextualized of all specificities and hovering from nowhere over all actual and possible experiences of all cultures and all linguistic traditions. For the relativist, humans do not have it (yet) in their power to create a universal language game that would be useful for passing judgments on every habit of every culture. The furthest Williams could possibly go in this direction is to affirm, in the manner of Wittgenstein, that moral language games may share, across themselves, family resemblances. But these resemblances are not and cannot be strongly cognitive, that is, serial, logical relations. Instead, the relations are historical and genealogical.

To pass an evaluative moral judgment on a behavior on the basis of family resemblances in ethical worldviews appears, and will always appear, to be either of two things: to speak thinly and in generalities or to speak thickly but, as it were, from another place: from the point of view of an other. Neither of these alternatives suggests, however, that such moral judgments are any less valid than one made from within a particular, shared worldview. The judgments are simply different forms of moral judgments. As such, even for the radical relativist, *some* morally evaluative cross-cultural statements, however at risk for meaninglessness on account of their generality and however interruptive their externality to the addressee, are perfectly possible because actors across cultures do believe, for example, that there are, generally speaking, *types* of behavior one can call right and types of behaviors one can call wrong, or that certain types of action can be said to be good while others are said to be bad, some proper and improper, some beautiful and others ugly. To engage in arguments, even merely conceptually, for or against the binary thinking involved in these pairings of terms is already to recognize their conceptual possibilities.

From here onward I examine the cognitive status of this idea of the conceptually possible in various kinds of ethical judgments. Ultimately, whether one is a believer in the rational validity of cross-cultural languages of cross-cultural morality or a relativist in the matter, the question for everyone is the cognitive status of the idea of the languages of morals as such, no matter if this language is said to be thin (sharing only a family resemblance) or thick (from the point of view of a particular form of life).

Another way of phrasing the same problem is as follows: Is there a possibility of a logical guarantee that cross-cultural actors may reach agreement about the rightness or wrongness of most highly specific, culturally or linguistically, contextual behavior? If yes, what provides the guarantee? If no, why not? These questions are relevant not necessarily in the course of primary, unreflective levels of social interaction. In fact, one hardly ever notices, in the normal course of ordinary lives, the logical incongruities and paradoxes that underlie much human inter-action. With the exception of those rare moments when reflection is forced upon actors by a breakdown in rituals that are everyday com-munication, the significance of our inquiry derives largely from the tech-nical domains of reflection and of thought. From this perspective, our problems belong with the questions already highlighted in the preface, introduction, and chapter 1. How consistent are all forms of reason within and across themselves? How is the unity of rationality possible? If rationality lacks an inner consistency except in its most abstract form (e.g., as pure apperception, as a supposedly supertranscendental subjec-tivity, or as merely figures of the mind), how, for example, might an anthropologist or a philosopher recording and judging the actual ac-tivities of a foreign culture have confidence that he or she has under-stood the real meanings of a culture or, within a culture, the thought of another? How is it ever possible to understand thickly another culture, another mentality, except from the "outside"?

To say that an understanding or judgment is "thick" is to suggest that it is highly specific and contextual. It implies that, in addition to the general understanding of the system of beliefs underlying a behavior understood or judged, the concrete contents of the behavior comprehended have also been accounted for in their causally explanatory relation to their general system of beliefs. To make a thick moral judgment, then, is to imply that one has understood the rational bases of actions directly resulting in a belief system that has been evaluatively, pragmatically comprehended in thought. To be able to make this kind of judgment the speaker must not only have seen what was done, but must also have understood for what and how it was done, from the perspective of the actor. To gain these two levels of understanding, however, one would need to, actually or vicari-ously, participate in the form of life and the language games of the culture and the customs in question. But the dilemma is that once one has so fully embedded oneself in a culture and its customs, there is no reason to think that, given the total-social character of culture and intentional practice, one has not lost one's "objectivity." How do we know that the interpreter is not henceforth rationalizing—that is, "understanding" in the sense of excusing—actions authorized by situations otherwise alien from the interpreter's original standpoint or background?[3] It is precisely this possibility, or probability, of rationalizing the potentially irrational (or the potential impossibility of knowing that one is not rationalizing the irrational) that motivates cognitive skepticism vis-à-vis claims to an objectively unitary, universal, and acontextual rationality. Another way to say this is that when it comes to making "thick" ethical judgments, one culture may not have the "right" kind of reasons to judge another culture —because the judged culture, even when the external observer is no longer just an outsider to it, tends to reassert the cognitive and moral sovereignty of the internal actor's point of view, whether this internal actor never was, or is no longer, foreign.

The relativism that this line of argument could lead to suggests that each culture has a capacity to develop systems of justification for its particular—and peculiar—value practices. It also leads to the assumption that it is always by a stretch that one moral judgment based on the values of one culture might be strongly made, especially uncharitably, about another culture.[4] While this position does not deny that cultures interact, influence, and even transform one another, the interactions, influences, and transformations are noted to occur not because anthropologists or philosophers cognitively decide upon and logically sanction authorizing such action ahead of time. Rather, the interactions occur because individuals leading their daily lives—with varying levels of self-awareness and unawareness; morally, immorally, and amorally—choose to assimilate or discard aspects of other cultures with which their own worldviews and practices come into historical contact. If one were to apply the traditional language of philosophy to this situation, it could be described as encounter, conflict, and transformation of cultural facts and values. The transformation may or may not lead successfully to partial or whole-scale cultural displacement of a people's previous self-interpretations or the moral norms of self- and other representations. But the mere fact that cultures do have in their vernaculars such representational or symbolic powers of both adaptation and resistance—powers that may or may not be cognitively obvious at the primary levels of less reflective social practices—invites one to determine precisely the cognitive claims of cultures to values, claims that are made at both reflective and unreflective levels of symbolic exchange.

Hilary Putnam indirectly takes up some of the challenges just noted in *Representation and Reality*. It is widely said that this book helped awaken Euro-American analytic philosophy from its twentieth-century dogmatic slumber. The work argues, in substance, that the classical correspondence theory of truth is wrong because the idea that a "nonpsychological" absolute fixes references to objects is totally unintelligible. Translated, this is plain denial of the idea that somehow it is nature itself—rather than the human mind—that determines what human words stand for. The correspondence theory of meaning—what Richard Rorty famously called philosophy as "the mirror of nature"—requires one to revert to, in Putnam's equally colorful language, "medieval essentialism" in order to account for experience and concept-formation. The medievalism consists in a belief that essential, self-identifying objects naturally populate the world—essences on the behalf of which, it is presumed, linguistic sign-relations are built, also naturally, to match an essential order of things. The contrary, nondogmatic position is that it is only from human mental constructions of nature that the law-like character of nature may be known.

To understand the true impacts of Putnam's and Rorty's works on these issues, one must distinguish between a rejection of the correspondence theory of knowledge of nature, on the one hand, and an embrace of relativism, on the other. Neither option necessarily entails the other. In fact, Putnam examined several brands of relativisms and ultimately rejected their claims. Instead, much like Quine, he looks in a different direction for the consequences of a post-Cartesian metaphysics of nature and postessentialist nonmedieval epistemology. Although he rejects the metaphysically relativistic and nihilistic idea that there is no reality "out there" independent of language games, Putnam nevertheless insists on the fuzziness at the boundaries between the spheres of nature, culture, and language. How can one delineate between the languages of fact, value, and interpretation? For example, how might one correctly conceptually mark the boundaries between the languages we use to describe present events versus past events? Or between the languages that describe one's own culture as opposed to an appropriate language for understanding a foreign culture? Putnam thinks that some versions of weak and differential relativism—for example, Williams's account of the possibility of scientific but not other kinds of "absolute" conception of states of the natural or social world—is, in the final analysis, too relativistic. (Williams's scientific absolute, Putnam claims, may not be cognitively relativistic but is certainly metaphysically so.)

Whether the questions are addressed to the cultures that demarcate everyday language from the technical uses of language in the sciences, to the languages we use to isolate the past from present cultures, or to those we employ to distance the local from the foreign, the problem of relativism, for Putnam, goes all the way from the metaphysical (beliefs about what "things" absolutely or ultimately are in themselves) to the rhetorical (the best choice in the use of words or descriptive metaphors). In the final analysis, Putnam does not think that one can linguistically speak about objects of thought, the things of words, in absolute terms, but only in a continuum from one extreme (of objectivity) to another (of subjectivity). How concepts and judgments formed along the continuum get "standardized" and routinized as truths and norms in any society or among communities of experts is thus conventional—though not entirely so. The distinction between the merely conventional and the entirely conventional is thus crucial. In a choice example, Putnam points out that when one says "This is a *star*," "This is a *constellation*," and "This is the '*Big Dipper*,'" the conceptual relativity of the language(s) is clear. But the relativism in the conceptual relativity is not absolute, as some explicitly argue or implicitly believe.

What, then, is a nonabsolute conceptual or nonmetaphysical relativism? There are some who think that this problem has been solved in the past few years. But a careful review of the evidence suggests that what has been attempted, and achieved with uneven levels of success, especially in the United States, has been to pragmatically dissolve the necessary questions. Starting, first, with Quine's "Two Dogmas of Empiricism" and Davidson's "The Very Idea of a Conceptual Scheme," then in Rorty's *Philosophy and the Mirror of Nature* and Dick Bernstein's *Beyond Objectivism and Relativism*, and the latest in Brandom's *Making It Explicit* and McDowell's *Mind and World*, the history of American philosophy in the past thirty years reflects a desire to solve old Kantian puzzles about reason and nature as much as an effort to prove that the puzzles are either epistemically irrelevant or pragmatically unhelpful. This American, though just as often non-American, pragmatic tendency in twenty-first-century philosophy is the will to overcome or neutralize key problems created and addressed in not just classical metaphysics but also in the epistemologies of Kantian and neo-Kantian transcendental idealism.

THREE VERSIONS OF PRAGMATISM

Pragmatism's philosophic will usually manifests itself in one of three related versions. The first version is presented as a call to *abandon* the classic problems of transcendental idealism by evasion. We could call this evasive strategy, following Rorty, pragmatic cunning. The second version is a call to *overcome* transcendental idealism and its problems. We could call this pragmatic heroism: a call to transcend transcendence by heroically realizing its inner meanings in the worldly creativity of action. (The promises of this creativity, it is argued, are best achieved in poetic, moral, and political imagination rather than "dry" philosophical analysis.) Finally, some, also in the name of pragmatism, prefer a Wittgenstein-like *silence* on protracted epistemological problems of rationality. Wittgenstein is implicated because he was active in similar debates during the first half of the twentieth century, particularly in what was known in the United Kingdom as the "rationality debates," and his later writings inspire hope in various current American analytic beliefs that philosophical abstemiousness might quietly lead to a nonproblematic re-anchoring of philosophical concepts about reason to forms of everyday empirical intuitions, to a kind of common sense. I will describe in fuller detail each of these responses.

The first version is best represented in the arguments of the earliest paragraphs of Quine's "Two Dogmas."[5] In what reads like a manifesto, Quine asserts, "Modern empiricism has been conditioned in large part by two dogmas. One is a belief in some fundamental cleavage between truths which are *analytic*, or grounded in meanings independently of matters of fact and truths which are *synthetic* or grounded in fact." These are dogmas, he claims, because they are based on "ill founded" reductionism, namely, "the belief that each meaningful statement is equivalent to some logical construct upon terms which refer to immediate experience." The reduction misleads not just in its implicit claim to foundationalism but also by one of its necessary consequences, notably, the "blurring of the supposed boundary between speculative metaphysics and natural science." If the boundary or dichotomy between metaphysics and natural science is *supposed*, it is because Quine anticipates the opportunity to exploit precisely the problems of the ill-advised dichotomy, and do so in ways that favor a shift to pragmatism.

Hence, though the immediate target of Quine's charge of dogmatism is Kant's analytic/synthetic distinction, the implications go way back to problems in pre-Kantian traditions. Hume's distinctions between relations of ideas or logical truths and matters of fact, Leibniz's similar distinctions between truths of reason and truths of fact, and Descartes's definition of the person as a dual combination of a thinking substance (the mind) and physical automata (body) are just some of the positions affected by this pragmatic critique of a supposed Kantian dogmatism. By insisting that no satisfactory account of body, fact, or matter has ever been produced in a way that shows how they are separate from mind, reason, and idea; that the claims about the laws of "contradictions" presumed to regulate the analytic a priori or logical statements are themselves prone to the same dogmaticity as the analytic/synthetic distinctions they are meant to prove; and that nothing philosophically indispensable is lost when the distinctions and the supporting apparatuses are abandoned in favor of a robust "pragmatic" conception of relations between human thought and actions in objective worlds of objects and values: these insistences permit Quine to revisit traditional sanctuaries of epistemic idealism in order to substitute the holy cows with pragmatic ones. Descartes's and Kant's loss is pragmatism's gain, for though the mind/body, reason/fact, and ideas/matter questions do not entirely disappear, each reappears transformed—beyond recognition—in the pragmatist's backyard.

In the second version, heroic pragmatism, a robust conceptual relativity is deployed to explain away and overcome metaphysical dualism. The history of this pragmatist move, like the first, is rooted in the history of disaffection with Kantianism. In fact, its effectiveness depends on Kant's insights into the idealized nature of form and function of the concept. But pragmatic heroism also promotes the kind of relativity of conceptual schemes about which, given the analytic training of most of its American proponents, it is easiest to argue for from the writings of Gottlob Frege, specifically from Frege's distinctions between *reasons* produced to justify the use of a concept versus naturalistic, physicalistically or non-physicalistically conceived conditions that may or may not *cause* production of the reasons. Frege laments the fact that though we correctly speak about "the task of logic as the investigation of the laws of thought," we constantly fall into error when we also depart from this to think that the laws of thought are one and the same with the laws of nature. That this and similar errors are common may be attributed to the ease with which one forgets that in laws of thought one is dealing with spaces of reason, spaces of autonomy and freedom, and not of mechanical causality. For Frege, in the laws of reason one ought to be concerned only "with laws which, *like the principles of morals or the laws of the state*, prescribe how we are to act, and do not, like the laws of nature, define the causal course of events."[6] "Logic," Frege thought, is technically speaking always a normative—not empirical—science.

But why not radicalize the conceptual normativity to the ontologically natural? From the point of view of logical or conceptual pragmatism, this kind of question about nature is simply moot. And that is where the work of Robert Brandom, one of the best interpreters of Frege, comes in. Brandom describes Frege's positions in something like this: Frege had little to say about causal modalities because his interests in the question were primarily semantic. From an exclusively semantic point of view, there is no particularly compelling reason ("reason" as explained earlier) to seek harmony, logical or otherwise, between the laws of reason and the casual laws of nature. Diversity of conceptions of reason is thus something to be welcomed, not abolished.

Semantically speaking, one set of laws may forbid certain kinds of logical moves while the other does not. For example, the "laws of nature," Brandom notes, "do not forbid the making of contradictory [semantic] judgments"—not even when the judgments are "clearly forbidden in a normative sense."[7] To use other examples, we can speak lawfully by reason yet lawlessly by nature; lawlessly by reason and lawfully by nature; lawlessly by reason and lawlessly by nature; or lawfully by reason and lawfully by nature. Careful readers of *Making It Explicit* will draw these conclusions as I have because Brandom sufficiently explains how this ought to be the case when he writes that though it may be *normatively* incorrect "to endorse incompatible contents," the conceptual incorrectness may not be spoken about the identity of the natural objects they may conceptualize.[8] That can only be because the law of conceptual justification (e.g., a good inference) is not the same as the law of natural causality (e.g., modal compulsion). To jump from one (the conceptual) to the other (the ontological) requires more explanatory grounds than are available in the justifications of correctness or incorrectness, rightness or wrongness, and so on in the normatively prescriptive pragmatic uses of concepts. This is a version of the conclusion I independently reached in the last sections of chapter 1, during discussions of the problems of defining the rational.

In this pragmatist's approach to the problem, however, both the Heidegger-like hermeneutic and the Husserlian phenomenological demands for further explanation are usually circumvented. They are circumvented through the pragmatist's two, essentially different but functionally related denials of the metaphysical dualism presumed to hold between the natural and the rational or between causality and freedom. The first kind of denial is both substantive and procedural and most easily seen in John Dewey's work. Dewey's so-called overcoming of metaphysical dualism is predicated on an argument from empirical definitions of reason: reason is a mental process regulated by biological nature. Unlike traditional metaphysicians who assign reason to the power of consciousness and the freedom of culture, and emotion to the power of unconsciousness and causal biology, Dewey believes that reason is not an additional element to natural experience but rather a means-ends orientation in sociobiological conduct. This orientation, rather than being superimposed on experience, is the very condition of experience. The rational orientation can thus be defined as *habitual* disposition of an agent that arises only because the agent is confronted by situations of diversity in the natural habitus.

For example, if an organism—say, an amoeba—is perfectly adapted to its environment, there can be no talk of "reason" or "rationality" either in regard to its general biological life or in specific contextual situations of its everyday survival routine. But in the case of complex biological organisms, there is what Dewey called natural "distance receptors" that enable the more networked organism to experience multiple, contradictory possibilities of response to internal and external stimuli. Because of the organic variation and distanciation across the distribution of motor receptors—literally, the emotive neural networks—responses to natural stimuli in complex biological structures can no longer be direct. They can only be mediated. Thus, rather than be directly evoked by the stimulus, as in the case of a simple organism, response to stimulus in complex biological organisms becomes not only mediately but also distantly transcriptive. Our response to our environment can be a delayed, reflective, and deliberate action. To say that we are "conscious" in this context means no more than that we have *awareness* of multiplicity in regard to potential courses of response to a stimulus, so that "thought" going into the response is merely the means-end evaluation of what constitutes effective, proper, right, good response. And both consciousness and thought are parts of the nature of the organism: they are responses to a situation of possibilities.

Lacking the transparency and environmental obviousness common in simple biological organisms, humans must resort to thoughtful coping with discontinuities in what could have been entirely habitual and non-reflective tracks of conduct. Thought, awareness, feeling, emotion: for Dewey all these are results of a permanent habitus where competing possibilities present themselves as likely responses to a stimulus. For example, they can be seen as an adaptive process for an organism that, for survival, must rationally coordinate actions with other actors similarly environmentally placed. In their naturalistic and social contexts, rather than feeling being opposed to thought, or emotion to rationality, the so-called duality is only the necessary evidence of a general state of awareness of tensions generated in a complex sociobiological organism by an equal necessity for reflective action within what could have been, in less complex beings, entirely direct and habituated environment. By characterizing and attributing thoughtful awareness to sociobiological condition, Dewey could argue that feeling and emotion are at the core of any rational expression. For example, as Dewey argues in "Objects of Thought," rather than being irrational, emotion—"the nerves," so to speak—is presumed, in humanity, to be a signal indicator of a general disposition to reason. And far from being the result of a "blind" memory, instinct and, generally, the powers of the unconscious are, Dewey writes, "the first ['rational'] universal . . . experienced in immediate sensation."9 Instead of being opposed to reason, or being a product of thought, the emotional life is thus simultaneously a moment of self-awareness and of reason.[10]

In the continuity that should therefore exist across nature and culture, or biology and logic, the Dewey pragmatist argues that logic is no more than an adaptive system in a many-tiered evolutionary pattern of the species. Indeed, logic, for neo-Deweyans like Kwasi Wiredu, is no more than a natural communicative protocol.[11] But Wiredu sought to make metaphysical dualism entirely disappear. (Quite surprisingly, Wiredu, who is one of postcolonial Africa's best philosophers, seems to deny that *he* did any such thing: he claims it was observations of the spoken Akan language that forced him to adopt his conclusions.) He goes as far as to say that the *causal laws* of nature are, *logically* speaking, continuously anchored in the normative requirements of concepts and of the grammatical, sentential structures of languages. Under this understanding of a concept of language use, Wiredu judges a statement as correct or proper on the basis of flexible but uninterruptedly deep biosocial, anthropological and cultural, structures. Yet in the final analysis, these structures are said to be governed by nature's own universal biocausal modality, for though acknowledging that particular cultures are historical signals of heroic transcendence of nature in society, both Dewey's and Wiredu's versions of pragmatism aim to explain culture as continuously—that is, without what I called a gap, ambivalence, or breach in tongue—biosocially grounded in nature and cultures.

But there is a second kind of heroic pragmatic denial of metaphysical dualism, a denial stemming precisely from recognition but also from an effort to clear away residual questions arising in connection with universally justifying the rationality of non-normative causal laws. Whereas Dewey and Wiredu are interested in re-anchoring the idea of the rational in logic (e.g., in the law of noncontradiction) to organic-habitual conditioning of our species, so that the *normative* validity of an act of judgment can be justified as logical or illogical, correct or incorrect, or proper or improper with reference to the naturalistic background, the promoters of the second strand of heroic pragmatism disagree. We already witnessed Frege's and Brandom's radicalization of normativity in the logical domain. In Wiredu and Dewey we saw the radicalization of the biosocial (the logico-habitually naturalistic) as the universal. But the two strands of heroic pragmatism seem to merge into one: both successfully evacuate epistemology of the metaphysical residue in the classical—for example, based in correspondence theory, what Rorty called philosophy as the mirror of nature—notions of causality. Both Wiredu and Brandom would hold, for example, that in Brandom's words, a "concern with the contents of concepts and judgments is inseparable from concern with the possibility of the concepts being correctly or incorrectly *applied*";[12] similarly, all would also hold that this is the idea of the correct which should apply, as Wiredu has argued, even to judgments about truth, values, or appreciation of beauty.[13] To apply the idea of the rational beyond this idea of the correct (e.g., to speak about the "right" reason at the level of causal nature) is, for either Brandom or Wiredu, to speak unintelligibly. If you ask what rationally lies beyond Wiredu's reason-as-objectivity of biosocial opinion, the answer can be more easily and most bluntly found in either Frege or Brandom: in nature "things happen as they happen" for no reason.[14]

The third and most recent version of pragmatism's efforts to overcome metaphysical dualism is represented in the writings of John McDowell. McDowell's work embodies a quietist, deflationary sort of pragmatism in which conditions of reason are anchored in the most intuitive practical dispositions. For McDowell, there must be a distinction between, say, "thing" and "mind," but the distinctiveness cannot be found in metaphysical worlds or by arguments about metaphysical absolutes. Instead, the difference is to be comprehended through concepts like receptivity and spontaneity, or appearance and judgment. On the surface, this distinction seems to embrace, without reserve, Kantian concept and intuition. Indeed, like Kant, McDowell believes that intuition without concept is blind, just as concept without intuition is empty. But in precisely this affirmation is to be found, for the pragmatist in McDowell, the problem of details—the proverbial domain of the devil. What does it mean to say that intuition and concept, though distinct in the domain of experience, are also inseparable? For Kant the answer was to be found in the idea of the synthetic a priori. The syntheticity of judgment does not obtain only in empirical knowledge: it applies as well to propositional procedure, for example, in the relation of addition in numbers. But it is just this idea of the synthetic that Quine describes as "dogmatic."

Finding the justifications of the synthetic a priori unsatisfactory in light of Quine's attacks, McDowell—in steps that evoke now Hegel, then

Aristotle, but ultimately the version of American pragmatism I have described as quietist—wants to argue against Kant's synthetic doctrine of the mutual relation between concept and intuition. McDowell says that the mind has a "glimpse" of realities external to it not because some unknown or unknowable Thing is "given" to mind in a concept—a concept which, in turn, may be said to be an exclusive product of an abstract Understanding. Against this picture of what is possible in experience, McDowell thinks that the primal conditions of experience require both that there be no myth of the given nor a myth of disembodied mind. What is phenomenologically called "appearance," he says, should be seen as a state of *receptivity*, as a form of presentation of the world in the senses. But receptivity does not mean "passivity," if by passivity is meant real or imagined, actual or metaphorical "blind" intuition. To the contrary, receptivity is a mental engagement—an interpellation—in the world of senses, but a world of senses that is naturally already equipped with a capacity for *conception*. McDowell contends that without this primordial capacity of the senses for conception as a condition of experience, not only meaning but also judgment of any sort would be impossible. Without the attribution of receptive conceptivity to the sensualities of appearance themselves, one would have the unenviable task of explaining how the not-self "relates" to the self, or how the non-mind world of nature interacts with free, spontaneous spaces of mind.

The traditions out of which McDowell makes this plea for a worldly zone of experience in which there is active receptivity is clearer when he writes, "We need to recapture the Aristotelian idea that a normal mature human being is a rational animal, but without losing the Kantian idea that rationality operates freely in its own sphere." Or: "We need to see ourselves as animals whose natural being is permeated with rationality, even though rationality is appropriately conceived in Kantian terms."[15] Beyond these sensible pleas, however, it remains to be seen how Aristotle and Kant may be harmoniously, seamlessly reconciled. Most would easily agree with McDowell's basic diagnosis of the Kantian problematic situation. It is quite convincing: "Animals are, as such, natural beings, and a familiar modern conception of nature tends to exclude rationality from nature. The effect is that reason is separated from our animal nature, as if being rational placed us outside the animal kingdom. Specifically, the understanding is distanced from sensibility. And that is the source of philosophical impasse." The solution to this impasse, as Mc-Dowell sees it, is "to bring understanding and sensibility, reason and nature, back together."[16]

About how this could be done, he affirmatively gestures to "the Kantian idea . . . reflected in the contrast between the organization of the space of reason and the structure of the realm of the natural law," but faults "modern naturalism" for forgetting the reality of what Aristotle called "second nature." Coupled with the Kantian position, naturalism left one with an unwelcome disconnect between rationality and the animal being. By emphasizing the idea of "second nature," McDowell hopes to reconnect to nature without losing sight of the Kantian development.[17]

A full-fledged Kantian-Aristotelian conception of second nature is viable because, as McDowell says, "it must be possible to decide whether or not to judge that things are as one's experience *represents* them to be." Simultaneously, though, how "one's experience *represents* things to be is not under one's control . . . it is up to one whether one accepts the appearance or rejects it."[18] If we are puzzled by the assertion that representation is something that "experience" presents to mind, or something over which the subject has no initial control, that is precisely what McDowell wants one to hear. "Representation," he argues, is not entirely blind because it is experience that presents it—the same experience that involves a capacity both to receive what is presented and to judge it. To be sensually receptive as an animal is to be so as an animal with second nature, that is, a rational nature. Experience thus simultaneously is first and second nature, a cognitive receptivity, for humans are passive even as rational beings.

McDowell also speaks of receptivity as impressions, appearances or "appearings," each term suggesting that events impress or appear representationally to some subject, a sensitive consciousness. On the other hand, appearances are rationally continuous with the reflective judgment of the subject because they not only provide external, objective, and empirical anchors to thought but also constitute, in an essential way, a part of the cognitive experience. Appearances are therefore part of the *reasons* for our judgments about the correct or incorrect, right or wrong conditions of objectivity in experience. It is in virtue of this simultaneity of passivity and agency that "it must be possible to decide whether or not to judge that things are as one's experience presents them."[19]

Critique of McDowell

On one level, it looks like McDowell has got it about right. For example, if one thinks about experience as a form of appearance, an appearance in and over which humans have no control in the ways we are struck by the natural objectivity of the world, then our judgments of experience cannot be seen as antinatural. But experience, on account of appearance and judgment, can be interpreted as intrinsically double-aspected yet continuously interpreted if we think of experience as first and second nature of the same rational animal. It looks as if metaphysical dualism may be elaborated away: while experience under one of its aspects cannot be correct or incorrect, right or wrong, beautiful or ugly (it just is), in another respect, the rational agent can still bring evaluative judgments and decisions to bear upon that which just is. This phrasing of the matter does not easily allow a return to the language that divides up "experience" between appearance (sense data) and representation (judgment). In McDowell, experience re-presents to itself the contents of the world to be judged. As he puts it: "*That things are thus and so* is the conceptual content of an experience, but if the subject of the experience is not misled, that very same thing, *that things are thus and so*, is also a perceptible fact, an aspect of the perceptible world."[20]

But it seems that we ought to make a distinction between successfully staging conviviality between Aristotelian and Kantian programs, on the one hand, and believing that the two programs have become seamlessly merged into one, on the other hand. Aristotle and Kant together create unanticipated problems for McDowell from two flanks. Those who wish to defend the integrity of Kant's transcendental idealism are not happy with the result of the merger, and those who wish to maintain the most robust picture of Aristotle's empirical insights are not pleased either. I will discuss two notable responses to McDowell, Michael Friedman's "Exorcizing the Philosophical Tradition"[21] and Barry Stroud's "Sense-Experience and the Grounding of Thought."[22]

From their flank, where idealists charge that McDowell is too empirical and not idealistic enough, Friedman explains why, even while accepting that McDowell shares with the idealists a "picture of the sphere of the conceptual as absolutely unbounded," the idealists do not share his view that the "rhetoric of absolute idealism" requires any constraints by "deliverances of receptivity."[23] After all, it is still the case that, in relation to this receptivity, and despite the receptivity's thoroughly conceptual character, the way humans are implicated in its *deliverances* must remain passive. Or at least that should be the case because, as Friedman also notes, there has to be the "difference between its appearing to us that such and such is the case in experience (concerning which we have no free choice) and our actively judging that such and such is the case in thought (concerning which we have some free choice)." Thus, though the empirical world consists "of *thinkable* contents belonging to the space of reason," from the perspective of the idealist, not even the best idealistic aspects of McDowell's conceptions are strong enough to grant the empirical world independence from "free and spontaneous *activity* of thought."[24]

From the other flank, empiricists charge that McDowell is too idealistic and not empirical enough. Barry Stroud, for example, seems to have plenty of good reasons to show why he believes that McDowell's second-nature solution to metaphysical dualism amounts to "the idea that having a sense-experience or impression, at least when things go well, is simply a matter of seeing or otherwise perceiving that things are thus and so."[25] But this would be rather odd, given McDowell's effort to illuminate the conceptual nature of receptivity. The faithful empiricist's argument goes something like this: Suppose one accepts that the "experience of seeing that something or other is so certainly involves receiving an impact from the world of the senses." Suppose, too, that "no one could see that *p* without understanding the thought that *p*." And suppose, finally, one accepts that both the first order of experience (impression) and its second order (judgment) are thus simultaneously constituted in what has been called experience. Therefore, to think is to have both the impact of the world upon the sense impression and the capacity to experience this impact as both impression and grounds for empirically based reasoning and judgment. In the judgment "that *p*," one also affirms that "*p* is an actualization of conceptual capacities in sensory consciousness." But this is precisely where the empiricist becomes the most dissatisfied and begins to suspect McDowell of a crypto-idealism. If seeing that *p* involves judging that *p*, then having an impression, an appearing, or what McDowell calls a "representation" of *p*, strictly speaking, does not. The empiricist's suspicion is that there must be hidden, somewhere in *Mind and World*, a requirement for another level of cognitive activity or commitment—for example, an activity of judging or committing to propositions in the order of which the *truth* of *p* is brought about. This, the critic argues, is a quiet idealism but too much idealism nonetheless.[26]

Thus we find that while some point out McDowell's idealism only to praise it (and want more), others see it as evidence of a half-hearted empiricist program. Lamenting the fact that McDowell merely "saddled" empirical content (or impression) with an assent, Stroud complains, "When the content of one's impression is things' appearing to be thus and so, it looks as if the impression that grounds the judgment involved in accepting that content must be the very impression in the receiving of which that judgment is made. There is nothing else that could serve as its ground. To insist that its ground must be found elsewhere, because a judgment can be adequately grounded only if it is based on an impression that does not involve making that very judgment, would lead to a skeptical regress: no judgment would be grounded."[27] The solution, from the empiricist's point of view, is of course more radical empiricism. For example, one should give greater substantive independence, and therefore cognitive significance, to sense data and their causal objects. Ideas could be thought of as "copies" or formal imprints of sense data in the understanding or memory. Without this, it is assumed that, in the long run, McDowell's anchor of perception in receptivity is so thin that the idea of receptivity can be easily relativized or even entirely bypassed without losing much—except for "the fact." But to lose the "the fact" in this way, for the empiricist, is precisely to lose almost everything.

THE IDEA OF CONCEPTUAL DIVERSITY

The conflict between the idealist and the empiricist pulls on McDowell hinges on how best to explain *both* the distinction *and* the relation between "inner" and "outer" sense. If impression goes in two directions, mind (subjective) and world (objective), we would have impressions of outer sense as we have impressions of inner sense. While one is bounded (because in it we are stuck in the world of empirical entities), the other is not so. While one offers material, content-full occasion to acquire a purchase on objective reality, the other offers only empty formal boundaries by judgment. The realist critic worries that the sort of nondualism implied in these directions leaves the door open to the conclusion that ultimately *our* world is a species-specific model of reality. The worry is that this conclusion is just a step removed from saying that not only human rationality but also nature itself is only a chain of signifiers.[28] As we shall see, some of those who object to pragmatism's many efforts to evade, transcend, or deflate metaphysical dualism do so also out of fear that pragmatism might easily be contaminated by Continental philosophy.

It is well known that in Heidegger's corpus, for example, philosophy and poetry compete with equal weight for philosophical engagements. It is also known that in the course of decades of reading Heidegger, evident in the influential *Of Grammatology*, Derrida radicalized Heidegger's antimodernism by advocating what amounted to abolition of the technical separation between philosophy and literature, and reason and rhetoric. Together, these German and French developments, among others, have been called the *linguistic turn*.

But far from a flat denial of metaphysics or "reality," as in common sense, what distinguishes the linguistic turn as far as the debates about rationality go is its theory of the relationships not just between word and thing but also between word and the act of writing, still-photographing, motion-picturing, and so on. Thing, word, writing, image, reason: How do acts of representation as such reveal and obscure the relationships between the representing subjectivity and the represented object? What would an extralinguistic or nonimagistic world look like? Does this idea of the "extra" refer to the unrepresentable, or to something captured in language or image but not of language or image?

Among many reasonable answers to these questions, the Continentalist says that if there is a nonlinguistic or nonimagined realm to nature, we cannot have cognitive access to it except through language or the idea of an image. This position is not inspired by metaphysics but by studies of structures of grammar and their relation to logic of perception. In *Rules and Representation*, for example, Chomsky argues that language itself is natural, so that we can read out of the logic of grammar the law of nature as such. We could call this dynamic nominalism. But in arguing that cognition is instrumental to human capacity for language, or that language use is governed by a universal grammar, a grammar

structured in the human mind and present in every language, the arguments of dynamic nominalism imply only what we had seen earlier in
Dewey: namely, that human capacity for language has a natural sociobiological basis. Dynamic nominalism is founded on an antidualist metaphysics of language. It leaves open the problem to what extent nature
and its laws may be said to be linguistic—a problem that Frege and
Brandom, for example, attempted to solve in the assertion of a distinction between the realm of logic (normative) and the realm of causality
(natural). But if a dynamic nominalism adopted this Frege solution, it
would still need to address the resulting questions, among which: What
does it mean that there may be circumstances under which the laws of
nature (causality) might indifferently contradict logical rules (norms)?
The unsatisfactory answer to this question, from both Frege and Brandom, is: So what? McDowell as well, though more subtly, conceptually
demarcates the space of reason. Much like the Continentalist claim, in
this American pragmatist tradition, the uses of the term "law" to characterize both normativity and causality are entirely equivocal, even only
analogous.

But what is the ontological status of logic as a form of representation
of the world? What kinds of questions can one reasonably ask about the
relationship of both continuity and difference between the space of reason and the realm of nature? What shall we understand by "second
nature"? Deconstructionist and post-philosophical criticisms affirm the
humanistic insight that "nature" or "the world" may not be one unitary
entity governed by one universal and univocal law. But if the "law" of
nature and of the world is not one, then concepts or representations of
nature or world are bound to be as diverse as human worlds and languages. In both modern and postmodern practices, particularly in recently postcolonized countries of Africa, South America, and Southeast
Asia, the consequences of these last arguments have perhaps always
been clearer than in other parts of the world. Less consumed by the
Analytic-Continental rivalry, the traditions of philosophy in Brazil, India, and Nigeria have generally insouciantly borrowed combined insights from linguistics, anthropology, literature, and the plastic arts.
Postcoloniality, hybridity, and multiculturalism are just some of the
themes that have allowed questions like "What is reason?" to be asked in
ways that shed new light on what is meant in claims to objectivity, truth,

and knowledge; to justice and injustice; to right and wrong; and in debates about the beautiful, the ugly, and the sublime. Whether this inevitable pluralism conducts one—the one desiring to universally standardize, stabilize, and harmonize the concept of reason—down the road of essentialism or foundationalism in matters of rationality and objectivity is a different question. Pluralism could, equally, lead down the path of doctrinaire relativism. In fact, historically, for some, pluralism appears to be a kind of invitation to outright irrationalism. (We see this, for example, among the German thinkers, just prior to the Romantic movement, who took pride in calling themselves "the Irrationalists"; in the French surrealism of the 1950s; and in the Afrocentric primordialism of the 1980s.)

If conceptual diversity is at the heart of reason, it would be equally irrational to try to make rationality look the way some of us wish that it were. If reason speaks plurally both to itself and to us, what rationally is to be done? If diversity is at the heart of reason and of language, any language, aren't we required to explain the conditions of the possibility of the *thought* of reason's unity in difference? To think reason as one-and-many is, on more than the surface of the matter, a paradox. First, I have argued that diversity is at the origins of thought. If this is so, how is it possible for reason to produce difference at the same time that it is itself a product of difference? It would be harder, however to think of the reverse: Why not? If diversity, on account of the time in reason, goes all the way down, why would it be surprising to think that there is no nondiverse concept of what constitutes the reason of reasons? The apparent paradox can be dispelled in this way: if we accept that an ordinary or vernacular theory of appearance of the rational is ultimately spontaneous and autonomous (in the sense of self-authorizing), it becomes clearer how a *productive* procedure of the rational (e.g., a justification produced as argument in support of a belief regarding objective or subjective conditions of a world) is central to reason's own internal self-definition. The differentiality presumed or authorized in the internal formation of acts of reason can therefore be seen in the fact that, in experience, a space of rational autonomy comes into being where none or nothing of such had determined it; the rational emerges out of its own historical fate: the fates of bodies and selves and their memories, out of histories of cultures, societies, and their institutions; even out of ideas of history as such. The thought that rationality freely *appears* or *comes to itself* in history requires that we recognize this emergence of reason in time in the form of what we ordinarily call experience.

Twenty-first-century phenomenology, especially as it is practiced in cultural anthropology, recognizes that any serious study of consciousness is also a study of experience in the contexts of the temporality of social institutions.[29] This is an insight already obvious in St. Augustine of Hippo. St Augustine attributes time to even the innermost constituent of the soul precisely because he believes that temporality marks both the freedom of the soul as well as all dimensions of the sociality of reason.[30] In Augustine what I *know* about the world is not only a reason *for* affirmation of the experience and of the world but also a reason *of* the world. Thus, in one and the same internally and externally dialogic experience, I come to a rational state of being not just on account of experience in general but also out of a particular experience of a world which, since infinitely susceptible to other reasons ("cities," as Augustine metaphorically calls them), also exceeds the reasons I have for the world and of the world at any particular time. Building on these Augustinian insights, a vernacular theory of the ordinary in reason must remain entirely historical. But methodologically the theory of the vernacular must also presuppose a moderate skepticism toward claims to ultimate epistemic foundations and must therefore substantively cultivate abstemiousness in regard to the dogmatic aspects of Augustine's metaphysical claims. Ours must be a vernacular theory of rationality which is neither relativistic nor radically skeptical. The designation "radical" is usually employed to mark relativism where relativism becomes so corrosive that it undermines all grounds for rational assent. Unlike radical relativism, ordinarily conceptual historical pluralism, in its ordinary productive forms as the vernacular in experience, exercises a healthy skeptical relationship not only to all that is dogmatic in metaphysics but also to radical subjectivism.

I can illustrate the critical-skeptical position of this theory of the ordinary and the vernacular by way of another comparison. In *The Consequences of Pragmatism*, Rorty shows how the relation of language to the world may be described as other than semantic. Like Aristotle, Rorty maintains that reason is a part of human nature, and therefore rationality is a Darwinian adaptive ("pragmatic") biological and historical phenomenon. Avoiding the Platonic position that the philosopher ought to become a politician if politics is to become rational (just as the soul must govern the body, and reason, appetite, so that one might live a life of reason), Rorty follows Aristotle in arguing the anti-Platonic plausibility that politics precedes philosophy. For Aristotle, reason is an organic part of life, so that, though humans are rational animals, this reason is not infused in humans from outside of the biological and political condition of life with others in community.[31] Building on these insights, Rorty proceeded to argue that one must abandon the Platonic model, not because there is nothing to learn from Plato's point of view, but because the technical discussions among philosophers of metaphysical concepts like "Truth," "Good," and "Justice" have become narcissistic. Pragmatism for Rorty is one way out of the narcissism. Just as Dewey argues that the most important task for philosophers is cultivating critical minds capable of sustaining institutions of democracy, Rorty believes that philosophy will do just fine focusing on affirming, in their contingent everydayness, liberal values such as dignity, human rights, and social justice.

To explain or defend these and similar values does not of necessity require that one commits to essentialist or foundationalist grounding of reason as Reason. Nor is a metaphysics of grounds essential for promotion of philosophy and the sciences. If the narcissism that, ironically, masks itself as metaphysics were shown for what it is, the optimistic view is that, along with metaphysics, debates about fact/value, truth/interpretation, and essence/accident would no longer be all that important. In Rorty we learn that both natural and social realities are, in themselves and in their relations, dynamic, diverse, and evolutionary. For example, the essence/accident demonstrations beloved of rationalists, the fact/value distinctions promoted by empiricists, and the debates in literary theory regarding truth/interpretation are, for the Rortyan pragmatist who wishes to deflate or evade Platonic metaphysics and epistemology, different and competing modes of descriptions of otherwise continuous, dynamic, and ever-changing experiences. Which description is best depends on what one considers useful or useless. But the judgment about the useful and the useless does not replicate the metaphysics or medieval epistemology implied in the essence/accident or fact/value distinction. The judgment about what is useful or useless is pragmatically made on the basis of—and as the partial appeal to Aristotle already suggested—democratic political values and in the name of social progress.

The postmodern pragmatist position Rorty represents shows how each community and nation has enough "rules of thumb" in experience to guide it in its judgments about good and bad, or useful and useless practices of politics or development. If these rules of thumb that normalize judgments should be deemed ethnocentric, the pragmatist does not find the solution to ethnocentrism in abstract universals. From this pragmatist's point of view, the endless debates about the true nature of Reality, Truth, Beauty, Justice, and so on are themselves no less ethnocentric.[32] Thus for philosophers to continue to insist—in the name of *philosophia perenis*—on greater clarity about metaphysical issues on which no clarity is available appears both narcissistic and ethnocentric. Such a philosophy itself requires, at the very least, that we ask why it is assumed that this is the best way to do philosophy.

PHILOSOPHY IN POSTCOLONIAL VERNACULAR

The postmodern pragmatist and postcolonial philosopher share commitments to certain projects: the clarification of values, especially values relevant to questions of social suffering. These sufferings often result from factors such as poverty and class division, racism and sexism, and colonial exploitation. Rather than merely developing analytical virtuosity, value pragmatism and postcolonial criticism can help to re-anchor the idea of philosophy and the practices of philosophical life in larger forms of social freedom and in conceptions of political liberty.

But in postcolonial philosophy, as in the picture of *The Consequences of Pragmatism* presented earlier, there is an interesting question: In overcoming philosophy, are there any grounds to distinguish what philosophers do from what, say, poets, novelists, journalists, and literary critics do? On one level, Rorty might not think there is any loss in this. He would probably go further and show that what philosophers do is not all that different from what the engineers and janitors do who build and clean our classrooms—except that while the engineers and the janitors build and clean tangible objects, philosophers build concepts and ideas, and clean the fuzziness and misunderstandings about the concepts and ideas. The goals not only are related but converge, for while the engineer or the janitor seeks to make our lives as teachers and students better, philosophers endeavor to see to it that their concept-building and criticism are equally beneficial to the larger society, including the communities we presumably share with the engineer and the janitor. Rorty's pragmatic dissatisfaction with analytical philosophy seems to result from a suspicion that this brand of philosophizing risks becoming little more than self-serving conversations among a few in a closed, academic club. In this club members sometimes seem to comfortably talk among themselves while forgetting that they—and especially their comfort—are part of a larger world of others who do not talk as the philosophers do, and whose needs appear to be irrelevant in the philosophical discussions.

Would there remain anything special in philosophy after Philosophy? Can one argue that philosophy would still have a technical mission—a mission that justifies its choice of difficult problems, if not the professional snobbery? If one answers these questions affirmatively, what descriptions best capture philosophy's unique mission? There is indeed room for philosophers to contribute to clarifications of important concepts: "democracy," "progress," "justice," "equality." Rather than leave definitions of these solely to politicians, poets, investigative journalists, or preachers, the argument could be made that precisely because of its independence and analytic proficiency, philosophy, however narrow its technical interests, can contribute to expanding the important conversations of societies and cultures. For this reason we should suspect that some of Rorty's arguments, if supported in some hands by a crude realism, express too much insouciance about, or even advocate abolition of, the most technical of the philosopher's work. The worst consequences of such crude realism would be the temptation in philosophy to confuse quest for social relevance with ideological positions less prone to criticism.

It seems that philosophy can best make its contributions to culture if it does not limit the range of *issues* that matters to it nor the *methods* it employs in the pursuit of knowledge about these issues. If one has not attributed too much importance to what might be only an unlikely consequence, it seems that *The Consequences of Pragmatism*, in places, denies at least a robust semantic response in the range of available *philosophical* (as opposed to literary, rhetorical, political, evangelical, etc.)

methods of social engagements and criticism. Unless postmodern pragmatism's real or pretended impatience with High Theory is tempered,
one wonders if there is some danger that pragmatism could lead to, as
Cornel West framed it, an American *evasion* of philosophy. To capture
what is most true in the continental tradition, therefore, one could think
that philosophy must insist upon the persistence of theory and guard
against hasty "overcoming" of certain questions in metaphysics or even
philosophy itself. Is there one, or are there multiple ways of causally
conceptualizing a nonsemantic relation to the world? Is there one
"world," or are there many worlds that can be so conceptualized? Does
the very idea of "conception" lose its meaning in a causalist framework?
Does nonsemantic explanation urge a one-size-fits-all response to these
questions?

Even when we adopt a realist approach of any sort in the search for an
adequate theory of reference, we can see that causal psychologism and causal ontologism are mirror images of each other, and that they appear to
exhibit too much traces of a reaction against Platonic dualism. One then
tries to treat this reaction by the various sorts of epistemic desire to "overcome" metaphysical dualism in the notion of one kind of psychology-
inflected causality or the other: for example, a causes b or q is caused by p.
But thanks to Hume we know that to say that "a causes b" is not enough
explanation when the goal is to know what is meant by "causality," or what
kind of epistemic claims the person who says he *knows* what causality
means might be making.

There is a plausible way for an ordinary, nonmetaphysical theory of
vernacular reason to avoid these questions about causality without falling into the problem of a reaction to Platonism nor to an embrace of
Hume's hyperbolic skepticism: Putnam's "disquotational" theory of reference.[33] Disquotationality holds that any true reference is reducible to
statements whose conditions meet conditions of assertability. But conditions of assertability, as Putnam notes in *Realism and Reason*, are
fulfilled neither by associating that word with a property (e.g., language
"hooks" unto reality)[34] nor by a theory of correspondence (e.g., as in
Hume's statement: "Ideas and impressions appear always to 'correspond'
to each other").[35] Disquotationality implies that one has a basis, and
therefore is entitled, to assert something as true by *learning* the *meaning*
of experienced facts. Such facts are themselves ordinary and plain, for

example, "Snow is white," the conditions required for asserting this fact being to know the truth of what one means to say: "'Snow is white' is true if and only if snow is white." Linguists call disquotational statements truth statements, or t-sentences. These are the type of sentences which represent experience by, literally, dis-quoting their values within what happens at one level of meaning (vernacular linguistic experience) onto another context of meaning (logic and explicit judgment).

Disquotationality can also be seen to have a direct relation not only to the vernacularly linguistic but also to a transformational theory of language. This is so because in the disquotation the mind "transforms" meanings—forms of experience—from one implicit level of meaning to another, more explicit. Chomsky captured the transformational aspect of language use in the phrase "generative grammar." Disquotationality refers to the grammatical power to engender—by following a rule, the rules of grammar—meanings already implicit or explicit in experience. The productive power of disquotationality thus functions like what we get when, in a vernacular language, one "lifts" or re-presents in the grammatic sentential structure of everyday meaningful statements what the speaker believed to be already in the deep structure of experience (what one has in "mind"). Disquotationality is thus not too much unlike the technique of improvisation in jazz or of sampling in popular music cultures, namely, the proficient capacity to generate or transform the vernacular and ordinary in experience so that the vernacular and the ordinary reveal their particular reasons at a higher level of universal structures. It is precisely in the enunciation of this universality and in its structures in judgment that disquotationality, like improvisation or sampling in music, elevates the common and the recognizably mundane in experiences to the highest levels of cognition, where the experiences can be apprehended in thought and feeling as both subjective and social sources of the self. (Under "The Idea of Conceptual Diversity," above, I partially defended an account of the sociality of mind, reason, and the self that must be presupposed by my appropriations of the theory of disquotationality.)

Ultimately, one quotes only because one is capable of experience. One quotes *as* a rational animal because both language (grammar) and expressivity in truth-telling are consistent with biological life, sociality, and subjectivity. One quotes because the capacity to learn rule-governed behaviors—that is , the capacity for disquotation—is a key dimension of the sort of life to which one can attribute "experience." A disquotational act is consistent with experience or the life of reason because knowing how to linguistically conform to rules allows one the freedom to generate or reproduce, according to a rule, what is learned from experience in the rules governing disquotation as such. To disquote is thus inherently a creative act: the improvisationality in which we make explicit in speech act or other forms of experience a capacity that is already implicit as a life of reason. The social and historical presentation or representation of the self and of the world as rational or as susceptible to reason is therefore an act of freedom in experience. Disquotationality thus refers to the communicative act in which a world of experience comes universally into view.

To disquote, finally, also can be seen as a form of translation: it is to state what one "meant" or what an experience meant. Mastering rules of speech, accordingly, is a kind of disquotational semantics or hermeneutics, for thereby one learns to speak in generation of truths about what the world is like, or what reality could mean, in acts of judgment on the basis of an experience. Standardized, the most common and succinct of such expressive truth-sentences remains in the form of "p is true if and only if p." But we have also explored the complexities of this form, including their hermeneutical limits, in the discussion of the idea of "form" in formal rationality in chapter 1.

In summary, the idea of disquotationality sidesteps not only the Platonism implicit in a strong correspondence theory of truth but also the echoes of Platonism in thick realism (e.g., the claim that language "tracks" an extralinguistic world or "hooks" onto objects). Disquotationality also avoids—it leaves in suspension—the dualism of essence/accident, fact/value, and truth/interpretation. Finally, disquotationality does not have handicaps associated with rhetorical excesses in lapidary statements such as "There is nothing outside of texts." Disquotationality, in short, is a vernacular theory of rationality and of truth-telling. It compares with Wittgenstein's views about language and meaning in the *Philosophical Investigations*. The difference from this Wittgenstein is in the transcultural and universal intentions obvious in disquotationality. Such an intention is, at best, entirely implicit in the *Investigations*: if language games are properties of "forms of life," and forms of life may have only "family resemblance" across them, it is not clear if there is a universal form of the forms of possible relations across forms of life, or what *that* form might look like in experience. Disquotationality sidesteps the potentially cryptic problem of "What is the resemblance, if any, across family resemblances?" because of its robust reliance on the linguistically vernacular and on the ordinary need to tell the truth of, the truth in, experience.

If Putnam and Chomsky are correct about t-sentences, then it is right to say that the capacity for subjective internalization of assertability conditions is the only process by which rational actors acquire what we could call linguistic and rhetorical socialization. In turn, it is this socialization in language—the acquisition of competence in reason-giving behaviors—that not only signifies a mastery of language use but additionally greatly facilitates procedures of meaning-making within a given society. In this picture, far from being a mechanical process, speech is revealed as a creative activity in which, by rules, the "us" addressed in a language could be as large or as small, as varied or monolithic as the speech community will allow. The success of a language would thus be as large or as small as its social prestige, and as the speakers' moral imagination and rhetorical expertise are prepared to extend it. Likewise, knowledge of what is useful or useless, right or wrong, just or unjust and so on in one culture could be, in principle, communicated and shared within internally diverse or across communities of languages. Nothing in the theory of disquotationality therefore diminishes the soundness of arguments in favor of my idea of an intrinsic diversity of rational expressions. Implicit also in the vernacular theory of the language of ordinary reason is a related proposition: that reason is not only internally dialectical and externally social but also is co-constitutive of the objectivity of the world. In a competent speech, more than passively mirroring what is presumed to be "out there," merely reporting what is in one's "mind," or giving passive assent to others' reasoning, when one makes a claim to truth, one demonstrates a learned behavior to make—*invent, invest the world with* —values that can be evaluated within contexts of an existing culture and society. The invention or investment of the new in reason to an objective world is meaning-making. So, to make a meaning is also to make a world.

THE SOCIAL CONSTRUCTION OF THINGS

But how "deep" is the "making"? After all, humans may make their social worlds, but they do not make these out of nothing. What does it mean to make a world in relation to the *natural* world? In *The Construction of Social Reality* John Searle offers some interesting insights. He accepts a distinction between constructed social reality and brute facts of nature. The dimension of nature that constitutes what we call the "real" world belongs to the latter, though this does not mean that humans have access to brute facts of nature in a conceptually unmediated way. To the contrary, Searle does not even think that Kant was right when Kant believed that there might be a *Ding an sich*, a noumenal "thing in itself" which must be supposed to somehow exist but the how of which we know not. Minimally, the commitment to the existence of "brute facts" of nature merely commits us to the thought that, though we make the world, we do not make it *ex nihilo*.

We construct the social world at least out of other social constructions of the world, and certainly by re/constructing material objects of nature. This position, furthermore, does not commit us to explain what "matter" or "nature" consists of in every state, nor how either is permanently in itself. It merely says that there are things out there that do not appear to be ourselves, and with which we interact when we make our world or worlds. In fact, some of these things we are barely able to notice, manage, or control: the volcano erupts, the tornado develops, the dog swims. By whatever name(s) we choose to call these and similar observations, or in whatever language, they are forces of the said not-us which, like the force of gravity, we must reckon with, and often reckon with on *their* own terms (e.g., we have little choice other than to vacate the earthquake zone or take out an insurance policy and wait for the earthquake to happen at its own causally "appointed" time). To say that these not-us-es which we have decided to call brute facts of nature can be "constructed" by humans might be to say something meaningful, but meaningful only in a special way. It is meaningful only in a very technical, limited sense.

Borrowing a previous example, we could say that the *constellation* of the stars and the *Big Dipper* are "constructed" by astrophysicists, without implying thereby that the stars themselves were somehow intrinsically fabricated by humans. In other examples, we might say that "race" as we know it today was an invention in modernity, similar to the way others say that America or Africa was "discovered" by so and so; or, as Heidegger, in his inimitable style, opined that Newton's law could not be true if Newton had not existed. To speak in any of these and similar ways is *not* to say that stars, race, America, Africa, or the law of gravity did not exist before the astrophysicist, the Indian, the African, the European explorer, or Newton made the respective "invention" or "discovery." This manner of speaking is merely, as Rorty would have it, a way of paying compliments to—or for others, and in some cases, expressing a more ambiguous evaluation of— the thing discovered, the discoverer, or both. Rorty is correct because "paying compliments" are just the right words for the kind of goodwill most people would like to express to a successful explorer, inventor, or scientist. Paying compliments to the genius of the explorer, the inventor, or the scientist is a way to acknowledge, for example, that we probably could not otherwise, or so soon, or without more cost resulting from the ignorance, have known that the invented or discovered places or peoples or laws existed. A population's gratitude, and therefore the compliments it pays to the curious and the gifted, or sometimes the lucky, is in propor- tion to the recognition of the fact that being ignorant of the nature of stars or other cultures or the law of gravity did not immunize the population against existing or future influences of the object of discovery. (That is perhaps why the discovery of laws of things or the lives and cultures of "other" peoples therefore is highly significant: such knowledge can con- tribute to a people's capacity for survival and well-being.) Since the discovery can also lead to new risks (e.g., expansion of economic or political exploitations that could lead to war, hunger and disease, repres- sion and cultural conflicts), it is the case that other sentiments than compliments (curse, disowning, etc.) may be offered by a people to some of its important discoverers. Whether rightly or wrongly greeted by laurels or threatened with fatwa, in drawing the attention of a people to new realities—that is, "inventing," "discovering," or "constructing" per- ceptions of realities in question—the inventor or discoverer presents or re-presents a world of meanings to a people. Through discovery of newer truths, a society constructs or reconstructs what it believes to be objec- tively "out there." There is no question that it is in the constructors' creativities and geniuses that societies come to appreciate—or better appreciate, because in more conscious ways—realities that have or potentially have significant influence on how one lives and dies.

There is yet more meaning to what is said when one speaks about social construction of reality. Consider the similarities between these three items: a university's academic program, a twenty-five-pence coin, and a laptop computer. How did some individuals end up as the particular composition, academic faculty and students? How did the mineral copper acquire its value as money? And how did columbite-tantalite—a.k.a. coltan—become a computer chip? Diverse as may be the qualities of the entities (human individuals and minerals) composing the objects in society, they share fundamental similarities. They all are objects found in nature (human beings, copper, and coltan). But in their worldly configurations they also become, via diverse routes and transformational processes, parts of a *social* reality—for example, an academic community, the change in my wallet, or my Intel iBook. Why, when, and by whom was the university community founded or the copper or coltan discovered? What transformations did the natural entities composing each unit of these social meanings have to go through in order to end up what they currently are: an academy, money, a computer? When does an item pass from a pure natural state to part of a social world? If the process is a series of continuities rather than absolute breaks, where does the significant, deciding change occur from one realm of existence to the other? Can an object in one state (e.g., a coin) be regarded alternately or simultaneously as both social and natural?

If the natural objects humans, copper, and coltan were socially constructed into, respectively, an academy, money, and computers, wouldn't this idea of "construction" have to be taken nearly literally—as a *functional mobilization* of stuff in various states of nature for specific social ends? Let's say, in these examples, that the ends are, grossly speaking, embedded in our society's cultural, economic, and technological interests. It can be seen that, remote or immediate, the idea of ends must be already implicated at the beginnings of an initial human orientation to nature. It is therefore reasonable to suppose that an aspect of nature was "discovered" (invented, created, etc.) precisely on account of the initial approach to nature as both an environment and as a means to satisfaction of ends. Whether a discovery is accidental or deliberate does not affect this idea of the structural and structuring function of ends in worldly orientation, an end being that in function of which an entity takes on meaning or newer meaning as a worldly object. Although it might even be the case that an interest was taken in an object before someone discovered the object's specific social ends, phrases such as "taking an interest" already betray the teleological character of the perceptual act: one *looks* at a thing *with interest*. In these examples, the interest could be how to build an academic program, how to overcome the inefficiency of trading by barter, and the need for the finest conductor of electronic pulses. Whatever the medium or longer term ends may be, in the orientation to them we easily recognize that elements of nature —including human nature—are hardly ever comprehended in thought with complete orientational disinterest.

The difference between the "natural" and the "social" is therefore best captured by a distinction between the more and the less conditional, according to the degree to which a perceptual orientation—my "seeing" of an entity as . . .—is also capable of being functionally thematized in the perception as an end. For example, to be able to create or invent a classroom starting from my perceptions of a group of young adults (or money out of copper, or computer chips out of coltan) is conditional to the extent that items out of which my inventions must be constructed already have existences in worldly social states. Owing to their "advanced" positions in the objective social processes, the general conditionality of the invented status of the items comes from the fact that as social objects they are not only invented on the basis of limited interests but are also constructed out of limited knowledge, including the limitations imposed on the newer processes of invention by incomplete knowledge of all of the object's possible ends.

The least conditioned states in the idea of social construction of nature consist almost entirely in the recognition that one cannot construct something out of nothing. Natural facts are therefore the least conditioned elements in any stages of a process of discovery, invention, and satisfaction of ends that we deem to constitute "reasons" or conditions for the same process. Whereas the brute facts of nature (humans, copper, coltan) independently exist prior to interested perception and technical transformation, they become social facts somewhere at those instants of the interested perceptions. While the ambitious desire of classic metaphysics is to explain what "the thing" is without reference to interested perception, the ambitious desire of modern epistemology is to gain a pure perception of the state of nature of the pure state of the thing. From our perspectives, the ordinarily postcolonial and vernacular, both desires must be seen as impossible desires because there is no absolute "outside" to objects or to our perception of objects. We always perceive this or that in relation to a background of a fundamental orientation: an orientation to nature, to a world without which there could not be, properly speaking, the idea of the rational in experience. Such a preconceptual background which nevertheless co-constitutes any act of perception per se gives importance to the argument that to at all see is to see as . . . , to at all think anything is to think something as . . . , and so on.

Should we conclude that it is the perceptual act itself—perceptibility, so to speak—that is responsible for our social construction of things? Our answer, for consistency, must be affirmative. But is perception itself socially constructed? One would have to answer affirmatively as well— again for consistency's sake, in light of our discussions of the mind and of consciousness in chapter 1. Though a perception that takes perception per se as the object of its own consciousness may be called a transcendental perception, the perception is, categorically speaking, perception in any case. Thus, whether in empirical or transcendental consciousness, the perceptual act must also categorically be seen as an act of orientation to a world, subjective or objective. But unlike the subjective idealist who attributes the grounds of a perception's claim to objectivity or universality to a pure transcendental subjectivity, we say in the vernacular that the experience of the transcendental subjectivity itself remains, like all perceptual acts, not without interest. We could, for example, call the ends of the subjective transcendental interest *self-regard* and, at its most extreme, a form of metaphysical or epistemological narcissism.

REASON IN HISTORY

We can also draw the following conclusions. First, there is neither in the purest conceptions of human rationality nor in the language of any cultures evidence that reason or language escapes time and sociality. This inescapability of historical fate by any rationality is, as we saw, entirely due to the character of experience. And it is only in experience that we can come to know what it is rationality must look like if it is to be considered an essential attribute of humanity. Second—and this is an even a stronger argument—it is time, ultimately, that marks experience with its particular form of the rational life. By way of language, it is memory and history that, dialectically, constitute the subjectivity of an individual. "Dialectics" should here be understood in its most elemental form: the conversation of the soul with itself. It is this conversation that I called experience. Finally, the discovery (invention, construction, etc.) in freedom of what the world must look or appear like to persons of reason is what we call freedom of thought, freedom of expression, freedom of association, and so on. It is thanks to these forms of freedoms that we are able to acknowledge that for both known and (yet) unknown reasons we construct forms of experience merely in the figure of ends the rational-ities of which extend as far as the animating ideas of freedom and the actual or potential scopes of their supporting historical institutions. I can illustrate this last point.

In 1613 an East African boy, Walda Heywa Zera Ya'icob, was sent by his father to the seminary to train for the Coptic priesthood. In the course of his studies Zera Ya'icob went though what, today, we could call a "crisis" of faith: the existential stirrings of freedom of thought vis-à-vis religious or theological dogmatism. As he described his experience, Zera Ya'icob felt that "the flickering light of reason" in the human soul ought to be bright enough to enlighten the reasons for the heart's desire for God, truth, goodness, and beauty. Relocating himself therefore from the comforts of the seminary to a cave in the wilderness, Ya'icob composes a series of *hatata*, treatises on methods for rightly conducting the reason on the paths to God, truth, goodness, and beauty. "To the person who seeks it," he writes in the first hatata, "truth is immediately revealed." He also specifically thinks that anyone "who investigates with the pure intel-ligence set by the creator . . . and scrutinizes the order and laws of the creation, will discover the truth."[36]

But Ya'icob's encounters with a freedom to think also reveal roots of his crisis in their institutional contexts. There are at least three such contexts, each vying with the others in competition for construction or reconstruction of the seventeenth-century East African historical objec-tivities. The first and perhaps most crucial of these contexts is Ya'icob's experiences of three diverse—and rival—world religions. One element in the conflicts is the struggle between Jesuit missionaries sent from Europe to Abyssinia to evangelize Africans and their Ethiopian hosts. Though already practicing an African Christianity in a tradition which goes all the way back to the earliest apostles of Jesus, Abyssinia was also home to the oldest traditions of Judaism as well as the largest population of an African tribe of Jews in Africa. Then there was Islamism, the spread of which was witnessed in East Africa faster than anywhere else in Africa south of the Sahara. Finally, there was the Animist factor: the Oromos in particular remained resistant to both the incursions of Judaism, Christianity, and Islam until well into the nineteenth century and early twentieth. In the competing systems of beliefs as well as the different modes of acquisition or acceptance of allegiances, Zera Ya'icob, like most thoughtful believers, must have experienced the peculiar intellectual bewilderment about the conflicting proliferations of faiths, each of which claimed to be the true and exclusive face of One God.

Similarly, in the emerging political dynamics of an incipient global commercial capitalism, Diago Cao anchored in the Congo River in 1482. A few years earlier a most cruel kind of trade, the transatlantic slave trade, had started. The king of the Congo at Mbaza, one of Africa's famous converts to Christianity who assumed the Christian name Alphonso II, wrote to Lisbon in 1526 lamenting the ravages of the new commerce. Addressed to his "royal brother," the letter, in part, speaks about slavery with less than diplomatic nuance: "You cannot reckon how great the damage is . . . so great, Sire, is the corruption and licentiousness that our country is completely depopulated."[37]

Further west of the continent, there were social and cultural movements for transnational transformations of societies and cultures. In 1481, a monarch in what is now Ghana, unsure what to make of the appearance of the Portuguese monarch's new zeal to convert in addition to trading, also wrote a protest to Lisbon. "I am not insensible to the high honor which your great master, the chief of Portugal, has this day conferred on me," he began. "Your friendship I have long endeavored to merit by the strictness of my dealing with the Portuguese, and by constant exertions to procure an immediate lading for their vessels. But never until this day did I observe such a difference in the appearance of his subjects; they have hitherto been only meanly attired, were easily contented with the commodities they received; and so far from wishing to continue in this country, were never happy until they could complete their lading, and return. Now I remark a strange difference. A great number richly dressed are anxious to be allowed to build houses, and to continue among us."[38]

In the midst of these historical realities, Zera Ya'icob's question appears to be a simple one: What is the freedom of the African subject? In answer to this question, his choice of philosophical method speaks volumes. *Hatata* in Ge'ez means "searching," "asking questions," or "dialogue." Beyond an isolated quest for a privatistic experience of the self, Zera Ya'icob's method takes on new meanings beyond the previous, narrowly theological contexts. Hatata henceforth became a cultural and political idea: a hermeneutical suspicion of the social constitutions of freedom in a given, conflicted, world. "Those who wanted to rule the people," Zera Ya'icob wrote, "said: 'We are sent by God to proclaim the truth to you'; and the people believed them. Those who came after them accepted their father's faith without question: rather, as proof of their faith, they added to it by including stories of signs and omens. Indeed they said: 'God did these things'; and so they made God a witness of falsehood and a party to liars."[39] In this the hatata constituted a form of an intellectual declaration of independence. In one particularly important passage, we are asked:

> Is everything that is written in the Holy Scriptures true? Although I thought much about these things I understood nothing, so I said to myself: "I shall go and consult scholars and thinkers; they will tell me the truth." But afterwards I thought, saying to myself: "What will men tell me other than what is in their hearts?" Indeed each one says: "My faith is right and those who believe in another faith believe in falsehood, and are the enemies of God." These days the Frang tell us: "Our faith is right, yours is false." We on the other hand tell them: "It is not so; your faith is wrong, ours is right." If we also ask the Mohammedans and the Jews, they will claim the same thing: each group would say its faith is the right one. And who would be the judge for such kind of an argument?[40]

In this climate of cultures, What is truth? How do we come to know it? How best to justify and redeem both its private and its public validity?

In the twentieth century, Wittgenstein casually—you might say, glibly

—floated a similar problem, at the expense of those whom his time (the time of British colonialists) was fond of calling the "natives":

> Is it wrong for me to be guided in my actions by the propositions of physics? Am I to say that I have no good grounds for doing so? Isn't it precisely this that we call a "good ground"?
>
> Suppose that we met people who did not regard this as a good ground, and who did not regard that as a telling reason. Now how do we imagine this? Instead of the physicist, they consult an oracle. And for that we consider them primitive. Is it wrong for them to consult an oracle and be guided by it?—If we call this "wrong," aren't we using our language game as a base from which to combat theirs?
>
> And are we right or wrong to combat it? Of course there are all sorts of slogans which will be used to support our proceedings.
>
> Where two principles really do meet which cannot be reconciled with one another, then each man declares the other a fool and a heretic.[41]

Wittgenstein's predicament (if we can call it that) does not escape the terms in which Zera Ya'icob had framed his own context. "I said I would 'combat' the other man," Wittgenstein wondered, "but wouldn't I give him reasons?" The answer: "Certainly, but how far do they go? At the end of reasons comes persuasion. Think what happens when missionaries convert natives."[42]

Whether he was fighting for a personal space of reason, for freedom of thought, or for freedom of religion, or in critique of imperial and colonial politics, fundamentalist global movements of capital, or racial and cultural prejudice, Zera Ya'icob shows that some of his seventeenth-century questions have remained ours as well.

3

Science, Culture, and

Principles of Rationality

Philosophy is essentially its language. Philosophical problems are by
and large problems of language. The alleged independence of language
from things that is found in the so-called positive sciences does not
apply in the same way for philosophy.—THEODOR W. ADORNO,
Philosophische Terminologie, author's translation

Conclusions which are merely verbal cannot bear fruit. I approve of
theorizing only if it lays its foundation in incident, and deduces its
conclusion in accordance with phenomena.—HIPPOCRATES,
On the Sacred Disease, translated by Frances Adams

FREEDOM OF SCIENCE

Twentieth-century philosophy in Africa did not, luckily, face the kind of
intemperate competition between the Analytical and Continental factions that characterized philosophy in the same century in many parts of

Europe and North America. The credit for the convivial character of African practices in modern and postmodern philosophy can hardly be accounted for by the notorious "I am because we are" folk philosophy attributed, sometimes unwisely, to every African personality. After all, African philosophers, as individuals, are no more capable of professional friendships and collaboration or fierce independence and territoriality than fellow academics anywhere else. The ecumenical spirit of philosophy in today's Africa should be attributed, instead, to a singular history of cultural domestication of philosophy's most technical questions. For example, because the continent is geographically and culturally a meeting point of many historical influences—Greek, Islamic, Jewish, Christian, German, French, British, Portuguese, Arabic, North American, and many more—philosophical practices in Kenya, Nigeria, Senegal, South Africa, and so on reflect analytical interests that, clearly, show African philosophers' expertise in languages and cultures that encompass not just the foreign but also Kikuyu, Yoruba, Igbo, Zulu, Luo, Fon, and so forth. *Eclectic* and *universal* are the terms that most come to mind when one thinks about the current state of the discipline on the continent as well as in the African diaspora. Yet, precisely on account of this diversity, much more remains to be done in regard to critiques of philosophy and the diversity of its traditions and cultures in Africa. I wish to take steps in this chapter toward meeting this challenge. I will organize my remarks around the theme of method, the question of method in philosophy but also in the sciences generally. At what ends does philosophy aim in contemporary Africa? What human needs—individual, social, and historical—does philosophy claim to be a response to in the experiences of societies and cultures in Africa and in Africa's postcolonial, transcontinental diaspora? What are its methods?

It is easier to recognize these as questions touching on the needs of scientific methods when we approach the African experience in modern philosophy by analogy. In the book *Setting the Moral Compass: Essays by Women Philosophers* Cheshire Calhoun explains how, forced by the requirements of methods, women writers constantly compose philosophical questions in ways they do not intend. Or at least, this is what Calhoun claims happened to her: questioning the reasons of method leads her to produce a philosophy book she didn't think she intended to. "When I first thought about creating a collection of work in moral philosophy," she writes, "my first thought was to do one in feminist virtue ethics. But as I began the work of selecting contributors and writing a proposal, I found myself increasingly disinterested in the task. Indeed, I began to think about all the women moral philosophers I have read . . . and admired . . . I wanted to see their work in one place because it seemed to me that there was some important way in which they are kindred philosophical minds. But there was one sizeable obstacle to publishing such a collection: there didn't seem to be a rationale for bringing the diverse set of philosophers I had in mind into a collection. *There was no obvious principle of unity.*"[1] What would be an obvious principle of unity *in* thoughts on virtue ethics, moral theories, or any field of knowledge produced by women? What grounding rationale—beyond the biographical—gives an overarching yet particularly feminine or feminist identity to a body of work? Even if one concentrated on finding a principle of unity or a founding rationale for works done by women only in one area of a large discipline, such as Calhoun tried to do within philosophy, a suspicion remains that, purely on its intellectual merits, no such principle or rationale could be provided. The reasons for this suspicion are varied.

On the one hand, Calhoun points out that while some of the philosophers whose works are in question did "explicitly feminist philosophical work addressed primarily to other feminist thinkers," others did other things.[2] They focused on, for example, "nonfeminist philosophical conversations with other moral philosophers, most of whom were men." What methodological principle could make nonfeminist philosophical conversations into, after all, feminist conversations? Rejecting the thought of such an alchemical methodology, Calhoun sensibly notes about her project, "This couldn't be a collection of feminist ethics." What, then, is the book about? Should we conclude that there can be no feminist virtue ethics because there is no obvious thematic unity? If "the sorts of moral philosophy" women do in conversations among themselves as well as in conversation with men are "quite different" among and across them, shouldn't we therefore conclude that there are only good moral philosophy and bad moral philosophy? By this reasoning, and if selections are narrowed to virtue ethics, shouldn't the only further rationale or principle of unity pertain to how we avoid mixing good and bad moral philosophy under one cover? On the other hand, if the question is about how best to honor philosophers who also self-identify as women philosophers, what is the value to philosophy of the principle of gender? I think this is what Calhoun is getting when she wonders if "the only alternative" isn't "to envision the book as a kind of festschrift": it would be an anthology to celebrate the lives of "women who have contributed in important ways to moral philosophy." Like the first, abstract universalist option however, this identitarian definition of principle falls short. A celebration of biography would be wonderful but not enough because, as categorically affirmed, "what I wanted to bring into view was the nonaccidental fact that all of the philosophers I felt were kindred minds were women."[3]

Key terms are *nonaccidental* and *kindred minds*. Is this the philosophical significance of gender? The terms are meant to convey a conviction that "in the end," gender makes a difference, a difference seen as evident in the kinship shared by a diversity of minds on a range of related and competing topics. It is the noted nonaccidentality of the kin relations in thought that, it seems, endows gender with its power in difference. "The difference [gender] makes," Calhoun writes, "is sometimes subtle, often unpredictable," but in any case it is said to be also "compatible with deep philosophical disagreements among women philosophers."[4]

If kinship does not mean unanimity, and difference does not equal accidentality, what is the enduring difference that gender—and culture, geography, or race—makes or should make in a wide range of topics and problems of philosophy? If one does not wish to pose the core questions about the idea of difference in thought in this manner, what better alternatives exist for capturing and highlighting what, clearly, constitute not just a claim to difference but also a search for universally relevant methods as important principles of inquiry? What would be a universally neutral method in thought?[5]

Assuming that not only intellectual kinship but also a philosophical principle can be sustained on the difference that gender makes, can similar assumptions be made about race, culture, and history? Judging the result (rather than a self-aware problematic justification of method) in *Setting the Moral Compass*, one could say that Calhoun's claims about gender difference are not opposed to, but certainly are more fundamental than, the merely conventional and culturalist views of identity might allow. In fact, it is clear from the titles of the main parts of the book that she was staking out larger, disciplinarily transformative aims. The difference made by gender, in this reading of it, is ultimately a difference in the thoughts about what should count as ethical and unethical, moral and immoral, normative and non-normative. The difference in thoughts also extends to issues relevant in debates about the nonconceptual and conceptual status of emotion and reason and unreason in critiques of moral knowledge. Though *Setting the Moral Compass* does not argue that these themes and the diverse styles and modes of their explorations can be divided into male and female, it does make claim that women's arguments over the matters in a range of issues in ethics and morality have come to matter as both philosophical *and* feminist.

The difference gender makes is, in this sense, in fact no more than an assertion of the difference in philosophy that occurs when the perspectives of arguing women are explicitly introduced in discussions of general problems in moral theory. But it has been an easy step for me to extrapolate, by analogy, the methodological issues involved in internal dialogues of arguing women philosophers to similar questions and arguments over methods in twentieth-century African philosophy.[6] Is the saying true: where gender is, there is culture (cultures of race, class, etc.)?

Some who believe that the category gender is a point of view determined—and exhausted—by other categories (race and ethnicity, religion, nationality, or class) also argue, in parallel, that "racial" identities are not, or at least not just, about biology. For those who argue thus— let's call them cultural conventionalists—if "African" were meant as a racial category, then African philosophy is no more than examples of traditions of racially neutral philosophical reflections in places and cultures commonly understood as Africa and African. The problem with this conclusion is not, of course, in the conclusion: it is in the presuppositions. Even after we make allowances for the problematic scientific status of the idea of "race" as well as the historically dynamic character of what constitutes modern African identities, the task remains to explain what is—if the analogy with gender holds—the import of "racial" or "African" experiences not only in substantive philosophical themes but also in philosophical method. Beyond deconstructions of the concept of race and of the idea of Africa, what is left of the culturally "African" identity *even as a historical thought*? What, if any, should *that* remainder amount to not just by way of philosophical explication of issues but also in the way of methodological constitutions of—or is it merely orientations in?—philosophical subjectivities?

Surely, what makes race, ethnicity, or gender relevant in philosophy must extend beyond the fact that humans appear to be different in meaningful ways by reason of national origin, culture, or sex. If these were all there are to the matter, then politics, cultural geography, and biology would be sufficient to study the idea of the relevant differences, similarities, and sameness. Additionally, should one require merely a philosophical *perspective* on the empirical disciplines of the difference, we could appeal not to a self-standing discipline of philosophy but to bridge disciplines like political philosophy, philosophy of culture, or philosophy of biology. So by raising directly and quite narrowly the question about the significance of gender, race, or cultural differences within the discipline of philosophy, we have clearly chosen to foreground a concern about *method*—not gender, racial, or class cultural identity—in philosophy. This concern, if understood well, has relevance also to the philosophy-dependent interdisciplines.

From the point of view of my own procedures, two recent publications have been most illuminating. In the earlier, *Africa and the Disciplines: The Contributions of Research in Africa to the Social Sciences and Humanities*, the editors state the book's motives as follows: "African Studies, contrary to some accounts, is not a separate continent in the world of American higher education. Its intellectual borders touch those of economics, literature, history, philosophy, and art; its history is the story of the world, both ancient and modern. This is the clear conclusion of *Africa and the Disciplines*, a book that addresses the question: Why should Africa be an object of study in an American university? This question was put to distinguished scholars in the social sciences and humanities, prominent Africanists who are also leaders in their various disciplines. Their responses make a strong and enlightening case for the importance of research on Africa to the academy."[7] What is the importance of research *on* Africa *to* the academy, and specifically to the North American academy? In *Africa and the Disciplines* an economist shows us "how studies of African economies have clarified our understanding of the small open economies"; an art historian "uses the terms and concepts that her discipline has applied to Africa to analyze the habits of mind and social practice of her own field"; a literary theorist confesses that African literature "confounds and enriches" American literary theory; and a political scientist shows how studies of Africa contribute to knowledge of processes of political modernization, pluralism, and problems in Western theories of rational choice.[8] Together with similar examples from history, anthropology, and philosophy, *Africa and the Disciplines* wants to "attest" to the importance of research on Africa for the North American universities' academic curricula. The editorial arguments and contents of the collection are such that one could have easily imagined for the book a different title: Twentieth-Century North American Intellectual Adventures in Sub-Saharan Africa: A Selected Reading. The plausibility of this formulation is suggested by the more obvious title of the second book.

In *The British Intellectual Engagement with Africa*, the editors state, "We write of the British intellectual engagement in order to separate our particular interests from a more general history of enquiry that would include political, commercial and missionary relations between our country and Africa."[9] This separation seems quite necessary, for there are more aspects to the British intellectual engagement with Africa than are reflected in the academic debates about either the North American or the British universities' curricula. In fact, both the editors and the contributors to this volume make clear that the earliest interests motivating British-sponsored researches on Africa at the end of the nineteenth century through the twentieth were neither primarily academic nor university-based. Nor do the texts discuss events such as transatlantic slavery. The periods covered by this book are the centuries of active colonization, commerce, and religious missionization. The editors point out other limitations as well. In the preface, for example, they note, "Following a common distinction between Africanist and Arabists, our Africa is the region south of the Sahara."[10] The *common* factor on which this distinction is based is frankly acknowledged: "ideologies of Islam and Christianity." These ideologies date as far back as much earlier traditions of anthropology and philosophy of history, when it was taken for granted that there must be three Africas: the Arab Africa, a European Africa, and Africa's own Africa. Hegel, Conrad, and other academics and novelists considered the last of these—because last to be conquered by either adventuresome Arabs or Europeans—the Dark Continent.[11]

What do these books reveal about our interest in the problems of method in philosophy in Africa? How might resources from philosophy explain the modern experiences of postcolonial Africans and African-descended peoples in the contexts of the conventionalist claims to cultural "difference"? As we see in the discourses of gender, there are definitely many good reasons, and a variety of kinds of reasons, why claims of difference are not more than an expression of a desire for a historical nonaccidentality. In this regard the editorial intentions, and practices, of *Africa and the Disciplines* as well as *British Intellectual Engagement* are largely unimpeachable in their desire to inclusively universalize. Even when this desire for universality is expressed from particular localities, the practices of the desire raise questions not about the nature of particularity of intents but rather regarding a general idea: What is a mind from nowhere? When we ask about method in African philosophy, it is not at all to fuel particularistic claims to an African difference. My concern with method, like the previous elaborations on rationality in general, is entirely historical. What difference does history make to thoughts of method? What difference, in turn, does choice of method make in the conception and execution of programs of research? If this interest in an ordinary idea of difference really makes any difference, how should it be figured in the discourses of postcolonial, postracial, and nonsexist practices in philosophy's methodological subjectivities?

FREEDOM OF CULTURE

Science of Freedom

In the question about philosophy's method, one should be interested in determining the contours of philosophy's scientific dialogue with itself. This idea of a dialogue interior to philosophy derives from a concern with historical forms of reason as elaborated in the previous chapters. What would be an exemplary contour of a scientific philosophical discipline whose methodological subjectivity is grounded in spaces of a historical freedom? I can already hear both the Afrocentric and the Eurocentric critics say: But yours is a Cartesian idea! Aren't you asking, Under what conditions is the African "I think" possible? Well, first of all, we shouldn't be surprised at the chorus: the opposing voices are mirror images of each other, and there is hardly any geographical distance between the crosscurrents. Second, the charge cannot hold—certainly not on the scientific merits—before damaging itself in endless qualifications. When we ask questions about method in philosophy with respect to the modern African or Black experiences, the references are to a singular, or a series of singular, and theoretical contexts. These contexts are in fact postcolonial and post-Cartesian complexes. They are historical spaces of reason that could not be conceived particularly nor primarily, stereotypes notwithstanding, as markers of "race," geography, or even culture —certainly not any more than Descartes or any other philosopher and his or her historically contingent contexts could be said to have been so marked. Both the specificities and the generalities of contexts that distinguish my own projects about method in philosophy in the postcolonial or nonsexist African experiences must therefore be found elsewhere. And this elsewhere can be nowhere but in the questioning of our very orientations in method, the questioning particularly of our conceptions of what counts or cannot count as a guiding—that is, a reliably descriptive and justifiably normative idea of—method in scientific and philosophical research.

The empirical and normative aspects of my concern about methods in African and historically Black traditions in philosophy are highlighted in the practices of the social and most strictly historical sciences, such as anthropology, sociology, linguistics, history, art history, and literary criticism. What distinguishes the variety of methods in these historical and theoretical sciences of contemporary African thought? What distinguishes the issue of method in philosophy from the problems of method in the rest of the scientific and theoretical disciplines that constitute Africa and its elements of experience or the physical environments as objectivities in fields of both academic and nonacademic inquiries? What are the relationships between philosophical methods and the historical questions embodied in the general composition of objectivities in the hard sciences, or of the historicities in the social and moral sciences?

In this last question we can hear the critic, this time, perhaps, with a better argument: How can a post-Cartesian, post-Négritudist cogito claim, in the name of method, a context that, in the end, seems to be raising questions not only for its particular will but also for the particular as such? There is, frankly, no bottom to the puzzle in this query. This is easily seen if we remind ourselves that, at core, the concern about the methods of philosophy, perhaps unlike in some of the other sciences, is not in the end about philosophy's relations to a particular time or place. The core issue, at least for me on this occasion, is about philosophy's relation to place and time in general. If a contemplative and normative—which is to say, rationally free—essence of philosophy emerges, if it can emerge *only* as an internal dialogue of the soul with itself, then it is clear that a postcolonial practice in African philosophy, in thinking about its own methods, is also thinking this method first and foremost as a problem of the time of thought. What does the freedom of philosophy look like in a modern or postmodern, postcolonial, postracial, and nonsexist African time? In fact, what is philosophy in time—any time? However generally these questions may be related to the narrower issues that framed my particular points of departure, the way the idea of method touches on the broader question of history, and in particular the histories of the subjects of reason in African thought, I cannot see anywhere in the issues the much debated opposition between the general and the particular. For how can thought *in* freedom be opposed to the thought *of* freedom?

An anecdote might be instructive. A few years ago the South African journal *Philosophical Papers* solicited an essay for a special issue titled "African Philosophy and the Analytic Tradition."[12] Implicit in this framing of the title is the question of method in African philosophy—specifically, method in African philosophy in regard to claims also about method in the traditions of a specifically twentieth-century theoretical understanding and institutional practices of philosophy largely in leading English-speaking universities.[13] If the history of the development of analytic philosophy is disciplinarily complex and institutionally messy, the same characterization could be applied to the origins of what, today, some of us wish to practice as modern or postmodern, postcolonial and nonracialized, African philosophy. For example, it is also certainly true that the terms "Africa" and "tradition" are not equivalents, just as the terms "philosophical" and "analytic" are not equivalents. What binds each couple of the terms is their times, their histories. Whereas one aspect of the coupling speaks to the history of philosophy in Africa, the other speaks to the history of the analytic approaches to philosophy. But these histories—and hence the traditions—of the analytic method in philosophy and of traditions of philosophy in modern Africa are also undoubtedly intertwined. The history of philosophy in postcolonial Africa cannot be decoupled from the history of the analytical traditions in philosophy in Anglophone Africa. Beyond the most visible figures of some Nigerian and Ghanaian contemporaries of Moore and Russell—one easily thinks of Peter Bodunrin and Kwasi Wiredu—what must be meant in the title of the call for papers except this: Is there a tradition of the analytical method in the history of philosophy in today's Africa? If there is, what is Afro-analytic about the methodological tradition? If not, what methods distinguish the African traditions in philosophy from the analytic? After all, despite the examples of thinkers like Senghor, Du Bois, and Hountondji, it is clear that when one speaks about "Continental" philosophy in Africa it must be only through a rethinking of the idea of the Continental that African Marxists, existentialists, or phenomenologists might be said to be not just transatlantic in their scientific orientations but also "Continental" in the narrowly historical sense of the term.

A cursory search of the subject heading "analytic + philosophy" in any decent university library reveals the significance of the many implicit conjunctions that *Philosophical Papers* wished to address. For example, published in two volumes, R. J. Butler's *Analytic Philosophy* contains about forty essays organized under "Modality," "Quantification," "Causality," "Method of Analysis," "Intentionality of Sensation," "Propositions," "Nonentities," and more. The titles cannot be said to reflect the idiosyncratic choices of an editor, for they are representative of the field of the analytical in philosophy, at least in the 1960s and 1970s. I surmise that *Philosophical Papers* presumed that the history of African philosophers' arguments over themes such as these might raise methodological and perhaps other fundamental questions about the enterprise of the analytic traditions in general. And I have no reason to suspect that this self-given task—to discern in African arguments general issues in analysis of modality, quantification, causality, and so on—is not ongoing. Yet the reality of the quest has turned out to be not so simple. Doesn't the generalized point of view beg the question of what constitutes *the* analytical tradition? Besides, if we intend to speak so generally, what is the sectarian self-nomination also implicit in the formulation "African Philosophy and the Analytic Tradition"? The meanings of this sectarianism, if one chooses to look at it that way, cannot be interpretatively exhausted. In what manner, for example, is it a renovation of the form of a particular kind of claim to Africa as a field of primary data for a secondary research: philosophy *and* the study of Africa?

Whether or not one agrees with the arguments of the proponents— arguments about what philosophy should or shouldn't be about —there are two propositions on the basis of which the idea of the *analytic* derives its traditional power. The first is the idea that human rationality is not only indivisible and universal but also positively transcendent of time and culture; hence the expectation that philosophy should be only an a priori science. Second, though, like the first, in some ways Platonic and Cartesian in inspiration, is the belief that although it is a method, philosophy must function like a catalyst: it analyzes but must remain unchanged by the analytical process. While philosophy can analyze numbers, forms, and concepts, philosophy itself must remain, like the chemical catalyst, unchanged by the very things whose analysis makes its activity possible. And when philosophy takes an interest in the analysis of itself, this self-analysis must be called *meta*philosophy.

But we ought to ask in what ways these characterizations might have been based on a false understanding of how method actually works in any science, and especially in the science of philosophy. In contrast to many classic analytical ideas about method, Pierre Hadot argues that there has never been "a philosophy or philosophers outside a group, *a community*." As he puts it: even a "philosophical school" whose influence may or may not be delimited as national or continental, or correspond to any other geographical or cultural circumspections, can be shown to correspond to the members of the school's "choice of a certain way of life." We can understand this idea of *choice*, following Sartre, as one among many elements in a philosophy's existential options. That there are existential choices a philosopher must make demands from the individual thinker or a school of such thinkers not just an abstract use of an abstract method but also, again in Hadot's words, "a certain desire to be and to live in a certain way."[14] From at least this angle, as well as on the evidence from the history of traditions of academic philosophy on many continents, it can be said that both contexts and substances of thought— the Sartrean existential "situation," Fanon's "lived experience," or Gadamer's "tradition"—make possible not just a certain vision of experience and of the world but also specific philosophical procedures. These procedures prove their enduring powers not only as interioristic practices of egologic methodological subjectivities; they are also forms of culturally rooted practices of freedom of thought. In fact, this idea of rootedness can be considered a kind of facticity and therefore an empirical objectivity: it is the sum of customs and more or less prereflective social practices which make it possible for the scientist or the philosopher to think in freedom as well as think about freedom itself in its forms of historical objectivities.

The observation that philosophical thoughts can be constituted in communities and in existential choices oriented by objective forms and institutions of life helps to explain the apparent mystery of how philosophical traditions appear in historical constellations. Each constellation is, at core, an intellectual revolution—certainly an intellectual movement. We find examples of this throughout the history of philosophy in most cultures. In fact, the temporal and geographical distribution of traditions of philosophy is obvious evidence for this claim. Sometimes the distributions are reflected all the way down to the cultural conflicts that animate substantive philosophical positions. The Germans' historical debates about *Naturwissenschaft* and *Geisteswissenschaft* (or, in the English-speaking world, the "two cultures" of science) are cases in point. Debates about methods thus almost always map themselves not only on the backs of geography as well as epochs but also within the elements of a disciplinary identity. The other example is Descartes's doubt which, throughout the seventeenth century, made the *Discourse on Method*, a treatise on how to "rightly conduct the mind and seek truth in the sciences," today's equivalent of an academic best-seller. So were Bacon's *Novum Organum* and Vico's *Scienza Nuova*. Today, these works have their approximate parallels in the so-called professional philosophy and ethnophilosophy methodological debates in Africa, and most recently are best represented in Hountondji's classic *African Philosophy: Myth and Reality*. In all these cases the debates were at core primarily methodological. In all cases the major claims are claims of rights to the methodological new: the *new* logic, the *new* science, the *new* professional practice. Each of the claims to the new was, invariably, polemically directed against what was seen as a preexisting methodological orthodoxy.

Against what is widely known about Bacon and unlike Descartes or Hountondji, Vico's claim to the new came neither from the model of mathematics nor from the aspiration of the natural and the mechanical sciences. Vico's idea of the new presented itself as a search for grounds and procedures by which autonomous subjects, as individuals and groups, understand their self-constitution in society as meaning-making agents. Under what conditions, and by what methods, are social and cultural norms historically legitimated? In the Vico model, instead of mathematics, geometry, or mechanical calculation as the privileged kinds of the rational, we find that languages—the languages of culture, history, and interpretations of symbols—constituted the main sources of experiences of reason. We see in Vico perhaps the first Western thinker to claim that the logic of the natural sciences can tell one very little about the logic of human, free and inventive, actions—and this insight way before Kant, and later Frege and Brandom. "The world of civil society," Vico writes, "has certainly been made by men, and . . . its principles are therefore to be found within the modifications of our own human mind."[15]

It was Vico, then, who helped to convince his audience that Descartes's insistence on egoistically conceived clear and distinct ideas (corresponding perceptually to metaphysical substances of the soul and of nature), if applied to the analysis of the symbolic and opaque social, cultural, and historical realities that constitute the bulk of the everyday in human experience, is inadequate as paradigmatic of the rational. Vico's first two books accordingly contain original ideas on what would be methods in the study of the then neglected fields of culture and society. *On the Method of the Studies of Our Time* and *On the Oldest Wisdom of the Italians* are attempts to persuade the reader about the importance to philosophy of historical and ethnographic critiques of languages, legal institutions, religions, and literature. The influence—an influence often underrated—of these works on subsequent centuries was not limited to their Italian examples; they were generally influential in subsequent European scholarship in fields as varied as theology and religious studies, anthropology and history, politics and law, and literary and art criticism. Hegel, Collingwood, Berlin, and Bergson were some of the inheritors of the Vicoan vision in Germany, England, and France.

If we surveyed not simply philosophy's choices of subjects of study (in the manner of "research on") but also, and above all, its choices of ideas about methods of scientific practices in Africa, what are the metatheoretical configurations? What is the lay of the land of thought in "our

Africa" rather than simply out of it? In what internal debates might we notice constellations of traditions—bodies of arguments, texts, institutions, and professional societies—committed to competing and easily stable historical forms? Where such forms of freedom of thoughts and the disputes exist, do they overlap with broader cultures? Do they extend themselves merely into the narrowly academic?

There is no denying the clerical intent to the formations of philosophical traditions in postcolonial Africa. Minimally, we must see in the current configurations in thought, within and outside the continent, a reflection of the varied faces of a singular humanist movement. If we read the signals of this humanism primarily within the confines of the discipline of philosophy, what I can see is no less than an intense struggle over the life and death of the mind. Postcolonial African philosophy remains one of a few accessible arenas in which to stage the embodiments in thought of the humane struggles of our souls against forces that seek not only to silence our internal conversations but also to negate the historical shapes of our freedoms.

It is often said that philosophy can defeat past evils, but future evils always defeat philosophy. In the antagonistic relations of African thoughts to their local and diasporic environments in the past few centuries—an antagonism whose modernity, albeit encumbered by an untenably naïve naturalism, we glimpse in the works of Zera Ya'icob—how can postcolonial and nonracialized African philosophy think the impossible: a history of its future? Lessons from past degradations of our humanity, degradations of humanity *tout court*—slavery in the seventeenth and eighteenth centuries as well as the reconquests symbolized by political decolonization in the twentieth century—are certainly fresh not only in subjective memories but also in critical public institutions. Within as without Africa, broadly speaking, the internal debates in philosophy reflect this bifurcation, and have often taken two different and antagonistically related turns. On the one hand, there are tightly scripted appeals to cultural difference as a reason for Africans' claims to—indeed, demands for—respect of their premodern and ancient, modern and colonial, and postmodern and postcolonial heritage.[16] The premodern and ancient inheritances are portrayed as embattled by contacts with forces of traditions and cultures from other parts of the world, particularly the Arab and European. The value placed on the idea of the autonomous, which is *not* to say exclusionary or separatist, African cultures in these encounters with foreign traditions may not be absolute, but claims about the values have certainly always been presented as a conflict—or, as in Senghor, a "marriage"—of universalities. We can call these the arguments for African or Black difference. It is a position best represented in the writings of, in addition to Senghor, Soyinka and Du Bois.

On the other hand, there is what you might call the antidifference faction: the cultural conventionalist position. This position abhors what Mahmood Mamdani memorably called "culture talk": the suspicion that culture might be mistaken as some sort of an involuntary twitch passively endured by an individual or a society. The conventionalist sees culture talk as essentially an ideological politicization of cultural inheritance, in which it is pretended that each culture has a tangible essence that defines it, an essence that must therefore be universally recognized as an inalienable historical right. Mamdani, like most critics of culture talk, frequently points to what some consider the wasted years of ideological *authenticité* in Mobutu's Zaire, an ideology that also happened to have suited the interests of general politics in the old war period.

Whichever way you choose to look it, "culture" has been a vehicle for expressions of philosophical initiative and creativity in postcolonial Africa and throughout its diaspora. In fact, just below the surfaces, the so-called postcolonial conflicts between "tradition and modernity" in the African experience are an ongoing conversation about the universal nature of freedom, creativity, and autonomy. The culturalist arguments are therefore nothing to be praised or condemned. Though given a culture (peoples are in some important respects *products* of cultures), individuals and societies nevertheless *do* fashion and refashion for themselves, and according to changing needs, new cultural inheritances. In fact, the entire tradition of culture wars within societies, sometimes across generations even in one family, is without doubt evidence of the fact that the relations between individual subjectivities and social totalities are inherently characterized not just by agreements but also conflicts, negotiations, and renewal. Postcolonial African philosophy has contributed to accentuating the agential elements in the reception or rejection of that which one is given as cultural heritage. It is as both legacy and agency that the roles of history and individuality in formations of cultural identities emerge the most clearly. If, today, one *makes* of and for oneself and others one's sense of self out of what was bequeathed, the debates of African philosophers have succeeded in placing the emphasis where it ought to be: on the idea of the *work* of making, the task of the self, the course of socially and historically remaking a world that, clearly, as most philosophers believe, requires transformation and even repair.

That emphasis in thought has been crucial in highlighting the fact that individuals choose to make themselves in renewing a heritage. The philosophical discussions have revealed all sorts of acts of choice, the choice to fashion for oneself and with others a useful identity or multiple identities at a particular time from particular cultural resources available by birth or by learning. Yet, at any time, the process of identity formation is fraught with uncertainty and therefore anxiety. Because one fashions and refashions an identity or multiple identities in the present but also in the expectation that the identity or identities are both now serviceable and transmissible, the process seems to be unavoidably pierced by a structure of anticipation and by hope. The hope is there as a marker of a point of risk; in fact, hope marks a double risk. If we choose culture work over culture talk, the work is driven by the hope that our confidence in the identity passed down to us has been not just serviceable but right. It is this confidence in not just the efficacy but also the rightness of the forms of the past that, as if by entailment, nurtures the other side of the expectation: working in the hope that the future of the present will go on. These double acts of hope constitute an act of faith in the work of culture. The faith is a reminder that no matter how right and how hard one gives oneself or one's time to the work of culture, it is a kind of work whose outcome is essentially without guarantee.

THE CHARACTER OF FREEDOM

That culture work requires confident hope is a fact. We hope that the past had reasons we call good, but the goodness which we may not fully grasp in the same way as the past understood what must have been the good, its own hopes and its own present. And we hope that events in the future will be in line with our own hopes. These are the anxieties internal to hope which make the subject of culture such a contentious topic. The sources of the contention are to be found in these three consequences of the culture-of-hope. First, that it is by trust or hope in the work of culture, past and present, that we are able to project the only context within which an individual or society may be able to think the meanings of autonomy and of freedom. Second, that cultures are where we find both independence and belonging, which makes independence and belonging non-culturally neutral values: they cannot be neutral. Finally, that we can say all this without undermining the idea that freedom is grounded in the natural condition of humanity.

Cultures and traditions shape practices of freedom and agency. If by nature we are disposed to both individuality and sociality, to freedom and agency, it is precisely this disposition that also counts as the human origin of culture. The strongest cultural and social arguments one can make on behalf of freedom is thus to say, for example, that freedom is what cultures and societies make out of individuals whose natural endowments dispose them to exercises of life in liberty. In this formulation, culture talk can be seen as a denial of the realities of subjectivity. Abandoning culture talk, by contrast, means that one is willing to accept that personal identities are no more constrained by culture and society than humans, in general, can be considered incapable of escaping the reality of natural freedom.[17]

The basis of this dual allegiance to freedom and to culture is more obvious if one considers the differences between freedom and liberty. Though freedom and liberty are mentioned interchangeably and often in the same breath, the differences in their origins provide an insight into the conflict *within* the idea of culture. The etymology of *freedom* is the Sumerian *ama-ar-gi*, a "right of return" or "going home to mother."[18] As was true in ancient Sumer, in many of today's traditional societies children, particularly the boys, are sent away from their parents to distant tribes, where they live and learn trades with well-known artisans. The youth were not permitted to go home until the end of their apprenticeship. At the end of the apprenticeship, however, and usually after the child had been an adult for many years, one celebrated the freedom of the end of apprenticeship and the onset of adult responsibility as a right to return to the "motherland": a right to go home. Going home is a right to freedom because home is that community where one belongs by right. Freedom in this ancient sense is a freedom *to* community, a right of belonging. We can hear echoes of this enduring understanding of what it means to be free not just in traditional societies in Africa, Asia, and the Middle East but also in the language of Gandhi's political democratic work and in the movement for *civil rights* in the Americas and Europe. Civil right implies the idea of what Martin Luther King Jr. idealized as the "beloved community": a national space where one is at home because one has the rights and responsibilities that come from being treated as a full citizen. Citizenship, with its rights and duties, means that one is a protected member of a national "family."

In contrast to freedom, liberty has a different history. The etymology is Greek: *eleutheria*. Taxonomists give the generic label *Eleutherodactylus* to species that have well-developed digits, usually toes and fingers. Neonatal doctors, too, declare a baby *eleutherodactylic* when it has no webbed toes or fingers. The Latin word *libertas* derives its origins from the Greek *eleutheria*; both English *liberty* and French *liberté* retain the ancient and classical roots in their current meanings. For example, we understand quite clearly Patrick Henry when he declared "Give me liberty or give me death," or when the French took time to enumeratively affirm the relations in "*liberté, égalité, fraternité*." In the two revolutionary movements the word "liberty" meant something like "Independence now or we will die fighting for it." In "in-dependence" we hear individuality, autonomy, initiative, agency, even a dignified aloneness: all these connotations are in one way or another reflected in what became the outcomes of the historical movement for liberty. The independence movements in twentieth-century Africa as well as other Third World nations continued the historical traditions: the colonized countries wanted to exist or regain their existence as sovereign states, independent of the colonizing states. While these historically entrenched meanings of liberty are not opposed to the idea of freedom-as-a-right-to-belong in a community, the difference in the emphases points to tensions beyond the semantic. Freedom and liberty need each other, but they are not the same—and they do not always happily belong together. To belong, but as an individual: that is a tension at the heart of every social life.[19] Our uses of the terms freedom and liberty, together and enumerative, suggest an intuitive awareness of their conflicted inseparability.

The tension within and between liberty and freedom provides us with a model to think the conflicts within cultural forms. If we think about freedom as advocating a tightly scripted idea of cultural belonging, then liberty should be seen as advocating a more loosely scripted one. "Script" here means the depth of investment of one's sense of self in one culture or in a number of cultures. In reference to particular cultures and specific individuals, one might therefore speak in terms of tight culturalists and loose culturalists. One moves from one end of the range to the other depending on where one draws the line on the cost of culture in relation to individuality. Where one draws such a line can be easily determined, for the same reason that fictions like the 1993 movie *Indecent Proposal* fascinates. For what prize would one be willing sell even that—in this case, a relationship—which one ordinarily considers priceless or sacred? When the relationship in question is cultural belonging, the tight culturalist (TC) and the loose culturalist (LC) draw the line at different thresholds.

The reasons for the difference between the TC and the LC are as varied as there are individual needs and interests: security in conventional morality and public opinion, concern for ethical principles that transcend the conventionally moral, desire to conform to privatistic values or traditions inherited from religious or secular affiliations, and so forth.[20] Of course, the difference should be made more complex since, in the real world, the selves in the situations of choice are hardly culturally neutral. Individuals and personalities are always already differently enculturated and at various depths. The enculturation is partly responsible for shaping our sense of what is important and what is not. But even then it would not only be morally wrong but also philosophically contradictory to imagine that, because of cultural conditioning, an individual could never freely enough successfully assume a cultural belonging or belongings to societies other than those into which one was born or had been the earliest educated. (I rejected this philosophical view of human nature in the arguments against culture talk.)

Yet we can understand where the TC is coming from. Although a general relation to a culture does not rise in depth to the level of investment of self in a particular individual by, say, parentage or legal union, we can appreciate the position of even the most extreme TC by making an imperfect analogy. At the extreme, and putting the best light on it, the fundamentalist cultural nationalist, for example, is like someone who would not exchange a particular spouse (parent, child, etc.) for another individual or for whatever amount of money. You could argue with such a person all you want: There are many other individuals willing and ready to be your spouse (parents, children). How much really did the person love you in the first place if he or she could not understand that it is good for your individuality to exchange that love for a million dollars? Would you rather die poor in obscure honor or enjoy the celebrity? This example does not sugges that a TC's relation to a community's local or national culture is in fact as sacred as the primal affections, love, or the rights and obligations that exist in the intimate relations to the individuals in one's private life. But the deepest sentiments at the most personal levels illuminate the sentiments at the public and most general levels. For example, whether they are or are not legally supported as public rights and obligations, and if one does not wish to argue that existential sentiments like love are beyond reason, is it not possible to imagine that there are formal continuities between the reasons why one loves a parent, a child, or spouse and the reasons why one wants to feel self-invested in a local or national community's traditions? However stronger or weaker one set of feelings is than the other, aren't the reasons for attachments to family, tradition, and country ultimately simultaneously —or at least continuously—grounded in the two inseparable but, in the Kantian sense in which we interpreted them earlier, antagonistically related moral needs: belonging and independence, freedom and liberty?

Of course, the material and immaterial cultural objects one considers sacred may be only metaphorically so. However intrinsically useful the ideas, symbols, and institutions of a tradition might be *in their own right*, it is also true that *we in culture* have personally or socially invested moral values in them in such a way that they exercise over us the authority of the sacred or the aura of the priceless. There are reasons, also individual as well as general, why we make the investments. We may consider some of these reasons good and others bad. The fact is that for good and for bad—and, as we shall see, most of the time for good—cultures and social values exercise important powers over individuals. The most crucial good reasons for the roles a culture plays in the life of the individual are explained by Aristotle in the *Nichomachean Ethics*. Habit, Aristotle recognizes, is essential for formation of character.[21] As *second* nature, habit is far from blind: it surreptitiously reconciles the untrained (the "animal") part of an otherwise rational individual to the accumulated wisdoms of a society. Cultures and traditions are accumulated habits—and most of them wise habits.

"We don't do that," "That's not done," "It is immoral," "I can't imagine anyone from our people doing that" are often mere expressions of taste. But more often they are not.[22] They may also be shorthand for passing on knowledge about which ways of accomplishing a particular task have been tried and found to be useful or useless, proper or improper, or right or wrong. As a matter of content (morality, values, interests, etc.) and process (enculturation, learning, development, etc.), there are therefore good reasons to defend a cultural tradition. Moreover, the reasons why it may also be the case that such a defense is better done collectively, rather than left entirely to the private judgments or expertise of the individual members of the culture, are, as we shall see, equally obvious.

A culture bridges the necessary gap between implicit and explicit social knowledge. It allows us to become that which makes us who we are by making ourselves into that which we believe makes us who we are. Culture defined in this sense functions as both actual and hypothetical a priori: as a more or less trusted guide in everyday conduct. Although in the next chapter I will explore in detail what it means to trust a culture, I can already explain here why we develop the sense of a culture or a tradition as easy—that is, readily available—reservoirs of potentially good reasons. The problem is that bad reasons, too, become habits and second nature. But this is certainly not an argument to discard or absolutely relativize the potentially moral content and functional processes of enculturation. It is, rather, an argument to promote the good aspects of any culture, including the virtues, for example, openness, debate, and innovation.

The philosophical works of Paul Ricoeur, Hans-Georg Gadamer, and Charles Taylor and the political theories of Iris Young, Sheila Benhabib, and Will Kymlicka show in what ways the Aristotelian insights might still be quite valid even in our modern and postmodern world. But my favorite examples of defense of the role of culture in formation of character occurred in another world, and in tragic circumstances. Granville Sharp, a founder of the eighteenth-century British abolitionist movement, recounts a meeting with an African monarch who has come to London to support the abolitionist cause. Sharp suspects that the king is less moved by stories of individual slaves that had been cruelly beaten by their masters or mistresses than by stories of what the royal himself considered "insults" to Africans in Europe. The king reportedly said that he could imagine himself forgiving someone who bit a slave, but not someone who "took away" the African's character. "Being asked," Granville recalls, "why he would not extend his forgiveness to those who took away the character of the people of his country, he replied:

> If a man should try to kill me, or should sell me and my family for slaves, he would do an injury to as many as he might kill or sell; but if any one takes away the character of Black people, that man injures Black people all over the world; and when he has once taken away their character, there is nothing that he may not do to Black people ever after. That man, for instance, will, beat Black men, and say, *Oh, it is only a Black man, why should I not beat him?* That man will make slaves of Black people; for when he has taken away their character, he will say, *Oh, they are only Black people, why should I not make them slaves?* . . . That is the reason why I cannot forgive the man who takes away the character of the people of my country.[23]

"Character," in the sense the monarch uses it, is not an individual attribute, like, for example, wit. It is something shaped in community, by culture.

Culturalism and Multiculturalism

The loose culturalist cannot be seen as against culture per se; after all, everyone has a culture, and just as often many cultures. Instead, the loose culturalist presents himself or herself as against *culturalism*. By "culturalism" I mean a form of traditionalism: an uncritical embrace and immersion in a particular, usually exclusivist cultural tradition for no other reason except that the culture can be claimed as one's own by tribal, national, ethnic, or religious heritage. Culturalism is therefore not only traditionalistic but also—on account of the various exclusivist definitions of rights to inheritance—potentially chauvinistic. At the extreme, tribal, national, racial, or religious chauvinism might even grow beyond exclusion of those considered Other to its defined cultural community. It can expand inward to the level of explicit intolerance of those within defined memberships but who are suspected of holding dissenting views on a set of beliefs considered central to the tribe, nation, race, or religion. And the internal discrimination can also be more superficially coded, such as we hear about in "brown bag" or "pencil in the hair" tests once employed in the United States and South Africa as measurements to determine whether one was, respectively, Black or White and Black, Colored, or White. Needless to say, these tests often yielded bizarre results: a child may be classified as belonging to one race while the pair of biological parents are classified as belong to a different race.[24]

No doubt, it is in part the apparent irrationalities of the previous practices of racial and other kinds of ethnocentric and exclusivist culturalism that, naturally, fuels some of the current popularity of *multi*culturalism.[25] But the same condition also at least partially explains why some critics of culturalism are equally reticent to embrace multiculturalism as a counter- or alternative ideology. If one does not have a favorable view of culturalism to begin with, substituting the sort of strict allegiance to one culture implied in culturalism with a similar allegiance to many cultures does, in fact, remove some, but only some, of the unattractiveness. For example, from the perspective of an advocate of cosmopolitanism, multiculturalism might blunt the chauvinism and the potential intolerance implied in monoculturalism. But the reverse effect may also be true. Certainly, monoculturalism and multiculturalism may clash but, unsurprisingly, also ideologically fuel each other. Thus some cosmopolitans may criticize multiculturalism by arguing that it is an ideological counterimage of culturalism. Such a consistent cosmopolitan criticism objects to culturalism in every form, mono or multi. Even if it were shown that multiculturalism successfully blunts the explicit chauvinism and the potential intolerance encoded in the definitions of heritage in the monoculturalist idea, the multiculturalist remedy does not address, in specific, the traditionalism of which devotion to one or many cultural inheritances can still be suspected.

Can we go along with the radical cosmopolitan's suspicion that every culture is, in essence, traditionalistic? The answer to this question is not obvious. Given any culture's aim—at its best, to maintain or pass on what we call accumulated wisdoms of a people—it is impossible to turn around and think that a culture does not have or would not be the most prone to its conservative instinct. This aspect of a culture merits even further attention for the following reason. We generally think that a culture incapable of conserving itself is not a "real" or "true" culture. If we call a culture, for example, "disposable," it may be a descriptive observation about how individuals or groups use the culture, but it may also be construed as a judgment about what we think the culture is worth: it is all right to resort to it on an ad hoc, need-based fashion. The cultural item in question, material or immaterial, this judgment implies, is either not valuable enough to warrant the trouble of maintaining its existence as, for example, an antique or a classic. Either the disposable culture is not all that important or, if it is, its example is very common and cheap and can easily be replaced.

The idea of an antique or a classic already implies the idea of inheritance in the way the mono- or multiculturalist would have it: this item is something important, which is why it has been handed down from the past. It is an easy step from considering something antique or classic to investing it with an aura. The aura might be simply that of a secular respect for what is intrinsically important and rare, and therefore rising to the level of the precious on account of the combined value of importance and rarity. But it could also be a mythical and quasi-religious aura, for example, a veneration for influential past figures: actors, politicians, religious personalities, and so on. The veneration turns the classic or the antique into an icon or relic. (Beyond its secular value, the relic or the icon is additionally supposed to be a medium for spiritual communion with the figures, ancient or already divine, for which the relic or icon becomes a stand-in.) This aura returns to exercise on the present lives of the members of the culture a quasi-divine effect; let's call this a traditional belief in the "sanctity" of culture. Given the power of culture to invest its past with an aura, it is not surprising that the modern and postmodern mind should be, rather than instinctively conservative about culture, instinctively suspicious of it.

It is purely redundant to say that a traditional cultural mind-set is more readily disposed to accept than critically question the postulates of a tradition; that is why the mind-set is called traditionalism. The good reason why critics of traditionalism suspect the traditionalist's defense of traditional values is not because the critics do not recognize the traditional culture's morally edifying values; it's not even because they think traditional cultures may transmit the bad along with the good aspects of the past. (For example, there is nothing that inherently makes the avant-garde in modernist and postmodernist movements lack judgment in terms of making epistemic and moral distinctions between the good and the bad, the true and false, proper and improper, etc. in social morality.)

Rather, the critics of tradition are quite simply opposed to cultural impositions of the past on the present, whether the imposition is done by overt force or covert indoctrination. The critics of traditionalism explicitly adopt an antagonistic attitude toward the past—the past that traditional cultures are seen as transmissively mediating—*because* of their principled commitment to specific conceptions of subjectivity. The postmodern cosmopolitan, for example, prefers to be an inventor rather than a conservator of values. The values invented may or may not correspond or even conform to what past members of one's society or culture valued. The key interest, therefore, is to invent or reinvent, for example, one's identity, and the work of invention is postulated as a moral requirement. As if they were philosophical descendants of Nietzsche, critics of traditionalism go as far as to say that the greatest evil is the thought that one is subjectively uninventive, unimaginative, and conformist. Even when the postmodern cosmopolitan embraces tradition, what is embraced is tradition as understood and interpreted in new modes of self-expression. The key virtue in this expressive relationship to tradition becomes the act of invention in the forms of deconstruction, transgression, boundary crossing, or hybridity.

In a curious historical clash, then, the traditional and the progressive or post-traditional appear to collide *on moral grounds*. Theorists of modernity like Weber, Senghor, and Habermas understand very well this conflict, even if some of them try to show that the two cultures of cultural traditionalism and cultural progress are not, in the end, irreconcilable. Critics argue that even as it rejects the past as traditional or pejoratively classic, the progressive modern mind fails to notice a leveling of subjectivity occurring because of the modern processes as such. For Weber and Marx these processes were industrial and economic (capitalistic rationality). For Senghor the sources of the modern antihumanism were equally rooted in capitalistic and colonial rationalities. For Habermas the forces of what Marcuse called the eclipse of reason are mediated by money, power, and technology. But a cosmopolite's response to these humanist and neo-humanist critiques of both modernity and postmodernity does not suggest an abandonment of modernity's ideal (e.g., a universal world-is-my-culture idea of subjectivity); instead, the cosmopolitan returns with emphasis to insist on the reasons for his or her idea about, as well as practical standpoint of antipathy to, traditionalism: no matter whether it is the premodern past or the modern or the postmodern present behaving traditionalistically (i.e., denying the interests of objective historical institutions of freedom that enable the subjective expressions of individuality), a critical attitude is called for on moral grounds. In recognition of the supposedly more subtle but widely pervasive instruments of colonization of society and subjectivity in modernity, for example, critics of the modern and the "classic," such as Foucault, recommend that Nietzsche's type of critical attitude must be directed as much at the self as at social and political institutions.

In the cosmopolitan critiques of traditionalism, then, the negative parts of the judgments are clearly aimed at the fact or perception that, mostly, inherited cultures uncritically mediate the past—even if not exclusively so. Furthermore, unlike the criticisms directed at modern and postmodern exercises of bio-panoptical power, the cosmopolitan takes special care to point out that the worst kind of social control of the individual—the disempowerment of autonomy and agency—occurs when, in answer to questions about why one is morally required to do something, one is told: "Because that is the way we do it in our culture." The affront to the cosmopolitan imagination in this dictum may be because he or she suspects that the culture has commanded a substantive wrong or illiberal kind of conduct. But it could equally be because of the inherently modern or postmodern attitude of the cosmopolitan: the attitude that a culture, in principle, has no right to tell individuals how to live their life—or at least not without offering reasons.

The cosmopolitan, in principle, rejects the idea that an individual's identity is authentic only if it derives from a traditionally inherited and tightly scripted culture. This makes the cosmopolite also usually socially liberal because, for the cultural cosmopolitan as for the social liberal, statements like "We do it this way because that is the way our mothers did it, and that is how we want our children and our children's children to do it" are not sufficient to declare the practice so justified automatically morally acceptable. Where the principled cosmopolitan differs from the mere social liberal is when the former further believes that the deepest commitment to one's culture or to several cultures (the target of criticism is usually the deepest *and* exclusive commitment to one culture) is always traditionalistic. Remove the traditionalistic elements (arguments from a privileged and exclusive inheritance, for example) and the cosmopolite cannot see any good and exclusive reasons why, all things being equal, the deepest commitment to *this* culture rather than to *that* makes any morally important difference. Unlike commitments to specific individuals (e.g., members of a family, a friendship club, a professional guild), the cosmopolite's conception of culture is so general that almost any culture of freedom and liberty is as morally justifiable as the next.[26]

The TC's objection to the cosmopolitan ideal thus derives from a primary disagreement over the proper attitude to culture, both inherited and invented.[27] The TC need not be a cultural nationalist (it is even less likely that he or she is an ethnic chauvinist or a religious fundamentalist), but certainly operates from a more positive view of what constitutes appropriate individual relation to a culture and to a tradition, especially the relationship of the individual to morally valid aspects of one's own or other people's culture. If the main criteria for accepting or rejecting a culture were the requirement of choice *and* a capacity for critical affirmation of this choice, the TC will point out that not even the cosmopolitan could claim to be sufficiently aware of the reasons for every significant cultural belief a cosmopolitan individual might hold. If one is considered neither uninformed nor morally diminished because one cannot say why one walks out the door with the right foot first instead of the left, there is no reason to think that the TC, because perhaps insufficiently able to understand in order to critically accept or reject the correct reasons behind every observable aspect of a tradition, is thereby either less culturally intelligent or less capable of universal acts of morality. In fact, the TC and the LC may agree that even when a cultural practice is traditionalistic, the moral drawback, if any, in traditionalism does not consist in the more or less insufficiently reflective attachment to traditional beliefs by individuals or groups; it consists instead in the fear of potential fundamentalism suspected to exist in an inability to imagine, tolerate, or respect different moral viewpoints. But if this is true, the great risk in culturalism is not, after all, unique to the TC. The LC, whether cosmopolitan or liberal, especially if he or she does not live up to the rhetoric of the chosen ideal, may be equally prone to the risks inherent in an insufficiently reflective moral imagination.

From whichever ideological standpoint, then, culture matters. And culture matters not least because, in one way or another, it just is. Moreover, an attack on a culture may be an attack on the freedom of the individual. As the abolitionists' arguments showed, an attack on the freedom of an individual may also be an attack aimed at a cultural and ethnic group. Today, the United Nations declarations on genocide support this complex view of a people's relations to their cultural traditions. The declarations acknowledge that intentional attack on a free and open culture can be construed as attempted genocide, for the same reason that a morally evil culture is destructive of individual character.[28] Recent judgments and ongoing trials at the International Court of Justice and its tribunals put in practice this view of the cultural dimensions of genocidal crimes.[29]

Similarly, nothing I have said suggests that cultures are discrete entities subsisting in isolation like monads. Though I have provided ideal-type descriptors in order to explain why individuals or groups might internalize and cling to culture at various degrees of depth, the culture-types may be easily found cohabiting in one country, in the same neighborhood, or within a family. As my discussion of the etymologies of freedom and liberty suggests, one individual can experience two conflicting attitudes toward a particular aspect of his or her own society's cultural heritage. In classic modern liberal theories, Rousseau and Kant recognized this individual psychology as a key problem of social and political life in modern cultures. If the modern individual is an autonomous moral agent, their political writings asked, what kind of community is best suited for a society of such individuals? Instead of thinking the question of culture in any particular one-dimensional direction, especially in the direction of unanimity (how to achieve a promise of harmonious togetherness, or *sensus communis* as the ancients would have it), both thinkers grappled with issues about how to reconcile individuality and sociality around the transcendent demand of freedom as the essential element. As we saw, Kant rethought the problem as a task of finding a workable theory of what he less idealistically called unsocial sociality of mankind.

The remaining ambiguities in our own descriptions are therefore not a result of lack of clarity in the concepts; it is the nature of sociality as such that is unclear. The problem of culture, as I have tried to describe it, comes from the fact that no theorist has been able to decisively resolve the sorts of practical and historical questions reportedly posed to the anthropologist Jared Diamond while he was working in Papua New Guinea.

Why is it, he was challenged by an informant who spoke almost like Marx, that your people have "so much cargo and we New Guineans have so little?"[30] (There is a variation on this theme: "Why is cargo distributed so unequally both within and between our societies?")[31] There is therefore only so much clarity theory or even description can bring to bear on cultural explanations: culture matters, but culture may or may not be the explanation for every significant social and historical phenomenon. I have therefore not addressed the question why a culture may or may not be worthy of defense even when it is, visibly and in important respects, less materially prosperous in comparison to others.[32]

SCIENCE OF "RACE"

Race: What's the Idea?

In order not to rise to the human condition men sink into the dark depths of the zoological doctrine of race.—FRANZ KAFKA, in Gustava Janouch, *Conversations with Kafka*

Parce qu'on vous a trop fait dans le passé sentir votre race, il arrive que vous en soyez encombrés, que vous la retourniez comme un défi, qu'elle devienne pour vous, une obsession orgueilleuse.—EMMANUEL MOUNIER, *L'éveil de l'Afrique Noir*

Kafka could have intended to be dramatic when he said the above, but he certainly was correct to point out that race is a *doctrine*, a zoological one. Even when we take into account Aristotle's statement that the human person is a *rational animal*, it is still easy to see that the doctrine of race, when applied to humanity, makes a mockery of much of what we call rationality. When improperly employed as a concept, or a pseudo-concept, rather than held as dogmatically doctrinal, "race" as a thought is characterized by a special kind of antirational migrancy. It may describe a religious tribe (e.g., the Jew), a national identity (e.g., the Nazi's idea of a Germanic people), a linguistic group (e.g., the Ibo), a political-economic class (e.g., India's Aryan castes), an ethnic or ethnographic identity (e.g., Enoch Powell's idea of the English), a cohort of allele (in population studies), or a universal (the "human race").

It is because "race" can be used to explain so many different kinds of self-identification that some writers have argued that races are conceptually fictive.[33] In a recent essay in the journal *The Progressive*, the political scientist Adolph Reed extends this critique of "race" to the idea of "racism." Writing specifically about the post-Katrina flood in the southern United States, Reed argues:

> The language of race and racism is too imprecise to describe effectively even how patterns of injustice and inequality are racialized in a post–Jim Crow world. "Racism" can cover everything from individual prejudice and bigotry, unself-conscious perception of racial stereotypes, concerted group action to exclude or subordinate, or the results of ostensibly neutral market forces. It can be a one-word description and explanation of patterns of unequal distribution of income and wealth, services and opportunities, police brutality, a stockbroker's inability to get a cab, neighborhood dislocation and gentrification, poverty, unfair criticism of black or Latino athletes, or being denied admission to a boutique. Because the category is so porous, it doesn't really explain anything. Indeed, it is an alternative to explanation.[34]

But it is not only the status of the substance of "race" that has been put into question by the unclear scientific status of the concept. The historical conditions under which the imaginary and dynamic ideas of race are generated, and the disciplinary procedures by which knowledge of races and the social histories of the idea of race and practices of racism are produced, have also recently been brought under critical scrutiny.

The more current critical reception of race in contemporary discourses of the social sciences is largely driven by the rise of new biological, particularly genetic, sciences. This is obvious in the recent call for scholarly papers on race and medicine. Potential contributors were told, in August 2005, "With the first patent being granted to 'BiDil,' a combined medication that is deemed to be most effective for a specific form of heart failure when used by members of a specific 'race,' namely, African Americans, the ongoing debate about the effect of an older category of 'race' has been renewed." A key question was posed: "What role should 'race' play in the discussion of genetic alleles and populations today?"[35] While expressing surprise that genetics has not managed to make further empirical sense out of the concept "race" (or at least more progress over the past fifty years), scholars of race seem to wonder aloud: What are the new

reasons for the new urgency to pharmacologize race? Pharmacologization usually presupposes an underlying knowledge of a biological or
psychological condition subjected to medication. What is the biology (we
cannot say, strictly, "psychology" since this is about knowledge of heart
disease) of Blackness?

The relation between the medical gaze in view of pharmacologization
and claims, or lack of claims, to biological knowledge of race becomes
obvious when one reads some of the arguments in support of BiDil in the
dailies. The *New York Times* editorialized, "Race-based prescribing
makes sense only as a temporary measure." But one should wonder also
about how to understand this idea of the "temporary," say, from the
perspective of the history and philosophy of science. Certainly, in research procedures, there is nothing unusual about taking an idea as a
heuristic, a guiding notion or hypothesis in virtue of which a research
program cannot start, a notion whose confirmation or disconfirmation
is the very end of the scientific process. But what happens when the idea
of the heuristic is extrapolated, as has been done here, to medical *pre-
scription*? There are, I think, many levels at which philosophers might
intervene in this debate. Philosophizing about the science is just one of
them. The other could be in the form of an ethical inquiry: the ethics of
medical practice. To what extent must medical prescribing be based on
objective knowledge? What constitutes objectivity in this regard, and
who ought to determine when the constitutive conditions have been
met? Is it (still) science when a doctor prescribes medication to a patient
based, decisively, on the patient's subjective racial identification, regardless of whether or not the biological sciences have reasonably established
the existence or nonexistence of races?

If one interprets the temporality of this medical science of race as if the
concept were a placeholder in thought for a something whose substance
is yet to be empirically established, what is the ethical status of this idea
of research subjects? Who or what qualifies as objects of the research?
Who is medically doing what to whom, while, in the meantime, research
scientists explore the actual genetic makeup of the, obviously, already
speculatively racialized individuals? The journal *Patterns of Prejudice* has
taken seriously just such questions. In a recent call for papers, it asked
scholars to examine, from both biomedical and sociological points of
view, "Who defines 'race'?": a self-defined group, a government, a re-

search funder, or the researcher? "Does 'race' present both epidemiological and historical problems for the society in which it is raised as well as for medical research and practice?" "What does one do with what are deemed 'race-specific' diseases such as 'Jewish genetic diseases' that are so defined because they are often concentrated in a group but are also found beyond the group?" and "Are we comfortable designating 'African-Americans' or 'Jews' as 'races' given their genetic diversity?"[36] In short, what are the grounds, beyond the genetically yet unfounded argument that, by statistical reports based on subjective racial self-identifications, a measurable fraction of a sample of citizens of the United States who say they are Black appear to benefit from a particular new heart medication?

By the reading of it, some suspect that in addition to enabling the social success of race science, normative race theories and racial beliefs are themselves commercially profitable.[37] In their own take on it, organizers of a recent Massachusetts Institute of Technology conference on "The Business of Race and Science" remark that "advances in genetics have renewed interest in sciences and technologies of race." They are concerned that "although humans may share 99.9% of their genes, there may be much that is interesting, even profitable, in the remaining 0.1%," since this nearly nonexistent empirical definition "has fueled rapidly growing interest in a range of products that claim to take advantage of differences between human populations." They therefore ask participants to consider in what ways businesses "now market race-specific medications and vitamins, and other racial therapeutics." Even more basically, we know now that "competing laboratories offer genetic analyses of race and ancestry," a commercial development that some commentators refer to as "recreational genetics." Certainly, "racial science has infiltrated [popular] discussions of topics as wide-ranging as cosmetics and forensics." Are these developments, the MIT folk ask, "appropriate uses of new understandings of race?" They want to know whether "commodification of racial science helps or harms the targeted populations and society at large." "Who speaks for populations in endorsing or sanctioning the use of racial difference?" "How will the controversies play out in different countries and contexts?" and "How will attending to the business of racial science help [us] understand the science itself and clarify its role in our world?"[38]

It seems that, along with the science of medicine, twenty-first-century anthropology, sociology, psychology, and political studies have rediscovered that the idea of race persists, as both objective and methodological concept, in their core areas of specialization. But it also seems that in fields with scopes wider than the interests of empirical research—philosophy, arts and literature, and critical and cultural theory—there has not been indifference to the newer debates about the empirical content, if any, of the concept of race. In the philosophical literature, debates about why it could be thought that Africans, or at least all "Black" Africans, belong to a "race," as Europeans are said to belong to a "White race," the Asians to the "Oriental race," and so on, have acquired the status of both conceptual and historical problems. Understanding the historical elements in the conceptual debates requires one to make distinctions between at least three broad stages. *Grosso modo*, the stages comprise the religious or mythical speculations about divine origins of races, modern scientific theories about "human varieties," and the postmodern and postcolonial critiques of both the sciences and pseudo-sciences of race. Each of these stages and the mixtures of conceptions and misconceptions have consequences for how the humanities seek to interpret and critique identity formation in the contemporary world.

The first of the stages is tied to speculations about primordial processes of identity formation. Psychologically, it is presumed that geographical limitations allow isolated and self-absorbed ethnic groups to think that, beyond their own geographical borders and the security of their own order of life, something resembling social and metaphysical disorder abounds. Such active "ignorance" of the "outside" world, combined with limited security afforded by the ignorance, function to establish antagonistic relations to extended worlds considered not just different and distant but also imagined as Other. Conforming images are accordingly produced to mark, and idealize, the boundaries of those isolatable signs through which "they" are different from "us." Where the usable signs are hard to come by, it is not difficult to imagine ideal difference strong enough to generate believable contrast. ("They look like us only on the surface: inside they are *really* different." "They behave like us during the day, in general society, but at home, in private, they feed on the blood of little children." "During the day they are normal like you and me, but at night they turn into witches." "They are secretly cannibals: no one of an outside race has lived to tell.") In antiquity,

Herodotus exploited this genre. In *History*, for example, he described educated Greeks' image of Antipodes, "men on the opposite side of the earth," who were believed to be either "dog-headed" or entirely "headless."[39] Similarly, in Plinian anthropology of the early medieval world, educated Europeans believed in the existence of foreigners who lived where "the sun rises when it set on us," "walked with their feet opposite ours," and, unsurprisingly, remained unknown and anonymous: they "had no names."[40] In *The Monstrous Races in Medieval Art and Thought*, John Block shows us how the category "Other" functioned in the medieval mind. The peoples and cultures put under that category, real or imagined, invariably existed outside the boundaries of the esteemed life of the self-selected "humanity." It was *our* European race, culture, and religion against the unknown—incomprehensible, strange, or terrifying —theirs. "They" existed always in places far away, unreachable places. In a kind of manipulation of time and space, the distance between us and the distant places of unknown peoples fertilizes the imaginary work of bridging precisely that distance with horror, the exciting, and the exotic. There are always people lurking, excessively sensual and seductive or menacing (they amount to the same thing: they threaten disorder), at a distance from the very center of the planet—in the *Far* North, in the *Far* East, or in a *Dark* Continent.

Paralleling the impulse to externally orient the ordering of the cosmos as our world versus theirs, our known, familiar places versus the their unknown, terrifying outside, mythology and the archaic in religions tend to reproduce the divisions internally as well, within cultural totalities.[41] Differences of sex, skin color, hair texture, or some other visible particulars usually become fantastically coded in sensibilities and language meant to justify internally stratified and constantly reinforced social, economic, and political relations. For example, apparently sanctioned by Hindu religious beliefs, some Southeast Asian cultures provide fertile ground for such locally oriented systems of social divisions. A traditional Hindu society may be composed of racial castes: the Brahmins symbolically coded White, the Red Kshatriyas, the Yellow Vaishyas, and the Black Shudras. Then there is the lowest of the low, the Dalit, the Untouchable.

The order and hierarchy vary from one society to another, from culture to culture. But in whatever order, the racial categories produced in archaic religions claim to describe the "nature" of members of a given society, and the descriptions are always aimed to be both material and moral.[42] The descriptions are usually materially justified by appeal to oppositions presumed to be visible between male and female, day and night, right and left, and, ultimately and by just a little stretch, the moral and the immoral. That these supposedly natural and metaphysical binaries are felt to require replication in social relations helps to account for the apparently culturally universal constructions of essentialities that, in turn, regularize hierarchies of values and norms presumed guaranteed by natural law. As these binaries touch on racial and sexual hierarchies, Sartre and de Beauvoir's works show how non-neutral were their origins in the exercise of social identity. In the "racing" and "gendering" of individuals, one faction in society supposes itself judge on the scope of the freedom of the other. The facts of race and sex, as we call them, for Sartre and de Beauvoir are facts-as-interpreted. Because for them race and gender are social signs and sites of struggles about individual freedom, we can see in what sense it is possible to claim, as Sartre's metaphysics of freedom does: Hell is the other. In *Black Skin, White Masks*, Frantz Fanon recounts, "You are in a bar in Rouen or Strasbourg, and you have the misfortune to be spotted by an old drunk. He sits down at your table right away. 'You, African? Dakar, Rufisque, whorehouses, dames, coffee, mangoes, bananas.' You stand up and leave, and your farewell is a torrent of abuse."[43]

The more modern-scientific and empirical approaches to the conflated questions of racial and cultural differences dates to 1653, in a schema developed by the Dutch mapmaker Georg Hornius and included in an atlas published by Jan Jansson. On the map one finds a tripartite division of human species: the Yellow Semites, the Black Hamites, and the White Japhetites.[44] Hornius's atlas is notable because it includes a seven-sheet spread of Palestine (*Iudaea*), an older Peutinger table of Roman roads, and an explicitly racial geography of the territories. In these productions, particularly in the introduction of the geographical spirit in racial and cultural anthropology, the fields of scientific raciology progressed beyond what the historians of antiquities like Herodotus or medieval theologians like Pliny could have imagined. Over decades in the remaining part of Hornius's geographically scientific seventeenth century, ground would be laid for the emergence of the field of natural history. In 1735 Linnaeus published his *Systema naturae*. From this, the most influential book of its kind, one learned that "Homo" was a universal stem-genus branching worldwide into four "races." Claiming to refine Hornius's system by greater attention to wider empirical evidence, Linnaeus classified the Asian as Yellow, the American Indian Red, the African Black, and the European White. Each racial type was explicitly assigned, in categorical terms, corresponding—obviously by sight—to physical, cultural, moral, and temperamental contents. Yet the physical appearance of the Yellow and White races included, for example, "black hair and dark eyes."[45]

It is tempting, at the dawn of the twenty-first century, to declare *Systema naturae* a mere historical curiosity. After all, compared to the biological sciences, "natural history" is now a quaint hobby. It is also easy to recognize but then dismiss the Linnaean system's debt to the classical Hippocratic medical doctrine of the "humors." In Greek and Roman medical sciences, the four Galenic humors were highly regarded medical facts. But in Linnaeus, as later in natural taxonomists like Kant, the distribution of the humors was mapped onto anatomically "racial" differences (eye and skin colors, hair textures, size of the nose, etc.). These racial anatomies were then correlated to presumably biologically determined bodily fluid types: yellow bile, black bile, phlegm, and blood (the Sanguine).[46] The presumed biological differences were, finally, distributed along supposedly innate mental and moral dispositions. But it would be unwise to dismiss these antecedents because they are still the "racial" territories or their non-existence, upon which, today, the genetic sciences seek to shed some light. Archaic as some of the ancient and classical categories may sound, it is indeed the Hippocratic-Galenic and Linnaean taxonomy that, residually, informs today's most influential biological thinking in the areas of racial science.[47] At the popular level, too, and in many parts of the world, including the most scientifically advanced, the Linnaean system, nearly unchanged, informs the most basic categories of race thinking in public policy debates. In the United States today, citizens are every day asked to choose self-identification by racial classificatory systems whose biological outlines are so obviously Linnaean.[48]

There cannot be a better explanation of this phenomenon—the persistence of clearly unsuccessful centuries of efforts at scientific glorification of the idea of "race"—than to see it as a result of social and cultural imperatives to produce racial hierarchies. The fact that pro- and anti-racialist sciences have come to rely on the resulting racial discourse does not negate the initial condition, within contexts of racial domination, which first produced race as a domain of scientific analysis. In addition to Linnaeus's *System*, one must note in this regard the racial biology work of Moreau de Saint-Méry, when a mathematical scheme was generated to assign racial composition to individuals of mixed racial heritage. In his *Description topographique, physique, civile, politique et historique de la partie française de l'isle Saint-Domingue*, Médéric Louis Elie Moreau de Saint-Méry, in order to calculate the scope and rate of racial mixture in what is Haiti, postulates the idea that each of the races he studied (Black and White) was composed of 128 units of (White or Black) blood. According to this rule, a *mulâtre*, for example, is composed of 64/64 Black/White units of blood. But in a context of at least eight possible kinds of basic units of racial mixture, the mulâtre is derived by this, improbable, arithmetic:

> Sacatra: 112 units of Black and 16 units of White blood
> Griffe: 32 White and 96 Black
> Marabou: 48 White and 80 Black
> Mulatre: 64 White and 64 Black
> Quarterton: 96 White and 32 Black
> Métis: 112 White and 16 Black
> Mamelouc: 120 White and 8 Black
> Sang-mêlé: 126 White and 2 Black

It is pretty easy to see the logic of 16, 32, 48, 64 on the one hand, and 2, 8, 16, 32, 64 on the other, even if, ultimately, this belief system no longer makes sense in terms of today's science of blood types, genes, or phenotype.[49]

The helpful question, therefore, is: Where did Saint-Méry's base numbers (2 and 16) come from? No other tradition of natural history, biology, or a proto-statistical science can be found in the previous centuries to match Saint-Méry's ingenuity. Does his pseudo-scientific Haitian tradition inevitably correlate with the then emerging development of histories of legal—rather than biological—arguments for the "one drop rule" of race in North America? How was this quantification requirement, in blood, measured? Doris Lorraine Garraway's "Race, Reproduction and Family Romance in Moreau de Saint-Méry's Description" presents a sanguine view of this and other kinds of pursuit of a scientific method of classification whose truth does not lie in the science. Given Saint-Méry's background in colonial jurisprudence, and his formal status as an ambassadorial spokesperson in the colony, his classification system must have aimed, Garraway argues, "to disclose" an "ideology of family romance and reproduction." Under this reading, "Moreau's racial science represents a sexual fantasy for white colonials whose libertine practices threatened the fragile demographic balance of colonial society." Thus, even when recognizing and treating as a social fact the reality of racial *métissage* in the revolutionary Haiti, Saint-Méry nevertheless "revises Enlightenment ideas about racial degeneration and infertility to arrive at an original hypothesis for the biological reproduction of colonial humanity," a humanity that "places the control of such procreation squarely in the hands of white men."[50]

If there was an empirical content to the concept "race" in the eighteenth century, I have yet to find it. The closest is in Kant, when he claims that a chemical compound called phlogiston, in the blood of some races but not others, is responsible for the varieties in the species we attribute to racial difference. We know, at least since Joseph Priestley's experiments, that phlogiston is what, today, we call oxygen. There is no empirical science that at this time claims that the oxygen in some races or ethnic groups is different from the oxygen in others. Yet, "race" is both implicitly and explicitly ubiquitous not only in Kant but also in most other important eighteenth-century texts. How does one account for this historical discrepancy between concept and content?

Genes

Most of the variation between people is to be found within any given population. But most of the variation we think of as diversity is the variation between populations. When I ask for more diversity in a classroom, I am not asking for a wide assortment of random alleles. I am looking for "racial" or "ethnic" diversity. When I look for diversity in a neighborhood, I might also be looking for variation in age, class and forms of household living arrangements, all things (I believe) unrelated to genes and all forms of diversity (I think) are important.—BARBARA KATZ ROTHMAN, *Genetic Maps and Human Imaginations*

Regarding questions about if and how to racialize current traditions of scientific practices of medicine, the journal *Patterns of Prejudice* is correct to point out the fuzziness with which established public forums like the *New York Times* address—beyond differences in skin pigmentation —the empty scientific core of "race." The genetic science of race, it seems, has not provided clear and convincing support to justify pharmacologization of race rather than, say, the consequences of ethnic inbreeding and racism, either internalized or socially and institutionally mediated. Even at the moment of giving the pharmacology a pass, a *Times* editorial bluntly, some would say courageously, states, "Race is too superficial and subjective a concept, mostly based on skin color, to match up well with any underlying genetic or physiological differences that may affect how an individual responds to a disease or a drug treatment." It is widely known, the editorialist further admits, that medical scientists "are using race as a *crude surrogate* for what they *assume* are genetic differences yet to be identified."[51] But if the concept "race" is a stopgap word in genetic research, a *temporary* measure, what—in light of the long, sometimes dark histories of race-thinking and race-making —is the meaning of this temporality? When *is* race? What time of race are we living in at this obviously dynamic temporality?

Given the fuzziness and the loud silence in the science, might today's impulse to pharmacological racialism be driven by past, better, science studies that show high correlations between race and class and inequalities in national health care? It is indeed notable that the scientific debates about race and medicine occur at a time when many in the United States, including law-making institutions like Congress, are concerned about discrepancies in medical care delivery across racial groups. In 2002 the National Institutes of Health published a study revealing that racial minority citizens systematically get inferior health care throughout the country. This appears to be the case even when there is no disparity in income and insurance coverage between the members of the minority groups and their majority counterparts. The scientists who conducted this research investigated several likely causes of the disparity but were led by the evidence to conclude that the culprit is "subtle racial prejudice."[52] The report argues, based on what it calls "indirect evidence," that doctors' medical decisions were improperly influenced by *racial perceptions*. For example, all things but racial perceptions being equal, African

Americans are 37 percent less likely to undergo angioplasty and other heart procedures, including bypass surgery, than Whites. The study also found that in 90 percent of cases in which an African American patient did not undergo the appropriate surgery, the attending doctor did not offer the possibility of that treatment to the patient. In interviews conducted with the same doctors, the researchers discovered that the doctors held "classic negative racial stereotypes," for example, *assumptions* that Black patients would be less likely to participate in follow-up care.[53] Along with many recommendations, the scientific panel concluded that the racial factor in the practice of American medicine is "a very serious moral issue."

If these congressional and Harvard University studies are to be believed, is it really surprising that Black heart patients may not be eager to subject themselves repeatedly to "negative racial stereotypes" and racially prejudiced heart specialists, or any other doctor, for that matter? It is significant that BiDil was meant to treat heart ailments. If one of the causes of racial disparity in health care is doctors' classic racial prejudice, what would be considered a "cure" for this social problem? How might BiDil contribute to improve medical practitioners' racial attitude, where such improvement is necessary for achieving parity in health care outcomes? Might BiDil, in addition to whatever positive effect it may have in the body of a given individual, become an indirect incentive for the doctor to take a second look at the patient whom the doctor might have been initially, prejudicially predisposed to overlook? Or would BiDil become merely another example of a heroic medical practice? According to the acclaimed nineteenth-century Philadelphia physician Benjamin Rush, a "heroic" medicine is one in which a patient is subjected to an uncertain but, in one way or the other, costly procedure of unknown cure (e.g., bleeding) for a disease the cause of which the treating physician is either completely or insufficiently aware. The heroism in heroic medicine is, clearly, largely the patient's.

There are a few diseases linked to climates. Malaria, for example, happens to be endemic in the Euro-Mediterranean basins (parts of Spain, Turkey, Greece, and Azerbaijan, for example), several parts of Africa (countries in the east, central, and west, but not south), Asia (Korea, Malaysia, Burma, Butan, Vietnam, Cambodia, India, Pakistan, Indonesia, Thailand, etc.), the Arab world (Saudi Arabia, Oman, Yemen,

Iran, Syria, Iraq, United Arab Emirates), Latin America (Argentina, Venezuela, Peru, Paraguay, Honduras, Bolivia, Mexico, Costa Rica, Colombia), the Caribbean (Guyana, Suriname, Solomon Islands), and the Philippines. Yet suspicions abound that malaria, and other pathologies dependent on repeated malaria inflection (e.g., sickle cell anemia), might be a racial disease. Moreover, in cases where climate and geography or historical and social dynamics have isolated populations, leading to constant inbreeding, genetic diseases have been shown to exist within ethnic or cultural groups. In almost all these cases, however, the underlying causes of the disease have not been identified, and no one suggests that the illnesses are therefore "racial," in the sense in which we indicate race by skin color.

It is ironic, if in a White supremacist society the Black body is both sign and site of experience of the racially Other, that it is considered a legitimate practice of heroic medicine to "treat" the Blackness. After all, to a race-conscious mind, to what extent is the *moral* problem of race attributable to the existence of, literally, Black and Brown bodies of humanity? If the social constitutions of the bodies of an identified racial group were thought to be one of the sources of a social problem, to what extent is it clinically permissible to target palliatives according to racial divisions, no matter how subjective and confusing the divisions might appear in the truths of the more empirically biological sciences?[54]

"Race," ethnicity, and culture—including the cultures of poverty and systemic racism—are also potent factors that determine how much stress one suffers over a lifetime and how many years of productive and enjoyable days one can hope for. And it is indeed the uneven distribution of life expectancy across racial and other social divisions that makes very appealing, to a government and doctors alike, the thought that, perhaps, there is something *racial-genetic* one should do to remedy problems in public health. If one thinks that race has something to do with genes, though one is not sure exactly how, it might still be irresistible to turn away from data even remotely suggesting the most minimal correlation between subjective racial self-identifications and medical treatment outcomes.

Thus, even without objective science, BiDil appears to have succeeded in legitimizing the science of race. Steven E. Nissen, a Cleveland Clinic cardiologist, explains: "What we're doing here . . . is using self-identified race as a surrogate for genomic-based medicine." He adds, *"I wish we had a gene chip."*[55] The dilemma facing the future of gene-based race medicine must be how to account for whatever there might or might not be of genetic causes to diseases within and across populations.[56] What are the complex interactions between ethnic and cultural habits that affect health (e.g., diet, parenting skills), the biochemistry of actual individuals (based on inheritance and personal hygiene), and empirically based generalization by other indexes, such as age, weight, height, sex, class, or other group types?

Paul Finkelman has suggested an overlapping frame of identification of the objects of research: social medical issues (e.g., diseases that are associated by poverty, diet, life style), social/genetic diseases that are connected to life-style and diet but also have genetic components, and the diseases that are purely or mostly genetic.[57] Yet this formulation leaves too much room for doubt regarding whether there is anything "purely" genetic about race.[58] Recent studies indicate that genes are not immutable, even within an individual. For example, genetically identical twins grow genetically apart as the years pass. If one's genetic code itself does not change, the expressions certainly do. This is because the chemical changes *after* one's birth "alter the way [one's] gene is expressed."[59] Research on the dynamic, historical, processes of gene expression have grown sufficiently in recent years to constitute a subfield in biology, epigenetics. In the epigenetic study of twins already cited, the authors write, "We found a direct association between the remarkable epigenetic differences observed and the age of the monozygotic (identical) twins: the youngest pairs were epigenetically similar, whereas the oldest pairs were clearly distinct." The study concluded that "environmental factors, such as smoking, diet and exercise, affect DNA directly."[60]

If the DNA itself cannot be environmentally neutral, this is because it is influenced, at its core, by culture and society, time and history. In addition to the obvious mutations that may occur with aging, the epigenetic processes, in themselves, are capable of profound ontological transformation, known as "drift." On that basis philosophers of biology and anthropologists have cast doubt on the idea that there might exist some universal genetic "essence" of race waiting, ontologically out there, in nature, to be discovered in an ahistorical purity. Lenny Moss, for example, writes, "When one speaks of a gene for blue eyes, or for cystic fibrosis, the gene for breast cancer, or for Marfan Syndrome . . . one is using a concept of a gene that is defined and specified by its relationship to a phenotype. I call this sense of the gene, Gene-P. What allows something to satisfy the conditions of being a Gene-P is some predictable relationship to the appearance of a certain phenotype. While defined by a predictable relationship to a phenotype, Gene P, by contrast, is *indeterminate* with respect to DNA structure, that is, with regard to specific nucleic acid sequence."[61] In a review of works by Mendel, William Johansen, and Watson and Crick, Moss explains what he thinks is at stake. "My principal interest," he writes, "has to do with how we should *now* understand the phenotype." After examining the double uses—the determinate and indeterminate employment—of the concept in the discourses of the sciences, Moss affirms that "on the basis of strictly current scientific and clinical usage . . . there are two distinctly different senses of 'the gene.'" Each usage, he notes, "discloses something about the phenotype, but . . . properly understood neither suggests that the phenotype can be decomposed down to an ensemble of genes—indeed quite the contrary."[62] This makes gene talk in contemporary culture more hyperbolic than naturalistic. The language of the "gene as program, blueprints, and the like," the sort of talk which, as Moss writes, "has been very successful in finding its way to the public ear," is a result of confusion: "an illicit conflation" of otherwise equivocal meanings of the term "gene." This is so because

to speak of a Gene-P for a phenotype is to speak as if, *but only as if,* there was a definite certain something that was transmitted between generations and that dictated a distinct phenotypic outcome. But as we've already said, Gene-P is indeterminate with respect to its physical referent. It is indeterminate with respect to its DNA sequences and so there is not a certain something that is being transmitted, but rather an uncertain something. How can this be? Would it not simply be a matter of empirically fleshing out what the structure of the physical referent would be? The answer is no. And the reason the answer is no is that what one almost always, if not always, finds in cases of Gene-P, is that it is not the presence of some specific sequence that correlates with the appearance of a phenotype, but rather the absence of some "normal" sequence resource that is at issue, and there are always many ways for something to be absent.[63]

If "gene" does not just *refer to* an absence (the state of the "non-normal") but may also *be*, in principle, an absence, then no wonder experimentalists like J. Craig Venter drew the conclusion that "race," as we know it in everyday life and in popular culture, cannot be a genomic fact.

In 2002, Craig Venter, who led the first group of researchers to complete a draft of the human genome sequence, explicitly stated, "The concept of race has no genetic or scientific basis." This, he explained, on the basis of the 2001 study, was because all "humans share 99.9 percent of their genome with one another."[64] According to the science, therefore, in the human genome, which is made up of about 3 billion nucleotides strung together in a specific order along the chromosomes, all but .01 percent is identical from one person to another, no matter the person's race, ethnicity, continent of origin, or economic and social status. The most common type of variant in the 3 billion genomic nucleotides is the single nucleotide polymorphism (SNP), which usually occurs in regions where the nucleotides are known to be doing nothing. But it is not just that the SNPs do not have any known *racial* function. The .01 percent of our 3 billion nucleotides represents an estimated 10 million whose variations track population movement rather than what we know as racial difference.[65] For example, as Hoffman notes, most so-called racial or genetic diseases, such as sickle cell anemia, are, at root, directly or indirectly malaria-borne diseases.[66]

The recent haplotype map research project, "a catalog of common genetic variants that occur in human beings," conducted across the United States, Canada, Nigeria, China, Japan, and the United Kingdom, reaffirmed findings in earlier studies, for example, that "human DNA consists of more than 3 billion building blocks whose sequences form genes, just like letters spell a word. For any two unrelated people, these letters are 99.9 percent the same. But that leaves millions of single-letter differences, called SNPs that provide . . . patterns of tiny DNA differences that distinguish *one person from another*" rather than across what we think are racial groups.[67] Moreover, for the minuscule number of genes (in the 2007 revised estimate, .07 percent) suspected to code for phenotypic variations like skin color and hair texture, no other biologically significant function can be determined. Attributing phenotypic variation to race is either inconclusive or contradictory. "A possible, in-principle explanation for why a DNA sequence does not determine a specific phenotypic trait," Moss writes in *What the Genes Can't Do*, is that "any particular DNA sequence can in itself only contribute to any number of different, and often even antithetical, phenotypic outcomes." Further, because these different and antithetical outcomes cannot be predicted, they "can never be adequate to the task of narrowing down, or specifying, which of these [outcomes] would come to be the case."[68]

Identity

If at the deepest ontological levels environmentalism, historicity, and indeterminacy also mark the essential character of DNA, what conclusions should philosophers draw as the appropriate epistemic consequences? The first, certainly, is that our understanding of ourselves even as biological organisms is conditioned by the contexts of historically contested social identities. It is also to say that questions about identity are, in turn, irreducibly culturally conditioned. Because of that conditioning, we cannot neatly separate questions arising from the science of genes from issues in identities which arise in social relations and are, inherently, not just economic (particularly in market-driven models of social relations) and political but also susceptible to ethical, normative critique. The social history of the biological science of genes cannot, a priori, claim to be politically, economically, and socially neutral.

This background provides us with a context to reopen the issues from my earlier critical observations: On the basis of biological attributes present in DNA, what scientific explanations might justify the mythical, cultural, and modern moral ascriptions (or the social and cultural distributions of values) of race to individuals and groups? Barbara Katz Rothman cautions that though "the Human Genome Project is often said to be 'mapping the human genome,' this language can be misleading because it is in fact not a map." "Map," she writes, "makes it sound like there *is* a human genome, like there is a name BARBARA that can be read, or a downtown Brooklyn that the third grade can go out and map." If individuals are clones of each other, then such a map can be drawn; if we are not, *the* map—one map that represents each and any other person's genetic landscape—cannot be drawn. Thus, Rothman concludes, "We are the same in 999 out of 1,000 DNA base pairs. That is a lot of similarity. We are different in 1 in 1,000 out of the total 3 billion base pairs. And that is a lot of variation."[69] If most genetic variation between so-called racial groups is to be found within rather than across any given racially defined groups, then genetic scientific support for racialization seems, indeed, a dead end.

This must be one of the reasons why, in 1998, the American Anthropological Association took a public stand on the issue. The social idea of race, it declared, is a cultural invention.[70] However, the organization also stated that the invented character of race does not diminish its social potency. Racial narratives serve modern societies as a shorthand for classifying citizens; for self-identifying with a chosen religious, ethnic, or transnational group; and for capturing social and cultural dynamics that otherwise might appear even more mysterious. The idea of and ideas about race have produced a variety of consequences. These consequences range from the benevolent and benign to the malevolent. "Race" has both promoted and destroyed the self-respect of groups. It has promoted both solidarity and clashes within and across otherwise relatively stable societies. Race consciousness has been a tool for both negative social prejudice and discrimination and positive, affirmative remedies against prejudice and discrimination.[71] Yet, because popular racial beliefs tend to fuse together behavior and physical features, they invariably impede development of better explanations for individual biological variations and social behavior. We can see why, far from denying the cultural, social, political, or economic salience of race consciousness, twenty-first-century cultural and social anthropology affirms the empty biological concept of race precisely because the sciences want to better understand race's real foundations in social relations and in history.

One of the most serviceable social and historical theories of race remains the one proposed in twentieth- and twenty-first century economic and political theories. From Georg Simmel and Robert Park in sociology, Sartre and Fanon in philosophy, and Zigmunt Baumann in cultural analysis, we have come to appreciate how difficult it is to think "biological" race without the economic, social, and political racialism (i.e., the belief—the ideology—that races exists and, as in various regimes of apartheid in Africa and North America, should be segregated). Because of racialism, it is also difficult to think race without thinking racism. Because of past political and social racialism and the accompanying racism, one can be certain that even where it is known that the material content of the concept "race" is physically arbitrary or entirely naturalistically empty, the word "race" persists. The persistence can be rationally accounted for *because* the concept appears to retain its social, political, and historical ideological power. It is an ideology that enforces itself as a norm that both encodes and fuels multivalent ideological struggles. The intersections of these struggles around normative race with class, gender, and postcolonial issues have been widely explored in contemporary critical theory. We can be certain that race exists wherever there is the social will to enforce it by those who also have the means to enforce it.

Where such will to race triumphs, it both organizes—and distorts—social relations. I this sense Robert E. Park was correct to argue that race "is a name for relations that exist between individuals conscious of racial differences."[72] Similarly, in a more recent empirical comparative study, *Race in Another America: The Significance of Skin Color in Brazil*, Edward E. Telles notes the existence of a consensus in current sociology, namely, that "race is a social construction" which "exists only because of racist ideologies."[73]

Beliefs in the existence of races are thus embedded in social practices, giving the social and cultural concept a great influence in worldwide social organizations of power.[74] It is this sociological and cultural reality of race—the normative system of culturally and socially anchored racial systems of beliefs—that current theoretical issues (in philosophy, critical legal studies, and sociologies of race) can best illuminate. These critical projects justify themselves by the fact that, regardless of the verdict of the natural sciences about races, these verdicts are unlikely to diminish race's strong sociological and cultural power. Moreover, owing to the supreme linguistic manipulability of the concept, the idea of race can be counted upon to change and adapts itself successfully in diverse environments, wherever there exist a will to racialism and racial prejudice (a "white" person in Brazil or Jamaica may be "black" in the United States; a "white" person in the United States may be "colored" in South Africa; a "white" South African may be "brown" in Brazil; and so forth).[75] To conceptually transcend race through critical understanding of its conceptual motility is thus to unmask race's claims to all kinds of empirical and normative legitimacy; it is to hope that, by thinking through the permutations of the idea, damage done to individuals and social identities in the name of race may be judiciously exposed.

In critical theory, not even the pharmacological practices of racial medication can ignore the fundamental conceptual issues associated with the underlying biological science. How one understands what is being treated in the medical treatment of race—genetic or epigenetic, nature or nurture, or biology or society—is relevant. After all, science is not satisfied if all we know is that a medicine "just works." Even in cases where the interest in knowing should be deemed subordinate to the imperative of healing, the scientific questions cannot be considered marginal to the requirements of, say, philosophy and history of science; nor can it be claimed that the sciences *themselves* are beyond race and its problems. In this approach to racial pharmacology, we may be left no choice other than to conclude, following Joseph Margolis, that critical theory cannot "for a moment concede that correspondentism works in the physical sciences. . . . Even in the physical sciences, where the would-be laws of nature are said to be formulable in extensionless ways, it is reasonably clear that their acceptance depends on idealizations that cannot be easily reconciled . . . with severe constraints that naturalizing would impose."[76]

ETHICS OF THE UNIVERSAL

Pursuit of objectivity in both the physical and the moral sciences regarding race is predicated on a capacity for an ethics of critique. But this is an ethics menaced from several sides by false universalism. False universalism is achieved by bad generalizations from individuality to type. We see this most vividly in current ideological theories of culture clash. In *The Class of Civilizations*, for example, under the guise of universalizing, Samuel Huntington's seemingly accurate observation about the "double standard" readily degenerates into confusion between universal*ism* and universal*ity*.[77] He complains that "hypocrisy, double standards, and 'but nots' are the price of universalist pretensions" when "democracy is promoted but not if it brings Islamic fundamentalists to power; nonproliferation is preached for Iran and Iraq but not for Israel; free trade is the elixir of economic growth but not for agriculture; human rights are an issue with China but not with Saudi Arabia; aggression against oil-owning Kuwaitis is massively repulsed but not against non-oil-owning Bosnians."[78] With this mischaracterization of the "universal," the solutions offered to contradictory plurality in values (double standards) becomes a theory of impregnable "zones" of difference. Akeel Bilgrami, among others, responded to this challenge.[79] In "The Clash within Civilizations," Bilgrami shows what a false universalism looks like up close when he refuses to elevate the historical "other" (the neighbor deserving of ordinary dignity) to the Other (a quasi-sacred object of worship or fear; a superior object of envy and resentment; an inferior object of pity). This refusal of the political psychology promoted in the name of a doctrine of a clash of cultures was necessary because the doctrine is preceded by what Dieter Senghaas calls an idée fixe: it requires justification by an unacceptable political theology.[80] Rather than mediate—analyze, understand, explain, or debate and negotiate—existing differences on historical grounds, guided in all that by ascertainable interests, the political theology which underwrites the false universalism of a clash of cultures must resort to a default mode of ethnic relations: chauvinism. Rather than produce accounts of histories of cultures and civilizations, the false universalist, preferring the language of conflict and war, apocalyptically appeals, in the name of an ahistorical metaphysics of History, to a unipolar and hegemonic construction of an idea that must then be made to triumph and supervise the meanings and conceptions of any and all cultures and histories of peoples.[81]

The latter-day metaphysics of History is a far cry from the traditions of political theories familiar to us from Locke and Rousseau, or of their synthesis in Kant. In the name of an antiliberal liberalism, the Enlightenment hope of "perpetual peace" is put to an extreme test. When Kant asked, "Is the human race continually progressing?," he sought to reconcile the strife and discord inherent in the human condition (humanity, Kant famously wrote, is a "crooked timber") under the fate of an open-ended, not closed, moral imperative. Surely, Kant's political morality recognized the inevitable: "Man has gregarious inclinations, feeling himself in the social state more than man by means of the development thus given to his natural tendencies. But he has also strong anti-gregarious inclinations prompting him to insulate himself, which arise out of the unsocial desire (existing concurrently with his social propensities) to force all things into compliance with his own humor; a propensity to which he naturally anticipates resistance from his consciousness of a similar spirit of resistance to others existing in himself." But Kant also took for granted the moral requirement that, though society and civilization owe everything to the natural conflict, the moral humanity, in society, becomes more than the natural human in nature. Society awakens in humanity "all the powers of man" by driving this man "to master his propensity to indolence, and in the shape of ambition—love of honor—or avarice impels him to procure distinction for himself amongst his fellows." But further yet, society is only "the first steps from the savage state to the state of culture, which consists peculiarly in the social worth of man: talents of every kind are now unfolded, taste formed, and by gradual increase of light a preparation is made for such a mode of thinking as is capable of converting the rude natural tendency to moral distinctions into determinate practical principles; and finally of exalting a social concert that had been pathologically extorted from the mere necessities of situation into a moral union founded on reasonable choice."[82] This idea of "reasonable choice" implies a morality and agency that cannot be reduced to the results of acts of coercion or brute force by authoritarian, colonial, or imperial states.

4

Languages of Time
in Postcolonial Memory

The past is something we can never have. We can only represent it.
—JOHN LEWIS GADDIS, *The Landscape of History: How Historians Map the Past*

COLONIALISM AND HISTORY

In December 1949 a controversy erupted when J. H. Huizinga, a brilliant Dutch journalist, returned from an important assignment: an eight months' commissioned tour of Africa as a special correspondent for the *Manchester Guardian* and the *Nieuwa Rotterdamse Courant.* Huizinga's return from Africa was controversial because, apparently well aware that he was being provocative, he "attacked the principles, the policies, [and] the aims of the various European rulers" of Africa. Studying the journalist's report more than half a century later, what strikes the reader about the controversy the report must have caused is how startlingly counterintuitive the so-called attack on colonialism is. Huizinga writes, "West

African Home Rule means Self-Government, Self-Government means Secession, Secession means the end of Western culture."[1] Thus, against the nationalist movements in Africa which advocated cultural decolonization, political sovereignty, and popular democracy, the controversial report hailed instead the "political maturity" of British colonial rule in, among other places, the Gold Coast.[2]

The maturity of British colonial rule in Ghana, Nigeria, Kenya, and Zambia, by Huizinga's account, was in stark contrast to what the author describes as the "backwardness" of the occupied peoples of West, Central, and East Africa. In light of that difference—maturity versus immaturity—between the colonizer and the colonized, Huizinga claims that he has no choice but to defend "the very unfashionable cause of colonialism." Then, curiously, he takes pains to explain why he doesn't think of himself, and fears that others might misunderstand him, as a racist. "If I show myself from the outset a defender of . . . colonialism," he writes, "I do so not on *racial* but on *historical* grounds."[3]

What sense can one make out of his conceptual disjunction of race and history? Is race-thinking unhistorical? Was colonial history nonracialized? Assuming that a decoupling of the concept of race and of history in the colonial—particularly colonial African—contexts is at all possible and also desirable, what idea of history is at work in Huizinga's kind of colonial judgment?

In this chapter, in addition to the above questions, I discuss these: What idea of race underpins Huizinga's (and other writers') colonial conceptual maneuvers? What were the existing bodies of background historical and anthropological knowledge from which were derived Huizinga's and similar colonial explanations of history and international politics in the culturally conflicted contexts? By what authorities were these explanations considered analytically scientific, scholarly, and therefore expressions of objective, "mature" political judgments? By giving Huizinga's theory of colonial history the benefit of conceptual doubt, at the end of my exposition the reader shall be able, I hope, to address these ancillary topics: What is the right kind of material history—that is, culture and civilization—necessary for a people's national self-determination? What wrong kind of history, or a particular theory of presumed absence of history, renders a people suited for colonization?

A significant strand in classic postcolonial theory, as an academic discipline, stakes its reputations on questions raised by colonialist historians and writers such as Huizinga. The subjects of critical postcolonial theory therefore invariably lead to a reopening of the material lives and the intellectual resources of the colonial archives—in Africa, Latin America, Southeast Asia, and the Arab world. In a dialectical fashion, the general contexts of the emergence of postcolonial critiques of the modern idea of history can thus be easily understood if the reader has any familiarity with recent works by scholars whose specialties in the humanities and the social sciences study the adventures of European states in many parts of the world. Cumulatively, even in the midst of their diversity in terms of geographical and cultural formations, the body of writing in the anticolonial framework presents an embodiment of an image, a spirit of an age: the Postcolonial Age. Within the discipline of philosophy this age carries within itself particular kinds of dissatisfaction with, but also attempts to reenchant traditional theories of colonialism, since the traditional theories were ambiguously tainted by racist, capitalist, and ethnocentric issues of "maturity," culture, democracy, progress, modernity, and so forth.

In contrast to traditional theories of colonialism, critical theory in the postcolonial age, in its many facets, carries forward the promise of emancipation embodied in aspects of the Enlightenment and modernist discourses. But it also seeks to hold the processes of modernity and the European-inspired Enlightenment accountable for the false conceptual frameworks within which they produced, for example, the idea of history as something in the name of which peoples outside of the narrow spheres of Europe appeared to many of the European states as legitimate objects of capitalist enslavement, political conquest, and economic depredation. It is in these dual intentions that the *critical* element in postcolonial theory is to be understood. It is only this understanding of postcolonial theory that can adequately elucidate how one might rethink the idea of history not just from the point of view of the colonizer but also from the perspective of the experiences of those subjected to colonization in the name of history.

The postcolonial task in theory thus requires, and in fact is the conceptual correlate of, a historical consciousness more rigorous and more attuned to the vernacular languages of history. There is no way that the critical memories and the emancipatory imaginaries deriving from the enduring consequences of colonial injury can be ethically discounted from such critical theory of either colonial or postcolonial history. The project—and prospects—of critiques in the postcolonial vernacular thus make more explicit and more multiple the meanings embedded in what, already, passes as studies of history in the modern experiences of colonial conquest. It is from the point of view of elucidation of the vernacular historical consciousness that the spirit of postcolonial critique enables one to ask fresh questions about what, for other kinds of conceptions of histories, might otherwise be unquestioned standards of historical objectivity and universality.

Of course, some will point out that historical conceptions of Africa by journalists have changed since 1949. It will also be said that conceptions of African history since the 1950s have, in the hands of the experts, changed. Writing around 1995, Steven Feierman recounts how "African history was largely ignored by the established historical profession of the United States until relatively recently. In the mid-1950s graduate students of history at Harvard, Princeton, Chicago, Berkeley, Columbia, and almost all America's other historically white universities lived in a world where the field did not exist. None of these major postgraduate institutions offered courses in the subject. In 1958–59 the American Historical Association surveyed department chairs on the major fields of their graduate students. The total number of graduate students was 1,735; the number reported as concentrating in African history was one."[4] Much, it seems, has changed since the 1950s. The question might therefore be: *What* exactly changed and by *how much?* According to Feierman:

> The expansion of Africanist knowledge in the years since 1960 has had profoundly subversive effects on general historical learning. One of the first effects of the appearance of African history (and of other history like it) in the world of established scholarship was to dissolve world history, to make it impossible to write clear and coherent narratives tying together the world's parts. But this was only the most obvious and superficial effect of the incorporation of new knowledge. Much more important has been the tension between the accustomed language in which historians construct their explanations, and the historical experiences of Africans, which cannot be encompassed by the language. Because African history breaks the bounds of historical language it

undermines general historical thought and, in the end, cuts beneath its own foundation.[5]

Some would undoubtedly praise this conceptual revolution not only because of the quantity of existing knowledge but also for the qualitative transformation in the discipline—particularly in the methods of construction and production of what counts as, respectively, objects and means of historical knowledge.

However, I can also imagine others rightly resisting to be convinced that much has been gained by moving from the position that Africa had no history to the position that this history exists but (a) it exists in languages with which history cannot account for it, (b) its language "undermines general historical thought," and (c) the insurgent histories of peoples previously theorized out of history cannot only name themselves but, after all, cancel out the basis of hope for any language that could name its own experience. In fact, we can hold these reservations because we cannot ignore the premises of Feierman's immediate concerns, namely: What was so *general* about the so-called general historical thought? What was so *foundational* about the generality in the historical thought that had previously provincially proclaimed itself the exclusively general?

No one these days seeks to find, or defend claims to have found, "purely African narratives" about colonialism or anticolonialism.[6] But to speak from a postcolonial standpoint is to raise, from definite and vernacular sites of experience, memory, and theoretical elaboration, questions about unresolved conceptual themes not only in the ideas of culture, tradition, historical progress, and modernity, but also about history writing as such. The self-critical standpoint of the vernacular in postcolonial experience and its theoretical contestations marks a point of return to the origins of ideas—such as ideas about history—a return that could never have happened, in my point of view, from the perspective of a colonially commissioned writer like Huizinga.

Writing about the peculiar conjunction of questions concerning historiography and the projects of British colonialism in India, Dipesh Chakrabarty notes that developmental or stage conceptions of history as either modern, premodern, or nonmodern were deployed to justify, first, arguments against India's independence and then, after independence, the political derogations of peasants in terms of a modernized or modernizing national elite. The body of Chakrabarty's work is an example of how accounts of both the intellectual aspiration and actual mass movements for independence in postcolonial history require fundamental revisions of the colonial narratives about universal history. The first, and perhaps most important, of these revisions consists of "at least a practical, if not theoretical, rejection" of the colonial historian's tendentious preframing of the history of peoples outside of Europe as neatly packaged and distinctly marked premodern, nonmodern, and modern.[7] In practice at least, the rejection of *this* view of history preconditioned, Chakrabarty believes, "the nationalist elite's own rejection of the 'waiting room' version" of the colonized's history, when this version of history was used as the justification for denial of self-government to the colonized.[8] The second revision is also a form of transvaluation of a colonial, modernist metanarrative of history; it understandably evolved from the nationalists' debates about the historical status of the peasant. What was the role and status of the peasant in the new nation "long before he or she could be formally educated into the doctrinal or conceptual aspects of citizenship"?[9] This second issue should be quite familiar to Africanists not only from the writings on India but also in the works of Amilcar Cabral in Central Africa and Walter Mignolo and Enrique Dussel concerning the Americas.[10] Whether one speaks therefore about Africa, India, or the Americas, what was meant when it was said that the "native," on account of history, required conquest and occupation rather than self-determination and sovereignty? What could it have meant to say that because of history the peasant was not historically ready for citizenship?

It would be an obvious mistake to think that these questions provide only frameworks of justifications of colonial and postcolonial political acts. Their issues go much deeper than their political contingencies. As Cabral knew from studies of the political behaviors of the Portuguese in Guinea Bissau, the idea of history precedes and constrains the conceptual assumptions about the political as such. It is useful therefore to try to make these assumptions—including the morality of history presumed in their political acts—more explicit. What if there is a historical self-misapprehension on the part of colonialism and its projects? What if this self-misrecognition lies in the belief that the structures of the political in the colonies must mirror key preconceived ideas, preconceptions on the basis of which a picture of the colonized society emerges as, in principle, conceptually "not ready" for history and therefore as inviting conquest by history? In what ways were the a prioris of colonial thoughts on histories of societies translated as invitations to the would-be subjects of the colonial project to suspend their political will and identity in the interests of the colonialist *concept* of history.

What could have been meant by conceptual education to citizenship? Lurking behind this question, it seems, is the problem of colonial reason in relation also to conceptions of modernity. The idea of the modern is a problem not only on account of its colonial roots or branches but also on account of conceptions of history in modern social thought. To question colonial history is, indirectly, to also question the idea of the modern. How must one rethink the colonial experiences of the modern if the so-called national elite emerge in their own right—in politics as in history writing—but in this emergence still show no adequate signs of having completed, or having adequate interests to complete, the apparently prior and required schooling in the colonizer's idea of the modern? Would such be an authentic historical emergence? What happens when a Kenyan novelist, an Indian bourgeois, a postcolonial Jamaican historian, or a twenty-first-century Guatemalan nationalist makes epistemic demands on languages of history in a manner that exceeds the confines of the norms preestablished in the colonialist's idea? What would be the appropriate languages for a postcolonial idea of history?

POSTCOLONIAL HISTORICAL REASON

Suppose we ask, in a neutral manner, What is history? The answer will not appear by a process of abstract definitions. One would come to an answer only indirectly, from the point of view of experience. For example, when we affirm a circumstance as an experience (an encounter with an object, actuality, values, or means and ends), the affirmation is usually by reason that this or that is the case. In the affirmation one brings to bear on an object or the extended world generally a glimpse of an internal dimension of mind: what one *knows* about this world and its order as experienced becomes not only a reason *for* the affirmation of the world but also makes this reason a reason *of* the world. "Experience," in this sense, is an early form of historical thought: it is the bringing to view of a world-in-time. In experience, thinking spontaneously not only brings together its own ineffable grounds as essentially subjective freedom but also foregrounds the conditions of objectivity of the things we perceive as things, the objects, and of the rest of the world that surrounds persons and things. To rethink colonial interpretations of history involves, fundamentally, postcolonially rethinking the idea of experience in relation to the history of the colonized. After all, colonialism was a disruption in actual as well as possible courses of experience of a world.

Owing to the uncertainties involved in the historical tasks of revision and reconstruction of not just objective artifacts of a world but also the subjective acts of remembering of the world, contingency is in the unavoidable structures of the reasons of postcolonial history. The great sense of time and the contingency implied in the colonial experience stems from the traumatic realization that there is no guarantee that world history can continue as an entirely coherent narrative. Were a god to give assurance from its divine view of the world that history will go on, the writing of the postcolonial rupture in experience shows that not even the gods are safe from the vicissitudes of the ordinary. This is why the displacement from traditional colonial theories of history to postcolonial critical theory of the times of colonialism and their aftermath, when the critique functions from within a vernacular register, must always present itself as a problem in *method*. Its assumptions about both the idea of history and of the science of history writing cannot be taken for granted. In fact, one recognizes in the question of method in history writing a problem beyond the domain of professional practices of the historian. The answers to the question of the status of reason and conditions of truth in historical arguments—or in any kind of attempt at representations of the past—are embroiled in metaphysical and epistemological problematics. What passes as a historical argument? What is representation? What about the past is re-presentable? How does one go about a project to rethink the idea of history as such in light of colonial memory? From what critical standpoint may the postcolonial thinker come to think history from the perspectives of those whom Edit Wyschogrod described as silenced by history?[11]

In raising these questions in the search for an adequate method, I seek to discern the contours of claims to an adequate postcolonial historical rationality. What could reason in postcolonial history hope to achieve for itself theoretically, practically, and aesthetically? Because of its relation to time and to the past, the concept of reason that functions in the processes of production of historical truths, obviously, must be thought not only in its empirical positivity but also negatively. How does one think the brokenness in language—the brokenness *of* language in postcolonial memories of time?

Wyschogrod is correct: there is indeed an ethical issue at the heart of critical postcolonial approaches to history writing; it is an ethics of memory. But because memory is not history, and history writing cannot reduce all its practices to an act of memorializing, the place of the remembered in the historian's imagination of both the crafts of history and the world of the past needing representation, not to say repair, must be seen to require negotiations of acts of memory that the living and their future generally think they owe to the dead in the name of a past. Just a few decades ago, it was not unusual to encounter works in colonial anthropology that framed its historical questions—or rather its ahistorical questions about history—in languages such as this: Do the natives think? How do natives think? Do the natives think universally? How do the natives form the Idea of the universal? ("Can the subaltern speak?," of course, was an appropriate response to those earlier colonial questions.) But all of them are haunted by a subtext, and all the questions reduce themselves to it: Are they of the same *time* as we are? All the questions, and similar others, are therefore, to begin with, anthropological provocations.

Works by postcolonial anthropologists and critical historians like Fabian and de Certeau demonstrate in what senses this attribution of the provocative can be sustained.[12] But the provocation is so particularly in the sense in which Jörn Rüsen argued that history has an eschatological feature *simply by epistemology*.[13] On account of the historian's intersubjective relationship to the past, history writing leaves open the possibility —the promise—of a transformation in the consciousness of the present owing to "voices" from the past. Yet even for Rüsen this eschatological potential has to be already implicit, or as he says, "invested in the past by the intentions, interpretations, and by the sufferings and actions of those who brought about what was the case."[14]

But in postcolonial experience, what was *the* case? If we cannot return to the writing of history as if colonialism had not sowed in itself the seeds of the subsequent rupture of that metanarrative, then as a practice, history that derives from the postcolonial vernacular must readily confess its anthropological reliance on the memory of the colonial event. The question about how best to capture that anthropological element in historical experience—the question of method in the postcolonial science of historical thought—can thus be seen in the relationships of both belonging and conflict between memory and judgment, between remembrance and truth. I think this is why Rüsen acknowledges that "the ethics of the historian's work discloses the philosophy of history as its own condition of possibility."[15] In *Verité et l'existence* Sartre, too, considers history writing an event. Event, as he defined it, appears only through subjectivities, but it is also transcendence because it exceeds every subjectivity. In fact, the event is the occasion in which to each subjectivity is revealed a different aspect of the event and of the subjectivity itself.[16] To write history from a critical postcolonial point of view— to write the worldly vernacular *experiences* of colonialism as an event— is therefore to acknowledge that one's writing was expected by voices from the past; it is to write a history of the postcolonial present as if to remake the past in the form of a promise.

Because it was in the name of history that the "native" was consigned to an ahistorical past and a colonial present, colonial reason obscures the reality of the truly universal. It forgot that no one—not even the so-called primitive—lives in the fullness of time. New Age essentialism and mystical animism notwithstanding, no culture has harnessed—except in myth—the resources to make reason or time eternal and only eternal. This does not make the nonmodern or the premodern culturally or conceptually "not ready" for history; it merely reveals the underlying truth that the world means nothing to humans—any humans—except on account of small t time, small r reason, and small h history. This is so because, in order to get around in the world structured by a past and a future, one must devise, in time, ways of identifying or categorizing experience of the world and the relations of one object to another. One must order reality based on apprehensions of events in space and time. And this apprehension is itself none other than systematization of timely representations. To represent this or that to oneself and others is thus to generalize a concept by selecting now this feature, then that feature, in order to arrive at a class, type, or mental picture that allows us to think of different things as naturally or socially, cognitively or affectively—in any case, in one way or another, meaningfully—related. This is the only possible condition for the formation of empirical concepts of objects but also of our ideas of self, time, history: the past, the present, or the future. What is true about the formation of language, the concepts of empirical experience, is even more true in the formation of a sense of time as event.

LANGUAGE AND TIME IN POSTCOLONIAL EXPERIENCE

Ironically, we can best explore the eventful processes of composition of colonial memories by looking at postcolonial historical fictions.

What conceptual issues emerge, for example, in the modern African literatures when we try to think together the necessary relations between postcolonial writing, time, memory, and history? For a start, we can assume, as hypothesis, that it is not conceptually possible to separate the problem of postcolonial history from the question of language, in this case the language of writing. This is so because the nature of language is itself a problem not only for epistemology in the abstract but also concretely for matters concerning historical representation. For example, when examining the uses of language in works that harbor postcolonial memory in Africa, it is evident that if we must isolate a common element in the works of the writers, that element should be concerned with experiences of the historical break in Africa's language traditions. In Anglophone Africa, one could think about the earliest works by novelists or poets: Chinua Achebe (*Things Fall Apart*), Ngugi wa Thiong'o (*Weep Not Child*), Christopher Okigbo (*Labyrinth*), and Wole Soyinka (*Death and the King's Horseman*). In Francophone Africa, Camara Laye (*African Child*), Cheik Hamidou Kane (*Ambiguous Adventure*), and Léopold Sédar Senghor's numerous poems and critical essays come to mind. The African writer, it seems, not only writes about African cultures as "broken" by the experiences of colonialism (and the economic forces of an ideologically cultural modernity), but also appears to experience language itself—in this case, the language of writing—as a reenactment of otherwise de-centered traditions. The writers mentioned seem to write the modern histories of Africa's traditions as a series of events—as historical process. This observation is more than the allegation that all postcolonial writings are allegories of the nation or an imagined community. Made with only the temporality of the language of the writing in mind, it is to say that the African writers' discourse on tradition, much better than some exclusive colonial scientific claims about Africa's pasts, presents itself as a site of a different kind of historical signification.

Rather than repeat the valid arguments about the national allegoricity of most postcolonial writings, I want to show how the discourses of modern African writings operate on several other historical levels. On one level, the tradition writers presumably write about, or out of, is experienced by the writer as alive—a source of inspiration and creativity. But on another level, the writer also knows that the tradition in question has been "damaged" and transformed in an irreversible manner. In fact, the act of writing is itself a mark of the time of deconstruction, transformation, and renewal. This multilevel experience of history in language is not all that peculiar to the modern African writer. Its universality is apparent in, for example, the Irish experience as represented by Yeats and the Anglo-American experience, as can be seen in T. S. Eliot. In Germany in the 1930s, Jewish writers who wrote in German knew that the tradition of Jewish writing in the German language was under a specific kind of stress: the writing tradition itself was confronted—as Hannah Arendt remembered about some of her German Jewish colleagues—by the possibility of its own extinction.[17] Thus, much like Soyinka's preoccupation in the 1960s and 1970s with issues of "transition," we can read, in a general way, in the dilemma of the African writer faced during those decades with the possibility of a useful past and a historically hopeful but anxious future, both the reason for writing and reasons for choice of a language of writing. Caught between a series of African artistic traditions in need of a modern retrieval and the exciting but uncertain future of a new and untested form of postcolonial existence, the transition the African writer had in mind must be seen as a form of work of both artistic invention and existential repair.[18]

But an act of invention or reinvention is always accompanied by an acute sense of the contingency of history. Because theirs was a time of colonialism, a time out of joint, the language to mend time itself is one through which the writers strove to invent new meanings of culture for themselves and for their societies. Among the writers mentioned, Achebe, it seems, was the first to grasp—and in a series of criticisms, aesthetically articulate—the full dimensions of the modern African sense of tradition as that which is in need of artistic healing and repair. In addition to the title of his first novel, *Things Fall Apart,* in an interview we had on January 11, 2000, he argued that writing in general is a way of weaving what he called a second handle on reality.[19] This practice would be consonant with an idea, a theoretical ideal which I elaborated earlier, of how a thinker, a writer, or an artist might go about mending a broken tradition, a tradition in ruin. Such a tradition certainly demands of its subjects a second handle—second, and perhaps third and fourth, points of view.

In his introduction to Michel de Certeau's book, *The Writing of History,* Tom Conley argues that historians, often in the name of pursuit of the shape of evidence of *a* past, end up silencing *the* past.[20] This is a significant methodological problem. Today's best historians deal with it. In addition to de Certeau, there is John Gaddis, Joseph KiZerbo, Michel Rolph-Truillot, and Dipesh Chakrabarty. In their different ways, when they explicitly write historiographically, Rolph-Truillot and Chakrabarty, for example, eloquently analyze the reasons for the unusual phenomenon: the phenomenon of historians silencing—for a second time, as it were—the past in the name of a search for acceptable scientific evidence of the truth of the past.[21] Departing from an intuitive certainty that "the writing of history can begin only when a present is divided from a past," as Conley puts it, we can explain how this apparently simple act of division also profoundly constitutes an original act of exclusion: it marks a separation between current time and past time, between the living and the dead. Once this act of division and separation has been committed—and it must be committed if the science of history, the act of writing history, will start at all—the historian begins the work of objectification. Thus, the work of writing an objective history derives its objectivity precisely from that initial act—the labor—to objectify the past. For how can one write history objectively unless the past about which one writes can itself be objectively positioned in the past, as the past? In this, though, we can see quite clearly in what ways this same objectivity has been dearly purchased. History, it seems, can occur as history only through the requirement that the historian breaks what Henri Bergson called duration—an inner experience of time—in order to posit the pastness of the past. In addition to Bergson, St. Augustine, in the *Confessions*, understood the meanings of this problem in history writing. As if bargaining with the Devil, in an initial and absolutely necessary methodological act to divide and separate the past and the present, the historian finds the past, but only by repressing it: the past is *not* the present.

The ideal task of the scientific historian thereby appears heroic. On one hand, in order to be able to objectively attribute meaning to the past, the past both must and cannot be present. It is only by establishment of the boundaries of this time that the historian is able to legitimate his or her interpretation of evidence as recovered fact. Without this time-boundedness no *history* of the fact can be produced. And it is precisely in this act of production of histories of facts that the historian justifies his or her commitment to a profession, to a science of the past. Scientific representation allows the past to emerge as, literally, a different time.

For the rest of society, however—and without denying the objectivity of the past as objectified by the historian—it is easy to see that, because of its own paradoxes, the scientific account of the past cannot be the end of history. Even after we acknowledge the absolute requirement that the scientific historian—say, an archaeologist—must draw a line between brute facts, the evidence of the past, and the presence of interpretation, between the two kinds of time, past and present, we should ask: Can we hope, can we reasonably expect, that historiography itself will also be able to address every silent and murmuring aspect of truth about the past in history? If we cannot unequivocally answer yes, how do we explain *that* other fact: the fact that precisely when, to borrow from de Certeau, the historian advances "a sense of loss" (the past is not present) the historian also must "immediately fill the void" (here is the past)?[22] These and similar questions, constantly encountered in the mature works of many professional historians as well as literary critics,[23] partially account for the insistence with which I pressed Achebe along the line of his insight, the insight regarding the historical significance of fiction in postcolonial histories of Africa. The answers Achebe offered then were even more pointed than the earlier ones: "If art may dispense with the constraining exactitude of literal truth," he said in a reprise of an argument he had developed elsewhere, "it does acquire in return incalculable powers of persuasion in the imagination." Art, he said, is the human "effort to create for oneself a different order of reality from that which is given to one; an aspiration to provide oneself with a second handle on existence through the imagination."[24] These observations may apply, of course, to almost any writer anywhere, or in any discipline, such as history, in which the science of writing is also an important art and craft. In fact, Achebe admits that it is hard to imagine humans—individuals or collectives—who do not periodically inhabit, for all sorts of reasons, instrumental and noninstrumental, worlds that are make-believe. One is therefore justified to want to know, as I did, what about his remarks were so peculiarly African.

I started the interview with an intuition that, for one interested in the philosophy of modern African history, African fiction seems to be a privileged place to understand the most recent historical experiences of the people. But whether or not a philosophy of history—that is, a systematic reflection on the rationality of history—can also be developed out of modern African lives in fiction is a question I thought and still think worthy of a theoretical exercise. If you ask "How fiction?," I would answer: Because, as has been precisely put, in its function as a second handle on reality, fiction appears to allow a disabled tradition, a broken time, to appear at another level of consciousness as intense, if suspended, history. Yet, how does one historically think this suspension—a fictional suspension of the historical? What does the thought of history in fiction tell us about suspended histories of peoples, traditions, societies, and cultures in modern Africa, including Africa's experiences of its own past? Although each of these questions is, in its own right, riddled with layers of complexity, I can say that, cumulatively, the questions—with relative freedom in the selection of the literary authorities in the address—are in search of a fundamental distinction between questions of history as (scientific) records of facts about the past and history as a source of wisdom about the meaning of time. Whereas the first idea of history aims at establishing truths about past events, the second aims at recovering a wisdom of experience. Whereas in questions of truth one expects or demands a fidelity to facts (what Ranke called the *wie es eigentlich gewesen*, the event as it happened), the search for a meaning of an experience (what I have called the wisdom of history) is, to the contrary, a search for hidden reasons why, beyond habit, a historical tradition might be deemed worthy of transmission. Thus, whereas fiction may be an unreliable guide to the first form of history, it is a privileged place for the discovery of the second idea: the African fiction allows one, I think, to extend the problem of truth in history from questions about recovered facts of the past to the issue of tradition as in itself a form of historical experience.

But the question must be asked about the sense in which one might consider modern African fiction as a form of experience of tradition in history writing, if fiction prides itself not in facts and literal truths but, precisely, in make-believe. An explanation of this apparently odd situation must rely on the distinctions I established earlier: fiction asks one to suspend belief, and for this reason it is essentially suited to understanding the modern experiences of the African traditions. Consider these issues: Who can believe some of the truths about the colonial experience, from racial slavery through the colonial atrocities in the Belgian Congo to decades of apartheid in South Africa? How can one believe the horror of the many national wars for self-determination—including the one I barely survived as a child, the genocide which was aimed to stop it? The truths about these facts read like fiction, like horror films. Similarly, on what grounds must one commit to believe the factual claims to truths represented in the "traditional," precolonial African cultures, when these are traditions and cultures some of whose failures—in the face of racially self-whitened and ethnocentric versions of modernity, including projects of colonization—were spectacular? It could be argued that, in reframing these facts of history and their subjective impacts on experience in the form of fiction, even the most unbelievable of them is given a second chance at credibility. The persuasive power of the literary imagination renders accessible the wisdom of that which might be, literally, beyond belief. As I said earlier, whereas truths invite one to believe in facts, wisdom is a form of trust in one's own—particular, historically locatable—forms of experience. This kind of trust cannot be called naïve: it's already chastened.

So, without denying that it is in the truths of facts about the past that the science of history must emphatically acquire its cognitive authority, in the case of the search for meaning in histories whose courses were horrifically disrupted, or a tradition whose truths fell apart, it seems entirely consistent to ask not about the truth of history in fiction, but about the reasons why a writer might have no choice but to make a life of writing out of historical materials that are both less and more than truth.

In the case of the modern African writer, this reason is obvious: writing is a process of imaginative recovery and affirmation of the very idea of history as a form of existence.[25] As such, modern African writing circumscribes the possible answers to an unspoken, universal question: Why trust *any* form of narration of individual or collective totality? Why trust the terms of recovery of a decentered, dispersed account of a historical experience? Why trust that traditions or cultures whose violation was so obvious in the colonial experience were ever worthy of confidence? To the extent that these questions are answerable, the works of modern African writers do not necessarily justify the past: it is a past whose own reliability the writers are themselves often the first to put into serious doubt. But the questions do allow one to estimate the value —metaphysical, epistemological, moral, and aesthetic—of writing itself as an act of mending not only an individual's memory, but also the historical self-understanding of a people, a culture, or a tradition.

For those who inhabit it, that a tradition may be dispersed or diasporic merely heightens for the people a need to determine a sense of their history. This is why, it seems, the most important aspects of African writing as a process of cultural re-memorialization of selves and societies can be found in the experience of the languages of the writing itself, for it is in language that both time and memory are made the most manifest. What happens when a culture's tradition breaks down? Well, one could say, history reveals in a remarkable way *its own* constitution as contingency, and it is then that the meaning of time is most obvious. In fact, it is doubtful whether one may appropriately speak of history, any history, prior to such an experience of brokenness in time. By revealing the broken nature of time, the language of the ruin points out the truth of the normal time of normal experience when cultures have elaborate mechanisms for provisioning their subjects with a sense of continuity in experience. All cultures thrive through maintaining for themselves and their people a kind of virtual continuity of experience. What is arguably equally virtual is a history achieved seamlessly through vicarious enactment of forms of real or pretended self-dispersion, or national and historical catastrophes.

In the cases of modern African literature, the enactments of time are often ritually, which is to say rhythmically, structured around the culture and cult of seasons. The cult itself is predicated largely on the dictates of a conception of nature. (That is why it is easy for some to think that a cyclical conception of history is exclusively "African," or exists only in "primal" cultures. But this is hardly the case—unless, of course, all cultures of the world are, in addition to anything else, also African or primal. It is truer to say that it is on account of contingency—on account of time—that any people, any culture, must constantly wrestle with nature in view of establishing a coherence in experience, the sort of coherence usually associated with identity, whether individual, social, or historical.) That one not only instrumentally, pragmatically, adapts but also symbolically, even magically, mimetically borrows from nature a "story" or stories about the self, other, and the world is a fact about cultures, any culture. Among Christians, for example, a year may comprise the birth of God's son (the result of a miraculously immaculate encounter of God's angel and a virgin) at Christmas; then follows the agony and horrific death of this Son on a Friday impossibly called Good; and finally a triumphant return of the Son from the dead: an act of triumph over death-as-such as an inauguration of the possibility of Eternal Life. If many of these claims to a divine plot sound too abstract (or, from a historian's point of view, empirically problematic, beyond belief), they are nonetheless also a historically powerful narration of time: the times of existence of humans, nature, and God.[26] The historical power of the Christian story is evident in such facts as that, in the cycle of a year, on every seventh day of the week, usually Sunday, the outlines of a theologically sanctioned ritual murder is reenacted, and what looks to a complete outsider like symbolic cannibalism is permitted. What better nourishment for the weary traveler through history than the body and blood of a self-sacrificing god? The Christian sense of movement or progress through time—the idea of the Christian as a pilgrim on earth— is enacted in these recurrent celebratory procurements of otherwise horrible and ghostly acts of scapegoating, suffering, and terror presented as, and in service of, ritual acts of love.

That is the way it is only because rituals are the mechanisms through which a tradition invents a human community. It is also the medium through which a tradition or community manages its own history by framing its experience as a flow in time. Within this background one can understand the breakdown of history that a tradition may suffer. One can also understand why it is precisely in the ruin of such a tradition that the meaning of time and the reasons of history may become the most obvious. One may also, finally, understand why this or that detail of the ritual or tradition can become unimportant: these are not matters of fact seeking credence, but of wisdom in search of trust. In non-Christian cultural schemas it may not be an angel and a virgin meeting, but an animal and a human, a man and a woman, or even a "coupling" of ideas like necessity and plenty. What is common to all, however, is the human need to repair the brokenness of time, to articulate an existence that must be lived in temporal crises, and thereby redeem humanity from an Original Fall. Modern African writing shows that it is precisely these serious pretend enactments of cosmic existence in the quotidian that were shattered through a series of catastrophes of tradition. What the writer in such a tradition is obliged to do cannot be—as for a Christian theologian, for example—merely a celebration of history. The writer must first establish, or resolve, the question of whether or not there is a history at all to celebrate. Writing in this context is done in dread and anguish, even despair, because the terms of the conflict concern the conditions of the possibility of experience itself.

That this is the situation of key colonial and postcolonial African writing is obvious from the materials. Recall, for example, Wole Soyinka's *Death and the King's Horseman.* The drama in the play is precisely about a metaphysical order that is put into question when a colonial authority intervenes to prevent a ritual process that it understands as murder. The confusion that follows would clearly occur if, comparatively, a foreign army intervened to prevent the pope or the queen of England from celebrating Mass because, it feared, the social order may not tolerate the story of the judicial execution of a god's only son. For the postcolonial writer, the crisis of this and similar sorts of colonial intervention—and disruption, in this case, of a Yoruba social and cultural enactment of a historical rhythm dictated by or attributable to life itself—raises questions of loss beyond this or that event of tradition. Its essential questions concern an act of time and tongue. The literal and symbolic colonial interruption interdicts many of Africa's and other peoples' religious, social, and cultural proclamations of history by inauguration. The past is not present: here is the past. In this interdiction we ought to recognize a metaphysical speech act violently interrupted. What is put in question is the existential coming-to-form of a world itself. What is threatened is not one man's or woman's farm, a day's work, or a day's joy: it is the very construction of a sense of home on earth, no matter how transient, that has been forcibly rendered, however momentarily, ritually impossible. In Achebe's as in Soyinka's imagined traditional communities, it is no wonder that massive, spectacular, and otherwise unaccountable anxiety about chaos ensues whenever there is this type of ordinary cultural misunderstanding between Africans and Europeans.

HISTORY AND THE POSTCOLONIAL EVENT

Speaking specifically about Achebe's and Soyinka's works, these observations hardly need additional arguments for their support. Culture, for these modern Nigerian writers, is the triumph of time and meaning over death, of fragile harmony over chaos, and of chastened beauty over the ugly in nature or social experience. This, I think, is why Achebe might write, in the *Anthills of the Savannah,* "The story is our escort; without it, we are blind." When asked, "Does the blind man own his escort?," the answer is obvious: "No, neither do we the story; rather it is the story that owns and directs us."[27] In the poignant scenes that constitute a "Hymn to the Sun" in the same book, the emphasis which lends the poetry of the hymn stylistic depth and pathos revolves, without question, around the protagonist's articulate need "to tell the new grass of the savannah about last year's brush fires."[28]

Writers in other colonially "stressed" cultures often faced or face the forms of historical crises of traditions which emerged for them in experiences parallel to those of, say, the African Achebe. Consider Palestine. From Moses and the Old Testament prophets to the writers in Germany of the 1930s, we see various kinds of Jewish responses to a series of challenges that presented themselves as threats of loss of traditions. Arendt thinks that this kind of loss was not the loss of one or two aspects of a ritual to a Gentile influence; it was, rather, the threat that a tradition, similar to that of Achebe's Igbo, though alive in the people it inhabits, might nevertheless become incapable of transmission.[29] Although a tradition in crisis might experience itself in fragments—as remnants of a once organic form of life—it is also aware of its irreversible standing as a catastrophe of history, and as thus requiring a general language, a historical frame, to explain itself to itself. These questions take on importance, and their resolution a sense of urgency, because they go to the philosophical bottom of experience: What is truth? How does one celebrate a tradition whose sense of time and history has been shattered? How does one conserve a culture essentially defined by acts of violent dismemberment, exile, and diaspora?

From a comparative framework, Kwaku A. Gyasi notes, "Many great literary figures have, at one time or another, expressed themselves in tongues other than their own."[30] Speaking specifically about Kafka, Gyasi notes, "If Kafka, a Jewish intellectual living in Czechoslovakia and one of the few Jewish writers who spoke fluent Czech, Hebrew, and Yiddish, wrote in German, he never forgot the influence of his mother tongue on his other languages. In one of his journals translated into French he writes: 'Voyez-vous, je parle toutes les langues, mais en yiddish; See, I speak all the languages, but in Yiddish.'" Similarly, Gyasi points out that "Nabokov, Borges, Conrad, and Beckett wrote some of their major works in foreign languages," emphasizing that "these bilingual or multilingual writers continually confront their work in terms of what else it might be, and in fact, what it has to become when their works are translated into other languages."[31] These observations return us to the question I posed to Achebe: Is there anything all that unique in the experience of bilingual or multilingual postcolonial African writers, within Africa or elsewhere? Gyasi's own position on this question is well worth repeating in full because of its conceptual affinity to the hypothesis I assumed at the outset of this chapter:

> While the Nabokovs, the Conrads, and the Becketts who choose to write in a foreign language are few and far between, writing in a foreign language is a common plight for the many African writers who decided to "discard" their native languages in favor of that of the erstwhile colonizer. While the Becketts and the Conrads do not have to deal with the power relations that govern languages, while their choice of language may not be governed by a situation of diglossia, and while they may not be bothered by identity crises when they choose one language over the other, or when they express themselves in different languages, African writers, because of their past or present circumstances as (de)colonized persons, have to live and deal with all the difficulties, contradictions, and alienations in their use of language.[32]

It is the texture and tone of these difficult experiences—the contradictions and the alienations, but also the fruitful tributaries and fertile issues—that I will closely examine.[33]

Gilles Deleuze and Félix Guattari also studied Kafka and language, and their analysis provides some entry points into a closer scrutiny of the situation of language in a postcolonial setting. Under the notion of "minor literature," Deleuze and Guattari argue that Kafka's literary style shows how a new literary genre can transform its dominant linguistic and generic environment. What results from such transformation, they say, is not merely an extension of the dominating literary environment; rather, what develops is an essential mutation, an innovation which, though mutating from and innovating upon the older and generic, is radically new enough that only designation as a different tradition can successfully characterize the difference. Thus, this is a mutative constitution of a new literary tradition which, though minor in relation to the larger historical and cultural contexts, is nevertheless subversively self-standing. In this view, Kafka's work should be recognized not just as a German-language work but also in its constitution of the Jewish German as a nomadic minor. Kafka's work hence dislocates and relocates itself distantly enough in relationships with the larger, dominant, German-language environment, to a point where this Jewish German work's character, on its own, is able to make the dominant German take "flight on a line of escape."[34]

To a great extent, I can compare this reading of Kafka to what I believe about Achebe's postcolonial writing. To borrow from Ranajit Guha: both are intellectually insurrectionary.[35] I can also draw the analogy in another way: Kate Cook, among others, has good reason to judge that Achebe's fiction offers the reader "an alternative function of history and storytelling."[36] Finally, when Deleuze and Guattari say that in Kafka's writing, his use of the Czech language stands as the vernacular (or rural), the Hebrew as the religio-mythical, and Yiddish as the nomadic, we can conclude that, strictly speaking, it is obviously Yiddish which "de-territorialized" German. By its insurrectional motility, Yiddish dislocates and reworks its own and the German tradition by a tactile relocation. All the resulting literary constitutions—for example, Kafka's so-called Prague German—may be, without too much of a stretch, favorably compared to Nigerian "pidgin." Both are dynamic versions of "ideal" languages. A successful minor literary practice thus creates a tradition—the becoming-minor—by making it possible for a writer to write as "a sort of stranger" within the major language, even when this language is *also* his or her own tongue.[37]

But the analogy ends there. It ends for at least two good reasons. First, if Deleuze and Guattari think that the dominant literary tradition is not only eased out by the decentering acts of writing minorly, but also rather explicitly takes flight in virtue of the minor's insurrection, an obvious question, at least in the case of European languages in Africa, is: Escape to *where*? Escape with *what*? The culturally and politically tactile insurgency of "broken" postcolonial languages in modern African literatures is significant but not only because of its capacity for movement. It is also significant in virtue of that which it moves.

Second, paradoxically, we cannot fail to see that, in many African contexts, when we describe a literature as minor, the presumably minor may in fact be representatively major (compare, for example, the diverse cultures, publics, and contexts of the use of standard and pidgin English in Nigerian writing, or the generic uses of Kiswahili rather than standard Arabic or English in Kenya and Tanzania). In these contexts of motility in language—across ethnolinguistic regions, economic classes, or facility in educational access to means of cultural production—one can note that when many prominent postcolonial African writers thought about their cultural freedom, they often did so in the language of *rerooting* the Africa of their experience, the Africa after colonialism, in sensibilities and epistemologies of, sometimes, nostalgically idealized real, authentic, or traditional Africa. By and large, postcolonial African literature, where we find the liberatory gestures of minoring (even if only metaphorically speaking, and also speaking about African literature in select twentieth-century European languages), it is possible that, relative to the "foreign" languages, the modern works of African literature appear to hide, within their artistic imaginary, the denotative fabrics of many and easily multiplied levels of national, sometimes nationalistic, consciousness. The minoring, liberatory practices of this kind of writing as expression of postcolonial imperatives to the modern, are representative of self-inventions which, though recognizable universally in this modernity, are nonetheless primarily forms of migrant circulations of meaning within and across communities of, literally, invented identities. Rather than just culturally *minoring* by politically inflected processes of *deterritorialization* in the strict sense of Deleuze and Guattari, modern African literature is blatantly *nationalizing* by culture and *territorializing* by politics. These observations should make us ask whether it is true that the literary inventions of modern African identities—if one closely examined the forms of invention rather than simply their claims to supposedly primordial African contents—are in themselves veiled as well as veils. We should ask if, similar to the classical masks of Black Africa, even the most authentic of modern African literature is, within is own artistic self, simultaneously conceived and concealed in explosive forms of connotations.[38]

For at least these two reasons, one could argue that it is in the considerations of the specificities of what Abiola Irele describes as African experience in literature (no one needs to argue about whether the writings constitute a tradition or multiple traditions) that we ought to discern both similarity and difference in our reading of this literature (e.g., Achebe or Soyinka) and what Deleuze and Guattari have done with Kafka's German Jewish work. What marks the languages of modern African literature—and I think it is only in terms of this way of speaking that there might exist a slight risk to believe that any aspects of, or all of, the literature's traditions may be minoring when they are not—are their capacity to speak in self-concealments and by indirections. The *tones* of such modern African usage in language and their existential expressions are just as important as the *that* in experience which either the language as such or its writing claims to express. So, on one level, postcolonial African writing is a language in movement: it is a language *in* time. On another level, however, just like the best of modern African music, such a language, literally and figuratively, composes itself and its "what" in hiddenness: it is a language *of* the movement of time.[39] Because of this dimension of the hidden in experience as well as the residue of the hiddenness even in aesthetic expressions, it would be quite accurate to assume that even the most vital meanings of modern African cultural and political experience in literature are simultaneously occult and obvious.[40]

The postcolonial experience in Africa, particularly around the issue of tongue and language use, is thus more internally complex than the pictures we have so far generated as their representations. Engagement with the literature is also, at the moment, arguably vastly more interesting than the preoccupation with most things that currently go on under

the cloak of discourse analysis. For example, in the element of lamentation over dispossession in language, a lamentation so obvious in *Decolonising the Mind: The Politics of Language in African Literature*, Ngugi wa Thiong'o recapitulates some of the key questions that, for decades,
set apart twentieth-century African debates about the relationship between the writer and language. There is at this time perhaps nowhere
else to start discussion about the materiality of writing in any Third
World cultures better than from this work.

First of all, it was dedicated "to all those who write in African languages, and to all those who over the years have maintained the dignity
of the literature, philosophy, and other treasures *carried* by the African
languages."[41] In the preface we learn that parts of the contents were
delivered as a series of lectures at the University of Auckland in New
Zealand during one of the university's celebrations of Maori Language
Week. Of his travel to New Zealand, wa Thiong'o notes, "There is a lot to
learn from the culture of Maori people, a culture which has such vitality,
strength and beauty: the vitality, strength and beauty of resistance. I was
happy therefore that my lectures on 'The Politics of Language in African
Literature' coincided with Maori language week. Long live the language
and the struggling culture of the Maori people!"[42] This, it seems, presents the problem of language-and-history as a universal problem of
minority literature. But it is easy to see that whereas wa Thiong'o writes
in English—as, for example, Eliot wrote in American-inflected English
and Kafka in Yiddish- and Czech-inflected German—it could be argued
that wa Thiong'o writes otherwise than the English. There is at least in
his latter work a clear sense of affirmation of another time, a time that
the writer affirms, even invents, in the very act of writing. This adds
layers of philosophic and artistic complexity to the work. It is as if in the
writing, the writer historically inaugurates a different order of language
and time, *a different sense of place.* (Beyond the evident elements of a
mystical, messianic, or merely aesthetic claim to other time in experience, the stereotypically modern or postmodern writer makes claims to
otherness, but as almost always altogether internal to the spaces of Europe or European cultures. Such claims do not qualify as the same as
what a writer like wa Thiong'o expects when according to his own declaration in 1986, he refuses to write any more in English.) It is on the
strength of this kind of act of writing as a form of inauguration of history

of a (post)colonized people—as other than English or French or German or Portuguese, in this case—which an inquiry into the materiality of the language of African literature must focus. It is also on this account that critics must resist the temptation to characterize the struggles with language of some modern European writers in the same terms as the struggles of African writers. Yes, the encounters of African writers with colonialism or even with European traditions of writing may be points of departure and reference for some of their complaints against history, and specifically the history of imperialism. But their own writing as a form of language of historical repair, their work as a universal expression of African and general experience of time, history, and destiny, is clearly radically located elsewhere: let us just say, simply, in "Africa" (which, I presume, is why some of them call themselves African writers).

HISTORY AS THE FUTURE OF MEMORY

Wa Thiong'o, for one, is very explicit on these matters. "If," he says, "I criticize the Afro-European (or Euro-African) choice of our linguistic praxis, it is not to take away from the talent and the genius of those who have written in English, French or Portuguese." Instead, he is "lamenting *a neo-colonial situation which has meant the European bourgeoisie once again stealing our talents and geniuses as they have stolen our economies. In the eighteenth and nineteenth centuries Europe stole art treasures from Africa to decorate their houses and museums; in the twentieth century Europe is stealing the treasures of the mind to enrich their languages and cultures.*" "Africa," he concludes, "needs [to take] back its economy, its politics, its cultures, its languages and all its patriotic writers."[43] It is quite natural that the justness of these economic, cultural, and political feelings of violation articulated around the issue of praxis of language— acts of tongue—appears as a moment in an understanding of modern history. The material themes announced were, they still are, historical problems.

I am aware that some African creative writers, not just the critics, sometimes refuse to consider wa Thiong'o's protest in its literal terms. They say that the protest is a nice "gesture" but impossible practice. They say that the formulation is too rigid and doctrinaire. They accuse the author of confusing art and life, aesthetics and economics, or symbols and what symbols are made of. They say this is a pure piece of ideology with little of art. According to an anonymous reviewer, "Among the problems with *Decolonising the Mind* is its political and ideological slant," namely, the belief that there are "two mutually opposed forces in Africa today: an imperialist tradition on one hand, and a resistance tradition on the other." The critic says that "Ngugi's worldview . . . is still profoundly Marxist" and that one must "question how useful this simple division—imperialism versus resistance—is at the beginning of the 21st century." Finally, we are told that wa Thiong'o "also focuses on art-with-a-purpose: be it pedagogic or political or helping preserve traditions or forge identities, all the literature he considers serves a purpose," so that "the simple beauty of art isn't at issue for him—in part, no doubt, because he does not want to admit that politically incorrect art . . . might still have some value."[44] One or two of these criticisms may be valid. However, a central issue hidden in the same book but which can always be poached from a close reading—for example, by reading and critiquing beyond familiar slogans—is the problem of the materiality of writing itself.

What if even the most rarified artistic expression eventually, dynamically, moves not only itself but also its significations toward the world as it is? Heidegger's luminous reading of Van Gogh's peasant's pair of shoes in *The Origin of the Work of Art* is instructive in this regard. We can see, through that reading, in what ways one can argue that wa Thiong'o's book problematizes the art of writing in the context of the postcolonial African artist's material relations to Africa's historical—often, but by no means exclusively, peasant and working-class—languages. Wa Thiong'o poses the issue of language as a problem for both art and history: as an issue of (a concept representation of) time in experience. Through these multiple levels of *Decolonizing the Mind*, one can indirectly reread many works of modern African fiction and their imaginings of history. In its wider historical contexts, wa Thiong'o's writerly voice in this book does not appear just as one person's class-conscious protest against a people's earned or unearned economic and social suffering; from one angle, the book is an African voice in time: in fact, a voice *out* of time, a time of generic global commodification of too many aspects of experience in Africa by a particular and, in wa Thiong'o's view, virulent version of "modernization." This perspective suggests that there might exist more or less hidden situations within acts of both writing and reading, situations that suggest what may be lost without a reorientation in consciousness. Wa Thiong'o's protest allows one to see, or at least ask, to what extent time and history are themselves material artifacts of concepts and language. We should understand "artifact" in this sense as both the profound and the fake, material and symbolic, or real and fetish. If we entertain the possibility that the writer's language might be artifacts of what are themselves already artifacts of time and history, then it doesn't make sense to crudely claim that *Decolonizing the Mind* is also a crude materialist reduction of the writer's language.

This hypothesis gives one a chance to think more fruitfully about in what terms it can be said that a writer's language as such is both proper/ty and alien/ated—and thus a legitimate article of trade in chains of local and global exchange. (We should understand the phrase "legitimate article of trade" in all its historical echoes.) From this point of view, if we want to disagree with wa Thiong'o analysis or with his conclusions, we ought to at least try harder to uncover the premise. We should ask, more basically: What is language? Moreover, if we do not wish to subtract the critic from the consequences of such an inquiry, we should go further and ask: What does it matter whether or not one reads a theory about the language of African writing in Portuguese, English, or French rather than in Igbo, Twi, or Gikuyu? But these are no more than extended versions of an original dilemma: How is it possible to expect that a poem or a novel can—without sacrificing itself—be a reliable source of knowledge about past events? Since we are not developing a natural science of African history (recall my consideration of de Certeau versus Achebe), is it not fairer to the literary or other critical reflections on the cultures of the Africa of this history, if the critic not only focused on the idea of history in Africa's fictions but tried (as some critics have productively done) to expose other kinds of historical entanglements of its literature? For example, there are good works on the anthropology of African literature, the sociology of the African novel, the politics of the African drama, the economics of writing and reading in Africa's country or ethnic group a, b, or c. How can one articulate, in the abstract, a metaphysics or a theory of the language of a history, when some of the material references of the history in question are unsure of their own status as subjects of science? Of what value is the history of an experience abstracted—as literature has already done—from the facts of the traditions that are, supposedly, the object of both literary recuperation and the critique of this literature? Is not the critic, in this situation, enacting in his or her own act of writing a double shift of gaze away from the thing of experience? How might the critic overcome the certain knowledge that the tradition and history which inform his or her critical questions are, so to speak, literally twice overlooked?

The feeling of unease in the face of this list of questions may of course be entirely mine. But it is also entirely the product of a context. We cannot forget, however accidental the causes of the historical encounters, that it was in the name also of history—tendentiously, the history of Europeans in Africa[45]—that African languages and cultures were confronted with a good deal of their experiences of so-called crises of modernity. Hence, one must remember the sense in which those issues that bother the fictional writer of Africa's most modern experiences are also problems for the critic of that literature. As can be seen in the case of the idea of history, some of the common conceptual problems have been deposited—like both debris and ruined treasure after Katrina-like hurricanes, except that these are non-natural events: slave trading, colonialism, cold wars—on landscapes dialectically occasioned in Africa by Europe's supposedly one and only idea of civilization, modernity, or the free market. How is it going to be possible for us to *think* both modern and Afro-historically, in awareness of the ruptures in the economic, cultural, and political experiences on the continent, while acknowledging that these experiences, often violent in the extreme, were regularly initiated and conducted in the name of a civilizing reason? Caught between Europe's knowing assertions about lack of reason in Africa and the equally European resentment of the reasons for Africa's own premodern or nonmodern histories, shouldn't an African philosopher of Africa's aesthetic modernity, as a matter of procedure, first figure out how to circumvent his or her dilemma as African *and* critic, in order to turn the apparent prohibitions deriving from his or her position into a unique source of insight? In this and in other ways, whatever the principles of method the critic chooses to rely upon, he or she is, arguably, merely conceptually mimicking the landscape of the subject matter: the landscape of Africa's history.

Modern African literature—as, today, African philosophy—was once uncomfortably hinged between the claims of European writers about Africa for European cultures and traditions of history writing, and the claims of African writers about Africa and Europe in African history writing. (Achebe's well-known problem with Conrad is one, but by no means nonrepresentative, example of this.)[46] A critique from either standpoint must take into account the African thinker's questions about both the productivity and the limits of a history and a reason in the names of which knowledge of Africa has been both generated and obscured. Then, focusing on the temporality of Africa's traditions of writing colonial and postcolonial experience, and focusing on the critiques of that writing, we can hope to discern how, more or less, the implicit rationalizations of history on both sides can become more nearly universally articulated. The result of such articulations (in empirical, historical content) as well the history of the forms of articulation (a kind of meta-conceptual history, a history of forms of concepts) can also justly be called, quintessentially, African experience.

This, it seems to me, is one way a postcolonial critique of aesthetic modernity in Africa may construct a window, the sort of thing Achebe characterized as a second handle on reality, through which we can gain a view to explain to ourselves, without mystifying the sources of our material alienation (the sort of alienation lamented by wa Thiong'o), Africa's historical landscape, the same African landscape which so frequently appears to both enchant and baffle Arab, European, African, and other subjects. Even in success, however, a reflection such as this must remain highly circumscribed. Success would consist, for example, in making known reasons why, far from the din of celebrations of postmodernity in Europe or the United States, the postcolonial African writer or critic may instead choose to insist on lamenting (to take up, again, the choice word of wa Thiong'o) a series of specific, concrete modern events. Is it possible that the writer or critic not only laments this or that loss of an African good (though these, as we also saw in wa Thiong'o, are important), but also writes the meaning of loss as such? If this suspicion is correct, it means that the critic must see in the African writer's sorrows—after the complaints about which or whose language or tradition was stolen and by whom, and assuming settlement of the question can be fairly possible—a speech reaching beyond known events of artifacts stolen, to the fact that theft has been suffered. The writer, we already agreed, mourns specific acts of violation. But should we not also suggest what appears to be the case of a stronger reason for lamentation—stronger because historically irreparable and thereby a greater loss—namely, the coming-to-aware-ness, the historical awakening to the fact, that a culture or tradition *can* be so traumatically violated?

To use an inadequate but handy example, you may see this cup broken or that plate shattered, but it is another thing altogether to conclude from these observations that transience is the nature of all objects, and that time is the broken thread structuring all reality. As materialistic or elemental as this example may sound, it is precisely *that* sort of story that the philosophic critic of the traditions of self-writing in modern African history should insist upon. The modern African writer speaks in the faces of colonialism and racism about the difficulties of projects of self-apprehension (Soyinka) or of race retrieval (Achebe); about a searching African soul (Senghor); the yearning to return to an ancestral shrine (Laye); or the maternal or paternal shrine, like Idoto, at which the writer's persona may be awakened when stitches—the stitches of time—are sewn (Okigbo). In these writers' imaginations, the act of writing is not an effort to repair this or that disposable material aspect of a tradition or culture; it is their attempt to grasp and re/write the idea of history, and do so from an all-too-human, fragile, broken, and ruined ideality of that idea in experience. If this is true, then one of the historical notes—an unremarkable remark but which we will always remember—is that the crisis of history *seems* to have been dialogically, though in some known instances also diabolically, provoked for the modern African writer by a *seemingly* unbounded experience.

I could hesitantly venture to characterize—following in the footsteps of social and political theorists like Weber and Senghor—that the supposedly unbounded experience was a result of an unremitting appearance of unreason. I could also think, from reading some of the prescient diagnoses of the issue in Hegel's *Phenomenology of Spirit* together with his *Philosophy of Right,* that more than a few elements of the appearance of unreason in Africa (and some other places around the globe) were transported by traceable excesses—some say, excrescences—fueled by a rabid version of capitalism which, at its origins in a socially expanding postfeudal Europe, created far more problems than it could solve.[47]

I can say, returning for a moment to the subject of the art of self-writing as the work, that what we regularly call the modern African experience may well be the most meaningful anguish the African writer has produced in the encounter with colonialism's forces and their questionable rationalities. I use the word "anguish" in the sense in which Kierkegaard deeply understood it: an ecstatic kind of suffering out of (a normal run of) time. To the extent, therefore, that the African writer writes his or her sorrows and lamentation about a tradition that "fell apart," about a language "stolen" to enrich the nondeserving (or at least at the expense of the deserving), and to the extent that the writer may or may not feel unsettled by the fact that his or her lamentation is expressed also in the language of the wreck or of the theft, then the critics of the writing can take a few observations for granted. First, does it matter if it was a virulent capitalist version of modernity and the comprador bourgeois that constituted the chain in the theft of the good, or the wreck of a tradition of production of such good? Certainly, wa Thiong'o laments the theft of cultural products. But he also laments and celebrates his own triumph of consciousness over the facts and the idols of the market. We can also see that the writing consciousness could have been represented by *Weep Not Child, Things Fall Apart*, or *Death and the King's Horseman*. The tradition in question could have been Gikuyu, Igbo, or Yoruba. The issues could have been framed as Nigerian, Kenyan, or simply African. Either way, the modern African writer, I think, reveals something which is already and, it seems, always a possibility: his or her work points out a reality which exists ontologically, not just phenomenologically, as a constant threat. This threat is the knowledge that time, and therefore history, is unreliable; it is unreliable because it can fail those whose experience it makes not only meaningful but even possible.

Let me conclude, then, with indications of the obvious. As is evident in the long scholarly tradition of wrestling with the question of language in African writing, to say that the African writer's historical condition cannot be seen in any better terms than the above is to admit that only the writers themselves—better than anyone standing however close but outside of the facts of the life of the craft—should be believed to be in a position to best understand the social and historical situations of the writing. The truth of this matter can be grasped in reverse. The most successful and least nihilistic of the writers, unsurprisingly, are those who, in addition to writing in languages borrowed out of turn and out of time, tried to maintain the continuity of cultural traditions by writing in the *time* of African languages.[48] Whether these experiments have meant a return to creative use of Yoruba, Igbo, or Gikuyu, or whether they are simply the heroic reassumption of a sense of flow of time in experience and through traditions by writing "broken" or "rotten" forms of English (e.g., Gabriel Okara or Ken Saro Wiwa), these experiments are scattered testaments that Africa—like other cultural regions of the world before or along with it—articulated some stories of their experiments in modernity as stories of fragile traditions broken and, however imperfectly, reinvented.

But since radical acts of self and world renewals are always caught between yearning for a recovery of the past and desire to create a future out of whole cloth, it is this tension which explains the residual and persistent concern, among some African writers, that even the experience of the violated and reinvented tradition may not be entirely safe from threat. After all, is it not the case that, in the real events, a thief may murder the individual stolen from, not because of a prior intent to commit murder but—where the thief thought no person of reason was present at the scene of the crime—as an attempt to cover up? In a larger historical frame of reference, and if modern African writing may be considered a witness to a crime scene on the continent as out of it, why is it not possible to imagine that the writing, as a work of memory, may itself be indiscriminately co-opted?

If this sounds too far-fetched, I ask that we grant it merely the status of a thought experiment. Unless one is willing to do at least that, there is little chance for us to comprehend the depth of feeling in, for example, the complaints of wa Thiong'o. If languages were mere conveyor belts on which cultural goods move spatially or temporally from one place to another, or from one generation to another, we could ask: Wouldn't any language serve for any writer? Does it matter if it is Gikuyu or French, Igbo or German, or Kiswahili or Portuguese delivering the goods—as long as goods are being delivered? Moreover, what if the "foreign" language ("foreign" in scare quotes because often the foreign language has, in reality, become as native to the speaker or writer as the supposedly authentic mother or father tongue) does the job better? Does not pragmatism or healthy respect for efficiency—economy, orthographical familiarity, printers' requirements, ready-made markets and channels of distribution—make it wise not to lament, if merely for political reasons, the surpassing of one linguistic delivery machine by another? Referred to my earlier considerations, however, one discovers that none of these arguments leads us to the formation of appropriate images for the existential and historical crisis I have tried to formulate. The inadequacy of the mechanical picture and the solution that that picture suggests confirm, by negation, my earlier diagnosis of the issue as a problem of history. For what is in crisis—but not captured in the mechanical picture of language presented—is the reality that the African "minority" language writer's more-than-normal linguistic suffering (including the political protests, if indeed they were ever merely political) is not primarily aimed against or in favor of this or that language, which may or may not have become familiar. It seems to me that what is at issue is far more complex, hence the value of the crisis as an unparalleled source of both risk and creativity for the writer.

For example, I have already drawn attention to the similarities but also the limits of similarity between the modern and postcolonial traditions of African literature and what Deleuze and Guattari theorize about Kafka's German Jewishness. Because of that limit, I have also labored to emphasize the important differences. These differences are crucial because the significant concern for the modern African writer is not whether or not his or her native language will do. The problem is instead the idea that language itself—any language—can fail the writer. Put yourself for a moment in this writer's position: assume that today it is Gikuyu or Yoruba that is on trial, but tomorrow? Could English be next? Or French? In the African writer's apparent "political" effort to conserve and renew a tradition or language, can we not hear the more profound anxiety about the fragility of every language? If one might be working to salvage the English language tomorrow, a language to which, today, one has entrusted one's inspiration and genius—"seeds," as some of the writers, especially the men, think of it—what could be more anxiety-provoking than if one did nothing, today, to rescue those languages to which one's ancestors entrusted *their* own genius and their memory? If one lacks today the will or skills to save Kiswahili or Twi, how will one know what to do when the memory in English becomes also radically confronted by history, by contingency and threats of intransmissibility? If, today, the African writer feels that by negligence or distraction, he or she is guilty of a profound act of betrayal—if one lets the spirits of the ancestors die—what claim does one have or could one make on the future generation to preserve one's memory as theirs?

Could one not say, then, that it is a historical accident—it just so happened—that it is in the failure of the languages of his or her native cultures that the modern African writer confronts the problem of the possibility that language as such can fail the storyteller? The threat at the heart of this problem for the storyteller can be simply framed as follows. One writes in English, French, or German, but how does one know that this in time will not fail to bear and transmit one's memory and the experience of a people? How does one know that one's work is not being confided to the dead rather than the living? Framed so simply, one easily grasps that beneath but through the question of language lies the problem of time and of history itself. How does one know, the postcolonial African writer seems to ask, that time will allow memory to go on?

LANGUAGE AND EXISTENCE

There is obviously a relation between language and existence, a relation whose absence raises for the writer or the cultural thinker the specter of inauthenticity. I am not raising this question of relation, as is sometimes done, in the name of "soil": the idea that a language has an authentic root in a land, a geographical territory.[49] So if it is not a relationship to soil, what is lost when a language is lost? What is feared when a tradition breaks down?

When in a broken language the vulnerability of all languages becomes made evident, or when in the loss of one tradition questions about any tradition's transmissibility are made possible, we can say that in those moments there arises a sort of recognition of history which puts speech or writing into question. In those moments the use of a language—or, if you believe some of the artists, the use of oneself by language—experiences the transient nature of tongue and of writing as well as the contingency, the "borrowed" nature, of time. Modern African writers, I think, have been engaged in reimagining time and memory because they are among those who have felt the most need to do so.

Serious writers anywhere may claim that they write because they *have* to, or even that they must write in order to live. But beyond these existentially generic claims, writing, for the African writers I have discussed, is the act of reinvention of the possibility of experience itself: they write as if to re-create conditions of a possible existence. This kind of inventiveness or creativity, like the enchanted process of ritually constituting the best aspects of life, within or without a religious context, reenacts the processes of a secular modernity in a historical context that, you might say, needed Europe's imposing colonial fantasies and the inflicted traumas as greatly as one needs a bullet in the head.

In the regular religious idioms, Judaism and Christianity may represent history as a condition of lack caused by a Fall, and therefore await a Messiah who will return in the fullness of time; in Buddhism one recollects the self and nature in a progressive longing for transcendence of materiality into a state of Bliss known as Nirvana; in Islam one must learn what was already said from the Qur'an because this book of wisdom is apparently immune not only to heroic translation but also to historical ruination. It is well known that the religious sensibilities of animist and traditional cultures in Africa are quite different from any of these. Polytheistic animism operates in a peculiar form of narration of time—a time that colonialism, with its equally peculiar capitalist appetite for a particular kind of historical development, apparently resented. Because of the conceptual difference on this issue of time, when African writers argue over "authenticity" or "inauthenticity" of language or experience, often they are operating outside the regular contexts of what is vaguely called the times, or timelessness, of ritual and religion in other cultures. Similarly, when these writers lament the loss of a native "tongue," one can understand the depth of the mourning from the perspective of the idea of what is claimed to have been lost. The adoption of such resistant, countercolonial, and vernacular perspectives on time and tongue requires one to ask: What is time? What is a tongue? What is an authentic tongue?

Clues for answers may be found in several places. I will consider three of the most accessible, if rudimentary, presentations. The first is a Nigerian Fulani creation story, in a collection by Ulli Beier, *Origins of Life and Death*.[50] Among the many remarkable mythologies about the origin of existence available in Africa, this one must rank among the most vivid in imagery. In the beginning, the story says, "the sky was large, white, and very clear. It was empty; there were no stars and no moon; only a tree stood in the air and there was wind. The tree fed on the atmosphere and ants lived on it. Wind, tree, ants, and atmosphere were controlled by the power of the Word. But the Word was not something that could be seen. It was a force that enabled one thing to create another." Those familiar with this kind of creation narrative in other religions will recognize this form. For Christians, in the beginning was the Word, and the Word was God, and He became flesh, and so on. In the Fulani tradition, however, there is an investment in language that makes it such that when the language is put into question as a result of historical scrutiny, it is to the rituals of religion that one turns, to cope with whatever experiences motivate the demands of history. But without what is then a proper use of the language in ritual, the human risks a second and—because this would be a falling out of memory—more severe Fall than the first; one would fall back into wordlessness, and the world itself would fall back into the nameless, into nothingness.

As the Fulani theological poet has it, there is no world without word; existence in a fallen state of namelessness would be nothing but unceasing, meaningless stuff. But one cannot even say that this world would be just "stuff," for this, too, is a word. In short, one would be free to imagine *that* as a "world" of death—except that it would be difficult to say what "life," and therefore death, would be. The most succinct Fulani assertion of the metaphysical impossibility of a condition of world without word—and therefore the proposal of the cardinal role of language in the constitution of self, society, and culture—is wisdom available in all ages and to all peoples. Certainly, one might choose to question the details of the elements of its narration, as one might any philosophical fiction. Apart from the holy books, we have them in the technical writings of Plato and Aristotle, Hobbes's *Leviathan,* Heidegger's *Being and Time,* and even Derrida's *Of Grammatology.* Each story implicitly or explicitly admits to itself that it is a story about that which is nearly unknown, a glorification of the human instinct to language, and therefore the validation as beautiful of that which is already so judged.

My second example is from Sartre. In *Nausea* he imagines—or tries to imagine—experience without words. A character in the novel, Roquentin, imagines himself daydreaming as he sits in a coach of a tram. Suddenly, he feels lost to himself because deserted by words. Knowing neither where he is nor where he is going, the world appears to Roquentin only as chaotic, without order, and meaningless. In his "world" anything can be anything, so that all he feels is one mass of unmediated, unremitting, nonobjective because nonobjectifiable, sensation. It is not accidental that Sartre chose his own name for this wordless sensation for the title of the novel: *nausea*. Hegel, too, describes such a nauseating ontological sensation of unknown and unknowable as residue of experience as the ugly or "foul."[51]

In the confusion of not knowing *what* he is, *where* he is sitting, what it means to *sit*, Roquentin elaborates on his crisis of consciousness, on the metaphysical implications of the condition, and on the epistemological problems by describing another experience he remembers having at a park. Lost once again to himself on account of a loss of language, he claims, this time around, that it was the "word" in his mouth that had "refused to go and put itself on the thing." With word not being what it is because not doing what it does—make stuff some thing by naming—all Roquentin can affirm is that "things are divorced from their names," and that even his own existence, as nothing in nothingness in a sea or desert of nothing, is "nameless." Yet instead of recognizing himself as a servant of words—an agent of acts of naming—Roquentin reports himself as a person locked in loneliness and despair: as an object of pity. Wailing but without words or the power of word, he feels not only defenseless but unworthy of defense. "Things"—every thing and any thing—only scare and threaten him and exacerbate his feeling that senseless things, as pure sensation, are offensively but senselessly surrounding and menacing his raw feeling. He believes that under the park bench on which he sat was a chunk of the root of a chestnut tree, but he "couldn't remember it was a root" because "words had vanished and with them the significance of things." So there he sat, "stooping forward, head bowed, alone in front of this black, knotty mass, entirely beastly, which frightened [him]." All around without words, "there it was, clear as day: existence had suddenly unveiled itself." So what does bare existence look like?

> It had lost the harmless look of an abstract category: it was the very paste of things, this root was kneaded into existence. . . . All these objects. . . . How can I explain? They inconvenienced me; I would have liked them to exist less

strongly, more dryly, in a more abstract way, with some reserve. The chestnut tree pressed itself against my eyes. . . . It was the only relationship I could establish between these trees, these gates, these stones. In vain I tried to count the chestnut tress, to locate them by their relationship to the Velleda, to compare their height with the height of the plane trees: each of them escaped the relationship in which I tried to enclose it, isolated itself, and overflowed.[52]

Without words, without their concepts, existence bares itself as a mere concreteness, but a concreteness that means nothing, represents nothingness.

When language fails, it is experience itself that fails to occur. Without experience, there is no knowledge, no truth, no beauty, no intelligence, no memory, and no hope which we associate with, as both constitutive of and as deriving from, experience. Without significance, bare existence appears not just dull and raw but also frightening and inexplicable. Experience, then, is that of time and place, where word and world are related even if not exactly completely and equally matched. Yet that which gives existence its even greater significance is not mere experience as memories of experiences that were once intuitive and close. Thus a deprivation in language is not just the loss of one species of vocal mechanics or another: it is a problem arising from the very idea of speech, the capacity for "tongue," by way of challenge to a particular tradition of experience and of memory. Without its capacity for speech, a tradition's hope that consciousness could cultivate and humanize existence is fundamentally thrown into doubt. Beyond the needs of an isolated individual, without words and the skilled use of them, a community's anxiety that an otherwise foreign reality (or nature itself) could be culturally transformed into their only experience and memory, or that the work of knowledge, truth, and beauty, or of intelligence, memory, and hope might not go on, cannot be muted or reasonably contained.

My third and final example comes from a position antithetical to Sartre's Roquentin. It is antithetical in that it can be seen as an epistemic reversal of Sartre's egocentric phenomenology, particularly in regard to the function of the word and the processes of concept formation. Within the structure of what Senghor liked to call the "Negro African aesthetic," the experience of the word, its gift or loss, is supposed to be the reverse of the disconcerting procedure that Sartre articulated in *Nausea* and in his other existentialist essays.[53] Ontologically, rather than being the frightening nothingness that Sartre attributed to it (or respectively, death and the ugly which the Fulani poet and Hegel attributed to it), Senghor's position on "concrete" existence can be interpreted in at least three ways. He could be said to deny that existence is ugly or threatening, or otherwise something consciousness should be afraid of. He can also be interpreted to mean that there is something foul, worthy of fear, and inconveniencing in existence; but rather than this foul or threatening "thing" being existence as such, it is the human's cultural "word," or at least something deriving from the species' capacity and need to make names. Finally, Senghor could be said to suggest that neither raw existence nor pure word is innocent of the violence of the ugly, or of the frightful and its inconvenience.

It seems, however, that on account of Senghor's obvious, even innate, optimism, there is a fourth possibility. It is only not knowing enough or lack of courage that leads humans to think that *either* existence is foul and threatening and our words pure and nonthreatening, *or* everything, as Schopenhauer might say—existence and word—is foul, threatening, and inconvenient.[54] For Senghor, in any case, what (either or both) existence and word demand from humans is *not* flight from existence into the concept; such flight would be empty, illusory, and inauthentic.[55]

In Senghor's work, if there is any ugliness (and in the long run it is not clear that this doubt translates into an affirmation that there is), it is in the concept as such—in the abstraction we form out of the mouth, so to speak, and of our own egocentric will. Thus, instead of existence befouling the concept, as Sartre would have it, the reverse may be the case. Under his conception of values—including the meaning of any concept that would mean anything existentially referential—Senghor can be seen to deny what Sartre says about the concept, namely, that it is "the *harmless* look of an abstract category."[56] From Senghor's perspective, rather than being harmless or merely abstract, the category itself—or perhaps the willful search for category—constitutes the major source of Roquentin's (at best) pretended helplessness or (at worst) ontological resentment. It is a kind of resentment because instead of plunging into existence through participation in the activities of an existing state of the nothingness of the nameless (no)thing, Roquentin—as a Senghorian would read him—seems to dread not really loss of the word but loss of self, a self constructed in turn on the basis of a particular, historically situated conception of consciousness. Is it not possible that what really troubles the hero or antihero of *Nausea* is that the "paste of things" might, through uttering the word, literally stick to his person? Is it possible that what Roquentin desires is an impossibility: he wants only the pure concept that can *guarantee* for him a world of triumph of *his* will over existence? This interpretation would not be antithetical to Sartre's other works and autobiographical examples, whose themes are invariably the need for choice, the need for action, and the need for engagement even of thought itself.

Not finding such a pure, total, and universal guarantee of a category of domination, our antihero is reduced by his own either/or to the status of not only ontological, but also social sense of self-insignificance. Instead of lacking in intellectual lucidity, however, Roquentin appears to have, in fact, too much of it. What he really laments is not the absence of word, concept, or category; he laments the absence of a word, a concept, or a category powerful enough to guarantee his sovereignty over existence *with all the gain in the world but at no cost to the self.* We may therefore conclude that instead of, as self-reported, the word in his mouth "refusing to go and put itself on the thing," it was Roquentin who—either strategically or resentfully or both—refused to spit out the word. Rather than considering *Nausea* and its main character as a treatise on the metaphysics of being, a Senghorian might believe that Sartre has produced, even if inadvertently, a metaphysics of power.

Whereas Roquentin believes he is "powerless" and "defenseless" faced with what he must think of as the Other to language, this fake dilemma must be a form of neurosis and, additionally, entirely capitalist, modern, and ethnocentric.[57] When he launches into his own sympathetic portraits of what he calls the Negro African "participant reason," Senghor sees, in what he believes European thinkers misdescribe as ugly or raw existence, the opportunity for engagement of the Other to the self by which humans assume the power to restore the self to a world and to a universal community of mankind. Senghor claims that where the capitalist modern European mind is objectifying, analytical, and mechanical, the Negro's reason is subjectifying, intuitive, and communicative. From the latter's point of view, existence is therefore not foul, because for Senghor there is no need to think *abstractly* or think thinly the realm of the self as mortally at risk of pollution or taint by "concrete" nature. He conceptualizes the relation between thing and self as a world whose dynamism is constituted by the interplay between word and stuff, essence and existence, and subjective categories and nature. But even in this dialectical interplay, the last word, Senghor goes further to assert, always already belongs to the paste of that out of which both the self and the world must be consciously made.[58]

A phrase we could use to describe Senghor's basic approach to the relation of the word to the thing might be *rhythmic alignment* of consciousness with the structure of existence. He communicated this sentiment in such aphorisms as "I dance the Other, therefore I am." Dance, song, and poetry—not abstract categories or theories of such categories —are, for Senghor, the most obvious forms of self and of social existence. Against some of even his Marxist allies who chose to see in his "African" metaphysics or epistemology the possibility of a nonbourgeois disalienation of consciousness, Senghor insisted that the implied issue of social antagonism in the forms of class conflict might also be entirely a problem intrinsic only to modern capitalist European cultures. Some French communists who supported Senghor's work may therefore assert that the liberal and bourgeois reason of the Cartesian ego met its match in what Senghor proposed as the African authentic consciousness, or that the colonized African societies will save the colonizing powers from their egocentric European projects of domination, or prevent a capitalist metaphysics of consciousness from realizing its aim of an unqualified domination of human nature by tools. But it would seem that these dichotomous ways of framing the issues are themselves antithetical to, ideally, Senghor's hopes about the ways in which consciousness functioned in what he preferred to call *Africanité* and *Arabité.*

LANGUAGE AS TRADITION

For us to say that an ontological anxiety about inauthenticity arises when the relation between language and existence is threatened necessarily raises this question: In this age of technological manipulations of the very idea of the human, what does it mean to appropriate the language of the authentic and inauthentic? Taking Senghor's claims seriously—if only in the manner that we have hypothetically recuperated his postcolonial theory of the African experience of capitalist colonial modernity—allows us to entertain the idea that perhaps it is precisely the "thing" (the noumenal aspect of nature which frightened the mind of modern Western philosophy) that Senghor, as if by wisdom grounded in a chastened trust, wished to conceptually embrace. But consistent with my suspicions at the beginning of this chapter, one should ask if Senghor practiced this form of thinking *in the name of* the Serré, the Senegalese, or the African in general. It is of course true that Senghor believed there must be a form of thought unique to Black peoples everywhere; he believed that this form of thought was closer to what he outlined in his own writings than what Descartes, Hegel, or Sartre had presented on the related subjects. And he believed that beyond the Black world evidence exists—in Bergson, Chardin, Einstein, among others—that twentieth-century, post-Enlightenment, European science and the humanities were, finally, coming around to adopting noncolonial, noncapitalist, social democratic African and Black forms of thought. Such a universal emergence in thought and culture, Senghor believed, would eventually lead to what he optimistically characterized as *Civilization de l'Universel,* wherein all of humanity will—thanks to the Africa-inspired harmoniously environmental way of thinking—develop a new kind of metaphysics, epistemology, and multicultural social forms of shared existence.[59]

So it is plausible that even at the most universal moment in his speculative philosophy of history, Senghor maintained the "African" signature as the dominant in the idea of the would-be universal. Whereas Sartre and, arguably, Ulli Beier's unnamed Fulani poet seem to claim that the subject of language must live in terror of the danger of a relapse of consciousness into nothing, Senghor seems to embrace the Otherness of existence by imagining existence not as the Other *for,* but as the Other *of* consciousness. Where Sartre's bourgeois ego is nauseated in fear of the concrete and loss of self (after all, Roquentin is troubled because he cannot *count* the chestnut trees, he cannot *logically* relate them to the stones, the gates), in short, where the bourgeois ego is threatened by fear of loss of reason to a vastness that, apparently, might engulf the sovereignty of the self-consciousness and the secret of its desire, Senghor implies that this metaphysical anxiety is existentially unfounded. He even suggests that it is unethical. Rather than enhancing one's knowledge of the world, Roquentin's attitude, as Senghor might theorize it, in fact *stood in the way* of another, expansive path to greater self-knowledge.

The issue about in/authenticity ultimately has to do with the metaphysical and epistemological status of the "real," that is, the question of existence in regard to truth. Where writers in the classical modern European phenomenology saw and agonized over the "absurd" (Camus) or "senseless" matter (Sartre), Senghor recognized in these the outlines of a misdiagnosed form of experience. Where Europeans wrote of the darkness of the soul, the modern African writer, not only Senghor but Achebe, Soyinka, and Okigbo—through the artistic figures of Mask, Agwu, Ogun, or Idoto—derived and dramatized theories of experience and history that encode duality *in* existence. Rather than oppose an "essential" self to an "inessential" existence, African writers explored the transcendent issues of reason and time in experience and in the writing of experience.

But I have also argued that the issue of authenticity versus inauthenticity in language, even as African critics of Eurocentrism present this, cannot be, in the final analysis, about Africa versus Europe. The modern African writer's anxiety over tradition has far more to do with the issue of language as such than with the irreversible transformations of the continent and its cultures. After all, historical change, even if it appears threatening to the African writer, is so not because it is "Other" to the African self; the "West" is implicated only because in the acts of colonialism, as we saw in wa Thiong'o's lamentation, Africa recognized—on a scale previously unimagined—the vulnerability of its languages to severe forms of contingency and transience. Therefore, wherever it appears that the modern African writer values the language of authenticity, it is because tradition, which is nothing more than the constant human effort to conserve and transmit the universal in the form of particulars, lends itself only too easily to temporal breakdown. The language of authenticity—when one makes a claim to it by saying that an artwork is "antique" and "genuine" and therefore valued at enormous cost—is, as Walter Benjamin understood quite well, a particular kind of metaphysical claim to aura: it is a declaration that *this* artistic work, like a tradition unto itself, has defied time and clime in its capacity to encode and husband the universal in human experience, in history.

Behind the aura of timelessness and the reality of its bearer's hidden hunger for the eternal, the authentic is also practically useful—as a standard of judgment. Whether the judgment is aesthetic or also moral, that which comes with aura is pragmatically necessary, as it offers to a community that understands it not just immediate suggestions about enacting aesthetic sensibilities in the present but also ideas as to the practices of the same in the future. Beyond ad hoc adjudication of disputed taste, the authentic carries within itself accumulated wisdom and the hidden principles of possible future experience.

One can see, then, why a writer would lament the various forms of loss of language in his or her tradition, or decry a historical wreck of language in any tradition. In the case of Africa, writers like wa Thiong'o certainly think that to fail to re-collect a tradition of language stranded in a colonial catastrophe is, for the cultures involved, to truly lose a sense of "home" in a time and in a place. Regardless of the legitimacy or illegitimacy of backing up this claim with essentialist or nonessentialist metaphysical scaffolds, modern African writing makes clear that it is a form of existence that colonialism put, historically, into question. For a culture thus shaken out of its time, or from its anticipated historical evolution, the consequences of the ontological and epistemological questions about the nature of language are, at bottom, about the issue of integrity of tongue: the integrity of self, history, and the capacity for use of language.

Is it possible that the African writer who operates, for example, in a Senghorian model—and many of them do—is concerned that by writing in a foreign tongue he or she encourages theft (as wa Thiong'o put it)? Although the notion of integrity may be a slippery one, we have a sufficient glimpse of its consistency, even if negatively, in Roquentin's existential disposition. Is it possible that, in parallel to Sartre's Roquentin, African writing may be suffered by the writer as a loss of speech, as words that refuse to "go and put" themselves "on the thing"? If this last thought is at all beholden to reason, what would be its grounds? Is the African writer in non-African language(s) prepared to say that his or her "Africa" does not exist? Might the writer think that speech, any speech, is always implicitly a process of recovery of experience, and therefore already sufficiently a gain for any loss of a world?

I am often asked: If you Africans are so concerned about your native languages, why don't *you* write your African philosophy, or "afrohistorical reason," in Igbo (or Yoruba, etc., depending on which language the speaker thinks must be my "native" tongue)? From practice, I avoid mentioning to such critics that African writers *almost* answered the question in Kampala in the 1960s, when I was too young to be in elementary school. I do point out, however, that there are today more African writers writing in African languages than there were forty years ago. I also draw parallels with prior struggles of intellectual traditions that, in their early days, were considered "minority" and vernacular: Descartes, for example, wrote all his early works in Latin and only the later ones in his native—and at that time, vernacular—French. Similarly, Kant wrote his dissertation and published his earliest writing in physics in Latin, and only later wrote the books for which he is today best known in his native—again, at that time, backward and "primitive"—German language. Furthermore, the superior development and global expansion of the English language occurred merely two centuries ago. Hume, writing in the mid-1770s, lamented, "We have no dictionary of our language, and scarcely a tolerable grammar." Referring to the emerging writer and stylist Jonathan Swift, Hume noted that "the first polite prose" in the modern English language "was writ by a man who is still alive."[60] Clearly, by comparison, some African languages (Yoruba, Swahili, Igbo, Hausa, Zulu) seem to fare quite well: they have today, as perhaps never before, excellent dictionaries as well as numerous studies and experiments that point to future ways in which they may be fruitfully taken up and developed into languages of not only commerce, politics, and diplomacy (as some of them currently are), but also of studies in the liberal arts, science, and technology.[61] The lesson of history in this regard is eloquent: languages are not only metaphysical realities but also historical things; like any cultural institution, a language is subject to the rise and fall in the historical fortunes of the women and men who use and are used by it.

5

Reason and Unreason

in Politics

A superficial reading may suggest that this last chapter is an attempt to defend philosophical reasoning against unphilosophical encroachments by contextualist social morality and politics. Such a reading would be surprising because, according to stereotype, very few expect African philosophers to speak of philosophy, morality, or politics in noncontextualist fashion. The truth, however, is that most African intellectuals believe that to do philosophy well, a distinction—which is not necessarily to say a separation—between philosophy, morality, and politics, with philosophy and politics at the extremities of the distinction, needs to be maintained. This chapter is therefore an attempt to test this less stereotypic argument. I have chosen to use some of the justifications provided for South Africa's Truth and Reconciliation Commission (TRC) —specifically, the idea of *ubuntu* articulated in works by theologians and literary figures such as Desmond Tutu, J. M. Coetzee, Antjie Krog, and Njabulo Ndebele—as a test case for this philosophical experiment.[1]

It is useful to keep in mind that as I imagine it, the extremities in the distinction between philosophy and politics are not extreme enough to warrant an inflexible framing of the relationship and its tensions as a fundamental problem of philosophy versus politics. The difference between philosophy and politics is, however, so natural and morally significant that we need not attempt to assimilate this difference into an easy image in the usual metaphor, as points on a continuum. It is a particular concept of reason, and philosophy's greater readiness to defend this reason, which makes the distinction between philosophy and politics so significant. It is only to the extent that philosophy is willing to stand up for this reason—by making it philosophy's own reason, as it were—that philosophy may have a chance to indirectly participate in political society as a moral voice, or public face, of reason.

MORALITY AND POLITICS IN A
POSTRACIAL DEMOCRACY

In Ndebele's recent novel, *The Cry of Winnie Mandela*, one of the main characters says, "You, all of you, have to reconcile not with me, but with the meaning of me. For my meaning is the endless human search for the right thing to do."[2] What is the best way to go about this search? What is the best language in which to articulate its ends? I raise these questions in awareness of the complex moral situation Ndebele's character inhabits—or better, the moral conflicts that inhabit that character. "I am," she says, "hell and heaven," "beauty and ugliness," "pride and shame." I also ask these questions taking into account a larger social environment—including the context of the novel itself—namely, contemporary South Africa. Of this society, another of the novel's narrative voices says, "South Africans have an intriguing capacity to be disarmingly kind and hospitable at the same time as being capable of the most horrifying brutality and cruelty." She then enumerates these specific examples:

> We saw strange armies of black men terrorizing townships, hacking children's heads with matchettes. We abandoned patients to their deaths in hospitals because we were on strike; we held hostage people doing their work; trashed university campuses; blocked highways; burned to death old women we accused of being witches; abused our children and raped our women; engaged in

brutal taxi wars in which, if passengers miraculously escaped death from stray bullets, they would surely die once the reckless minibuses of death charged down the highway in a frenzy of speed. All this while we celebrated the advent of democracy, human rights, and victories in sport; abolished the death sentence, declared free medical care for pregnant women, and continued to receive and welcome guests into our houses with legendary hospitality.[3]

A careful reader's initial reaction may be to suspect that the characters in *The Cry of Winnie Mandela* are the creations of a nimble artist, a writer in love with the dialectics of opposites. But the more enduring and, incidentally, more accurate response is to think over the material basis of such dialectics—to systematically reflect on the significance of the moral oscillation in the lives of the individuals and society whose portraits the novel provides. This more reflective appreciation of the book might lead the reader to say to its characters: Welcome to humanity! Such an affirmation better disposes one to raise, along with the narrators, further necessary issues: What is—or what are—the cause(s) of the South African brand of moral Manichaeanism? Are these causes natural? Or do they have historical origins?

The narrators themselves give us some clues to possible answers. One of them attributes such moral extremism to something she calls "interrupted experiences." But what does this mean? The phrase is used to refer to a moral imagination that, in my translation, seems to abdicate the responsibility to reorder self and society in relation to an environment, and instead merely reflects this environment. The society is one in which, we are led to understand, individuals dramatically oscillate between—again quoting from the novel—comfort and discomfort, home and exile, hope and despair, honor and dishonor, knowledge and ignorance, heroism and roguery. In this apparently frenzied moral climate—and beyond the historical explanation in the form of interrupted experiences—from which other sources and perspectives may one seek to understand the meanings, the uses, of the oscillation in passions?

Passions, indeed, they are. And passion is the primary stuff of literature as well as of human nature, is it not? But in the case of individuals and societies, what does this appeal to nature amount to? Nature is historicizable, so that it is only in understanding the processes of this historicization of nature in experience—and by elucidating the logic of this experience in itself—that one can hope to shed light upon, and bring a measure of moral order to, that experience. The function of morality, in this context, is not at all a naked repression of the passion. Rather, it is the humanization, the socialization of nature. Moreover, it is on account of this idea of socialization that the concept of ubuntu—humanity—has come to be a powerful draw for many intellectuals within and outside of South Africa.[4] Ubuntu, it is believed, is the idea which will mobilize the moral imagination in such a way that the balance in the socialization processes is logically tipped in favor of honor, heroism, and knowledge.

My argument from here on is that this expectation is simultaneously too much and not enough. Ubuntu as a moral remedy from experience of the nature of the passion does not, I think, escape the radical dialectic of that same experience it seems primed to address. Ubuntu is too much because—if the portraits of the current African society it aims to speak to are accurate—as an ideology it relies too much on the extraordinary: luck, miracles, and an ambiguous concept of natural goodness. Ubuntu is not enough because it fails to supplement—or one might say moderate—its innate optimism about the natural goodness of humankind with what I call the ordinary. This ordinary—the unmiraculous and nonspectacular—has a caution born of experience and recognizes that the luck (the extraordinary) that attends to moral actions has an even chance of being as much *bad* as *good* luck.

Luck is the emergence in the everyday of that which is outside the ordinary. So is the concept of the miraculous. Morality, on the other hand, belongs largely to the realm of the everyday. In this regard the companion to luck is not only the miraculous but also the tragic. And the most ambiguous kind of moral disposition—one might even call it a tragic sense of life—is the one in which individuals (or society) try to convince themselves that they can manage the ordinary always by extraordinary means. One must be concerned that to adopt such a management philosophy—in business transactions as in morality—might be equivalent to having no philosophy of management at all. If this were merely a question of business management ethics, however, the stakes would not be so high. Instead, what we are confronted with is the possibility of questioning the idea (to stay with the analogy) of management as such. We are led to doubt the common understanding that the idea of morality involves the skillful negotiation of the passions of experience in the moral character, whether individual or collective.

What happens when, for whatever reason, ordinary passions are attended to by extraordinary means? Do we get the oscillations described in *The Cry of Winnie Mandela*? If so, what is the value of such oscillation in a framing of the moral outlook? And if not, how do advocates of ubuntu seek to address these issues? To get a fuller picture of the tragic faces of the passions, and their implications for moral reasoning, one's references must, for convenience, remain within the literary arts. Below are further examples with historical relevance to the cultures under discussion: Joseph Conrad's *Heart of Darkness*, Toni Morrison's *Beloved*, and Wole Soyinka's *Death and the King's Horseman*. In these novels and a play, all of which have some direct or indirect relevance to the contemporary African experience, evil is portrayed as the *necessary* road to a revelation of goodness, *sin* is the path to *salvation*, *love* is the path to *murder*, and *death* is the path to *life*. Thus, characters internally conflicted or antagonistically related do not hesitate to *exterminate* human populations in order to *civilize* them; mothers *love* their children so much that they *kill* them for no other reason than the love itself; and kings must commit *suicide* for the kingship to *live* on. Similarly—and on the basis of the same extraordinary logic—men love women so much that rape between the sexes appears inevitable; nationalists burn down their own countries in order to liberate them; and so on.

One easily gets the point: the passion of experience, in these contexts, eminently operates on what seems to be a dialectics of nature, and the writers and the poets who depict the passions in this light are fully aware of this fact in their constructions of the historical vicissitudes of their characters' moral imaginaries. It does not seem to matter to these artists whether the passion in question is love, faith, or greed. The poetic, tragic outcome is always the same. The individual or community whom passion possesses ends in moral—and quite often physical—self-disintegration.

It is precisely in order to remove, or at least somewhat shield morality from these forms of self-disintegrative nature and historical fate—the *bad* luck of passion—that an individual or society might choose to renounce oscillation as a self- or social management logic, as a system of morality. The philosophical search for a reasoned balance in moral and empirical experience is not, therefore, predicated on the grounds that one does not like *good* luck. It is instead an effort to renounce the principle of the extraordinary. The transition from the Greek poets to the philosophers might, in this context and for comparative purposes, be considered a significant and irreversible development in the public moral imagination. The transition from literary tragedy to the philosophical attitude—a transition of which the figure of Socrates seems to have been the most visible cultural marker—takes on an ominous, more transcendent cultural meaning. What would be the salient African experience in this comparative history of development of morality, politics, and society?

If I am not in error in suspecting that the idea of moral balance—what some ancients called the rational "mean"—was a classical form of moral appreciation of what I earlier referred to as the ordinary, then from this perspective of the everyday, to wait on the good luck of passion is to give up on the idea of morality itself. This is so because one is a moral animal only at those moments when one consciously seeks to understand the logic of nature, in order to steer this logic in the course of the good. Or when one invents such a logic of goodness, where nature itself seems to offer none.

In the South African context, Ndebele's book is indeed about the play of natural and social history in morality. Or at least it gives postapartheid morality a play in fiction, so that we are not surprised to note that the novel is often mentioned in the same breath as *Country of My Skull*, the award-winning, fictionalized report of the proceedings of South Africa's TRC by the poet Antjie Krog. *The Cry of Winnie Mandela* could be regarded as a Black feminist extension of *Country*, for both are narratives of the short elasticity between right and wrong—in a society or in an individual—when we leave morality to the vagaries of the spectacular. The context, once again, is the stress on the tissues of the moral fabric of a society in the process of transition from a racio-totalitarian state to a democratic one. But the implication of such elasticity, when staged as a conflict between an old social order and a new one, goes beyond the South African context. In its abstract relevance, it applies to questions about what constitutes the contents of everyday moral concepts about theft, honesty, and bribery.

Concerned that raids on farms she knows increased exponentially after the election that ushered in the democratic transition, Krog seeks to illuminate what she rightly considers an intriguing confusion in values —a confusion resulting, in turn, from a scrambling of the social scales across White-Black ethnic, cultural, and political divides. Krog, a White writer, asks a Black colleague, "Moshoeshpe's name means 'He who can steal as swiftly and silently as cutting someone's beard.' How can the deftness of stealing be a mark of honour?" And: "Why would Mandela write in his biography about the cattle he and his cousin stole from his uncle? Do we understand the same thing when we talk about stealing?" The colleague explains: "I grew up with the notion that stealing from whites is actually not stealing. Way back, Africans had no concept of stealing other than taking cattle as a means of contesting power. But you whiteys came and accused us of stealing—while at that very same minute you were stealing everything from us!" Likewise, when she asks a Black novelist writing in the Afrikaaner language why one of the main charac-ters in his novel condemns another, a murderer who has "ratted" on his co-murderers, without being condemnatory about the crime itself, the novelist answers, "Because black people must always stick together." Krog suggests an alternative moral perspective: "But the woman who saw a white man running away from Chris Hani's dead body didn't say, '[the murderer] was white, so I'll shut up'; instead this white woman witness of the murder of a black man said, 'The deed is wrong, so I speak out.'" The Black novelist responds by saying something to the effect that Whites are not only evil but indestructible, so that the only reason Blacks have not been entirely "wiped out" is that Blacks stick together as a counterpower.

One refreshing aspect of these conflicts in moral sense is that the characters involved are aware of the slippery-slope tendencies in their positions, the strained nature of their contextualist arguments in light of the multiethnic and multiracial society they must build, and the di-lemmas attending to conflicted moral points of view that relativize themselves. The formal outline of the South African context is more obvious if we look at how similar problems present themselves else-where within and outside of Africa. In Nigeria, Kenya, and Ghana, for example, where Africans are transiting out of the English colonial expe-rience, some of us are concerned that corruption in high and low places in and out of government wrecks the economy and saps the moral fiber of these modern societies. But then there are sympathetic critics—their opponents call them apologists—who argue that, for example, because of Africa's ancient traditions, the modern idea of bribery should be considered a relative term in moral judgment. The difference seems to be that in the case of South Africa, elasticity in this kind of moral imagination stretches not just to corruption in public administration but also to ideas about obvious theft and nonjudicial murder.

It is, therefore, far from surprising when one of the characters portrayed in *Country* says, despondently, "When Mandela was talking about white and black morality, how whites only care when whites die, he should have added: blacks don't care if whites die . . . they don't even care if blacks die."[5] It is within these African contexts—with special reference not only to the internal South African social relations it is supposed to address—that I wish to discuss ubuntu. It is supposed to be a philosophy, a statement of moral and political beliefs. I accept, then, that ubuntu might be a form of claim (because accompanied by self-justifications in the form of reason-giving) to a systematic approach to an African society's social and political morality. But I also take this claim seriously as a philosophical—that is, not just locally African—matter.

The conclusion I draw is that ubuntu—with partial but significant similarities to Négritude before it—succeeds as a kind of aestheticized, quasi-religious, political thought for a particular place and time. But I have reservations about the universality of its moral and political claims to philosophical, and particularly epistemic, justifications. Moreover, I hold this reservation not exclusively in the name of a philosophic "universal," but also in the name of ubuntu's African—and even South African—particulars. It is, then, accurate to say that I express caution about this newest African politicized thought not because of its relations to the universal or the particular; it might indeed be a morally decent thought-device for *action* on both universal and particular counts. Rather, I find the think-device unsatisfactory as a thought in itself, on the grounds of an ideal of reason that I espouse—an ideal that here as elsewhere I characterize as an ordinary, Afro-historical, form of reason.

If the reader is willing to entertain this thought of an epistemically qualified support for ubuntu's claim to status as a particularistic or universalizable philosophical thought, I can imagine the same sympathetic voice asking: If ubuntu is as good as you already acknowledge it to be, then why do we not grant it what you call "philosophical" protection, instead of defending your so-called ordinary philosophical reason against ubuntu or the political ideal it represents? A critic might also say to me: You are, are you not, covertly advocating what should be regarded as an idea of reason for reason's sake? To these I would respond: Thanks for the evident willingness to go along with the proposed thought experiments, but my primary reason for staking out a partisanship with ordinary reason—with the reason of philosophy—is not that I particularly wish to defend some kind of an ideal of "pure" reason or philosophy against contextualist morality and politics. Nor am I trying to produce a theory of the moral or political that covertly benefits my conception of reason, or covertly promotes academic philosophy at the expense of folk philosophy. The distinction I advocate between ordinary and extraordinary reason—between a philosophic temperament that takes this distinction seriously and a philosophic temperament that does not—or between philosophical conceptions of morality and politics in general and an action-oriented expression of political morality, is aimed to protect what I regard as the relative independence of philosophical reflection from contextual morality and political settlements.

I understand how unexpected, even puzzling, it may be to hear someone who does *African* philosophy speak of philosophy and politics in this way. But I believe that in order to do philosophy well—or insofar as philosophy is being done well, in Africa or anywhere else—a distinction, which is not the same as a separation, between philosophy and politics exists and needs to be maintained.

REASON AND UNREASON IN ART AND POLITICS

In J. M. Coetzee's *Elizabeth Costello* the eponymous main character says, in utter abandon, "I am offering myself to you in all my unreason. Let reason do what it wants with me. I am not an idea." She says this in the middle of a lecture in which she is struggling to explain the meanings, for her, of a common human experience: the reality of evil. By any means of evaluation, this is an unusual response to a traditional problem in theodicy. Unlike the traditional approaches to the problem in philosophy or even theology, Elizabeth seems to think that evil is inherent in the human condition, and that we must associate this origin of evil with the moral origins of the aims of goodness. But, unlike philosophers and theologians, she refuses to name—or at least pretends to refuse to name —the origin of the origins of good and evil.

As anyone who knows Plato, Aquinas, or Nietzsche—and Elizabeth should—must agree, this pretended self-abandonment to unreason is an extraordinary, and hasty, gesture. Yet *Elizabeth* is neither the first work, nor its heroine the only character, in and through which Coetzee has indulged an idea of the human right to the irrational. May one raise questions about the source of this artistic license? Or does the novelist's absolute right to celebrate reason in the form of the irrational trump even any surreptitious suggestion of "petit" philosophical discontent on the matter?

In an earlier Coetzee novel, *Disgrace*, an aging professor named David Lourie commits an indiscretion—David himself may not think the word "indiscretion" an appropriate term—with one of his students. This indiscretion leads to his resignation from his position. While he teeters on the borders of insanity with his conviction that only the mythical or the extraordinary—his own word is "revelation"—is a worthy source of morality for any usable human knowledge, David expects, waits, and drifts in the hope of being hit by some lightning of truth from the sky. His only source of intermittent consolation—an effort to compose an opera based on the life of the romantic poet Byron—allows him to regain faith in the worth of human existence, but only in the extremities. While he struggles to rebuild his life, he nevertheless finds more spiritual comfort in the company of animals than with his daughter, his three ex-wives, or the many prostitutes he frequently picks up. But even this affection for animals—dogs, cats, goats—depends on the fact that he has become a volunteer worker at an animal shelter that specializes in killing them: "There are too many of them, too many of *us*," is how David explains his fascination for the job. Not surprisingly, instead of some moral compass the reader might expect the practice of humaneness to grant David, we discover that his new choice of lifestyle is merely, as he puts it, "preparing to die."

With David, as with Elizabeth, there is only passion for the extremes, and the extremities of passion. The words "nature" and "natural" seem, for both of them, not only terms of endearment but the most important moral compliment humans can pay each other. When David considers why Byron left England for Italy, he believes it was because, unlike the English, "Italians were still in touch with nature." In his writing and lectures as in his supposedly amorous adventures, David consistently strives to attain the life "less hemmed in by convention," or the most "passionate." He claims to avoid rational analysis—of self and social relations—because such analysis is inferior to "revelation." And when he tries to explain this partisanship for the irrational, he insists on the belief that "without a flash of revelation there is nothing." Since it is only in the absence of mundane reason and rational analysis that the mystery of revelation can unfold (or strike), David sees the task of his life as an effort to keep "the imagination pure"—even when what is imagined are the unredeemable impurities in nature or existence. Thus, at fifty years, David is still able to prefer to admire his own sexual "animal magnetism," to think of himself as the libidinal "servant of Eros," and to propound, gloriously, that art is nothing but the work of unmediated instinct. "No animal," humans included, he says, "would accept the justice of being punished for following its instincts."

Yet—and this is an important "yet"—it is not that David has abandoned morality, even as we conventionally understand it. Rather, he thinks that the greater danger to morality is that a human, like an obedient dog, may become conditioned "to hate its own nature." In terms reminiscent of Foucault's studies of the modern invention of the panopticon in *Discipline and Punish,* David Lourie worries that everyday moralities turn a human into an animal whose natural instincts have been tamed, so that such a creature "no longer needed to be beaten." The beating becomes superfluous because the domesticated and normalized has become "ready to punish itself." When morality succeeds so well, David concludes, "it would have been better to shoot" the animal. It is in fact this belief that explains his mission at the kennel—or rather the animal mortuary. Yet, when his daughter asks if he has always felt this way, he answers, "No, not always. Sometimes I have felt just the opposite."

In David's dialectics of opposites, as in Elizabeth's, the choice appears to be to *either* allow instinct and passion to run their natural courses (the individual becomes, as David puts it, the "servant" of passion), *or* to extirpate instinct and passion (as David also says, they are "a burden we could do without"). The only grounds David can find to reconcile the extremities of passion is, this reader is led to believe, no "grounds" at all. One *either* waits for possession by divine or satanic mystery in the form of a revelation, *or* one actively cultivates the art of death against life in an irrational metaphysics of nature or myth. The nearest one comes to a "resolution" of these arbitrary tensions—the closest, therefore, that Coetzee's major characters come to realizing a properly moral existence— does not and cannot occur in daily life. Instead, resolution is pursued in what is called "Art," with a capital *A*. And Art, for this novelist, provides a unitary and totalistic vision of reality in which—alternatively or in conflict—good is not just "good" but also The Good, and "evil" is likewise The Evil.

One is not supposed to "see" the imaginary conflicts between these forces expressed in ordinary goodness, the daily and quiet heroism of life. David's and Elizabeth's cherished visions of the struggle between death and life are never less than *mystagogique*. Such a choice of resolution of conflicts in the moral character suggests, at the minimum, that only an artistic solution is legitimate in the question of production of moral principles (to the extent that one can legitimately call art a "principle" of morality). Left out of the high artistic equation are the ordinary powers of reason or common sense. As opposed to the miraculous expectation that all will be well in the end—or, alternatively, all will be bad—to dwell in the power of the ordinary is, for David, merely to engage in philosophy. But "philosophize," he says, only "when all else fails."

What is unexpected—because most strange—is not that David believes the individual has a choice to merely wait for nature and instinct to exhaust themselves in extremities of passions. Rather, one is surprised to read, in the twenty-first century, that David self-exhausts (or, more faithful to the logic of the novel, is exhausted), and might counsel such self-exhaustion, if not self-disintegration, *in the name of* what he calls "darkest Africa." In this Africa—where he is threatened by a madness so carefully constructed—David the professor of language recalls that he has a professional mastery of Italian and French, "but," he adds, "Italian and French will not save [one] here in darkest Africa." Instead of suspecting that the abandonment of reason in favor of a "natural" quest for "revelation" might be the source of his existential malaise and social ineptitude, David prefers to think that Africa and Africans are making him (to use his own expression) "helpless."

Thus, according to his own version of the gospel in *Disgrace*, David is not the author of his moral drift, but rather sees himself as "an Aunt Sally, a figure from a cartoon, a missionary in cassock and topi waiting with clasped hands and upcast eyes while savages jaw away in their own lingo preparatory to plunge him into their boiling cauldron." In his self-pity, learned helplessness, and self-exculpation from a question the natives may be entitled to ask—"Why are you here?"—and may have asked, since they are "boiling" him, David leaves himself no room for reason in the potential for affirmation of a common humanity across the line. Instead, he searches for the miraculous sign: "Mission work," he asks, "what has it left behind?" His answer: "Nothing." But when he thinks of Europe, or White Africans (whom, curiously, David still refers to as "we Westerners"), he sees only "a field of white light" that "stays before him," crying: "Save me."

One should note, parenthetically, that in this work, unlike the subsequent *Elizabeth Costello*, "Africa" appears merely as a receptacle into which the author pours David's "metaphysical" racial and sexual anxieties. In the latter novel's postscript, "Letter of Elizabeth . . . to Francis Bacon," Elizabeth, metamorphosing into the historical Lady Chandos, writes to Bacon about what she calls the "raptures" and "flaming swords" she has felt cutting into her by her husband's madness. Right after describing their nuptial "sorrows" and "affliction," Elizabeth says of Philip, her husband, "Soul and body he speaks to me . . . into me, soul and body he presses what are no longer words but flaming swords." Remarkably, neither Philip in his wounding word and thrusting sword, nor Elizabeth in her carefully constructed self-sacrifice, escapes the fundamental anxiety that binds them together. She repeatedly refers to this anxiety as "the plague" or "the contagion," but is at a loss to characterize it in any empirical detail. Instead, the plague is "[that which is] always . . . not what I say but something else."

As in *Disgrace* David believes his writing will save him, Elizabeth imagines that Philip's writing will cure him of the plague. But also like David in Africa, Philip knows all the ancient and modern European languages, but also that "not Latin nor English nor Spanish nor Italian" can contain the excess of his plague or the madness in revelation. In the same way that David pictures what he calls "the white West" as the savior, Elizabeth implores an equally idealized Bacon: "Drowning, we write. Save us." The difference, as far as one can tell, is that whereas Elizabeth understands pretty well what Philip, like most humans (or is this just the menfolk?) suffers from (himself), David pretends that it is "Africa" and Africans that are the source of his affliction. Unlike David, Elizabeth takes pains to ask the more self-reflective question, even in the context of her most intimate relationship with Philip: "How did our sorrows come to be?" Her answer, unimpeachable in its exploitation of memory, recalls that there "was a time . . . before this time of affliction, when he would gaze like one bewitched at paintings of sirens and dryads, craving to enter their naked bodies. But where in Wiltshire will we find a siren or a dryad for him to try? Perforce I became his dryad: it was I whom he entered when he sought to enter her, I who felt his tears when again he could not find her in me. *But a little time and I will learn to be your dryad, speak your dryad speech,* I whispered in the dark; but he was not consoled." This recognition—that the source of "the plague" is, in the final analysis, within—is what is artistically displaced upon Africa and the African in *Disgrace.*

Because of the pitiless absence of divine consolation to any world that would choose, in the name of racial politics, to divide the indivisible—humanity—into Black and White, it is no wonder that a country like South Africa confounds all sorts of moral Manichaeanism. "This place . . . South Africa," David admits not without some irritation, is a work of the "god of chaos and mixture." This irritation is most exacerbated when a Black farmer manages his farm "all very swift and businesslike" because, according to David, this is "all very unlike Africa." David tries—unsuccessfully, which adds to his melancholy—to persuade a "mixed" daughter to "return to civilization" (i.e., to Holland) because, he reasons, she cannot make a living "against" the Black African farmer who "arrived" at the family's farm "as the dig-man, the carry-man, the water-man" but is now only "too busy for that kind of thing." This White Westerner who wants to farm, it seems, has lost not only her Whiteness but also her Black labor—a labor which, in the first place, gave metaphysical meaning and economic value to that Whiteness. In the inimitable racial logic of either/or—and as far as David is concerned—you are *for* Westerners if you are one of them (or one of their servants), otherwise you are against them. There is no in-between, and little chance for the thought of founding a new human—and humane—society. For David and similarly invested characters, it seems that without the racial pecking order and exploitive labor practices, Africa is nothing but a "desolate yard."

I have argued that it is the pursuit of the logic of the exceptional which requires—and inexorably calls forth, dialectically—in places that include South Africa, the morality of the extraordinary, such as doctrines of "transformation," "reconciliation," and "forgiveness." In parallel to Elizabeth's or David's cult of irrationalism, morality in African contexts—in its transforming or reconciling or forgiving—stretches the boundaries of the ordinary and of common sense. Each term of this trinity escapes the logic of everyday life. Some might choose to celebrate this as a triumph of "African reason" over "Western reason," but it is precisely such a dialectic of opposites that I have isolated for scrutiny under a different, non-Manichaean, moral requirement.

Instead of being the imaginary creations of a middle-aged White man in Black Africa, it is apparent that in *Disgrace*, the transformation, reconciliation, or forgiveness of self that David achieves only in myth evokes the myth of reconciliation that some countries and cultures pursue in politics and religion. Like Elizabeth's celebrated sacrifice of the ordinary for the quest of the miraculous, the language of the TRC, for example, is one with which David also would have been entirely comfortable: We are offering ourselves up for truth and reconciliation. Let justice do with us whatever it wants. We are more than the ordinary liberal idea of justice. But this is a rhetoric that one rarely hears in ordinary social moralities as in law.

In religion, of course, yes. Consider what I refer to as the evangelical paradoxicals: "Those who want to save their life must lose it"; "The first shall be last"; "If you want to serve your Father in heaven you must abandon your Father on earth."[6] Or, to return to examples from the secular arts: Whitman boasting how large he is, and for that reason capable of containing what we ordinary mortals call contradiction; or Goethe, proclaiming through Faust, "Two souls, alas! Reside within my breast." In its postmodern version, this miraculous attitude in religion and the arts is obvious in novels such as *Life of Pi* by Yann Martel.

Tellingly, Martel wrote the book while living in India to research India's religions, so that the influence of what we usually picture as India's multireligious sensibilities saturates the novel from beginning to end. The main story is of a young man, Pi of the title, wrecked on the high seas on a boat reminiscent of Noah's Ark. The boat's animal inmates devour one another until only Pi and a tiger remain. To survive, Pi, through cunning, must tame the tiger in an imaginary cage. Miraculously, both animals (the tiger "humanized" and the man more or less formed in the ways of the animal) survive and wash ashore on the Mexican coast. The news spreads and a team of scientists is sent to investigate. The scientists want truths, the facts of the case, but the only fact Pi has, or is willing to tell, is about a miracle—the miracle of, in this case, a spiritual ordeal and survival.

At first the scientific examiners are incredulous: Pi's story, they reason, is unbelievable. But Pi does not contest their reasoned unbelief on the basis of the facts of his case. Instead, he argues that everyone believes the unbelievable, so why won't the investigators believe *his own* incredible story. If people believe in things like God and love, what difference does it make (he argues) and what objections can the investigators have, if one more miracle is added to this list of believed unbelievables? For Pi, how the scientists explain the facts of what may or may not have happened at sea is utterly irrelevant. "Be excessively reasonable," he cautions, "and you risk throwing out" not only this story but—incredibly, from the point of mortal reason—the entire "universe with the bathwater." Besides, if the scientists are able to establish the truth of the facts, won't *their* type of truth be just another story—another version of the "story" he has already told them?

Pi and his creator seem to justify these philosophical meditations on "truth" on the grounds that "just looking upon this world . . . is already something of an invention." If this statement is true, they argue, does it not make life itself a story? But, beyond the artistic posturing in this claim to a higher insight into reality, and in the name of an artistic vision of life itself, Pi admits to knowledge of what the investigators are looking for. He just does not think they are entitled to it. Or, at least, he is convinced that his own conception of truth is morally superior. "I know what you want," he says. "You want a story that won't surprise you. That will confirm what you already know. That won't ask you to see higher or further or differently."

One need not be quick to think that all premodern, modern, and postmodern examples of the dialectics of reason represent merely the classical claims of religion or art to superior forms of intuition into reality, or the nature of the human experience. When we notice that this dialectics is practiced as a form of morality or politics, we must wonder if such practitioners have not exceeded the natural boundaries of religion and of the arts, and intrude on moral and civil domains where the claims of natural reason and its own modes of intuition—for example, intuitions of self-respect, fairness, justice, or the law—may not be so easily sacrificed, even for the sake of religion or the arts. One could, of course, choose to argue otherwise, for example, in favor of theocratic societies or, in parallel, aesthetico-cratic republics. But common sense suggests that the best guarantor of freedom for religious belief as well as artistic pursuit is not necessarily secured under civil unions, where religious thought or artistic style in itself becomes a substitute for the authority of conscience, or of the sovereign or the universal will. It seems that only the natural and ordinary intuitions embodied in this conscience are secure grounds for the pluralism under which expressions of faith and taste may find their most extensive rooms. For this idea of pluralistic moral and social relations to self or others, one would have to seek to recover—in Africa as elsewhere—modes of reasons for political or cultural associations that depend neither on theocracy nor on artistic license. It is therefore not enough for our theologians and novelists, Black or White or Brown, Africanized or Westernized or Orientalized, to tell us that words and stories that words make up, and the worlds that the make-believes will into existence, are sacred and therefore superior to our ordinary and daily forms of moral intuitions—including intuitions into our historical constructions of the sacred or the artistic.

It is simply not enough in philosophy or in politics to sacralize or aestheticize the everyday. It is even more unsatisfactory to try to do so—romantically or tragically—in the name of an African exceptionalism. Yes, in Africa the dead and the living and the unborn may be metaphysically conceived to be in constant relations. And the realm of art may not be neatly separated from the boundaries of social life and from society's instrumental uses of culture. To go beyond these banalities of religion and art as part of the quotidian existence in Africa, and argue—ideologically—that all of life in Africa is but one, indistinct tissue of relations among the gods, or that daily life is shrouded in a mythical cloth, woven in a mythical "natural" world of the aesthetic, literary or otherwise, is to profoundly misunderstand the intricate ordinary reasons woven into the enduring fabrics of morality and politics in African cultures and anywhere else in human experience.

A Conceptual Division of Labor

The distinction between religion or art and reason, *as the distinction extends to the relations between politics and philosophy,* needs to be carefully thought and, for practical analysis, maintained. As noted in the beginning, the choice of South Africa's Truth and Reconciliation Commission as a point of reference is a contingent fact. It is obvious from the two preceding sections that I do not consider the TRC's substance or procedures deficient as political settlements. I merely think there is room to raise questions about some of its epistemological assumptions, especially the assumption behind the putatively philosophical and moral concept, ubuntu.[7] It is precisely the conceptual conditions of the legitimacy of a distinction that should exist, between the *political* questions of ubuntu and its merely *philosophical* justification, that I wish to trace.

I ask, for example, whether or not the languages of South Africa's or other countries' political "truth" and "reconciliation" commissions do not suggest—beyond the language of "amnesty"—the religious and artistic examples of comprehensions of truth and social relations that I have attributed to certain theologies and novels. Are the TRC's settlements not driven by unitary, aesthetic, and transcendental visions of community? Visions that—in their exuberance, we need not overlook—"override" the language of ordinary reason and this reason's understanding of, for example, the requirements of justice and the law? In this concept of "truth" or "reconciliation," is not one asked to suspend a specific kind of moral judgment—for the sake of survival of politics as such? Did not the same TRC show, and in a postmodern tone that Pi would have liked, how anything—religion, art, law, justice, truth—is, in the end, a political event?[8]

If one were to defend the reasons of philosophy from unphilosophical encroachments by the political, it would be on the grounds that there is no *necessary* equivalence between the philosophical and the political. What is good politics, for example, is not necessarily good philosophy— and vice versa. Similarly, what is good religious work is not necessarily a good work of art, or the reverse. So I insist that not every good artistic work is an important philosophical event—and that a good artistic work *need not* be a good philosophical treatise. To think otherwise is to willfully court a confusion of domains. The intuitive truths of these observations are apparent when, for example, we admit that the procedures for redeeming an artistic vision or religious yearning, or winning a political contest, need not be the same as the procedures for making successful— that is, disinterestedly convincing—philosophical arguments.

I am, obviously, operating with a specific idea of philosophy, an idea premised on several considerations. First, philosophy need not be asked to make compromises on the question of reason, or apologize for standing in defense of "reasonableness"—as Pi would have put it, with a hint of the pejorative. Contrary to David's understanding of philosophy (what one does "when all else fails") or Pi's definition of reasonableness (bourgeois primness), one need not believe that philosophy could ever become too ordinary. If philosophy is said to be synonymous with the defense of procedures of ordinary reason, and of reasonableness (as opposed to revelation, myth, artistic "vision," etc.), then reason eludes overextension: it is conceived as conceptually delimited by its own iterative, reflective, and bounded relations to the ordinary in experience.

Second, by affirming the quotidian and public—and the morality of the publicity of ordinary reason—philosophy absconds neither from sociality or politics nor allows itself to be confused with the exclusively religious, artistic, or political. Philosophy is just the opposite of intellectual preciousness or moral primness, and philosophical reason must have its own defined place and role in the public domain, even when confronted with experience of issues that arise in what should be considered nonspecifically philosophical spheres. I do not believe that there are ever sufficient or necessary *philosophical* reasons to plead—as Kierkegaard would have wished—for a teleological "suspension" of the rational or merely reasonable, when it comes to conceptions of the morality of social or political relations.

Third, this form of defense of reason in ordinary experience is also required for an equally ordinary principle of justice. Social life, whether religiously or aesthetically conceived, would be impoverished—in fact, made vulnerable as morally fragile—without such an ordinary conception of justice as a requirement of reason. Moreover, it is precisely the vulnerability of the social projects of reason—especially in Africa, and in relationships within industrializing worlds, across them, and with postindustrialized societies—that leads one to insist on the paths of defending this figure of reason and the equi-primordial concept of justice. The defense of reason and its justice will be valid even when it is acknowledged that modernity's industrial and commercial reason is merely an imperfect version of possible historical ideals of reason. It is, in fact, this potential in the capacity to conceive such "better" reasons that accounts for the necessity for a historical critique of reasons of the present.[9] Far from dogmatic or conservative, this is a critical, progressive theory of rationality.

Fourth, in defending such a resilient version of the capacity to say that one's beliefs are true as part of daily life, rather than only in extraordinary moments of revelation or forgiveness, I also maintain the right to consider modernist conceptions of reason in their historical accidentality—for I could offer defenses of reason at any other time or place in history, where the dominant ideal could have been other than modern. But by this same account, the modern version of a reason (in science, law, and morality) could also have remained available—if only *in potentia*—as an option to, for example, a humanity that might or might not have shared the radical and essential traits of the modern.

Highlighting the historical fragility of even my radical partisanship for this—admittedly burdened, imperfect, but serviceable—version of reason, should prevent my and my critics from the tempting but irresponsible turn of fixing all blame on "modernity" or "rationalism" as Africa's or the Third World's most primal curse. Such an attitude proceeds as if premodern or postmodern forms of life were morally perfect or could be imagined without their own irrationalities. The view of public reason that I hold may well be guilty of some of the charges leveled against it by defenders of premodern primordialism or a postmodern irony. But when justifications of these pre- or postmodern protests are framed with any substantive interests in mind—for example, material (economic,

political, social) and logical (epistemological, moral, aesthetic, etc.) arguments—one easily detects in these antimodern attitudes any number of
the following: a choice of critique of reason in the name of some religious
or secular "prophetic" posture within which reason is said to be inadequate (but this inadequacy, it is said, must be detectable only in the name
of an apparently "higher," unknowable version of reason); or the aesthetic
attitude (e.g., it is argued that reason represents a cult of analysis, division, and suffering, and that we must therefore think in ways that "heal"
experience with what such proponents, and they are romantics, prefer to
call the remedy of art); or the "realist" political disposition (e.g., reason is
nothing but power, and its exercise little else than practices of coercion
and force so that, all of us being caught in the capillaries of disciplines of
power, all are wittingly and unwittingly engaged in biopolitical agonism,
an agonism that may be full of "pleasure" for the body and mind but
could never be entitled to have happiness, *le bonheur* in its sight).

But throughout these critical posturings it is easy to see that those
making the various arguments do so in the hope that theirs are the most,
not the least, reasonable. That is, they claim to have higher or better
reasons, to have a clearer rational picture of how reason actually works,
or to offer better sermons, edification, and communal exhortations
about how to enjoy the life of desires and of reason. In any case, there is
presupposed a framework of possibility of persuasion across "reason,"
however the critic chooses to define reason (prophetic mandate, aesthetic desire, disciplinary power, etc.). This being the case, when disagreements occur over definitions of reason, what is called for is not a
rejection or abandonment of rationality as morally serviceable in any of
its most conventional—including the Afro-modern historical—forms.
Instead, it is precisely a greater thinking-through of reason's essential
multiplicities that is required: its historical identities, contemporary political affiliations, and demands of civil, cultural coexistence. From a
performative point of view, the opponent of ordinary reason may therefore be interpreted—against any metaphysical pretensions of the rhetoric of prophecy, revelation, nature—as advocating more pragmatic
(higher, clearer, more practical) forms of reason.

On the other hand, when radical partisans of modernity's rationalism
accuse *anyone* who critiques modernity or rationalism of advocating
"irrationality," there is no question that neither modernity nor its ordi-

nary ideals of reason need such extraordinary demonization of its critics. There is simply no cause to offer extraordinary justification of modernity or reason as such: it is precisely its abstemiousness in relation to grandiose claims—romantic or tragic—that distinguishes the claims of reason to ordinariness. Those of us Afro-modern rationalists who protest the romantic primitivization of reason and intellectual life in Africa do so regardless of whether such primitivization is pursued in the name of premodernity, nonmodernity, countermodernity, or postmodernity. By the same token we reject the claims of religionists—animist, Christian, Islamist, or other—that mysticism or the mystical frame of mind alone is "African" while "philosophy" is non-African. We are also opposed to New Age, neopagan artists who think that in Africa distinctions between science, religion, art, philosophy, and morality are nonexistent. We assert that there is simply no need to deify, in the name of "Africa," any form of art or aesthetic sensibility as such, at the expense of the public claims of reason or other forms of common sense. We Afro-modern rationalists can amply justify this reason and its processes of modernization without resorting to the spectacular tactics of most religious, artistic, and political movements in Africa. The legacy of European enlighteners who permitted themselves—at the moments of inaugurating their own movements—to be carried away by racist and sexist prejudices is hardly sufficient reason to indulge in the belief that enlightenment movements or modernization in Africa could not escape such racialist and sexist and class prejudices.

I should more directly answer the question: Why defend modernity and its irreversible process in the contexts of a history of reason in Africa? I do so in the name of morality and justice. The moral sense of self (e.g., integrity) that the idea of the rational being presupposes in acts of moral persuasion is best affirmed when this reason is provided with a rigorous philosophical defense. Likewise, in affirming the integrity of self I *de facto* postulate as equally morally, rationally defensible the individual's or collectivity's capacity to respond reasonably to demands imposed by sociality on grounds of justice. One thus affirms not only one's entitlement to self-respect and agency in the social domain, but also the rights of others to the same. If one chooses to call this ubuntu, so be it. Self-integrity and relational agency describe not just the requirements of respect for self and the other—as necessary for social life—but also the demands of the general interests of social or political agency in itself. If one were to come up with better ways to hold and defend these values—under whatever different name or names—such counterproposals would be compatible with the ideals of reason and justice that these concepts of integrity and agency aim to capture. Thus, by defending what I have called ordinary reason, I simply seek to enunciate the ways individuals and parties *who believe diversely* (religiously, politically, culturally, etc.) may argue and agree, and even secure agreements about difference, on any range of issues that matter to individuals and communities.

By holding that reason-giving is something individuals owe to themselves and to others, I propose a minimalist conception of reason that can hardly be charged, pejoratively, with "rationalism." My conception of the social reason is minimalist in that the person is imagined deflatively—with regard only to that which is most necessary for relation to both self and society—and held philosophically accountable for this and only this. The minimalist conception allows one to imagine a form of self-empowerment on the basis of which personal and social morality may be entertained without prejudice.[10] Furthermore, because of its formality, we may also characterize the private and public requirements of the moral minimum of reason in social relations as leading necessarily to a negative ethics: an ethics that does not provide a principle of what must happen, but rather of what must not be allowed to happen. (We cannot require, for example, that everyone must be wealthy; rather, the poverty or social deprivation of the many by a few is—on grounds of social justice or human rights or virtues like charity and duty—unacceptable.) In whatever positive terms these and similar principles may be framed, the principles themselves may be considered philosophically "negative" because they are secured by no metaphysical substance or noncontingent positivities. Because of its common cause with the ordinary in reason, an ethics of the ordinary or an ordinary ethics must, like its reason, remain intuitively secured by "natural" freedom in the form of autonomy of self (the requirement of integrity) and the respect owed to others (responsibility). Like ordinary reason's radicalness, the radical nature of freedom in these contexts is secured merely by freedom's natural form as the indivisible. Justice, like reason, grounds itself epistemically and morally because there is nothing else into which one can analyze reason's rationality or the morality of justice. In a sense, reason and justice—by their own natures—are what I call, respectively, "analysis" and "social morality."

The ethical and social significance of philosophy's ordinary reason derives from the fact that it is that which we can with certainty assume as protection against the excessive in claims—political, religious, or artistic—to the "miraculous." To affirm the rational as retention of critical attitudes toward *both* the charismatic *and* the demonic is to treat with due suspicion the dialectically linked claims of both the saint and the devil, wherever such claims may be found. It is to foreswear slavishness to the exciting, through affirmation of the mundane. Whereas possession or revelation may be virtuous by reason of luck or anointing by the gods, the just in the justice of reason is so only on account of the intuitive ordinariness of reason's requirement to treat oneself and others according to its rationally justifiable and nonarbitrary principle. But I have also refused to succumb to another kind of excess: the portrayal of the dialectics of reason and the irrational as that of a modern/antimodern, European/African, Western/Eastern problematic.

I can therefore be confident that I have defended the right of reason to maintain its sovereignty in the face of all dialectics driven by the principles of the passionate, the revealed, or the mystical. These have their proper and legitimate spheres—as philosophy is entitled to its sphere. Moreover, unlike some modern philosophers who share harbored prejudices against pre- or postmodernism, I have not attributed essential unreason to nonmodern rationalities. And instead of the Platonic desire for a reason that governs all—including the passions—I advocate reason's right to self-governance and philosophy's claim to defend the sovereignty of the moral sense, as seen only in the light of the autonomy and agency of this natural reason.

The Counterargument: Against the Autonomy of Reason

Following some authors, one could argue that there is already too much of the impact—the negative impact—of modernist, universalizing rationalization in Africa, so that the hyperbolic images of Africa's "traditional" cultures need protection from competing, idealized processes of modernity. This kind of critique of modernization as cultural colonization or economic imperialism has long roots in philosophical traditions, within as well as outside of Africa.[11] Since Weber and Senghor, it has become acceptable to blame secular rationality for the excesses of the commercial spirit of the market (globally unregulated capitalism), the ethos of rugged individualism (corrosive of family bonds and traditional ties to community), and the moral consequences of these burdens on institutions like marriage, child rearing, labor, and public service. So why, the critic asks, should anyone be expected to defend these colonialist or imperialist versions of reason or modernity anywhere, in the name of philosophy or anything else?

To frame the question thus is to misunderstand the perspective of my core argument: I have *not* attempted to shield the commercial reasons of modernity or the capitalist social conditions of modern philosophy from criticism. Instead, I have, more modestly, argued that any such criticism is not most effective when pursued in the name of revelation, tradition, or nature. I have also argued that only some specific understanding of politics (e.g., a nonmiraculous conception of the political) can provide the most effective, if nonetheless partial, grounds from which a viable critique of modernity's instrumental reason for the profit-motivated, labor-insensitive, commercial reasons of unregulated international capitalism.

The most reflective objection to this perspective can derive only from frameworks that are willing to take seriously my basic starting point: that of philosophical priority, and the consequent ordinary social and political morality. The critics could challenge this starting point by asking whether or not I have adopted too narrow a conception of philosophical reason, and therefore too narrow a conception of the justice that might be acceptable to this reason in the name of reason alone. One could also choose to criticize this perspective by saying that, for example, rejecting the primacy of what I have called the "ordinary," "everyday," or "intuitive" and its stricter sense of social justice does not mean that there cannot exist other forms of rationality or conceptions of justice—justice as forgiveness, or a total transformation of social systems; justice as the "right to knowledge"; "telling one's story" of crimes suffered. One could argue that the reasons for these other understandings of justice may be just as ordinary as any I could propose. For example, the proponent of the rationalities of revolutionary or transformational justice could argue that in suspending the basic, social, and intuitive idea of reason and justice as defended earlier, one is in fact acting on the basis of—and for the sake of a deeper understanding of—community and of common sense.

But I must repeat that I do not claim that there is one way to think about reason or morality or politics, whether or not this one way is ordinary. Instead, I have merely juxtaposed an ordinary understanding of reason and political morality with extraordinary ones. I do not wish to argue for exclusivity or superiority of my proposal. I have only asked, investigatively: Can there be a logical (dialectical) relation between the thinking that forgives in order to reconcile the community, and the thinking that demonizes in order to divide and punish? Is there a relation between the thinking that suspends the law in order to redeem its deeper morality, and the thinking that, say, destroys a village in order to liberate it? I am not, of course, making a *moral* equivalence between the poles of this dialectic; I am asking if there is a *logical* equivalence. To the extent—no matter how low in a measuring scale—one can imagine the possibility of such logical equivalence in the dialectics of these opposites, I have argued that one could anticipatorily escape the side of the logic that I do not find morally acceptable by giving up on the fervor for the morally "attractive" side of the dialectics.

I refuse the revolutionarily or spectacularly moral not because I do not like victories and transformations. Rather, my refusal is based on a principled reservation against the revolutionary and spectacular as a social or political ideal. Against the messianic, charismatic, or historically inaugural in moral, legal, or political thinking, I propose the merely deliberative, ordinary, and democratic. Instead of recourse to the revealed or the "inspired," why not rely on the merely reasonable? The contexts of my reservations are also clear: in Africa as in much of the Third World, there are too many gods and prophets and too few doctors, nurses, and engineers. In these countries—most of which already suffer from legacies of colonialism—why accept the risks of glorifying the "strong man" messianic (or demonic) models of leadership or social transformation, models which tend to reinforce the citizen/subject cleavages in these postcolonial societies? Why not, instead, promote in every possible way the ordinary ideals of citizenship and equality for all?

Unless one is against these intentions, the best challenge to my argument might be the following: What if it is the ordinary or everyday I defend which, in the first place, gives rise to the need for the extraordinary? For example, were not the judicial crimes of apartheid so banal, so everyday (because systemic) that they required a transformative suspension of the everyday and its systems of morally illegitimate law in order to inaugurate a democratic and legitimate order of law? I would not respond by accepting that apartheid—or any other judicial system of crimes against humanity—was ordinary in the sense that I have defined this term. Events like Black slavery, Jim Crow, the Jewish Holocaust, and apartheid, were—as should be easy to see—precisely results of "visionary," "inspired," and charismatic politics. These moral evils were often conceived by their creators in languages, and for purposes, of moral or social transformation (civilization, commerce, free market, purity of race, tribe, country, etc.). Even today, most catastrophes in history are often prosecuted in the name of "moral clarity" or conceptions of destinies whose manifest nature is claimed to have been inherited from, or revealed by, God or history.

Race, Nation, God: these are codes for the miraculous and the spectacular. They are the grounds of those messianic elements in politics which produce catastrophes that, in the name of transforming history seem only to wreck it. For this reason, the "banality" of evil or of the postcolony which some philosophers and political historians like Arendt and Mbembe have eloquently written about, needs to be placed in its proper contexts: Holocaust, colonialism, slavery, Jim Crow, and apartheid are banal or everyday only *after* their systems have been routinized. Keeping in mind the logical—not moral—equivalence that I think exists between the "inaugural" nature of the democratic *and* demonic forms of social transformation, is it not possible to suspect that (to return to my prime example) apartheid is precisely a historical instance of reasons for distrust of totalistic forms of thought that, I suspect, animate—as dialectical opposites—both slavery and freedom?[12] We cannot afford to exempt contemporary Africa—in the name of its Third World and internationally exploited status—from this philosophical critique of politics. We might find even in precolonial traditions of Africa—in the idea of "palaver," for example—reasons to support my rejection of politics-as-the-extraordinary. There are instances of First World countries also abandoning the everyday reason of pluralism in domestic politics and of diplomacy in international relations to embrace the irrational in uninhibited expression of revolutionary might. Whether such irrationalism is motivated by a religious zeal, a racial or national sense of entitlement, or market fundamentalism, its exceptionalist justifications do not affect my argument that revolution—in domestic as in international politics, and for whatever reason—provides the best cover for failures of, and threats to, everyday political freedoms and stable world orders.

REASON: AN ASCETIC IDEAL

It remains to consider an abstract, though indirectly practical question: Are there certain motives in the individual mind or collective psyches of societies which require humans to periodically discharge them into convulsive political fits of revolution? If the answer is yes, one could argue for some "metaphysical" necessity of revolution regardless of whether it be democratic, socially liberating, and empowering of the weakest members of society or antidemocratic, totalitarian, and gender-/race-/class-prejudiced. An affirmative answer to this question also implies that revolution is not only a philosophical possibility in the experience of individuals and societies, but also a logic of social and political relations whose moral and immoral potentials one must learn to live with, without regard to what anyone—artist, theologian, or philosopher—wishes to believe. Indeed, we must ask: Is revolution a necessary, permanent, and noncontingent part of the historical logic of evolution for any moral self or (even the most socially, ordinarily democratic) society?

There are several possible nonabstract ways to enlighten the issues thus raised, should one choose to embrace a metaphysics of the extraordinary as a requirement of the ordinary, or revolution as a necessary condition for any democratic process of natural or historical evolution of individuals and societies. One could ask: Instead of seeking to philosophically distance oneself from this necessity, should we not celebrate it in its inaugural events, and hope that these events will always dialectically "correct" their innate extremisms? If the rational and the irrational somehow deeply belong together and enable each other—presumably for the beneficial end of actualization of the good in forms of everyday institutions—then shouldn't dialectical thought be considered a highest metaphysical and social duty in philosophy and politics? We should then expect that revolution, like a pendulum, will inexorably lead to evolution in the everyday as evolution leads to revolution. The Emancipation Proclamation, decolonization of the Third World, the civil rights movement, Zionism, TRCs in Africa and Latin America would all be seen as historically necessary forms of grand, corrective gestures that respond to equally necessary events that were in their own ways grotesque in their grandiosities. But if it is assumed that the human psyche is naturally inhabited by irrationality and is periodically overtaken by madness, and if it is further believed that such natural attacks of insanity can be countered only by an equally irrational transhuman revelation or extra-ordinary inspiration in the form of political "miracles," then one should be concerned about the confusion of the ordinarily distinct domains of the natural, the religious, the artistic, and the properly political. Whereas it may be acceptable to evoke natural luck or divine intervention in the form of grace or redemption in religion and tragedy in the arts, shouldn't we worry about a conception of politics that decides to defend a redemption from evil or the tragic ideal of existence as its answer to questions that arise in the common processes of political interests?

If our critic—for the sake of the argument or out of hermeneutic charity—is presumed to be correct that "fate" somehow invisibly and inscrutably maneuvers individuals and societies into political situations where the extraordinary, miraculous, or (good) luck appears to be a necessary rational mode of political practice, the philosopher, as opposed to the politician, may yet reserve the right to distance his or her professional commitments from such a fateful understanding of nature or the historical. This is not to suggest that philosophy and its reasons thereby become ahistorical and apolitical: I have already defended a historical, not a divine or divinely inspired, theory of fate in the Introduction to this book. It is, rather, to affirm and maintain philosophy's right first to difference, and then to intervention in the public spheres of politics or civil societies of religion and culture—and to make its intervention in terms *motivated* by distinctly philosophical reasons.

Political violence and its posttraumatic reconciliation, unleashed as forms of discharge of natural or social psychic burdens, are common in the religious and artistic rituals of any premodern, modern, or postmodern culture. But instead of the abuses of historical reason and its intuitive understanding of freedom and justice (or autonomy and agency), as revealed in the politically spectacular, or perversions of ordinary morality or law in the name of such spectacular and spectral politics, why not confine such periodic outbursts—if this is what they are—to revivalisms in religion and carnivalism in the arts? After all, we all know that in religious celebrations, as in carnivals, it is precisely the ordinary that is ritually and dramatically suspended. One may imagine and enact all sorts of symbolic discharge of psychic contents along with their necessary emotions. One commits murder—suicide, patricide, matricide, even deicide—yet celebrates this as an act of individual or social redemption. Why extend such miracles to democratic political performances? And if the politician chooses to make this extension, why should philosophy be expected to capitulate?

I have conceded that mine is an apology for philosophical reason. And my *primary* effort has not been aimed at rationalizing politics or politicizing philosophy. Instead, I have argued that there are good reasons—philosophical and political—for us to maintain reason's interests to preserve for itself an autonomous space vis-à-vis politics. The conceptual distinction between spheres is good not only for philosophy but also for politics: by allowing reason the right to self-discipline and sovereignty, politics gains an ally whose independence secures—as a last resort, if it has to be so—the possibility of democracy as ordinary, not revolutionary, politics. As one does not expect to create wealth for a nation by luck—playing the lottery, say—but through careful and mundane acts of balancing predictable incomes and expenditures, so democracy, I believe, allows a political society to function not by "miraculous" acts that suspend—no matter how inaugurally—the everyday forms of social reasons. Rather, it is through the meticulous affirmation of mundane institutions of life—institutions that reference their legitimacy to intuitions embodied in nonradical, free and open forms of ordinary sociality—that political stability is achieved.

The reciprocity required by ordinary reason in the context of social relations is precisely that in the name of which the best democratic revolutions—the French, the American, and revolutionary de-colonizations of Africa and Asia—have been initiated and prosecuted. But it does not make such reasons for revolution any more rational to argue that the conditions that produce its necessity are themselves necessary. To argue that revolution is the reason for despotism is to place a historical effect before its logical cause. Revolution in this case would only appear necessary because there is already a prior "natural" failure, or historical repression of reason and freedom in everyday life. Likewise, it does not make sense, in the everyday perspective from which I speak, to say that this same everyday perspective naturally or historically requires—for political reasons—teleological suspensions of its ordinary reason for the sake of radical or transformative social ends. Politics, in my opinion, does not intrinsically require the extraordinary or revolutionary fervor—any more than the artist intrinsically requires the virtue of propriety at carnivals, or the prophet conformism in the pulpit. Yet the alternative is not *either* revolutionary transformation *or* no transformation at all. Vigilant, constant, reasoned practices of sociality in everyday life, I believe, provide for democratic politics its necessary radical requirements.

RATIONALITY AND THE POLITICS OF MEMORY

Some took issue with Derrida's claims, in a lecture delivered at the University of Durban, that "forgiveness is not, *it should not be*, normal, normative, normalizing," and that forgiveness "*should* remain exceptional and extraordinary, in the face of the impossible: as if it interrupted the ordinary course of historical temporality."[13] The counterposition coming largely from Black South African students is interesting, but the complexity of its reasons is yet more significant. What motivates victims of a universal system of human rights abuses—as in the once legal South African system of racial apartheid—to forgive their known or unknown abusers? Beyond *present* material needs and political interests of a state undergoing fundamental democratic transformation, to embrace a transitional accounting (instead of a strict discharge) of its duty as guarantor of justice for the citizens, what does it mean for victims of crime perpetrated in the name of systems of law, such as apartheid, to forgive the *past*? What does forgiveness mean in these contexts? And what kind of morality should govern its offer or the refusal to offer it, the request for it or the refusal to request it, and its acceptance or refusal to accept it? Likewise, is there an ethics that should govern such forgiving relationships, in terms of the necessary requirements of justice *and* the memory of past acts of state-sanctioned political and judicial crimes? This section is a meditation on the range of answers to these questions—answers that could be easily gleaned by any attentive observer from the practices of public memory in South Africa after apartheid. I hope to shed some light on the reasons for forgiving or not forgiving judicial crimes in general, and the ethical and political uses of public memories of gross, systemic, state-sanctioned human rights violations in particular.

It is often on account of obtaining knowledge of the crimes suffered, and the processes of public memorialization of this knowledge, that victims of systemic human rights violations—by themselves or through mediating instruments of state (e.g., negotiated political settlement, constitutional compromise reached between previously warring political parties, truth and amnesty commissions)—resort to the ideology of forgiveness or reconciliation as means to both establish facts about the crimes and promote democratic transformation of the general political culture, so that such crimes may not repeat themselves in the future. Hence, David Crocker has argued that this pursuit of "*knowledge* about the past is important in itself" because "victims and their descendants have a moral *right to know* the truth about human rights abuses."[14] South Africa's TRC was also explicit on this matter. In justifying the reasons for its offer of amnesty to judicial criminals of the apartheid state, the commission argued that since "secrecy and authoritarianism have concealed the truth" of the crimes "in little crevices of obscurity in our history," and as "records are not easily accessible, witnesses are often unknown, dead, unavailable or unwilling," it was in the interest of truth—and a matter of rights for the victims—to do everything necessary to establish and make public what happened in the particular instances of these crimes. In a language that thus traded truth for amnesty—ambiguously understood as official forgiveness of otherwise dire consequences of crime—the commission was ready to say that "truth, *which the victims of repression seek so desperately to know,*" is, "in the circumstances, much more likely to be forthcoming if those responsible for such monstrous misdeeds are encouraged to disclose the whole truth with the incentive that they will not receive the punishment which they undoubtedly deserve if they do."[15] Even those who raised moral objections against these arguments arrived at their position by considering the value of (public) display of what may not have been as hidden or "secret" as the commission believed.

Finally, it is on grounds of the moral and political value of this right to knowledge *and* the will to public remembrance that critics of these perspectives on amnesty, forgiveness, and reconciliation have based their criticisms. Soyinka, for example, asked, "Will the South African doctrine work? Will society be truly purified as a result of this open articulation of what is known?" His main skepticism grew out of the fact that "while we speak of 'revelation,' it is only revelation in concrete particulars, the ascription of faces to deeds, admission by individual personae of roles within known criminalities, affirmation by the already identified of what they had formerly denied." If nothing new is being revealed, then one is left with the impression that the state is trading—by negotiated political instruments and constitutional amendments—the due process of law for mere publicity on crimes arguably otherwise establishable as facts under extant bodies of evidence. "The difference," Soyinka believed, was that "*knowledge* is being shared, collectively, and entered into the archives of that nation."[16]

Might the political "transition," then, be understood as a memorial deferral of justice? The insistence on knowledge (the right to know) and public memory is, however, not only in a tension with a certain under-standing of the requirements of justice. This insistence, I believe, tran-scends the problem of the hidden and the revealed, or the previously obscured becoming universally manifest. The main discomfort posed by the situation to a standard theory of justice is in the tension between demands of forgiving as a means of "moving on" and requirements of a moral understanding of law. Whereas the language of forgiveness is, basically, individualistic and carries religious overtones, issues of demo-cratic political or constitutional settlements are, like the origins of the crimes they are meant to address, domains of civil or criminal law. How to reconcile a political ethic of forgiveness—or the morality of constitu-tional doctrines of amnesty for crime—with revelation of a truth about the same crime by the perpetrator? This question highlights not merely a circumvention of the normal course of law, but also—and this is quite remarkable—a plea for the public and the state to substitute the order of law for a higher, moral order.

When, in the interest of politically "moving on" as a nation, a national public forgives or reconciles with criminals but nevertheless insists that it remember their crimes, then clearly, reasons for a different and transformed principle of legality—or suspension of the normal run of justice, or, worse, legal interruption of the law directly or indirectly sanctioned by the state—are at issue. In addition to the fact that the civil or criminal procedures—which usually lead to recovery of any benefits of crime from its perpetrators, or punitive awards against the perpetrators in favor of the victims—are compromised, there is also the issue of compensation for collective and systemic State violations of rights in the form of material, usually economic deprivations that result from legislation, discriminatory public lending, employment practices, education, and so on. The debate that preoccupies those who study transitional democracy is this: Does not the desire to forgive but remember—motivated, as it is, by political considerations—compromise too much of the very political reasons of transformation in the name of which such languages of forgiveness and reconciliation have gained sympathy?

To speak, instead, of "transitional justice" brings no clear relief to the questions. The phrase itself sounds strange and highly ambiguous. The ambiguity derives from an intention to designate a form of limit—in this case, the limits of justice or democracy—but a limit left vague and unspecific. Is this the limit of what can be achieved *now* (time) in justice or democracy; the limit of possible justice and democracy achievable *here* (place); or, more radically, the limit of the principle of justice or democracy *regardless* of place and time?[17] A casual perusal of the literature on transitional justice and transitional democratic practices reveals the variety and internal complexity of reasons why one must speak at all of these transitionals.[18]

In "The Perpetrators Should Not Always Be Prosecuted: Where the International Criminal Court and Truth Commissions Meet," C. Villa-Vicencio makes transparent one of the motives for transitional justice, a motive that addresses one of my hypotheses about one of the reasons for transitional justice. "The question," Villa-Vicencio states, "is whether legal absolutism involving a 'duty to prosecute' is necessarily helpful or realistic in national and international disputes involving genocide, terror, and similar forms of lawlessness." He thinks that in some of these cases, the "popular perception of law as the 'bulwark of freedom' and being 'of God not man' . . . need[s] to give way to more humble metaphors that capture the tension between political vicissitude and the codification of the law." One of the consequences of this contextualist and contingent understanding of the duty to prosecute—and the reason this approach to justice must be seen as necessarily transitional (i.e., incomplete)—is clear: "Lawyers and judges need to adjust to what is required in a particular situation to meet a given goal. The necessity for this adjustment militates against the notion that a 'duty to prosecute' is a legal absolute."[19] Moreover, in "The Duty to Punish Past Abuses of Human Rights Put into Context: The Case of Argentina," Carlos Nino provides another argument in favor of this conception of transition: in a climate where rights violations are pervasive and systemic, as is often the case in the best known examples—Chile, South Africa, Rwanda—a "legal duty selectively to prosecute human rights violations committed under a previous regime is too blunt an instrument to help successor governments who must struggle with the subtle complexities of re-establishing democracy."[20]

It seems clear, then, that South Africa's TRC had the equivalent of these broader pictures of the place of the law in society. Hence the commission's observation that, though "every decent human being must feel grave discomfort in living with a consequence which might allow the perpetrators of evil acts to walk the streets of this land with impunity, protected in their freedom by an amnesty immune from constitutional attack . . . the circumstances in support of this course require carefully to be appreciated."[21] It then added, more bluntly, in the words of the commission's chairperson: "Amnesty is a heavy price to pay. It is, however, the price the [political and constitutional] negotiators believed our country would have to pay to avoid an 'alternative too ghastly to contemplate.'"[22]

These backgrounds, cumulatively, sum up what I call *a deferral of justice for the sake of the law.* This may also be characterized as a teleological suspension of the judicial, neatly captured thus: We forgive, or offer amnesty, but we shall not forget. In the case of South Africa, however, manifestations of this forgive-and-forget sentiment are shared across the races that were once divided as oppressors and oppressed, perpetrators and victims, or beneficiaries and sufferers of the apartheid system of law. The idea of justice as legally deferred could also be entertained because this idea does not suggest a moral equivalence of the racial oppression of majority Blacks by minority Whites, or an equally morally ambiguous ignorance of the facts that, even at its most racially intense, it should not be surprising if racial oppression affected different identifiable social groups—classes, genders, ethnicities, religions within and across racial lines—unevenly.

It is a truism that oppression per se seeks to sustain itself with the aid of divisions of all kinds, and that these divisions thrive only because they are based on structured *inequality*. For these reasons, it is only at the most abstract level that one might be able to make vague statements like "We all are victims" or "We are all guilty" and understand that consequently there are no crucial distinctions—moral, material, or political—that must be drawn among the "all" who victimized and suffered victimization. Even the moral suffering of guilt, shame, or loss of ill-gotten benefits that a repentant perpetrator of judicial crimes may suffer *because* of being a victimizer cannot be morally equated to the moral dilemma that the victim must confront in the processes of exercising the moral generosity implied in the radical, if momentary, ethical suspension of the law, as in "We forgive, but we shall not forget."

Underscoring the fact that "We forgive, but we shall not forget" could be heard from across racial, class, gender, and other defining lines of meaningful social and political distinction and legal status is helpful because it allows one to see, at the outset, the specifically moral—and thus by no means exclusively racial, class, gender, religious, ethnic, or otherwise parochial character—of the statement or its motive. Individuals of all ethnicities, classes, religions, and genders designed, executed, or otherwise facilitated apartheid; just as individuals of all ethnicities, classes, religions, and genders suffered from it. Alongside the primary victims of apartheid, repentant and transformed instruments of the legal but illegitimate regime, and all those who might be considered apartheid's universal collateral victims (including those who might claim, "I was following orders," "I was executing the law," "I acted legally"; or the many peoples around the world who felt that apartheid was a crime against a shared humanity, and fought against it, regardless of their own nationality or location, and with whatever means available to them) may also be heard to say: We may offer or receive forgiveness, but we shall not forget.

The question, then, is how (not) to forgive the unforgivable—and apartheid may be unforgivable for several reasons. May there be not only a right to know the circumstance of a crime suffered, but also a victim's natural *right to forgive* the perpetrator? And how can a victim who is dead offer forgiveness? Can a living relative, beyond the right to offer forgiveness for his or her own suffering from the crime against the dead, also have the right to forgive in the name of the dead? Or is it the state that, beyond its offers of politically motivated or constitutionally negotiated amnesty, should extend forgiveness in the name of the dead? If the state, beyond public memorials, has no moral standing to forgive in the name of the dead, can it forgive in the name of the living—or even merely "promote" forgiveness, as South Africa's TRC did reconciliation? Could a nation be "reconciled" or "healed" of gross human rights violations or crimes against humanity without the request, offer, and acceptance of forgiveness by individual perpetrators and victims? Or is forgiveness an entirely private matter? And then, what if the perpetrator asks for forgiveness but is visibly insincere in that asking; or asks sincerely and is not granted it; or receives (and accepts or rejects) an offer of forgiveness, without the asking?

Some have argued that these questions arise only because some of us are operating under an uncritical concept of forgiveness. In the case of apartheid, for example, it is said that to interiorize the idea of forgiveness in the individualistic, Christian-confessional model, is to ignore the fact that apartheid itself was a racial crime of a racial group (White) against other racial groups (Black and Colored). The suggestion, then, is to understand that forgiveness of the crime of apartheid is never something that one solitary individual asks of another solitary individual. If one were to use forgiveness as a metaphor, it is the society as a whole that needs to ask and receive forgiveness of itself. And such asking and receiving of forgiveness—as a previously racially divided but now more racially united nation—implies not only that the social institutions of apartheid have been dismantled, but also that the moral *and* material transformation for the better of the lives of the people who suffered the most under apartheid have been, and must be seen to have been, facilitated. Because apartheid morally corrupted all, and materially enriched the (White) few at the expense of the (Black and Colored) many, such global social transformation may be seen as the only useful form of forgiveness to be asked for, given, or accepted by the agents and beneficiaries of the perpetrating racial group and the victim racial groups.

It is to avoid this stretched meaning of forgiveness that some have chosen to speak only about uncovering "truths," about national reconciliation or negotiated amnesty, rather than forgiveness. Yet the TRC itself has been blamed for having, on precisely this account, an indistinct —even confusing—mandate. On the subject of its truth-finding mission, for example, Frederik Van Zyl Slabbert writes:

> The TRC is based on suppositions and assumptions that, even if they are demonstrably invalid, are nevertheless misleading and ambiguous. What is the notion of truth assumed here? It must be universal and transferable, otherwise the entire process is senseless. By definition it cannot be relativistic truth . . . if we want the same reconciliation *We must at least agree that we are referring to the same truth for which confession, forgiveness and reconciliation are being asked.* . . . So how do we get to this truth? Here it is not about verifiable scientific truth in the pure sense of the word. In a traditional society, truth is determined by the priest, a king, a captain or group leaders. In modern industrial societies, the truth of accountability is determined by the country's *prevailing* justice system. . . . This is the closest that we sorry sinners can get to the truth.[23]

Likewise, on the subject of the TRC's mission to promote reconciliation, Derrida notes, "When Desmond Tutu was named president of the Truth and Reconciliation Commission, he christianed the language of an institution uniquely destined to treat 'politically' motivated crimes. . . . With as much goodwill as confusion . . . Tutu, an Anglican Bishop, introduced the vocabulary of repentance and forgiveness."[24] Emphasizing the origins and the significance of this confusion, Derrida explains:

> The statute of the Truth and Reconciliation Commission is very ambiguous on this subject, as with Tutu's discourse, which oscillates between a non-penal and non-reparative logic of "forgiveness" (he calls it "restorative") and a judicial logic of amnesty. We would have to analyze closely the equivocal instability of all of these self-interpretations. Favoring a confusion between the order of forgiveness and the order of justice, but also abusing their heterogeneity, as well as the fact that the time of forgiveness escapes the judicial process, it is moreover always possible to mimic the scene of "immediate" and quasi-automatic forgiveness in order to escape justice.[25]

After recounting the story of a widow who refuses to forgive the murder of her husband by a police officer, even after this officer may have become eligible for amnesty, Derrida draws the following, partial, conclusion: "The anonymous body of the State or of a public institution cannot forgive. It has neither the right nor the power to do so; and besides, that would have no meaning. The representative of the State can judge, but forgiveness has precisely nothing to do with judgment. Or even with the public or political sphere." The wisdom of this conclusion lies in a fact that Van Zyl Slabbert notes in equally precise terms: the un-equivalence of truth in law and truth as such; the gap between the morally principled and the politically motivated; or between the right and the legal. This is why, for Derrida, "Even if it were 'just,' forgiveness would be just of a justice which had nothing to do with judicial justice. . . . There are courts of justice for that, and these courts never forgive in the strict sense of the word."[26]

The most sympathetic interpretation of the rationality of the South African TRC might be to see the commission as a venue where progressive citizens of a country desired, and worked, to make out of political transition a social transformation. With this assumed, it becomes legitimate to question the possibility, and the conditions of such possibility, of reconciling the dichotomy established by Van Zyl Slabbert or Derrida between, respectively, forensic truth and political negotiation, or the just versus justice. There exists a way to do this, not only theoretically—as a form of political philosophy—but also practically, in regard to existing bodies of reflection on the TRC by those who were part of the processes.

The most introspective critics of the TRC are critics on the grounds that the commission was never clear on what it set out to do, leaving the public with an impression of it as a hybrid, even contradictory character. Critics point out the commission's inability to satisfy the desires of those, including the state itself, who might have wished for a strict due process of civil and criminal law. They also point out the confusion between truth-seeking in the form of a search for (criminal) evidence, the moral or religious dispositions and legal requirements to confess to (ambiguously) either sin or crime, and the confusions between languages of amnesty and forgiveness. Some critics also believe that the TRC might have left some who cooperated with it on either side, victims and perpetrators, uncertain of what they had participated in—a moral and legal loophole for the truly criminal-minded to gloat in the thought that they escaped the consequences of judicial and political crime—making sought-after "closure" harder, if not impossible for victims.

Yet, it is hard to discard the opposite truths: that there were morally and socially "restorative" elements to the activities of the TRC, as of similar commissions in other societies. Those most sympathetic to the TRC—among whom I count myself—found precisely in the commission's apparently conflicted allegiances a revolutionary potential: the idea that restorative justice is not *either* morality *or* politics, the right *or* the legal, the just *or* justice. Instead, one can think of the processes of the TRC as that of a moral and ethical suspension of justice for an equally moral and ethical—and more universal—aim of *societal transformation.* This future-oriented aspect of the TRC project has been captured best by Njabulo Ndebele, in his arguments in "Of Lions and Rabbits: Thoughts on Democracy and Reconciliation." The constitutional and politically negotiated "preconditions for reconciliation," he writes, "were laid by acknowledging a common interest to preserve an imperfect zone of stability, in which the scales of morality were nevertheless seen to be tipped in favor of *an emergent order.*"[27] In the same spirit, Dumisa Ntsebeza reminds one of an often-overlooked but obvious section of the TRC's mandate: "Both the Preamble to the Promotion of National Unity and Reconciliation Act, No. 34 of 1995, and the Postamble of the Interim Constitution, Act No. 200 of 1993, recognize the need for reconciliation between peoples of South Africa in order for peace and national unity to endure, *and for the reconstruction of society to take place.*"[28]

In fact, there have been countercomplaints that those who read, religiously, forgiveness-as-redemption-from-sin of apartheid, or, naïvely, reconciliation as amnesty-without-cost-to-anyone, may have been confused by the *personality* of the chairman of the TRC and not by the words of the report or the constitutional mandate. Ndebele, for one, expresses this concern: "The more I read the Commission's Report, the more I became convinced that the predominance of religious connotation in the public discourse on reconciliation resulted from a tendency for many of us to focus on the Chairperson of the Commission as a man of God. The linking of reconciliation directly with forgiveness closed off many other angles of discussion."[29] Some of the angles thus closed off must, I think, include the higher social purposes that amnesty and the radical suspension of due process meant to serve. In this sense alone, it could be argued that while crimes may or may not have been forgiven, the impossible was done—or at least attempted: the forgiving of the "law" itself by a nation whose citizens had been long violated in the name of the law. This formulation would make sense if we remember that it was indeed the law itself that failed. Apartheid showed, vividly, the limits of the law—in other words, a legal lawlessness. Apartheid was an established disorder. The TRC was therefore at a point of crisis resulting from a prior crisis of the law.

But by refusing to acknowledge the moral equivalence of these levels of crises, and by insisting that between them must be instituted indirect reasons of social change, one can understand why—in the same foreword to the report—even the genial archbishop warns that national reconciliation is "not about being cozy; it is not about pretending that things were other than they were. Reconciliation based on falsehood, on not facing up to reality is not true reconciliation." Similarly, Ndebele notes, on the part of the previously racially violated, that there might remain "the fear that magnanimity has not only been misunderstood for weakness, but that it has, in fact, become weakness. There is the fear that the perception of a loss of face may restore old feelings of inferiority, or rage, in proportion to the increasing levels of confidence amongst those who lost very little else beside political power."[30] And in the same spirit, for Mamphela Ramphele, there is the concern that "the ghosts from the past" have refused to lie down: the ghosts of "continuing and growing inequality between 'haves' and 'have-nots.' "[31]

PHILOSOPHY, POLITICS, AND AUTONOMY

If politics-as-transformation is a manner of affirming a commitment that "tomorrow is another country," there are obvious lessons one can draw from the foregoing, and beyond South Africa's "miracle." First, "justice" need not be *either* strict (punitive, retributive, exact, procedural, etc.) and unrestorative *or* restorative (reconciliatory, truth-commissioned, nonadversarial, etc.) and hopelessly inexact. That is, neither a law nor a truth commission need be *either* narrow *or* nonsystemic in its social vision. The idea of the *transformational*—and not merely *transitional*—justice suggests that strict and narrow legal requirements of justice, and broader questions of social stability, may be found, however untidily, in the deeper yearnings of peoples and individuals who mutually recognize themselves as fellow citizens engaged in short-term and long-term projects of change at many levels of society.

Second, if some of those who critiqued South Africa's (as other similar) truth and amnesty commissions did so because the crimes of apartheid were so general and pervasive, and if it was in an analogous context of systemic crises of state, the Holocaust, that Arendt argued that too many were like Eichmann, making evil "terribly and terrifyingly normal," it becomes imperative that a cure, or the search for a cure to such evil, proceed first by breaking this "normality." The abnormal justice required here must be, paradoxically, at once legal and (morally and ethically) transcendent of law: it must itself be an inaugural moment of law. It must be a point in time—but also out of time—in which a people re/invents or fundamentally democratically renegotiates the terms of the social contract. That is why, along with the American and French revolutions, we must speak about the South African Revolution.

Van Zyl Slabbert, the chairman of the Open Society Initiative in South Africa, teased his friend Alex Boraine, who was "primarily responsible for the legislation that eventually resulted in the establishment of the TRC and later became Deputy Chairman of the TRC" and now teaches *transitional* justice at a university in New York, saying, "Alex, it is time [you] came round to *permanent* justice."[32] Thus third, and finally, we too ought to maintain a sense of humor, while at the same time being quick to point out that the real opposition is not, it seems to me, between transitional and permanent justice. There is, arguably, no permanent state of justice. Given the dynamic nature of society and the political and moral foundations of law—or any substantive, or lack of substantive instance of it, at any moment in history—it may well be that countries like South Africa are better off keeping their attention where it is: on responsible, credible, and ongoing democratic transformation of their ordinary institutions of morality, law, and society.

Notes

Preface: What Is Rationality?

1. See, for example, Edelman, *Second Nature*; Searle, *Freedom and Neurobiology*; Minsky, *The Emotion Machine*; Hauser, *Moral Minds*; Friedman, Scholnick, and Cocking, *Blueprints for Thinking*; Baron, *Thinking and Deciding*; Montague, *Why Choose This Book?*; Holyoak and Morrison, *The Cambridge Handbook of Thinking and Reasoning*; Moseley et al., *Frameworks for Thinking*; and Arnauld and Nicole, *Logic or the Art of Thinking*.

2. To mention a few: Pecher and Zwaan, *Grounding Cognition*; Forgas, *Feeling and Thinking*; and Billig, *Arguing and Thinking*.

3. See Spearman, "'General Intelligence' Objectively Determined and Measured."

4. For Piaget, see *La psychologie de l'intelligence*, *Biology and Knowledge*, *Logique et Connaissance scientifique*, *The Origins of Intelligence in Children*, and *Introduction à l'Épistémologie Génétique*. For Kohlberg, see *Essays on Moral Development, Vol. I: The Philosophy of Moral Development*, "The Claim to Moral Adequacy of a Highest Stage of Moral Judgment," and *From Is to Ought*, as well as Kohlberg, Levine, and Hewer, *Moral Stages*. For Gilligan, see *In A Different Voice*.

5. See, for example, Dennet, *Brainstorms*, and Damasio, *Descartes' Error*.

6. Margolis, "The Limits of Ethics and History," 181.

7. Ibid.

8. Ibid.

Introduction: Diversity and the Social Questions of Reason

1. For a good grasp of the many dimensions of the general dilemma, as a substantive issue rather than as the narrowly methodological concern which we make of it here, see Paul Ricoeur, *Oneself as Another*, trans. Kathleen Blamey (Chicago: University of Chicago Press, 1992).

2. See, for example, Tully, *Strange Multiplicity*, and Tully and Wienstock, *Philosophy in an Age of Pluralism*.

3. Adorno, *Negative Dialectics*, 8.

4. See, for example, Ackerman, *Heterogeneities*.

5. See, for example, P. Wood, *Diversity*.

6. Emerson, "The American Scholar," in *Essay and Lectures*, 64.

7. Kant, "Preface to First Edition," in *Critique of Pure Reason*, trans. Werner S. Pluhar (Indianapolis: Hackett, 1996), 26.

8. David Hume, *A Treatise of Human Nature: Being an Attempt to Introduce the Experimental Method of Reasoning into Moral Subjects*, ed. L. A. Selby-Bigg (Oxford: Clarendon, 1988), 269 [orig. pubd London: John Noon, 1739].

9. Ibid.

10. Ibid.

11. Ibid.

12. Ibid.

13. Ibid., 268–69.

14. Immanuel Kant, *Critique of Pure Reason*, trans. Werner S. Pluhar (Indianapolis: Hackett, 1996), 6.

15. Plato, *Meno*, trans. W. K. C. Guthrie, in *The Collected Works of Plato*, ed. Edith Hamilton and Huntington Cairns (Princeton: Princeton University Press, 1961), 353–420.

16. See, for example, Georg Wilhelm Friedrich Hegel, *Lectures on the Philosophy of Religion*, vol. III, *The Consummate Religion*, ed. Peter C. Hodgson (Berkeley: University of California Press, 1998).

17. See for example, Léopold Sedar Senghor, *Teilhard de Chardin et la politique africaine* (Paris: Le Seuil, 1962), and Gilles Deleuze, *Difference and Repetition*, trans. Paul Patton (New York: Continuum, 2005).

18. See, for example, Richard Wolin, "Michel Foucault and the Search for the Other of Reason," in Wolin, *The Terms of Cultural Criticism: The Frankfurt School, Existentialism, Poststructuralism* (New York: Columbia University Press, 1992), 170–93; Nickolas Kompridis, "Invoking the 'Other' of Reason," in Kompridis, *Critique and Disclosure: Critical Theory Between Past and Future* (Cambridge: MIT Press, 2006); and Hent de Vries, *Minimal Theologies: Critiques of Secular Reason in Adorno and Levinas* (Baltimore: Johns Hopkins University Press, 2005). According to de Vries and his supporters such as William D. Hart

(Hart, "Minimal Theologies," *Journal of the American Academy of Religion* 75:1 [2007], 179–82; quote on p. 179), to speak about the Other of Reason is to recognize that "theology, minimally understood, is an unavoidable supplement to critical thought." This, apparently, is because "secular reason makes claims for which it cannot give an adequate account on its own terms." Therefore, for the theologian there appears to be a need for philosophy to depend on, or appeal to, a religious Other of Reason in order to make sense of secular reason, and therefore of philosophy itself. In this book I have not presumed any need of this sort of recourse to theology, however minimal.

Chapter 1: Varieties of Rational Experience

1. Hobbes, *Leviathan*, "On Reason and Science," v. Online version of the original 1660 edition: http://oregonstate.edu/instruct/phl302/texts/hobbes/leviathan-contents.htm (19 October 2007).

2. Ibid.

3. Hobbes, *Leviathan*, "On Speech," iv. Italics added.

4. Hobbes, *Leviathan*, "On Reason and Science," v.

5. Ibid.

6. "Aristotle," Bacon wrote, "made his natural philosophy a mere bond-servant of his logic, thereby rendering it contentious and well nigh useless." Against the methods of Scholasticism he warned, "The logic now in use serves rather to fix and give stability to the errors which have their foundation in commonly received notions than to help the search after truth. So it does more harm than good" (Bacon, *The New Organon*, liv and xii). All quotations in this chapter from *The New Organon* are from the 1885 Oxford University Press edition, edited by G. W. Kitchin and available online at http://www.archive.org/details/thenovumorganonoooobacouoft.

7. Bacon, *The tvvo bookes of Francis Bacon*, xiii, 1–2.

8. Bacon, *Religious Meditations of Heresies* (1597).

9. Bacon, *The New Organon*, xxx, lxxviii, and lxxx.

10. Bacon, *The New Organon*, xxv. See also *The New Organon*, xvii, and *Advancement of Learning*, Book II, 3–4.

11. Bacon, *The New Organon*, cx.

12. Bacon, *The New Organon*, xcix.

13. Ibid., xxxviii–lxix.

14. Ibid., xli.

15. Ibid., lii.

16. Ibid., li.

17. Ibid., liii.

18. Ibid., lix.

19. Most would think of George Orwell's famous essay, "Politics and the English Language" or Chinua Achebe's "Language and the Destiny of Man." Both essays are observations on public uses and abuses of language. Achebe writes, "It has long been known that language, like any other human invention, can be abused, can be turned from its original purpose into something useless or even deadly" (Achebe, "Language and the Destiny of Man," in *Hopes and Impediments: Selected Essays* [New York: Doubelday, 1990], 127–37). But here is a story, the source of which escapes my memory, illustrating what I think Bacon had in view when lamenting the social consequences of *un*intentional corruption of language—especially when the language-users are unaware of consequences of the corruption. The prior of an American monastery whose cat had became a nuisance at prayer times developed the habit of putting the pet on a leash, then tying the leash to the door of the chapel, right before he led his monks in their four-times-a-day prayers. At every time of prayer, just before heading out to the chapel, the prior would call out to his novice assistant, "Brother John, tie the cat to the door." The conscientious assistant, to remind himself as well as the novice brethren who might one day step in to assist, wrote down and pinned to the community bulletin board the list of "Things to Do before Prayer." The first item on this list was "Tie the cat to the door." Now when a group of monks from this monastery was sent by the prior to Malawi as missionaries, the leader of the mission decided that it was important to write down the order's daily rules of prayer, so that even in Africa the monks could be sure that they were conforming to the practices in the brother monastery. An African missionary committee was therefore set up to draft the "General Rules of Prayer of the Monastic Order for Overseas Observances." In the final document, in the first chapter, "Preparations for Prayer," the first entry was "1. Tie a Cat to the Door."

20. Hobbes's own list of abuses or potential corruptions of language is as follows:

First, when men register their thoughts wrong by the inconstancy of the signification of their words, by which they register for their conception that which they never conceived, and so deceive themselves. Secondly, when they use words metaphorically—that is, in other than that they are [naturalistically] ordained for—and thereby deceive others. Thirdly, by words when they declare that to be their will which is not. Fourthly, when they use them to grieve one another, for, seeing nature has armed living creatures, some with teeth, some with horns, and some with hands, to grieve an enemy, it is but an abuse of speech to grieve him with the tongue, unless it be one whom we are obliged to govern, and then it is not to grieve but to correct and amend. (Hobbes, *Leviathan*, iv)

21. Bacon, *The New Organon*, xxxvii.

22. Ibid., xliv.

23. Ibid., xxxviii.

24. Ibid.

25. A critical reading of Bacon by the Indian postcolonial philosopher of science Ashis Nandy inspired this chart. See Nandy, *Science, Hegemony and Violence*.

26. I should note that, unlike our current usage, the word *logic* for Aristotle had a meaning closer to what we call *dialectics*. For the discipline of *logic* as we think of it, Aristotle's most proximate term would have been *analytics*.

27. Aristotle, *Analytica Priora*, Book I, 24b.

28. Aristotle, *Analytica Posteriora*, Book II 19, 100b.

29. Aristotle, *Analytica Priora*, Book I, 24b. For Aristotle, "the premises must be primary and indemonstrable; otherwise they will require demonstration in order to be known, since to have knowledge, if it be not accidental knowledge, of things which are demonstrable, means precisely to have a demonstration of them." See also Book I, 31.

30. Aristotle, *Analytica Posteriora*, Book I, 3, 72b.

31. Aristotle, *Metaphysics*, 1005b, 35.

32. See, for example, Wittgenstein, "Bemerkungen über Frazers *The Golden Bough*"; Donald Davidson, *Problems of Rationality*; and Rorty, "Problems of Rationality," a review of Davidson's book.

33. For a more extensive discussion of the uses of these rules, and their values as well as "precariousness" in logical demonstrations, see Robert Fogelin, *Walking the Tightrope of Reason: The Precarious Life of the Rational Animal* (New York: Oxford University Press, 2004).

34. Russell, "Dewey's New Logic."

35. Emerson, "Self Reliance."

36. From broad historical perspectives, the classic critiques of the Enlightenment rationality by Theodor Adorno, Max Horkheimer, and Walter Benjamin explore this problem. The works of Ashis Nandy, Bruno Latour, and Sandra Harding in philosophy of science are recent examples.

37. Heidegger, *The Principle of Reason*, 107.

38. Heidegger, *The Principle of Reason*, 108.

39. Ibid., 111.

40. Ibid., 100.

41. Ibid., 103.

42. Dreyfus, *What Computers Still Can't Do*.

43. Hume, *Treatise of Human Nature*, 1.

44. Hume, *Treatise*, 10.

45. In support, he gave this example: "I can imagine to myself such a city as the New Jerusalem, whose pavement is gold and walls are rubies, tho' I never saw any

such. I have seen Paris; but shall I affirm I can form such an idea of that city, as will perfectly represent all its streets and houses in their real and just proportions?" Hume, *Treatise*, 10.

46. Ibid., 3.

47. Ibid., 4.

48. Ibid.

49. Bayes, "Essay Toward Solving the Problem of the Doctrine of Chances."

50. Bovens and Hartman, *Bayesian Epistemology*, 2.

51. For a discussion of the general problem of error within as well as beyond the narrowly cognitive, epistemic issues, see Rescher, *Error*.

52. Bovens and Hartman, *Bayesian Epistemology*, 3.

53. For a treatment of fallibilism as methodology in science, see Popper, *The Logic of Scientific Discovery*. For a historical approach to the question of contingency in method within the broader field of philosophy of science, the canonical reference work remains Kuhn, *The Structure of Scientific Revolutions*. Also of interest is Kuhn, *The Road Since Structure*.

54. See, for example, Sternberg, *Cognitive Psychology*, and Decatanzaro, *Motivation and Emotion*.

55. See Paul Churchland, *The Engine of Reason, The Seat of the Soul*; Patricia Churchland and Sejnowski, *The Computational Brain*; Flanagan, *The Problem of the Soul*; and Chalmers, *The Conscious Mind*.

56. Lakoff and Johnson, *Philosophy in the Flesh*, 4.

57. Ibid.

58. Husserl, *Logische Untersuchungen*; *Untersuchungen zur Phänomenologie und Theorie der Erkenntnis*; and "Philosophie als strenge Wissenschaft." See also Husserl, "Phenomenology."

59. Husserl specifically asks, "In each case the reduction to the phenomenological, as the purely psychic, demands that we methodically refrain from taking any natural-objective position; and not only that, but also from taking any position on the particular values, goods, etc., that the subject, in his or her naturally functioning cogitationes, straightforwardly accepts as valid in any given case." *Husserliana*, IX, 238 and 243.

60. *Husserliana*, IX, 243.

61. Ibid.

62. Ibid.

63. *Husserliana*, IX, 243.

64. *Husserliana*, IX, 239.

65. Ibid.

66. *Husserliana*, IX, 245.

67. Ibid.

68. Furthermore, the "reduction to the purely physical brings us into the self-

contained nexus of physical nature, to which animal organisms, as mere bodies, belong. [Therefore,] scientific exploration of this area takes its place within the universal unity of natural science and specifically within physical biology as the general science of organisms in purely physical experience." Ibid.

69. *Husserliana*, IX, 593.

70. Ibid.

71. Ibid.

72. One of Husserl's most important multivolume books was titled *Logical Investigations* (1901), and the first volume was called "The Prolegomena of Pure Logic." Ten years earlier, Husserl had also written a dissertation on the logical properties of numbers, *Philosophie der Arithmetick* (1891).

73. *Husserliana*, IX, 240–241.

74. *Husserliana*, IX, 243.

75. *Husserliana*, IX, 247.

76. See Husserl, *Phenomenology and the Crisis of Philosophy*.

77. *Husserliana*, IX, 247.

78. Ibid.

79. Ibid.

80. Ibid.

81. Ibid.

82. Ibid.

83. Ibid.

84. *Husserliana*, IX, 248.

85. Ibid., IX, 249.

86. Ibid.

87. Ibid., italics added.

88. Ibid.

89. Ibid.

90. Ibid.

91. Ibid.

92. Ibid., IX, 490.

93. To take just a few of the examples: phenomenology's basic concepts are said "to be formed in originary genuineness." The development of the same concepts should be, *"from the outset,* free of any unclarity." Likewise, systematically, phenomenological ontology is preparation for "all the as yet ungrounded a priori sciences." Finally, the development of phenomenology is aimed at preparing the absolute grounds "of all empirical sciences into *exactly* rationalized sciences" (*Husserliana*, IX, 492, italics added).

94. Lakoff and Johnson, *Philosophy in the Flesh*, 3.

95. Ibid.

96. Descombes, *The Mind's Provisions*, 2.

97. Ibid., viii.

98. See, for example, Maurice Blondel's 1893 thesis *L'Action*.

99. See, for example, Pinker, *The Language Instinct* and *How the Mind Works*.

100. Butler, *Gender Trouble*.

101. On the idea of "extended mind," see Clark and Chalmers, "The Extended Mind"; Petit, "Groups with Minds of Their Own"; Goody, *The Domestication of the Savage Mind*; Robert A. Wilson, *Boundaries of the Mind* and "Collective Memory, Group Minds, and the Extended Mind Thesis."

Chapter 2: Ordinary Historical Reason

1. Virginia Woolf, "The Novels of E. M. Forster," in *The Death of the Moth and Other Essays* (New York: Harcourt, 1974), 162–75.

2. If would-be cross-cultural speakers are initially not playing the same language game because they come from backgrounds from different forms of life, initial cross-cultural judgments can be made only from a high level of generality: "What kinds of objects would you consider beautiful or ugly?" "In your culture, is it just or unjust to rob the rich to feed the poor?" "Do your people consider it civilized or uncivilized to commit judicial murder?" and so on. To sidestep this general level of conversation and directly judge that Mr. Thomas is ugly, that missing bread is the result of theft, or that Mr. Amadi's death was intentional murder could lead one to less informed conclusions. A judgment is universal because it is open to general, cross-cultural consensus.

3. To appreciate this dilemma in practical terms, consider the social anthropologist Daniel Jordan Smith's efforts, after many years of life and work in Nigeria, to explain the country's cultures of corruption. See Smith, *A Culture of Corruption,* particularly the introspective portions of the preface (xi–xviii) and the introduction (1–27).

4. For objections to this version of cultural relativism, see Wright, "Relativism and Classical Logic."

5. Quine, "Two Dogmas of Empiricism." References are to the revised version in *From a Logical Point of View: Nine Logico-Philosophical Essays* (Cambridge: Harvard University Press, 2006), 20–46.

6. Frege, *Posthumous Writings*, 147 and 148.

7. Brandom, *Making It Explicit*, 12.

8. Ibid.

9. Dewey, *Early Works of John Dewey, 1882–1898,* 454.

10. Dewey, "The Objects of Thoughts," in *Essays in Experimental Logic*, 157–82.

11. Wiredu, *Cultural Particulars and Universals*, 2.

12. Brandom, *Making It Explicit*, 47.

13. See Wiredu's dated but still influential essay, "Truth as Opinion," especially his original conception of opinion as objectivity: "To be true is to be opined." (See Wiredu, *Philosophy and an African Culture*, 114–27.)

14. Beaney, *The Frege Reader*, 289 (or Frege, *Posthumous Writings*, 144); Brandom, *Making It Explicit*, 13–30; Wiredu, "The Concept of Truth in the Akan Language," in E. C. Eze, ed. *African Philosophy: An Anthology* (Oxford: Blackwell, 1998), 176–80. Dewey arrived at similar conclusions about conceptions of the rationality of nature, though by an inverse process: if thought and reasons are causal-biological and habitually derived, then rationality cannot be justified beyond the rationally "natural" because questions about *ultimate* causality are moot.

15. McDowell, *Mind and World*, 85.

16. Ibid., 108.

17. Ibid.

18. Ibid., 11. Italics added.

19. Ibid., 62.

20. Ibid., 26.

21. Friedman, "Exorcizing the Philosophical Tradition," 34.

22. Stroud, "Sense-Experience and the Grounding of Thought," 82.

23. Friedman, "Exorcizing the Philosophical Tradition," 34.

24. Ibid.

25. Stroud, "Sense-Experience and the Grounding of Thought," 82.

26. For idealists of any stripe, passively received impressions are just that: passive. They become active experiences of an objective world (and thus impressions of outer sense) only by being *taken as such* by the active faculty of understanding, "by its being subject . . . to the perpetually revisable procedure through which the understanding integrates such impressions into an evolving world-conception" (Friedman, "Exorcizing the Philosophical Tradition," 40). For the idealist, this is the only way we can understand the idea of *world*.

27. Stroud, "Sense-Experience and the Grounding of Thought," 87.

28. In countries where the dominant philosophical models are analytical, critics of Continental philosophy frequently point out this problem by resorting to catchphrases such as "There is nothing outside of text"; "by language alone"; and "the death of nature." See, for example, Harpham, *Language Alone*.

29. See, for example, Castoriadis, *The Imaginary Institutions of Society*.

30. St. Augustine, *The Confession*, book XI, chap. 14: 17.

31. Aristotle, *Politics*, book VII, in *The Politics and the Constitution of Athens*, 166–94.

32. Rorty, "Stories of Difference."

33. Putnam, *Representation and Reality*. See in particular chap. 4, "Are There Such Things as Reference and Truth?," 57–67.

34. Putnam, *Realism and Reason.*

35. See Hume, Treatise of Human Nature, 4.

36. Ya'icob, "God, Faith, and the Nature of Knowledge."

37. King Alphonso II, quoted in B. Davidson, *Africa*, 177.

38. The letter writer was anxious that "men of such eminence, conducted by a commander who from his own account seems to have descended from the God who made day and night, can never bring themselves to endure the hardships of this climate, nor would they here be able to procure any of the luxuries that abound in their own country. The passions that are common to us all will . . . inevitably bring on disputes." King Asa, quoted in R. Wright, *Black Power*, 83.

39. Ya'icob, "God, Faith, and the Nature of Knowledge," 459.

40. Ibid., 457.

41. Wittgenstein, *Philosophical Investigations*, sections 608–11.

42. Ibid., section 612.

Chapter 3: Science, Culture, and Principles of Rationality

1. Calhoun, introduction to *Setting the Moral Compass*, v. Italics added.

2. Ibid., v–vi.

3. Ibid.

4. Ibid.

5. In its ramifications, this question entails: What, ultimately, do the existential and theoretical categories of gender and race mean in philosophy or to philosophy? What *is* the difference gender and race make in philosophical thought? In what ways could the argument be sustained that gender or race "makes a difference" by understanding the difference as a claim that, nonaccidentally, members of a subgroup within a profession share "kindred minds" or a mentality?

6. Sandra Harding was one of the first to systematically explore what she called "the curious coincidence" between both methodological and substantive debates in feminist and postcolonial African philosophy. Harding, "The Curious Coincidence between Feminine and African Moralities."

7. Bates, Mudimbe, and O'Barr, *Africa and the Disciplines*, i.

8. Ibid.

9. Rimmer and Kirk-Greene, *The British Intellectual Engagement with Africa in the Twentieth Century*, 1. The authors continue, "Nevertheless, we have not been able, nor have we wished, entirely to abstract from that broader context."

10. Ibid.

11. The similarities and divergences between *Africa and the Disciplines* and *British Intellectual Engagement* go even further. The latter notes, "Just as since the *coups d'état* of 1966 in Nigeria and Ghana no self-respecting political scien-

tist can think of writing about military rule without adding African data to his hitherto largely Latin American models, so in the prewar period a growing number of social anthropologists began to look to Africa as the laboratory for their field research" (Kirk-Greene, "The Emergence of an Africanist Community in the UK," 19). The debts of anthropology to Africa are so great that one could question whether, at least in Britain, there existed an independent academic field known as anthropology prior to the constitution of African studies. At least this is the impression this reader is left with in this marvelous Kirk-Greene essay. As in *Africa and the Disciplines*, there are in *British Intellectual Engagement* numerous examples of Africa as a mine of data that would ultimately transform, in North America and Britain, modes of thought and practices of teaching in fields as wide-ranging as medicine, game theory, and philosophy.

12. Eze, "African Philosophy and the Analytic Tradition."

13. It is not clear how analytic philosophy transformed itself from a description to a regulation. The late Bernard Williams is said to have been fond of pointing out that the difference between analytical and continental philosophy is like the difference between "Japanese cars" and "cars with front-wheel drive." For example, when historians of modern philosophy think about the term *analytic*, it is Kant's distinction between the analytic and synthetic in judgments that come to mind. But at some point in the twentieth century, particularly in England and the United States, analytic philosophy came to mean both a type of philosophy distinct from what was practiced in Continental Europe *and* a method of doing that type of supposedly non-European philosophy. Some believe that Bertrand Russell was a major figure in this development, particularly because of the impact of his arguments about "logical atomism." Part anti-Cartesianism and part Leibnitzian materialism, logical atomism brought together mathematics and analysis of logical propositions and allowed Russell to attack Cartesian dogmatic theism and Hegelian absolute idealism. See, for example, Russell, *The Principles of Mathematics*. Other early works in what became the analytic tradition include Bradley, *Principles of Logic*; Moore, "On the Nature of Judgment"; and Collingwood, *An Essay on Philosophical Method*. By 1936, Ernest Nagel could publish a fairly long article called "Impressions and Appraisals of Analytic Philosophy in Europe."

14. Hadot, *What Is Ancient Philosophy?*, 3.

15. Vico continues, "Whoever reflects on this cannot but marvel that the philosophers should have bent all their energies to the study of the world of nature, which, since God made it, he alone knows: and that they should have neglected the study of the world of nations, or civil world, which, since men had made it, men could come to know" (*The New Science of Giambattista Vico*, 331).

16. "Culture" is merely one of the modes of this particular line of conflicts. "Race," too, is a similar, if sometimes narrower, area of conflict. "Universality"

completes the trinity. These are the themes under which claims and counter-claims about the rationalities of identities were routinely debated among the intellectuals in nineteenth- and twentieth-century Africa. A closer look at the trinity (culture, race, and universality) shows that the histories of their discourses in the African contexts share some general patterns, which will be studied closely in chap. 5.

17. Without denying that individuals are products of particular cultures by birth and training, one should accentuate the fact that individuals and peoples do negotiate the cultures in which they come to hold dominant stakes. For example, knowing that societies and cultures get transformed on account of intercultural encounters—whether forced or voluntary, violent or peaceful—is crucial to theorizing freedoms of culture in postcolonial contexts. Instead of being thought of as mere "transacted" commodities, cultural values should be examined as indexes of freedom. In this view of cultures and their values, instead of cheapening and commodifying, we see why we value cultures and, in some cases, are willing to sacrifice lives—our own or others'—in their defense. This view also explains why we speak about cultures or traditions as priceless, invaluable, or even sacred. But the religious, aesthetic, and moral investments we thus make in material or immaterial cultures and traditions are warranted only because we see in them sources or evidence of morally transcendent values such as freedom and agency. What is defended in such contexts is not necessarily individual freedom in the abstract and without regard to community and history; rather, we defend the exercise of freedoms through morally meaningful allegiance to ideas of culture and society as necessary conditions for any history of liberty.

18. Fischer, "Freedom is Not Just Another Word." See also Fischer, *Liberty and Freedom*.

19. I have tried to show that there is an intrinsic tension between the culture of freedom and the culture of liberty. The tension is unresolvable and therefore comparable to what Kant captured in the concept of "unsocial sociability" of the human condition. In his 1784 essay, "Idea for a Universal History with a Cosmopolitanism Purpose," under his "Fourth Thesis," Kant explained, "By antagonism of this kind I mean the unsocial sociability of man, i.e., a propensity to enter into society combined with a perpetual resistance to that propensity, [a resistance] which is continually threatening to dissolve the social state" (46). Yet Kant knew "we should be grateful for the socially conflicted nature of mankind because it is a source of specifically human creativity and social progress." As he put it: "because but for these anti-social propensities, so unamiable in themselves, which gave birth to that resistance which every man meets with in his own self-interested pretensions, an Arcadian life would arise of perfect harmony and mutual love such as must suffocate and stifle all talents in their very germs."

Kant, "Idea for a Universal History with a Cosmopolitan Purpose," *Political Writings*, 43. Speaking about a twentieth-century example of the same problem, the historical sociologist Orlando Patterson noted that "two versions of freedom emerged in America": "The modern liberal version emphasizes civil liberties, political participation and social justice. It is the version formally extolled by the federal government, debated by philosophers and taught in schools; it still informs the American judicial system. And it is the version most treasured by foreigners who struggle for freedom in their own countries. But most ordinary Americans view freedom in quite different terms. In their minds, freedom has been radically privatized. Its most striking feature is what is left out: politics, civic participation and the celebration of traditional rights, for instance" ("The Speech Misheard Round the World").

20. See, for example, Kohlberg, "The Claim to Moral Adequacy of a Highest Stage of Moral Judgment." Also of relevance are Piaget, *Psychology of Intelligence* and *Psychology and Epistemology;* and Gilligan, *In a Different Voice.*

21. Aristotle, *Nichomachean Ethics*, 18–20.

22. For an extended, if somewhat dated, development of this insight, see Ravaison, *De l'habitude.*

23. Hazlitt, "Race and Class," 464.

24. Kidd, *The Forging of Races.* See particularly the prologue, "Race in the Eye of the Beholder," 1–18.

25. Multiculturalism, a product of twentieth-century movements in cultural anthropology, is a belief nicely captured by the Nigerian historian Kenneth Dike: "There is no criterion by which to compare one culture in terms of progress with another [as each] is the product of the environment and must primarily be judged in relation to the community," quoted by Apollos O. Nwauwa, "Kenneth Omwuka Dike," in Falola, *Dark Webs*, 309–28. In the United States, cultural anthropologists such as Margaret Mead, Franz Boas, and Melville Herskovits contributed to the shift to this conception of relationships across cultures.

26. For debates about this view of postmodern cosmopolitanism, see Appiah, *The Ethics of Identity, Cosmopolitanism,* "The Politics of Identity," and "The Case For Contamination."

27. Without imputing to the authors my own characterizations of the TC, the reader can imagine how the TC might respond to the cosmopolitan's objections to culturalism from the perspectives of the following works: Moody-Adams, "Reflections on Appiah's *The Ethics of Identity*"; Levy, *Multiculturalism of Fear* and "Contextualism, Constitutionalism, and Modus Vivendi Approaches."

28. According to the 1948 United Nations "Convention on the Prevention and Punishment of the Crime of Genocide" (UN General Assembly resolution 260 A (III), Article 2), the term *genocide* "means any of the following acts committed with intent to destroy, in whole or in part, a national, ethnical, racial or religious

group, as such: (a) Killing members of the group; (b) Causing serious bodily or mental harm to members of the group; (c) Deliberately inflicting on the group conditions of life calculated to bring about its physical destruction in whole or in part; (d) Imposing measures intended to prevent births within the group; (e) Forcibly transferring children of the group to another group." *U.N.T.S.* No. 1021, vol. 78 (1951), p. 277. Also available at http://www.un.org/Depts/dhl/resguide/r60.htm (accessed 30 January 2007).

29. See, for example, the proceedings of the International Criminal Tribunal for the Former Yugoslavia (http://www.un.org/icty/index.html) and International Criminal Tribunal for Rwanda (http://69.94.11.53/). See also the media reports, such as: LaFraniere, "Court Convicts 3 in 1994 Genocide across Rwanda."

30. Jared Diamond, *Guns, Germs, and Steel.*

31. Kerim Friedman, "What Is Wrong with Yali's Question," http://savageminds .org/2005/07/25/whats-wrong-with-yalis-question/ (accessed 2 August 2005).

32. In his conception of multiculturalism, Jacob T. Levy notes that whether we should condemn cultural identities or celebrate their beauty or diversity is beside the point. Cultural identities, he says, are simply facts; they are not likely to prosper or disappear simply because we like or dislike them. Similarly, one need not advocate preservation or perpetuation of any one cultural identity or community, for preservation or perpetuation of any one cultural identity or community "is not, by itself a political goal of high moral importance." Levy, *Multiculturalism of Fear*, 7. Similarly, we can say that neither is cosmopolitanism absolutely important, for encouraging the abandonment of attachment to particular cultural identities may or may not be a political goal of high moral importance. This clearly is an analytical approach to understanding non-attachments and attachments to cultures rather than an advocacy.

33. See, for example, Zuberi, *Thicker Than Blood*; Moss, *What Genes Can't Do*; and Kidd, *The Forging of Races.*

34. Reed, "The Real Divide."

35. Sander L. Gilman, guest editor, "Race in Contemporary Medicine," special issue of *Patterns of Prejudice*, 2006.

36. Ibid. For some implications of these questions, drawn from studies of medical practice in the previous centuries, see Dorr, "Defective or Disabled? "

37. See, for example, Troy Duster, "Race and Reification in Science," Alan Goodman, "Two Questions about Race," and Ann Morning, "On Distinction," all at *Is Race Real: A Web Forum Organized by the Social Science Research Council*, http://raceandgenomics.ssrc.org/Morning/ (accessed 5 February 2007).

38. See "The Business of Race and Science," http://web.mit.edu/csd/BRS/Welcome.html (accessed 5 February 2007).

39. Herodotus, *History*, 4: 191.

40. Pliny, *Natural History*.

41. See Eliade, *The Sacred and the Profane*.

42. About the notion of race in the Hebrew Bible, see Goldenberg, *The Curse of Ham*, and Lewis, *Race and Slavery in the Middle East*. For Europe's medieval period, in addition to Block, see Braude, "The Sons of Noah and the Construction of Ethnic and Geographical Identities in the Medieval and Early Modern Periods," and Boulle, *The Color of Liberty*, and John Block, *The Monstrous Races*. For fictionalized examples of the "racial" phenomenon in ancient African traditions, see Achebe, *Things Fall Apart*. For the most modern nonfiction examples, see Gourevitch, *We Wish to Inform You That Tomorrow We Will Be Killed with Our Families*.

43. Fanon, *Black Skin, White Masks*, 89.

44. Hornius, *Rdo. Dno. D. Adr. Stalpartio Abb. Togerlesi dignisod*.

45. For example, those classified as Yellow are said to cover themselves "with loose garments." They are morally "governed by opinion," temperamentally "melancholic, rigid or fevered, haughty, and covetous." The Red race is "erect, copper-colored, with black, straight, thick hair, wide nostrils, harsh face, and scanty beard." Culturally, they paint themselves "with fine red lines," and are morally regulated by "custom." Temperamentally they are "choleric, obstinate, and content." Members of the White race, have "yellow, brown, flowing hair and blue eyes." They cover themselves "with close vestments." They are morally "governed by law," and temperamentally "fair, sanguine, brawny, gentle, cute, and inventive." Members of the Black race possess "black, frizzled hair; silky skin, flat nose, and tumid lips." They anoint themselves "with grease." They are "governed by caprice." They are temperamentally "black, phlegmatic, relaxed, crafty, indolent, and negligent." For Linnaeus, since all the races are related to an original stem (i.e., "the four-footed, hairy, wild man") and are all "sapiens, diurnal, and varying only by education and situation," the scientific system of race must label as deviant "monstrosities" only the following, atypical, members of the species: the "small, active, timid Mountaineer," the "large, indolent Patagonian," the "less fertile Hottentot," the "beardless American," the "conic-headed Chinese," and "the flat-headed Canadian." Carl von Linnaeus, *A General System of Nature* (London: Lockington, Allen, 1806), 1–9.

46. Kant, *Anthropology from a Pragmatic Point of View*.

47. See Ereshefsky, *The Poverty of Linnaean Hierarchy*.

48. U.S. Census Bureau, http://www.census.gov/ (accessed 15 October 2005).

49. Saint-Méry, *Description topographique, physique, civile, politique et historique de la partie française de l'Isle Saint-Domingue*, vol. 1, 89–102.

50. Garraway, "Race, Reproduction and Family Romance in Moreau de Saint-Méry's Description . . . de la partie française de l'isle Saint-Domingue." See also Garraway, *The Libertine Colony*.

51. *New York Times*, "Toward the First Racial Medicine," editorial, 13 November 2004. The editorial goes on: "There is considerable genetic variability within any racial group, so it is likely that the new pill may fail some black patients, while white patients who could benefit may not get it because they don't fit the racial profile. The ultimate goal, still years or decades away, is to develop medical treatments based on an individual's genes and life experiences, not on membership in some poorly defined racial or ethnic category. Race-based prescribing makes sense only as a temporary measure."

52. *New York Times*, "Race Gap Seen in Health Care of Equally Insured Patients," 21 March 2002. For other studies providing a fuller—and more complex—picture of the issue of disparity in illness incidence and treatment outcomes, see the Duke University Medical Center press release "Black Heart Disease Patients Die at Higher Rate Than Whites," available at http://www.dukemednews .duke.edu/news/article.php?id=798 (accessed 2 February 2007). The Duke study concluded, "Black patients . . . did not receive the same aggressive treatment for heart disease as the whites did. In fact, the researchers found black patients were 40 percent less likely to receive angioplasty or bypass surgery. These differences in treatment appear to have led to slightly lower survival rates in blacks compared to whites." See also Preidt, "Blacks, Hispanics Hospitalized More Often for Diabetes, Heart Disease," which reported on research conducted in 2003 by the U.S. Agency for Healthcare Research and Quality, an agency of the U.S. Department of Health and Human Services. This study concluded, "Many cases [of minority patients' deaths] could have been prevented through better outpatient care" (http://www.omhrc.gov/templates/browse.aspx?lvl=1&lvlID=6, accessed 2 February 2007); In "Black vs. White: Unequal Health Care," Anne Underwood writes, "The Institute of Medicine may not seem like a revolutionary body. But in 2001, it issued a challenge to the nation—to strive for equal health care for all citizens, regardless of gender, ethnicity, geographic location and socioeconomic status. The impetus was clear: Too many studies were showing that African-Americans were receiving poorer medical care than whites. Five years later, how are we doing? Not so well, according to a pair of new studies." The follow-up study was reported in the *Journal of the American Medical Association*: http://www.msnbc .msn.com/id/15404055/site/newsweek/ (accessed 2 February 2007).

53. A recent Harvard study has drawn a *causal* connection between "attitudes about race" and "the way doctors care for their African-American patients." See Stephen Smith, "Tests of Trainee Doctors Find Signs of Race Bias in Care," *Boston Globe*, July 20, 2007.

54. For a defense of this view, see Vedantam, "Patients' Diversity Is Often Discounted."

55. Stein, "Heart Drug for Blacks Endorsed: Racial Tailoring Would Be a First." See also Stein, "FDA Approves Controversial Heart Medication for Blacks."

56. For how a philosopher looks at the issues, see, for example, Block, "How Heritability Misleads about Race."

57. Finkelman, *Medicine, Nutrition, Demography and Slavery.*

58. See Keita et al., "Human Genome Variation and 'Race.'" Keita et al. argue that the "human genome contains both enough variation for us all to be genetically unique individuals and little enough variation that it is clear we are all members of one human race. . . . It emerges that the widespread use of 'race' as a proxy is inhibiting scientists from doing their job of separating and identifying the real environmental and genetic causes of disease."

59. Fraga et al., "Epigenetic Differences Arise During the Lifetime of Monozygotic Twins."

60. Ibid.

61. Moss, "From Representational Performatism to the Epigenesis of Openness to the World?"

62. Moss, "The Concept of the Gene and the Future of the Phenotype."

63. Ibid. Similarly, Moss argues, "In the modern genetics clinic, traditional family pedigrees can be supplemented or even replaced by the use of molecular probes. Molecular probes are targeted to a specific sequence, but because a Gene-P is indeterminate with respect to sequence, because a Gene-P is characteristically based on the absence of some sequence, probes can only probe for particular ways of not having the normal sequence and never fully rule out the possibility of some *other* way of not having the 'normal' sequence."

64. See Venter, "Genome" and "Human Genome Promise"; and Adams et al., "The Independence of Our Genome Assemblies." In 2007, on the basis of additional research which used himself as object of analysis, Venter revised the level of universally shared genome from .01 to .07. However, since this new information is based on differences between individuals, not groups, racial or otherwise, Venter maintains that "race is a social concept, not a scientific one." According to him, the new information means that "we are in fact very unique individuals at the genetic level." See "First Individual Diploid Human Genome Published By Researchers at J. Craig Venter Institute / Sequence Reveals That Human to Human Variation is Substantially Greater than Earlier Estimates," http://www .jcvi.org/ (10 October 2007).

65. Henig, "The Genome in Black and White (and Gray)"; Goodman, *Race*; and Graves, *The Emperor's New Clothes.*

66. Hoffman et al., "Plasmodium, Human and Anopheles Genomics and Malaria."

67. http://hapmap.org. See also Henig, "The Genome in Black and White (and

Gray)." Henig notes that researchers hope that, like other promising tracks of genetic research in medicine, the HapMap will indicate how about a million SNPs form in patterns within an individual. It is hypothesized that an individual with a particular configuration of one SNP would be "highly likely to carry particular versions of other SNPs as well."

68. Moss, *What Genes Can't Do*. See also Moss, "From Representational Preformationism to the Epigenesis of Openness to the World?"

69. Rothman, *Genetic Maps and Human Imaginations*, 97.

70. See "Race: Are We So Different?," http://www.understandingrace.org/home.html (accessed 5 February 2007).

71. For a close examination of this double use of the social concept of race, see Morning and Sabbagh, "From Sword to Plowshare," and Lamont, Morning, and Mooney, "Particular Universalisms."

72. Park, "The Nature of Race Relations."

73. Telles, *Race in Another America*, 78.

74. Winant, *The New Politics of Race*.

75. Telles, *Race in Another America*, 78–79.

76. Margolis, "The Limits of Ethics and History," 187. See also Cartwright, *How the Laws of Physics Lie*, and Hacking, *Historical Ontology*.

77. Huntington, *The Clash of Civilizations and the Remaking of World Order*, 184.

78. Ibid.

79. Bilgrami, "The Clash within Civilizations"; Senghaas, *The Clash within Civilizations*, especially chap 1, "Intercultural Philosophy Today"; Marrouchi, "Islam and the West."

80. Senghaas, *The Clash within Civilizations*, 71–78.

81. Giorgo Agamben develops the essential problems in this quasi-theological idea, around the themes of sovereignty and claims to exception; see his *Homo Sacer*.

82. Kant, "Idea for a Universal History with Cosmopolitan Purpose," in *Political Writings*, 41–53.

Chapter 4: Languages of Time in Postcolonial Memory

1. Huizinga, "Africa, the Continent of To-morrow's Trouble," *African Affairs* 49 (1950): 120–28; quote from p. 122.

2. Ibid., 122.

3. Ibid., 121.

4. Feierman, "Africa in History," 40.

5. Ibid.

6. Ibid.

7. Chakrabarty, *Provincializing Europe*, 8.

8. Ibid.

9. Ibid.

10. Mignolo, *The Darker Side of the Renaissance*, and *The Invention of the Americas*.

11. Wyschogrod, "Representation, Narrative, and the Historian's Promise." See also Wyschogrod, *An Ethics of Remembering*.

12. de Certeau, *The Writing of History*, and Fabian, *Time and the Other*.

13. Rüsen, "Responsibility and Irresponsibility in Historical Studies," 205.

14. Ibid.

15. Ibid.

16. Sartre, *Vérité et l'existence*. Although I cannot accept Sartre's elaboration on history because it eventually collapses history into an ambiguous notion of a historical totality, it is useful to recall the general spirit of Sartre's dialectical conception of "committed" history: "Before manifesting my epoch to itself, before changing it into itself and for itself, I am nothing other than its pure mediation: except this mediation being consciousness (of) self and assuming itself saves the epoch and makes it pass over to absolute" (Sartre, *Notebooks for an Ethics*, 490).

17. Arendt, "Walter Benjamin."

18. For an interesting analysis of the concept of repair, from which I have adapted this phrase, see Elizabeth V. Spelman's *Repair* and *Fruits of Sorrow*.

19. Chinua Achebe, interview with E. C. Eze, Bard College, New York, January 11, 2000. For an approach to Achebe most similar to mine, see Kortenaar, "Beyond Authenticity and Creolization," "Fictive States and the State of Fiction in Africa," and "Chinua Achebe and the Question of Modern African Tragedy"; as well as George, *Relocating Agency*, and Gikandi, *Reading Chinua Achebe*. However, my current research has a different focus than these works do. I want to answer the question: What is the essential relation between language and time? And, having posed this question, what is the appropriate methodology to use in answering it in the contexts of postcolonial African literatures?

20. Tom Conley, introduction to Certeau, *The Writing of History*, 2–6.

21. Truillot, *Silencing the Past*, and Chakrabarty, *Provincializing Europe*.

22. Certeau, *The Writing of History*, viii; see also chap. 2, "The Historiographical Operation."

23. Klein, "Studying the History of Those Who Would Rather Forget"; Carr, *What Is History?*; White, *The Content of the Form*; Korhonen, *Tropes for the Past*; LaCapra, *History in Transit* and *Writing History, Writing Trauma*; Gaddis, *The Landscape of History*.

24. Achebe, "The Truth of Fiction."

25. In addition to the works by men cited earlier, see the works of women

writers Mariama Bâ (*So Long a Letter*), Tsitsi Dangarembga (*Nervous Condition*), and quite recently Ngozi Adichie (*Half a Yellow Sun*). We can even include the controversial—because often considered either anti-African or too eccentric— works by iconoclasts such as Yambo Ouologuem (*Bound to Violence*) and Dambudzo Marechera (*The House of Hunger*).

26. For histories of the Judeo-Christian God, see, for example, Cross, *Canaanite Myth and Hebrew Epic*; M. Smith, *The Origins of Biblical Monotheism*, *The Early History of God*, and *The Memoirs of God*; Dever, *Who Were the Early Israelites and Where Did They Come From?* and *Did God Have a Wife?*

27. Achebe, *Anthills of the Savannah*, 114.

28. Ibid., 28–30. The Angolan political revolutionary Amilcar Cabral once observed, "Denying to the dominated people their own historical process necessarily denies their cultural process" (Cabral, *Unity and Struggle*, 142). In light of the Nigerian Achebe's work, we may wonder to what extent the reverse is true: denying a people its cultural process constitutes a challenge to its particular sense of time and of history.

29. Arendt, "Walter Benjamin."

30. Gyasi, "Writing as Translation," 81.

31. Ibid., 84.

32. Ibid.

33. Gyasi focuses on problems in translation and translating. Other works that treat this topic directly include Berman, *The Experience of the Foreign*; Ricoeur, *Oneself as Another*; Steiner, *After Babel*; and Roger T. Bell, *Translation and Translating*.

34. Deleuze and Guattari, *Kafka*, 25 and (for further discussion) 26.

35. Ranajat Guha, "The Prose of Counter-insurgency," in Guha and Spivak, *Selected Subaltern Studies*, 45–88, quote on p. 45.

36. Kate Cook, "Historical Detection in *Waterland* and *Anthills of the Savannah*," http://www.thecove.nus.edu.sg/post/achebe/histeriaz.html (10 October 2007).

37. Deleuze and Guattari, *Kafka*, 27.

38. Some histories of Black Africa contain strands of neo-Hegelianism that frequently misunderstand what I have just noted about claims of authenticity. The neo-Hegelian theory recognizes the smoke-and-mirrors aspects of postcolonial societies in modern Africa, but chooses to interpret them as evidence of "counterfeit" modernity. The use of this word cannot be anything but misleading: What—and where—is the original? For a discussion of this question, see Comaroff and Comaroff, *Modernity and Its Malcontents*; Austen, "Coming of Age through Colonial Education"; and Apter, *Beyond Words*.

39. For examples of the many ways modern Nigerian artists, working in Nigerian languages, conceptualize these issues from the inside out, see the compositions of Akin Euba, including *Orunmila's Voices* and *Chaka*. For discussion,

see Nketia, *Ethnomusicology and African Music*, *The Music of Africa*, and "Musicology and Linguistics"; and Chernoff, *African Rhythm and African Sensibility.* Also of interest is Soyinka, "The Fourth State."

40. For signs of a need to explore systematically this idea of the hidden in African experiences of modernity, see, for example, Barber, *Africa's Hidden Histories*, and R. John Williams, "'Doing History.'"

41. Ngugi Wa Thiong'o, *Decolonizing the Mind*, 2.

42. Ibid.

43. Ibid.

44. "Decolonizing the Mind," *Complete Review*, http://www.complete-review .com/reviews/kenya/ngugi1.htm (accessed 9 January 2007).

45. Barely fifty years ago, Margery Perham could confidently claim that Africa was "without writing and so without history." Kenneth Dike, whose *Trade and Politics in the Niger Delta* is described by Nwauwa as "the first modern monograph on African history written by an African," was aware of Perham's colonial posturing. When Dike became the first African to teach African history at the University of Ibadan, he embarked on a project to reform the departmental curriculum, believing that "there is no criterion by which to compare one culture in terms of progress with another [as each] is the product of the environment and must primarily be judged in relation to the community." Apollos O. Nwauwa, "Kenneth Onwuka Dike," in Falola, *Dark Webs*, 320. See also Youe, "Moving Forward, Staying Still."

46. See Achebe, "An Image of Africa," and Achebe and Phillips, "Was Joseph Conrad Really a Racist?"

47. Hegel, *Phenomenology of Spirit* and *Elements of the Philosophy of Right.* See also Marx, *Capital*; E. Williams, *Capitalism and Slavery*; and Eze, *Race and the Enlightenment.* Aimé Césaire began his classic *Discourse on Colonialism* with the statement, "A civilization that proves incapable of solving the problems it creates is a decadent civilization" (9).

48. Barber, "African-Language Literature and Postcolonial Criticism."

49. See, for example, Richter, *Language without Soil.*

50. Ulli Beier, *Origins of Life and Death: African Creation Myths* (Ibadan: Heinemann, 1968), 1–2.

51. Hegel, *Aesthetics*; Desmond, *Art and the Absolute*; and Buck-Morss (one of the most versatile readers of Hegel in the past forty years), *Origin of Negative Dialectics.*

52. Sartre, *Nausea*, 127.

53. See, for example, Sartre's 1946 essay "Existentialism Is a Humanism."

54. Schopenhauer, *The World as Will and Representation.*

55. Senghor, *Liberté, Vol. 3: Négritude et Civilisation de l'Universel.* Some readings of Senghor suggest that he advocates the abandonment of the concept

and the "drowning" of consciousness in pure existence. Those who read Senghor in this fashion have textual support for it, including all his talk about the Negro as a "worm" with a pure sensation that "penetrates" the essence of the "real" in order to become one with the reality of the real. Although I suspect that this is a misreading of Senghor's work, I am not trying to produce an authoritative and "correct" interpretation of Senghor. Rather, I use Senghor's writings about the "Negro African" aesthetic as a jumping-off point to explain the concerns of African writers of his generation in their debates about language. My appropriation of Senghor's Afrocentrism is formal, methodological, and instrumental rather than an appropriation of substantive content. Like Senghor, I claim that Africans could read Sartre, Hegel, or Schopenhauer differently simply because they are writing about, and from the point of view of, African experience, without necessarily being ideologically Afrocentrist.

56. Sartre, *Nausea*, 127. Italics added.

57. Senghor, *Les Fondements de l'Africanité ou Négritude et Arabité*; Soyinka, *Myth, Literature and the African World*.

58. Senghor, *Les Fondements*.

59. For a recent restatement of these ideals, see Boff, "We Are All Africans." This essay postulates:

> Whenever they face a crisis, civilizations look back to their past, seeking inspiration for the future. We are today in the heart of a phenomenal world-wide crisis that affects all civilizations. The crisis could spur a leap towards a superior humanization, or it could be a tragic menace to our entire species. In such a critical moment, it is of great interest to explore our most ancient roots and that seminal beginning when we moved from being primates to being human beings. There must be lessons here that could be useful to us now. . . . Africa is not just the place of the origin. It is the primordial archetype, the source of the markers imprinted in the human soul, still present today, as indelible information, very much like that inscribed in our genetic code. It was in Africa where the human being worked out its first sensations, where the growing neuronal connections (cerebral) were articulated, where the first thoughts shone, where juvenility was strengthened (a process similar to youth, that shows plasticity and learning capacity), and the social complexity emerged that allowed language and culture to appear. Today the spirit of Africa is alive, and present, in every human being. . . . If we reincorporate the spirit of Africa, the crisis need not become a tragedy.

60. Hume, *Essays: Moral, Political, and Literary*, 91 [orig. pubd Edinburgh, 1741, as "Of Liberty and Despotism"].

61. In 1991 there existed, at a Nigerian university, a group of artists and intellectuals who called themselves the Ona Group. This group's mission was or is to ensure that, by the year 2010, "all dissertations on African art should be written in the indigenous African language of the artistic culture or artists being

studied." This position raises questions not just about whether this goal is realistic, by what date and in which disciplines; it also raises concerns about translation. But there are historical parallels to problems of this sort in other, similarly post-colonized (or, according to Hume, post-Despotic) countries. See Okediji, "African Sculptures," and William van Damme, "African Verbal Arts and the Study of African Visual Aesthetics," *Research in African Literatures*, 31, no. 4 (winter 2000), http://iupjournals.org/ral/ral31–4.html (accessed 9 February 2007).

Chapter 5: Reason and Unreason in Politics

1. *Ubuntu*—the generic form of *muntu*, or personality—literally means "humanity." *Ubuntu* is thus an abstract, neutral concept, but one that also contains an implicit ethical imperative. The concept underlies traditional abstract claims about freedom but also forms the basis of various sets of beliefs in many African cultures that "one is a person because of other persons," and therefore one must always treat each individual, oneself and others, from a standpoint of universal humanity. The politics of forgiveness and reconciliation in postapartheid South Africa often was discursively justified in this humanistic language.

2. Ndebele, *The Cry of Winnie Mandela*, 113. I use "postracial democracy" in the title of this section in a technical sense, as in the social transcendence of race. This idea of transcendence is thought through in my book *Achieving Our Humanity*. There is some overlap between the meanings of the terms *nonracial*, *multiracial*, and *postracial*. I prefer *postracial* because of its parallels to other terms that employ the same prefix, such as *postmodernism*, *postcolonialism*, and *postfeminism*. None of these designations implies an end to modernism, colonialism, or feminism. Instead, the *post-* refers to the irreversible disruption of a prior, older, classical intellectual or social order.

3. Ndebele, *The Cry of Winnie Mandela*, 70.

4. See, for example, Bell, *Understanding African Philosophy*; Shute, *Ubuntu*; Battle, *Reconciliation*.

5. Krog, *Country of My Skull*, 12.

6. These injunctions work powerfully in practice. For example, on November 14, 2003, the *Washington Post* reported on the funeral ceremony for an American soldier who died when a helicopter in which he was a passenger was shot down in Iraq. Knowing of the exemplary life of the deceased—and, of course, of the paradoxes which appear to confer on religions an aura of theological profundity—the pastor at the funeral proclaimed the Christian mystery of the struggle between life and death. "Don't fool yourself," he told the congregation. "When the helicopter went down, he went up." To this declaration, the reporter wrote, the congregation responded with "a chorus of a thousand 'amens'" (Arzua, "A

Man Who Touched 'Everybody's Life': Stafford Soldier Killed in Iraq Remembered for Bonds He Built"; my thanks to Katharine Baker for her perceptive comments about this event). For a recent scholarly study of the United States' ambiguous, but historically deep-rooted, narrative construction and rhetorical glorification of war's violence, death, and destruction as required elements of heroic service to the nation and to freedom, see Nudelman, *John Brown's Body*. Nudelman, like some other scholars (Fahs, *The Imagined Civil War*; Sweet, *Traces of War*; Trachtenberg, *Reading American Photographs*), argues that the real bodies of mass casualties in American civil and foreign wars are often rhetorically transformed into (by no means uncontested) triumphalist narratives of the nation. Nudelman argues that this transformation can be effected through "popular tune[s]," a "nationalist aesthetics of . . . abstraction," and other processes of idealization (12). For sympathetic treatments of the epistemology of faith, which nonetheless refrain from glorifying the noncognitive, see Wood, *Unsettling* ; William James, *The Will to Believe*; R. A. Putnam, *The Cambridge Companion to William James*; Alston, *Epistemic Justification* and *Beyond "Justification"*; Steup, *Knowledge, Truth, and Duty*; and Clifford, *The Ethics of Belief*.

7. The *political* cogency of the arguments for the TRC is irreproachable, and ten years after its exercises, the outcome of the process can, on empirical grounds, be considered a success. Even those inclined to disagree with this observation usually critique the TRC and the settlements prospectively: they know that these instruments have proven politically adequate, but argue for greater levels of social and economic "transformation" and for the vigilance to ensure that current gains in lifting citizens out of poverty—not just across, but also within, racial and other identifiable social cleavages—can be sustained.

8. See, for example, Van Zyl Slabbert, "Truth without Reconciliation, Reconciliation without Truth."

9. "Imperfect" because too often compromised in terms of race, gender, class, or some other status.

10. It is hardly convincing—and unacceptably ambiguous—to argue that this minimalist, historicized rationalism is in itself a form of prejudice. If this is a prejudice, then it is an epistemically justifiable one. It would be prejudice based on rationally acceptable principles, open to counterarguments, and—above all—subject to revision. These qualities are just the opposite of those commonly ascribed to prejudice.

11. See, for example, Habermas, *Theory of Communicative Action,* vol. 2, *Lifeworld and System: A Critique of Functionalist Reason* (Boston: Beacon, 1987); Momoh, *African Philosophy*; Gyekye, *Tradition and Modernity*; Weber, *The Protestant Ethic and the Spirit of Capitalism*.

12. It is ironic, is it not, so insistently to make the argument that revolution may never be a form of everyday politics. It is important to understand my

reasons: revolution is an exceptional event, and cannot always be relied upon (after all, there is always the possibility of counterrevolution) to guarantee the peace and security—let alone the social justice—in the names of which revolutions are usually carried out. More important, however, I object to the idea of the revolutionary in politics not on *political* but on *philosophical* grounds. Instead of debating, as some would prefer, the moral values of "good" and "bad" (or "progressive" and "reactionary" revolutions), and the points of view from which these distinctions are to be drawn, I have opted for the ordinary: a deliberative politics in which the touchstone is abstemious calculation based on the reasonable rather than the "original" or "inaugural." The original or the inaugural becomes a rational option only where this ascetic model of reason has already failed.

13. Derrida, "On Forgiveness," 32.

14. David A. Crocker, "Truth Commissions, Transitional Justice, and Civil Society," in Rotberg and Thompson, eds., *Truth v. Justice*, 100, italics added. Richard A. Wilson goes as far as to call this a doctrine of the "human right to a human story" (*The Politics of Truth Reconciliation in South Africa*, 56).

15. Azania People's Organization (AZAPO) and Others v. President of the Republic of South Africa and Others, 1996 (8) BCLR 1015 (CC), pp. 1027–1028.

16. Soyinka, *The Burden of Memory, the Muse of Forgiveness*, 33. Italics added.

17. Two dominant perspectives on justice in transitional democratic societies are evident. For the sake of convenience, experts characterize these perspectives as the *universalist* moral approach to democratic justice and the morally *contextualist* approach to democratic justice. Advocates of the former, represented by Dennis Thompson, argue from a universal moral principle of democratic constitutional justice, especially the requirement of due process: "The pursuit of justice . . . means . . . bring individuals to trial who are credibly alleged to have committed crimes and a seeking of a legal verdict and an appropriate punishment if they are found guilty" (Amy Guttmann and Dennis Thompson, "The Moral Foundations of Truth Commissions," in Rotberg and Thompson, eds., *Truth v. Justice*, 22–44; quote on p. 25). Under this perspective, therefore, "in a democratic society, and especially in a society that is trying to overcome injustices of the past, trading criminal justice for a general social benefit such as social reconciliation requires a moral defense if it is to be acceptable" (ibid.). The second perspective, represented by Andre du Toit, contextualizes even the moral foundation of this requirement of due process. "Transitional justice," writes du Toit, "need not be construed as a moral compromise, sacrificing justice for the sake of truth and reconciliation. The moral foundations of truth commissions require a closer consideration of the distinctive features and requirements of the circumstances of transitional justice, in addition to the general moral considerations underlying notions of justice familiar to established liberal societies" (André du Toit, "The Moral Foundations of the South African TRC:

Truth as Acknowledgment and Justice as Recognition," in Rotberg and Thompson, eds., *Truth v. Justice*, 122–40, quote on p. 123). This approach is contextualist because—largely on the basis of the South African example—du Toit argues that, "consistent with justice itself, understanding the moral foundations of truth commissions may require different principles applied in fundamentally different kinds of historical circumstances" (ibid.). Both perspectives, nevertheless, appeal to principle, morality, and democracy. They are principled because of the nonarbitrary derivations of their moral terms of reference; they are moral because predicated on the desire of associated individuals to live together in society by treating one another with respect and dignity; and they are democratic because based on an idea of the polity as governed by equality of rights, equality before the law, and so forth.

18. The main focus of my discussion in this section is on the moral meanings of forgiveness in relation to transitional justice, not democracy. But as David A. Crocker has observed, justice or democracy may be called "transitional" precisely because it is a process whereby "a fledging democracy reckon[s] with severe human rights abuses that earlier authoritarian regimes, their opponents, or combatants in an internal armed conflict have committed" ("Truth Commissions, Transitional Justice, and Civil Society," 100). This approach to justice, Crocker argues, is necessary because it seems to be the most suitable, if not the only reasonable, way for emerging democracies "to respond appropriately to past evils without undermining the new democracy or jeopardizing prospects for future development" (ibid.).

19. Villa-Vicencio, "The Perpetrators Should Not Always Be Prosecuted," 113.

20. Nino, "The Duty to Punish Past Abuses of Human Rights Put into Context," 2638.

21. Azania People's Organization (AZAPO) and Others v President of the Republic of South Africa and Others, 1996 (8) BCLR 1015 (CC), pp. 1027–28.

22. Tutu, "Foreword," 12.

23. Van Zyl Slabbert, "Truth without Reconciliation, Reconciliation without Truth," 68. Italics added.

24. Derrida, "On Forgiveness," 42.

25. Ibid., 42–43.

26. Ibid., 43–44.

27. Ndebele, "Of Lions and Rabbits," 146, 147.

28. Ntsebeza, "A Lot More to Live For," 101. It is, in fact, precisely in this sense that Andre du Toit compared some aspects of the work of truth commissions to work of writing a constitution: "Similar to a constitutional assembly, charged with the task of drawing up a new constitution, the TRC was not a permanent institution, but was meant to facilitate the launching of a new era. Unlike the [presumably entirely] forward-looking founding function of establishing a con-

stitution, the founding missions of truth commissions are, in addition to for-ward-looking, also backward-looking." Thus, as the "conjunction of the TRC and the Constitutional Assembly demonstrates in the South African case, these were not mutually exclusive alternatives," because "if truth commissions are back-ward-looking, they are so precisely as historical founding projects; they deal with the past not for its sake but in order to clear the way for a new beginning" ("The Moral Foundations of the South African TRC," 123).

29. Ndebele, "Of Lions and Rabbits," 152.

30. Ibid.

31. Ramphele, "Law, Corruption and Morality," 173–74.

32. Van Zyl Slabbert, "Truth without Reconciliation, Reconciliation without Truth," 68. Italics added.

Bibliography

Aba Commission of Inquiry. *Notes of Evidence Taken by the Commission of Inquiry Appointed to Inquire into Disturbances in the Calabar and Owerri Provinces, December 1929.* Lagos: Government Press, 1929.

Abiodun, Rowland, Henry J. Drewal, and John Pemberton III, eds. *The Yoruba Artist: New Theoretical Perspectives on African Arts.* Washington: Smithsonian Institution Press, 1994.

Achebe, Chinua. *Anthills of the Savannah.* London: Heinemann, 1987.

———. *Christmas in Biafra and Other Poems.* London: Heinemann, 1971.

———. *Girls at War.* London: Heinemann, 1973.

———. *Hopes and Impediments: Selected Essays.* New York: Doubleday, 1989.

———. "An Image of Africa: Racism in Conrad's Heart of Darkness." *Heart of Darkness: A Norton Critical Edition,* by Joseph Conrad, ed. Robert Kimbrough, 251–62. New York: W. W. Norton, 1988.

———. "Language and the Destiny of Man." *Hopes and Impediments: Selected Essays,* 127–37. New York: Doubleday, 1990.

———. *No Longer at Ease.* London: Heinemann, 1960.

———. *Things Fall Apart.* New York: Anchor, 1994.

———. "The Truth of Fiction." *Hopes and Impediments: Selected Essays.* New York: Doubleday, 1989.

Achebe, Chinua, and Caryl Phillips. "Was Joseph Conrad Really a Racist?" *Philosophia Africana* 10, no. 1 (2006): 1–10.

Ackerman, Robert John. *Heterogeneities: Race, Gender, Class, Nation, and State.* Amherst: University of Massachusetts Press, 1996.

Adams, Mark D., Granger G. Sutton, Hamilton O. Smith, Eugene W. Myers, and J. Craig Venter. "The Independence of Our Genome Assemblies." *Proceedings of the National Academy of Sciences of the United States of America* 100, no. 6 (18 March 2003): 3025–26.

Adichie, Ngozi. *Half a Yellow Sun.* New York: Alfred A. Knopf, 2006.

Adorno, Theodor W. *Negative Dialectics*, trans. E. B. Ashton. New York: Continuum, 1983.

——. *Philosophische Terminologie*, vol. 1. Frankfurt am Main: Suhrkamp, 1973.

Agamben, Giorgio. *Homo Sacer: Sovereign Power and Bare Life.* Stanford: Stanford University Press, 1998.

Agawu, Kofi, ed. "The Landscape of African Music." *Research in African Literatures* 32, no. 2 (2001) [special issue].

Alston, William P. *Beyond "Justification": Dimensions of Epistemic Evaluation.* Ithaca: Cornell University Press, 2005.

——. *Epistemic Justification: Essays in the Theory of Knowledge.* Ithaca: Cornell University Press, 1996.

——. *A Realist Conception of Truth.* Ithaca: Cornell University Press, 1996.

American Anthropological Association. "Understanding Race," http://www .understandingrace.org/home.html (accessed 5 February 2007).

Appiah, K. Anthony. "The Case for Contamination." *New York Times Magazine*, 1 January 2006, 30.

——. *Cosmopolitanism: Ethics in a World of Strangers.* New York: W. W. Norton, 2006.

——. *The Ethics of Identity.* Princeton: Princeton University Press, 2005.

——. "The Politics of Identity." *Daedalus* 135, no. 4 (fall 2006): 15–22.

Apter, Andrew. *Beyond Words: Discourse and Critical Agency in Africa.* Chicago: University of Chicago Press, 2007.

Arendt, Hannah. "Walter Benjamin: 1892–1940." *Illuminations*, by Walter Benjamin, 1–58. New York: Schocken, 1969.

Aristotle. *Analytica Posteriora.* http://etext.virginia.edu/toc/modeng/public/ AriPost.html (accessed 7 February 2006).

——. *Analytica Priora.* http://etext.virginia.edu/toc/modeng/public/AriPrio .html (accessed 7 February 2006).

——. *Nichomachean Ethics*, trans. Terrence Irwin. Indianapolis: Hackett, 1999.

——. *Metaphysics*, trans. Hugh Tredennick. Cambridge: Harvard University Press, 1979.

——. *The Politics and the Constitution of Athens*, ed. Stephen Everson. Cambridge: Cambridge University Press, 1996.

Arnauld, Antoine, and Pierre Nicole. *Logic or the Art of Thinking*, trans. Jill

Vance Buroker. New York: Cambridge University Press, 1996 [orig. pubd 1683 as *La logique ou L'art de penser: contenant outre les règles communes, plusieurs observations nouvelles, propres à former le jugement*].

Arzua, Lila. "A Man Who Touched 'Everybody's Life': Stafford Soldier Killed in Iraq Remembered for Bonds He Built." *Washington Post*, 15 November 2003, B, 3.

Augustine of Hippo. *The Confessions*. Indianapolis: Hackett, 2007.

Austen, Ralph A. "Coming of Age through Colonial Education: African Autobiography as Reluctant Bildungsroman." *Boston University Discussion Papers in the African Humanities*, 2000.

Azania People's Organization (AZAPO) and Others v. President of the Republic of South Africa and Others, 1996 (8) BCLR 1015 (CC): 1027–28. http://www.azapo.org.za (accessed 7 February 2007).

Bâ, Mariama. *So Long a Letter*. London: Heinemann, 1989.

Bacon, Francis. *Advancement of Learning*. London: G. W. Kitchin, 1881.

——. *The New Organon and Related Writings*, ed. Fulton H. Anderson. New York: Bobbs-Merrill, 1960.

——. *The New Organon: Or True Directions Concerning the Interpretation of Nature*. London: Typographium Regium, 1620.

——. *Of the Proficience and Advancement of Learning, Divine and Human*, 1605 original edition online at http://www.uoregon.edu/~rbear/adv1.htm.

——. *The tvvoo bookes of Francis Bacon, of the proficience and aduancement of learning, diuine and humane*. London: Henrie Tomes, 1605.

——. *The Works of Francis Bacon*, ed. James Spalding, Robert L. Ellis, and Douglas D. Heath. London: Longman, 1857–74.

Barber, Karin. "African-Language Literature and Postcolonial Criticism." *Research in African Literatures* 26, no. 4 (1995): 3–30.

——, ed. *Africa's Hidden Histories: Everyday Literacy and Making the Self*. Bloomington: Indiana University Press, 2006.

Baron, Jonathan. *Thinking and Deciding*. 3rd ed. New York: Cambridge University Press, 2000.

Bates, Roberts H., V. Y. Mudimbe, and Jean F. O'Barr, eds. *Africa and the Disciplines*. Chicago: University of Chicago Press, 1993.

Battle, Michael. *Reconciliation: The Ubuntu Theology of Desmund Tutu*. Cleveland: Pilgrim, 1997.

Bayes, Thomas. "An Essay Toward Solving a Problem in the Doctrine of Chances. By the late Rev. Mr. Bayes, F. R. S. communicated by Mr. Price, in a letter to John Canton, A. M. F. R. S." *Philosophical Transactions, Giving Some Account of the Present Undertakings, Studies and Labours of the Ingenious in Many Considerable Parts of the World* 53 (1763): 370–418.

——. "An Essay Toward Solving a Problem in the Doctrine of Chances." *Biometrika* 45 (1958): 296–315.

Beaney, Michael, ed. *The Frege Reader*. Oxford: Blackwell, 1997.

Beier, Ulli. *Origins of Life and Death: African Creation Myths*. London: Heinemann, 1968.

Bell, Richard. *Understanding African Philosophy: An Essay in Cross-Cultural Approach to Classical and Contemporary Issues*. New York: Routledge, 2002.

Bell, Roger T. *Translation and Translating: Theory and Practice*. London: Longman, 1991.

Benjamin, Walter. *Illuminations*. New York: Schocken, 1969.

Berman, Antoine. *The Experience of the Foreign: Culture and Translation in Romantic Germany*, trans. S. Heyvaert. Albany: State University of New York Press, 1992.

Beti, Mongo. *Mission to Kaka*. London: Heinemann, 1982.

——. *Poor Christ of Bomba*. Long Grove, Ill.: Waveland, 2005.

——. *Remember Reuben*. London: Heinemann, 1988.

Bilgrami, Akeel. "The Clash within Civilizations." *Daedalus* 132, no. 3 (summer 2003): 88–95.

Billig, Michael. *Arguing and Thinking: A Rhetorical Approach to Social Psychology*. 2nd ed. New York: Cambridge University Press, 1996.

Block, John. *The Monstrous Races in Medieval Art and Thought*. Syracuse: Syracuse University Press, 2000.

Block, Ned. "How Heritability Misleads about Race." *Cognition* 56, no. 2 (1995): 99–128.

Blondel, Maurice. *L'Action*. Paris: Presses Universitaires de France, 1993 [orig. pubd 1893].

Boas, Franz. *Race, Language, and Culture*. Chicago: University of Chicago Press, 1995.

Boff, Leonardo. "We Are All Africans." The Earthcharter Commission, http://www.ciranda.net/spip/article998.html?lang=en (accessed 22 May 2007).

Bovens, Luc, and Stephan Hartman. *Bayesian Epistemology*. Oxford: Oxford University Press, 2003.

Bradley, F. H. *Principles of Logic*. London: Oxford University Press, 1883.

Brandom, Robert B. *Making It Explicit*. Cambridge: Harvard University Press, 1994.

Braude, Benjamin. "The Sons of Noah and the Construction of Ethnic and Geographical Identities in the Medieval and Early Modern Periods." *William and Mary Quarterly* 54, no. 1 (January 1997): 103–42.

Buck-Morss, Susan. *Origin of Negative Dialectics*. New York: Free Press, 1979.

Budgen, Sebastian, Stathis Kouvelakis, and Slavoj Žižek, eds. *Lenin Reloaded: Toward a Politics of Truth*. Durham: Duke University Press, 2007.

"The Business of Race and Science," http://web.mit.edu/csd/BRS/Welcome.html (accessed 5 February 2007).

Butler, Judith. *Gender Trouble*. New York: Routledge, 1999.

Cabral, Amilcar. *Unity and Struggle*. London: Heinemann, 1980.

Calhoun, Cheshire, ed. *Setting the Moral Compass: Essays by Women Philosophers*. Oxford: Oxford University Press, 2004.

Carr, David, Thomas R. Flynn, and Rudolf A. Makkreel. *Ethics of History*. Evanston: Northwestern University Press, 2004.

Carr, Edward Hallet. *What Is History?* New York: Vintage, 1967.

Cartwright, Nancy. *How the Laws of Physics Lie*. Oxford: Clarendon, 1983.

Castoriadis, Cornelius. *The Imaginary Institutions of Society*. Cambridge: MIT Press, 1998.

Certeau, Michel de. *The Writing of History*, trans. T. Conley. New York: Columbia University Press, 1988.

Césaire, Aimé. *Discourse on Colonialism*. New York: Monthly Review Press, 1972.

Chakrabarty, Dipesh. *Provincializing Europe*. Princeton: Princeton University Press, 2000.

Chalmers, David J. *The Conscious Mind: In Search of a Fundamental Theory*. New York: Oxford University Press, 1997.

Chernoff, John Miller. *African Rhythm and African Sensibility: Aesthetics and Social Action in African Musical Idioms*. Chicago: University of Chicago Press, 1981.

Chomsky, Noam. *Rules and Representations*. Revised ed. New York: Columbia University Press, 2005.

Churchland, Patricia, and Terrence J. Sejnowski. *The Computational Brain*. Cambridge: MIT Press, 1994.

Churchland, Paul M. *The Engine of Reason, the Seat of the Soul: A Philosophical Journey into the Brain*. Cambridge: MIT Press, 1996.

Clark, Andy, and David J. Chalmers. "The Extended Mind." *Analysis* 58 (1998): 10–23.

Clifford, W. K. *The Ethics of Belief and Other Essays*. Amherst, N.Y.: Prometheus, 1999.

Coetzee, J. M. *Disgrace*. New York: Vintage, 2000.

———. *Elizabeth Costello*. London: Secker and Warburg, 2003.

Collingwood, R. G. *An Essay on Philosophical Method*. Oxford: Clarendon, 1933.

Comaroff, Jean, and John Comaroff, eds. *Modernity and Its Malcontents*. Chicago: University of Chicago Press, 1993.

Cook, Kate. "Historical Detection in *Waterland* and *Anthills of the Savannah*." http://www.scholars.nus.edu.sg/landow/post/achebe/histeria2.html (accessed 6 January 2007).

Crocker, David A. "Truth Commissions, Transitional Justice, and Civil Society." *Truth v. Justice*, ed. Robert I. Rotberg and Dennis Thompson, 99–121. Princeton: Princeton University Press, 2000.

Cross, Frank Moore. *Canaanite Myth and Hebrew Epic: Essays in the History of the Religion of Israel*. Cambridge: Harvard University Press, 1997.

Damasio, Antonio. *Descartes' Error: Emotion, Reason, and the Human Brain*. New York: Quill, 1995.

Damme, Wilfried van. "African Verbal Arts and the Study of African Visual Aesthetics." *Research in African Literatures* 31, no. 4 (2000): 8–20.

Dangarembga, Tsitsi. *Nervous Condition*. Emeryville, Calif.: Seal Press, 2005.

Davidson, Basil. *Africa: History of a Continent*. New York: Macmillan, 1966.

Davidson, Donald. *Problems of Rationality*. New York: Oxford University Press, 2004.

Decalanzaro, Denys A. *Motivation and Emotion: Evolutionary, Physiological, Developmental, and Social Perspectives*. Princeton, N.J.: Prentice Hall, 1998.

"Decolonizing the Mind." *The Complete Review*, http://www.complete-review.com/reviews/kenya/ngugi1.htm (accessed 9 January 2007).

Deleuze, Gilles, and Felix Guattari. *Kafka: Toward a Minor Literature*, trans. Dana Polan. Minneapolis: University of Minnesota Press, 1986.

Dennett, Daniel C. *Brainstorms: Philosophical Essays on Mind and Psychology*. Cambridge: MIT Press, 1986.

Derrida, Jacques. "On Forgiveness." *Cosmopolitanism and Forgiveness*, trans. Mark Dooley and Michael Hughes, 28–60. New York: Routledge, 2002.

Descombes, Vincent. *The Mind's Provisions: A Critique of Cognitivism*. Princeton: Princeton University Press, 2001.

Desmond, William. *Art and the Absolute: A Study of Hegel's Aesthetics*. Albany: State University of New York Press, 1986.

Dever, William G. *Did God Have a Wife? Archeology and Folk Religion in Ancient Israel*. Grand Rapids, Mich.: Eerdmanns, 2005.

——. *Who Were the Early Israelites and Where Did They Come From?* Grand Rapids, Mich.: Eerdmanns, 2006.

Dewey, John. *Early Works of John Dewey, 1882–1898*, vol. 2: *1887 Psychology*. Carbondale: Southern Illinois University Press, 1970.

——. *Essays in Experimental Logic*. Chicago: University of Chicago Press, 1916.

Diamond, Jared. *Guns, Germs, and Steel: The Fates of Human Societies*. New York: W. W. Norton, 1997.

Dike, Kenneth. *Trade and Politics in the Niger Delta: An Introduction to the Economic and Political History of Nigeria*. Oxford: Clarendon, 1962.

Diop, Alioune, ed. *Présence Africaine* 1, November–December 1947.

Dorr, Gregory Michael. "Defective or Disabled? Race, Medicine, and Eugenics in Progressive Era Virginia and Alabama." *Journal of the Gilded Age and Progressive Era* 5, no. 4 (October 2006): 359–92.

Dreyfus, Hubert L. *What Computers Still Can't Do: A Critique of Artificial Reason*. Cambridge: MIT Press, 1992.

Dubois, Laurent. *A Colony of Citizens: Revolution and Slave Emancipation in the French Caribbean, 1787–1804*. Chapel Hill: University of North Carolina Press, 2004.

Duke University Medical Center. "Black Heart Disease Patients Die at Higher Rate Than White." Press release, http://www.dukemednews.duke.edu/news/article.php?id=798 (accessed 2 February 2007).

du Toit, André. "The Moral Foundations of the South African TRC: Truth as Acknowledgment and Justice as Recognition." *Truth v. Justice*, ed. Robert I. Rotberg and Dennis Thompson, 122–40. Princeton: Princeton University Press, 2000.

Edelman, Gerald M. *Second Nature: Brain Science and Human Knowledge*. New Haven: Yale University Press, 2006.

Eliade, Mircea. *The Sacred and the Profane: The Nature of Religion*. New York: Harvest, 1959.

Emerson, Ralph Waldo. *Essays and Lectures*. New York: Library of America, 1983.

——. *Selected Essays*. New York: Penguin, 1982.

——. "Self Reliance" [1841]. *Self Reliance and Other Essays*, 19–38. New York: Dover, 1993.

——. "The Transcendentalist" [1842]. *Selected Essays*, 239–58. New York: Penguin Classics, 1982.

Engelhard, Jack. *Indecent Proposal*. New York: Pocket, 1993.

Ereshefsky, Marc. *The Poverty of Linnaean Hierarchy: A Philosophical Study of Biological Taxonomy*. New York: Cambridge University Press, 2000.

Euba, Akin. *Chaka: An Opera in Two Chants*. Birmingham, England: Touring Opera and Music Research Institute, 1998 [compact disc].

——. *Orunmila's Voices: Songs from the Beginning of Time: For Soloists, Chanters, Chorus, Dancers, and Symphony Orchestra*, 2002.

——. *Yoruba Drumming: The Dùndún Tradition*. Bayreuth: Bayreuth African Studies Series, 1990.

Eze, Emmanuel Chukwudi. *Achieving Our Humanity: The Idea of the Postracial Future*. New York: Routledge, 2001.

——. "African Philosophy and the Analytic Tradition." *Philosophical Papers* 30, no. 3 (October 2001): 205–13.

——. *Postcolonial African Philosophy: A Critical Reader*. Oxford: Blackwell, 1998.

——, ed. *African Philosophy: An Anthology*. Oxford: Blackwell, 1998.

——, ed. *Race and the Enlightenment: A Reader*. Oxford: Blackwell, 1997.

Fabian, Johannes. *Time and the Other: How Anthropology Makes Its Objects*. New York: Columbia University Press, 1983.

Fahs, Alice. *The Imagined Civil War: Popular Literature of the North and South, 1861–1865*. Chapel Hill: University of North Carolina Press, 2001.

Falola, Toyin, ed. *The Dark Webs: Perspectives on Colonialism*. Durham: Carolina Academic Press, 2004.

Fanon, Frantz. *Black Skin, White Masks*, trans. Constance Farrington. New York: Grove, 1994.

Feierman, Steven. "Africa in History: The End of Universal Narratives." *After Colonialism: Imperial Histories and Postcolonial Displacements*, ed. Gyan Prakash, 40–65. Princeton: Princeton University Press, 1995.

Finkelman, Paul. *Medicine, Nutrition, Demography, and Slavery*. New York: Garland, 1989.

Fischer, David Hackett. "Freedom's Not Just Another Word." *New York Times*, 7 February 2005, A, 21.

———. *Liberty and Freedom: A Visual History of America's Founding Ideas*. New York: Oxford University Press, 2004.

Flanagan, Owen. *The Problem of the Soul: Two Visions of Mind and How to Reconcile Them*. New York: Basic Books, 2003.

Fogelin, Robert. *Walking the Tightrope of Reason: The Precarious life of the Rational Animal*. New York: Oxford University Press, 2004.

Forgas, Joseph P., ed. *Feeling and Thinking: The Role of Affect in Social Cognition*. New York: Cambridge University Press, 1999.

Fraga, Mario F., Esteban Ballestar, Maria F. Paz, Santiago Ropero, Fernando Setien, Maria L. Ballestar, Damia Heine-Suñer, et al. "Epigenetic Differences Arise During the Lifetime of Monozygotic Twins." *Proceedings of the National Academy of Sciences* 102, no. 30 (26 July 2005): 10,604–9.

Frege, Gottlob. *Posthumous Writings*, ed. Hans Hermes, Friedrich Kambartel, and Friedrich Kaulbach. Chicago: University of Chicago Press, 1979.

Friedman, Kerim. "What's Wrong with Yali's Question." *Savage Minds*, http://savageminds.org/2005/07/25/whats-wrong-with-yalis-question (accessed 2 August 2005).

Friedman, Michael. "Exorcizing the Philosophical Tradition." *Reading McDowell*, ed. Nicholas S. Smith, 25–57. New York: Routledge, 2002.

Friedman, Sarah L., Ellin Kofsky Scholnick, and Rodney R. Cocking, eds. *Blueprints for Thinking: The Role of Planning in Cognitive Development*. New York: Cambridge University Press, 1987.

Gaddis, John Lewis. *The Landscape of History: How Historians Map the Past*. New York: Oxford University Press, 2002.

Garraway, Doris. *The Libertine Colony: Creolization in the Early French Caribbean*. Durham: Duke University Press, 2005.

———. "Race, Reproduction and Family Romance in Moreau de Saint-Méry's Description . . . de la partie française de l'isle Saint-Domingue." *Eighteenth-Century Studies* 38, no. 2 (2005): 227–46.

George, Olakunle. *Relocating Agency: Modernity and African Letters*. Albany: State University of New York Press, 2003.

Gikandi, Simon. *Reading Chinua Achebe: Language and Ideology in Fiction*. London: Heinemann, 1991.

Gilligan, Carol. *In A Different Voice: Psychological Theory and Women's Development*. Cambridge: Harvard University Press, 1982.

Goldenberg, David M. *The Curse of Ham: Race and Slavery in Early Judaism, Christianity, and Islam*. Princeton: Princeton University Press, 2003.

Goodman, Allen. *Race: The Power of an Illusion*. Los Angeles: California Newsreel, 2003 [video cassettes].

Goody, Jack. *The Domestication of the Savage Mind*. Cambridge: Cambridge University Press, 1977.

Gourevitch, Philip. *We Wish to Inform You That Tomorrow We Will Be Killed with Our Families*. New York: Picador, 1999.

Graves, Joseph L., Jr. *The Emperor's New Clothes: Biological Theories of Race at the Millennium*. New Brunswick, N.J.: Rutgers University Press, 2001.

Green, Judith. *Deep Democracy*. New York: Rowman and Littlefield, 1999.

Guha, Ranajit, and Gayatri Spivak, eds. *Selected Subaltern Studies*. New York: Oxford University Press, 1988.

Guillory, J. D. "The Pro-Slavery Arguments of Dr. Samuel A. Cartwright." *Louisiana History* 9 (1968): 209–27.

Gutmann, Amy. *Identity in Democracy*. Princeton: Princeton University Press, 2004.

Gutmann, Amy, and Dennis Thompson. "The Moral Foundations of Truth Commission." *Truth v. Justice*, ed. Robert I. Rotberg and Dennis Thompson, 22–44. Princeton: Princeton University Press, 2000.

———. *Why Deliberative Democracy?* Princeton: Princeton University Press, 2004.

Gyasi, Kwaku A. "Writing as Translation: African Literature and the Challenges of Translation." *Research in African Literatures* 30, no. 2 (1999): 75–87.

Gyekye, Kwame. *Tradition and Modernity: Philosophical Reflections on the African Experience*. New York: Oxford University Press, 2002.

Habermas, Jürgen. *The Theory of Communicative Action*. Cambridge: MIT Press, 1984–87.

Hacking, Ian. *Historical Ontology*. Cambridge: Harvard University Press, 2004.

Hadot, Pierre. *What Is Ancient Philosophy?* Cambridge: Harvard University Press, 2002.

Harding, Sandra. "The Curious Coincidence between Feminine and African Moralities." *African Philosophy: An Anthology*, ed. Emmanuel C. Eze, 360–72. Oxford: Blackwell, 1998.

———. *Science and Social Inequality: Feminist and Postcolonial Issues*. Urbana: University of Illinois Press, 2006.

Hargreaves, J. D. "Approaches to Decolonization." *The British Intellectual Engagement with Africa in the Twentieth Century*, ed. Douglas Rimmer and Anthony Kirk-Greene, 90–111. New York: St. Martin's, 2000.

Harpham, Geoffrey Galt. *Language Alone: The Critical Fetish of Modernity*. New York: Routledge, 2002.

Hauser, Marc. *Moral Minds: How Nature Designed Our Universal Sense of Right and Wrong*. New York: Ecco, 2006.

Hazlitt, William. "Race and Class." *Selected Writings*, ed. Ronald Blythe, 464–66. Harmondsworth: Penguin, 1970.

Hegel, Georg Wilhelm Friedrich. *Aesthetics: Lectures on Fine Art*, trans. T. M. Knox. Oxford: Clarendon, 1975.

——. *Elements of the Philosophy of Right*, trans. H. B. Nisbet. Cambridge: Cambridge University Press, 1991 [orig. pubd 1821].

——. *Phenomenology of Spirit*, trans. A. V. Miller. New York: Oxford University Press, 1979 [orig. pubd 1807].

Heidegger, Martin. *Basic Writings*. 2nd ed., trans. David Farrell Krell. San Francisco: Harper, 1993.

——. "The Origin of the Work of Art." *Basic Writings*, 2nd ed., trans. David Farrell Krell, 139–212. San Francisco: Harper, 1993.

——. *The Principle of Reason*. Indianapolis: Indiana University Press, 1996.

Henig, Robin Marantz. "The Genome in Black and White (and Gray)." *New York Times Magazine*, 10 October 2004, 47.

Herodotus. *History*, trans. A. D. Godley. Cambridge: Cambridge University Press, 1920–25.

Herskovits, Melville. *The Myth of the Negro Past*. Boston: Beacon, 1990.

Hippocrates. *On the Sacred Disease*, trans. Frances Adams. http://classics.mit.edu/Hippocrates/sacred.html (accessed 2 January 2006).

Hobbes, Thomas. *Leviathan: With Selected Variants from the Latin Edition of 1668*. Indianapolis: Hackett, 1994. Online version of the original 1660 available at http://oregonstate.edu/instruct/phl302/texts/hobbes/leviathan-contents.htm (accessed 19 October 2007).

Hochschild, Adam. *Bury the Chains: Prophets and Rebels in the Fight to Free an Empire's Slaves*. New York: Houghton Mifflin, 2005.

Hoffman, Stephen L., G. Mani Subramanian, Frank H. Collins, and J. Craig Venter. "Plasmodium, Human and Anopheles Genomics and Malaria." *Nature*, 415, no. 6872 (2002): 702–800.

Holyoak, Keith J., and Robert G. Morrison. *The Cambridge Handbook of Thinking and Reasoning*. New York: Cambridge University Press, 2005.

Hornius, Georg. *Rdo. Dno. D. Adr. Stalpartio Abb. Togerlesi dignisod. Lumen Historium per Orientem. illustrandis Biblijs sacris, Martyro-logio, et alijs multis. Concinn. Fran Hareio Antverpiae*. Leyden, c. 1653.

Huizinga, J. H. "Africa, the Continent of To-morrow's Trouble." *African Affairs* 49 (1950): 120–28.

Hume, David. *Essays: Moral, Political, and Literary*, ed. Eugene Miller. Indianapolis: Liberty Classics, 1985.

———. "Of Civil Liberty." In *Essays: Moral, Political, and Literary*, ed. Eugene Miller. Indianapolis: Liberty Classics, 1985.

———. *Treatise of Human Nature*, http://socserv2.socsci.mcmaster.ca/~econ/ug cm/3ll3/hume/treat.html (accessed 6 February 2007) [electronic version of original copy].

———. *A Treatise of Human Nature: Being An Attempt to introduce the experimental Method of Reasoning into Moral Subjects*, ed. L. A. Selby-Bigge. 2nd ed. Oxford: Clarendon, 1978 [orig. pubd 1739].

Huntington, Samuel P. *The Clash of Civilizations and the Remaking of World Order*. New York: Simon and Schuster, 1996.

Husserl, Edmund. *Husserliana: Gesamelte Werke*, ed. Ullrich Melle. Louvain: Husserl Archives, 1888–.

———. *Logical Investigations*. New York: Routledge, 2001–6. [orig. pubd 1901].

———. *Logische Untersuchungen*. Halle: Max Neimeyer, 1922.

———. "Phenomenology." *Journal of the British Society for Phenomenology* 2 (1971): 77–90.

———. *Phenomenology and the Crisis of Philosophy: Philosophy as Rigorous Science and Philosophy and the Crisis of European Man*, trans. Qientin Lauer. New York: Harper and Row, 1965.

———. "Philosophie als strenge Wissenschaft." *Logos* 1 (1913): 289–341.

———. *Philosophie der Arithmetick: Psychologische und logische Untersuchungen*. Halle-Saale: Pfeffer, 1891.

———. *Untersuchungen zur Phänomenologie und Theorie der Erkenntnis*. Halle: Max Niemeyer, 1901.

James, William. *The Will to Believe and Other Essays in Popular Philosophy*. Cambridge: Harvard University Press, 1979.

James, Wilmot, and Linda van de Vijver, eds. *After the TRC: Reflections on Truth and Reconciliation in South Africa*. Cape Town: David Philip, 2000.

Janouch, Gustava. *Conversations with Kafka*. New York: New Dimensions, 1971.

Jha, Ashish K., Paul D. Varosy, Alka M. Kanaya, Donald B. Hunninghake, Mark A. Hlatky, David D. Waters, Curt D. Furberg, and Michael G. Shilpak. "Differences in Medical Care and Disease Outcomes among Black and White Women with Heart Disease." *Circulation* 108, no. 9 (2003): 1089–94.

Journal of the American Medical Association. http://www.msnbc.msn.com/id/ 15404055/site/newsweek/ (accessed 2 February 2007).

Kaiwar, Vasant, and Sucheta Mazumdar. "Race, Orient, Nation in the Time-

Space of Modernity." *Antinomies of Modernity: Essays on Race, Orient, Nation*, ed. Kaiwar Vasant and Sucheta Mazumdar, 261–89. Durham: Duke University Press, 2003.

———, eds. *Antinomies of Modernity: Essays on Race, Orient, Nation*. Durham: Duke University Press, 2003.

Kant, Immanuel. *Anthropology from a Pragmatic Point of View*, trans. Mary J. Gregor. The Hague: Nijhoff, 1974.

———. *The Critique of Judgment*, trans. J. C. Meredith. Oxford: Clarendon, 1992.

———. *Critique of Pure Reason*, trans. Werner S. Pluhar. Indianapolis: Hackett, 1996 [orig. pubd 1781 as *Kritik der reinen Vernunft*].

———. *Grounding for the Metaphysics of Morals*, trans. James W. Ellington. Indianapolis: Hackett, 1981.

———. "Idea for a Universal History with a Cosmopolitanism Purpose." *Political Writings*, ed. H. S. Reiss, trans. H. B. Nisbet, 41–53. Cambridge: Cambridge University Press, 1991.

———. "Innate Characteristics of the Human Being Considered Throughout the World." *Race and the Enlightenment: A Reader*, ed. Emmanuel Chukwudi Eze. Oxford: Blackwell, 1997.

———. *Political Writings*, ed. H. S. Reiss, trans. H. B. Nisbet. Cambridge: Cambridge University Press, 1991.

Kaufmann, Walter, ed. *Existentialism from Dostoyevsky to Sartre*. New York: Meridian, 1989.

Keita, Shomarka, Rick A. Kittles, Charles N. Rotimi, Charmaine D.M. Royal, et al. "Human Genome Variation and 'Race.'" *Nature Genetics*, 9 November 2004: http://hum-molgen.org/NewsGen/11–2004/msg06.html.

Kidd, Colin. *The Forging of Races: Race and Scripture in the Protestant Atlantic World, 1600–2000*. New York: Cambridge University Press, 2006.

Kirk-Greene, Anthony. "The Emergence of an Africanist Community in the UK." *The British Intellectual Engagement with Africa in the Twentieth Century*, ed. Douglas Rimmer and Anthony Kirk-Greene, 11–30. New York: St. Martin's, 2000.

Klein, Martin. "Studying the History of Those Who Would Rather Forget: Oral History and the Experience of Slavery." *History in Africa* 16 (1989): 209–17.

Kohlberg, Lawrence. "The Claim to Moral Adequacy of a Highest Stage of Moral Judgment." *Journal of Philosophy* 70 (1973): 630–46.

———. *Essays on Moral Development*, vol. 1: *The Philosophy of Moral Development*. New York: Harper and Row, 1981.

———. *From Is to Ought: How to Commit the Naturalistic Fallacy and Get Away with It in the Study of Moral Development*. Burlington, Mass.: Academic, 1971.

Kohlberg, Lawrence, Charles Levine, and Alexandra Hewer. *Moral Stages: A Current Formulation and a Response to Critics*. New York: Karger, 1983.

Korhonen, Kuisma, ed. *Tropes for the Past: Hayden White and the History/Literature Debate*. The Hague: Rodopi, 2006.

Kortenaar, Neil Ten. "Beyond Authenticity and Creolization: Reading Achebe Writing Culture." *Publications of the Modern Language Association of America* 110, no. 1 (1995): 30–42.

——. "Chinua Achebe and the Question of Modern African Tragedy." *Philosophia Africana* 9, no. 2 (2006): 83–100.

——. "Fictive States and the State of Fiction in Africa." *Comparative Literature* 52, no. 3 (2000): 228–45.

Krog, Antjie. *Country of My Skull: Guilt, Sorrow, and the Limits of Forgiveness in the New South Africa*. Johannesburg: Random House, 1998.

Kuhn, Thomas. *The Road Since Structure*, ed. James Conant and John Haugeland. Chicago: University of Chicago Press, 2000.

——. *The Structure of Scientific Revolutions*. Chicago: University of Chicago Press, 1996.

LaCapra, Dominick. *History in Transit: Experience, Identity, Critical Theory*. Ithaca: Cornell University Press, 2004.

——. *Writing History, Writing Trauma*. Baltimore: Johns Hopkins University Press, 2000.

LaFraniere, Sharon. "Court Convicts 3 in 1994 Genocide across Rwanda." *New York Times*, 4 December 2003, A, 1.

Lakoff, George, and Mark Johnson. *Philosophy in the Flesh: The Embodied Mind and Its Challenge to Western Thought*. New York: Basic Books, 1999.

Lamont, Michèle, Ann Morning, and Margarita Mooney. "Particular Universalisms: North African Immigrants Respond to French Racism." *Ethnic and Racial Studies* 25, no. 3 (2002): 390–414.

Latour, Bruno. *We Have Never Been Modern*, trans. Catherine Porter. Cambridge: Harvard University Press, 2006.

Levy, Jacob T. "Contextualism, Constitutionalism, and Modus Vivendi Approaches." *Cultural Pluralism and Political Theory*, ed. Anthony Laden and David Owen. Cambridge: Cambridge University Press, forthcoming.

——. *Multiculturalism of Fear*. New York: Oxford University Press, 2000.

Lewis, Bernard. *Race and Slavery in the Middle East: An Historical Enquiry*. New York: Oxford University Press, 1992.

Linne, Carl von. *A General System of Nature*, vol. 1. London: Lackington, Allen, 1806.

Lugard, Frederick. *The Dual Mandate in Tropical Africa*. London: Frank Cass, 1965.

Lyne, Adrian. *Indecent Proposal*. Los Angeles: Paramount, 2002 [motion picture].

MacDougall, Hugh. "Amazing Grace." Posting to H-NET List for the History of Slavery. H-SLAVERY@H-NET.MSU.EDU (accessed 18 February 2007).

Malebranche, Nicolas. *The Search after Truth*, trans. Thomas M. Lennon and Paul J. Olscamp. Columbus: Ohio State University Press, 1980.

Marechera, Dambudzo. *The House of Hunger*. London: Heinemann, 1982.

Margolis, Joseph. "The Limits of Ethics and History." *Ethics of History*, ed. David Carr, Thomas R. Flynn, and Rudolf A. Makkreel, 172–91. Evanston: Northwestern University Press, 2004.

Marrouchi, Mustapha. "Islam and the West: Unequal Difference/Unequal Distance." *Philosophia Africana* 10, no. 1 (March 2007): 1–34.

Martel, Yann. *Life of Pi*. Edinburgh: Canongate, 2002.

Marx, Karl. *Capital*. New York: Gateway, 1999 [orig. pubd 1867].

McDowell, John. *Mind and World*. Cambridge: Harvard University Press, 1996.

Mead, Margaret. *The World Ahead: An Anthropologist Anticipates the Future*. New York: Berghahn, 2004.

Mignolo, Walter. *The Darker Side of the Renaissance: Literacy, Territoriality, and Colonization*. 2nd ed. Ann Arbor: University of Michigan Press, 2003.

——. *The Invention of the Americas*. Malden, Mass.: Blackwell, 2005.

Minsky, Marvin. *The Emotion Machine: Commonsense Thinking, Artificial Intelligence, and the Future of the Human Mind*. New York: Simon and Schuster, 2006.

Montague, Read. *Why Choose This Book? How We Make Decisions*. New York: Dutton, 2006.

Moody-Adams, Michele. "Reflections on Appiah's *The Ethics of Identity*." *Journal of Social Philosophy* 37, no. 2 (2006): 292–300.

Morning, Ann, and Daniel Sabbagh. 2005. "From Sword to Plowshare: Using Race for Discrimination and Antidiscrimination in the United States." *International Social Science Journal* 57, no. 183 (2005): 57–73.

Moseley, David, Vivienne Baumfield, Julian Elliott, Steven Higgins, Jen Miller, and Maggie Gregson. *Frameworks for Thinking: A Handbook for Teaching and Learning*. New York: Cambridge University Press, 2006.

Moss, Lenny. "The Concept of the Gene and the Future of the Phenotype." *Theoria: Revista de Teoria, Historia y Fundamentos de la Ciencia*, in press.

——. "From Representational Performatism to the Epigenesis of Openness to the World?" *Annals of the New York Academy of Science* 981 (2002): 219–29.

——. *What Genes Can't Do*. Cambridge: MIT Press, 2003.

Mounier, Emmanuel. "Lettre à un ami africain." *L'éveil de l'Afrique Noir*, ed. Alioune Diop, 207–18. Paris: Le Seuil, 1948.

Nagel, Ernest. "Impressions and Appraisals of Analytic Philosophy in Europe." *Journal of Philosophy* 33 (1936): 5–24.

Nandy, Ashis. *Science, Hegemony and Violence*. New Delhi: Oxford University Press, 1991.

Ndebele, Njabulo. *The Cry of Winnie Mandela*. Cape Town: David Philip, 2003.

——. "Of Lions and Rabbits: Thoughts on Democracy and Reconciliation." *After the TRC: Reflections on Truth and Reconciliation in South Africa*, ed. Wilmot James and Linda van de Vijver, 143–54. Cape Town: David Philip, 2000.

Nino, Carlos. "The Duty to Punish Past Abuses of Human Rights Put into Context: The Case of Argentina." *Yale Law Journal* 100 (1991): 2619–40.

Nketia, J. H. Kwabena. *Ethnomusicology and African Music: Modes of Inquiry and Interpretation*. Cape Coast, Ghana: Afram, 2005.

——. *The Music of Africa*. New York: W. W. Norton, 1974.

——. "Musicology and Linguistics: Integrating the Phraseology of Text and Tune in the Creative Process." *Black Music Research Journal* 22, no. 2 (2002): 143–65.

Ntsebeza, Dumisa. "A Lot More to Live For." *After the TRC: Reflections on Truth and Reconciliation in South Africa*, ed. Wilmot James and Linda van de Vijver, 101–6. Cape Town: David Philip, 2000.

Nudelman, Franny. *John Brown's Body: Slavery, Violence, and the Culture of War*. Chapel Hill: University of North Carolina Press, 2004.

Nwauwa, Apollos O. "Kenneth Onwuka Dike." *The Dark Webs: Perspectives on Colonialism*, ed. Toyin Falola, 309–28. Durham: Carolina Academic Press, 2004.

O'Hear, Anthony, ed. *Logic, Thought and Language*. Cambridge: Cambridge University Press, 2002.

Okediji, Moyo. "African Sculptures." http://h-net.msu.edu/cgi-bin/logbrowse.pl ?trx=vx&list=H-AfrArts&month=0701&week=a&msg=oRXxo8Q8Q9BXMK NiORA8YA&user=&pw= (accessed 9 February 2007).

Orwell, George. "Politics and the English Language." *Horizon*, April 1946. Available online at http://www.netcharles.com/orwell/essays/politics-english-lan guage1.htm (accessed 15 November 2006).

Ouologuem, Yambo. *Bound to Violence*. London: Heinemann, 1983.

Oyono, Ferdinand. *Houseboy*. London: Heinemann, 1991.

——. *Old Man and the Medal*. London: Heinemann, 1969.

Page, Scott E. *How the Power of Diversity Creates Better Groups, Firms, Schools, and Societies*. Princeton: Princeton University Press, 2007.

Park, Robert E. "The Nature of Race Relations." *Race Relations and the Race Problem: A Definition and an Analysis*, ed. Edgar T. Thompson, 3–45. New York: Greenwood, 1968.

Patterson, Orlando. *Ethnic Chauvinism: The Reactionary Impulse*. New York: Stein and Day, 1977.

——. "The Speech Misheard Round the World." *New York Times*, 22 January 2005, A, 15.

Peabody, Sue, and Tyler Stovall, eds. *The Color of Liberty: Histories of Race in France*. Durham: Duke University Press, 2003.

Pecher, Diane, and Rolf A. Zwaan. *Grounding Cognition: The Role of Perception and Action in Memory, Language, and Thinking.* New York: Cambridge University Press, 2005.

Peirce, C. S. *The Essential Peirce: Selected Philosophical Writings,* vol. 1, ed. Nathan Houser and Christian Kloesel. Bloomington: Indiana University Press, 1992.

Pettit, Philip. "Groups with Minds of Their Own." In *Socializing Metaphysics,* edited by Frederick F. Schmitt, 167–93. Lanham, Md.: Rowman and Littlefield, 2003.

Piaget, Jean. *Biology and Knowledge.* Chicago: University of Chicago Press, 1971.

———. *Introduction à l'Épistémologie Génétique.* Paris: Presses Universitaires de France, 1950.

———. *Logique et Connaissance scientifique.* Paris: Encyclopédie de la Pléiade, 1967.

———. *The Origins of Intelligence in Children.* London: Routledge, 1953.

———. *La psychologie de l'intelligence.* Paris: Armand Colin, 1991.

———. *Psychology and Epistemology: Towards a Theory of Knowledge.* New York: Penguin, 1972.

———. *Psychology of Intelligence.* New York: Routledge, 2001.

Pinker, Steven. *How the Mind Works.* Cambridge: Harvard University Press, 1997.

Pliny. *Natural History,* trans. H. Rackham, W. H. S. Jones (bks. 20–23), and D. E. Eichholz (bks. 36–37). Cambridge: Harvard University Press, 1938–52.

Popper, Karl. *The Logic of Scientific Discovery.* New York: Basic Books, 1959.

Preidt, Robert. "Blacks, Hispanics Hospitalized More Often for Diabetes, Heart Disease." http://www.omhrc.gov/templates/browse.aspx?lvl=1&lvlID=6 (accessed 2 February 2007).

Putnam, Hilary. *Realism and Reason.* Cambridge: Cambridge University Press, 1983.

———. *Representation and Reality.* Cambridge: MIT Press, 1991.

Putnam, Ruth Anna, ed. *The Cambridge Companion to William James.* Cambridge: Cambridge University Press, 1997.

Quine, Willard V. O. *From a Logical Point of View.* 2nd rev. ed. Cambridge: Harvard University Press, 1961 [orig. pubd 1953].

———. "Two Dogmas of Empiricism." *Philosophical Review* 60 (1951): 20–43.

Ramphele, Mamphela. "Law, Corruption and Morality." *After the TRC: Reflections on Truth and Reconciliation in South Africa,* ed. Wilmot James and Linda van de Vijver, 172–74. Cape Town: David Philip, 2000.

Ravaison, Félix. *De l'habitude: Métaphysique et morale.* Paris: Presses Universitaires de France, 1999 [orig. pubd 1938].

Reed, Adolph L., Jr. "The Real Divide." *Progressive,* November 2005, 27–32.

Rescher, Nicholas. *Error: On Our Predicament When Things Go Wrong.* Pittsburgh: University of Pittsburgh Press, 2007.

Ricoeur, Paul. *Oneself as Another*, trans. Kathleen Blamey. Chicago: University of Chicago Press, 1992.

Rimmer, Douglas, and Anthony Kirk-Greene, eds. *The British Intellectual Engagement with Africa in the Twentieth Century*. New York: St. Martin's, 2000.

Rorty, Richard. "Problems of Rationality." Review of Donald Davidson's *Problems of Rationality* in *Notre Dame Philosophical Review*, http://ndpr.nd.edu/review, 2005.02.01.

———. "Stories of Difference: A Conversation with Richard Rorty," ed. Gaurav Desai. *SAPINA Bulletin* 5, nos. 2–3 (1993): 23–45.

Rotberg, Robert I., and Dennis Thompson, eds. *Truth v. Justice*. Princeton: Princeton University Press, 2000.

Rothman, Barbara Katz. *Genetic Maps and Human Imaginations: The Limits of Science in Understanding Who We Are*. New York: W. W. Norton, 1998.

Royce, Josiah. *The Religious Aspect of Philosophy: A Critique of the Bases of Conduct and of Faith*. New York: Kessinger, 2006.

Rüsen, Jörn. "Responsibility and Irresponsibility in Historical Studies: A Critical Consideration of the Ethical Dimension in the Historian's Work." *Ethics of History*, ed. David Carr, Thomas R. Flynn, and Rudolf A. Makkreel, 195–213. Evanston: Northwestern University Press, 2004.

Russell, Bertrand. "Dewey's New Logic." *The Philosophy of John Dewey*, ed. Paul Arthur Schilpp and Lewis Edwin Hahn, 135–56. Chicago: Open Court, 1989.

———. "On the Notion of Order." *Mind* 10 (1901): 30–51.

———. *The Principles of Mathematics*. New York: W. W. Norton, 1996 [orig. bpud 1903].

Saint-Méry, M. L. E. Moreau de. *Description topographique, physique, civile, politique et historique de la partie française de l'Isle Saint-Domingue, avec des observations générales sur sa population, sur le caractère et les moeurs de ses divers habitans; sur son climat, sa culture, ses productions, son administration, etc. . . .* Philadelphia: Chez l'auteur, au coin de Front et de Callow-Hill Streets, 1797.

Sartre, Jean-Paul. *Existentialism and Human Emotions*. New York: Citadel, 1984.

———. "Existentialism Is a Humanism." *Existentialism from Dostoyevsky to Sartre*, edited by Walter Kaufmann. New York: Meridian, 1989.

———. *Nausea*. New York: New Directions, 1975.

———. *Notebooks for an Ethics*, trans. David Pellauer. Chicago: University of Chicago Press, 1992.

———. *Verité et l'existence*, Paris: Gallimard, 1989.

Schmitt, Frederick F., ed. *Socializing Metaphysics*. Lanham, Md.: Rowman and Littlefield, 2003.

Schopenhauer, Arthur. *The World as Will and Representation*. New York: Peter Smith, 1968 [orig. pubd 1819 as *Die Welt als Wille und Vorstellung*].

Searle, John R. *Freedom and Neurobiology: Reflections on Free Will, Language, and Political Power*. New York: Columbia University Press, 2006.

Senghaas, Dieter. *The Clash within Civilizations: Coming to Terms with Cultural Conflicts*. New York: Routledge, 2001.

Senghor, Léopold Sédar. *Les Fondements de l'Africanité ou Négritude et Arabité*. Paris: Présence Africaine, 1987.

——. *Liberté*, vol. 3: *Négritude et Civilisation de l'Universel*. Paris: Présence Africaine, 1977.

Smith, Daniel Jordan. *A Culture of Corruption: Everyday Deception and Popular Discontent in Nigeria*. Princeton: Princeton University Press, 2006.

Smith, Mark. *The Early History of God: Yahweh and the Other Deities*. Grand Rapids, Mich.: Eerdmanns, 2002.

——. *The Memoirs of God: History, Memory, and the Experience of the Divine in Ancient Israel*. Minneapolis: Augsburg, 2004.

——. *The Origins of Biblical Monotheism: Israel's Polytheistic Background and the Ugaritic Texts*. New York: Oxford University Press, 2003.

Smith, Nicholas S., ed. *Reading McDowell on Mind and World*. New York: Routledge, 2002.

Social Science Research Council. *Is Race "Real"? A Web Forum Organized by the Social Science Research Council*. http://raceandgenomics.ssrc.org/Morning (accessed 5 February 2007).

Soyinka, Wole. *The Burden of Memory, the Muse of Forgiveness*. Oxford: Oxford University Press, 1999.

——. "The Fourth State: Through the Mysteries of Ogun to the Origins of Yoruba Tragedy." *African Philosophy: An Anthology*, ed. Emmanuel C. Eze, 438–46. Oxford: Blackwell, 1998.

——. *Myth Literature and the African World*. Cambridge: Cambridge University Press, 1972.

Spearman, Charles Edward. " 'General Intelligence' Objectively Determined and Measured." *American Journal of Psychology* 15 (1904): 201–93.

Spelman, Elizabeth V. *Fruits of Sorrow: Framing Our Attention to Suffering*. Boston: Beacon, 1998.

——. *Repair: The Impulse to Restore in a Fragile World*. Boston: Beacon, 2003.

Stein, Rob. "FDA Approves Controversial Heart Medication for Blacks." *Washington Post*, 24 June 2005, A, 15.

——. "Heart Drug for Blacks Endorsed: Racial Tailoring Would Be a First." *Washington Post*, 17 June 2005, A, 1.

Steiner, George. *After Babel: Aspects of Language and Translation*. 3rd ed. New York: Oxford University Press, 1998.

Sternberg, Robert. *Cognitive Psychology*. Belmont, Calif.: Wadsworth, 2003.

Steup, Matthias, ed. *Knowledge, Truth, and Duty*. New York: Oxford University Press, 2001.

Stroud, Barry. "Sense-Experience and the Grounding of Thought." *Reading McDowell*, ed. Nicholas S. Smith, 79–91. New York: Routledge, 2002.

Sweet, Timothy. *Traces of War: Poetry, Photography, and the Crisis of the Union*. Baltimore: Johns Hopkins University Press, 1990.

Telles, Edward E. *Race in Another America: The Significance of Skin Color in Brazil*. Princeton: Princeton University Press, 2004.

Tempels, Placide. *La philosophie bantoue*. http://www.aequatoria.be/tempels/Melang3.html (accessed 20 February 2007).

Thomas, Alexander, and Samuel Sillen. *Racism and Psychiatry*. Secaucus, N.J.: Carol Publishing, 1974.

"Toward the First Racial Medicine." *New York Times*, 13 November 2004, A, 14 [editorial].

Trachtenberg, Alan. *Reading American Photographs: Images as History, Mathew Brady to Walker Evans*. New York: Hill and Wang, 1989.

Truillot, Michel-Rolph. *Silencing the Past*. Boston: Beacon, 1997.

Tully, James. *Strange Multiplicity: Constitutionalism in an Age of Diversity*. New York: Cambridge University Press, 1995.

Tully, James, and Daniel M. Wienstock, eds. *Philosophy in an Age of Pluralism: The Philosophy of Charles Taylor in Question*. New York: Cambridge University Press, 1994.

Tutu, Desmond. "Chairperson's Foreword." *Truth and Reconciliation Commission of South Africa Report*, vol. 1, chap. 1. Cape Town: Juta, 1998.

Underwood, Anne. "Black vs. White: Unequal Health Care." *Newsweek*, 24 October 2006.

United Nations. *Durban Declaration of the World Conference against Racism, Racial Discrimination, Xenophobia, and Related Intolerance*. 2001. http://www.unhchr.ch/html/racism (accessed 9 February 2007).

———. *General Assembly Resolution 260 A (III)*, 1948.

———. *International Criminal Tribunal for Rwanda*, http://69.94.11.53/.

———. *International Criminal Tribunal for the Former Yugoslavia*, http://www.un.org/icty/index.html.

———. *U.N.T.S.* No. 1021, vol. 78 (1951), http://www.un.org/Depts/dhl/resguide/r60.htm (accessed 30 January 2007).

Van Zyl Slabbert, Frederik. "Truth without Reconciliation, Reconciliation without Truth." *After the TRC: Reflections on Truth and Reconciliation in South Africa*, ed. Wilmot James and Linda Van de Vijver, 62–72. Cape Town: David Philip, 2000.

Vedantam, Shankar. "Patients' Diversity Is Often Discounted: Alternatives to

Mainstream Medical Treatment Call for Recognizing Ethnic, Social Differences." *Washington Post*, 26 June 2005, A, 1.

Venter, J. Craig. "Human Genome Promise." *R&D Magazine* 41, no. 7 (1999): 40–43.

———. "Genome." *Nature Medicine* 6, no. 11 (2000).

Vico, Giambattista. *The New Science of Giambattista Vico*, trans. Thomas Goddard Bergin and Max Harold Fisch. Ithaca: Cornell University Press, 1968.

Villa-Vicencio, C. "The Perpetrators Should Not Always Be Prosecuted: Where the International Criminal Court and Truth Commissions Meet." *Emory Law Journal* 49 (2000): 101–18.

wa Thiong'o, Ngugi. *Decolonizing the Mind: The Politics of Language in African Literature*. London: James Currey / Heinemann, 1986.

Weber, Max. *The Protestant Ethic and the Spirit of Capitalism*. New York: Routledge, 2001.

White, Hayden. *The Content of the Form: Narrative Discourse and Historical Representation*. Baltimore: Johns Hopkins University Press, 1990.

Williams, Eric. *Capitalism and Slavery*. Chapel Hill: University of North Carolina Press, 1994.

Williams, R. John. "'Doing History': Nuruddin Farah's *Sweet and Sour Milk*, Subaltern Studies, and the Postcolonial Trajectory of Silence." *Research in African Literatures* 37, no. 4 (2006): 238–39.

Wilson, Richard. *Boundaries of the Mind: The Individual in the Fragile Sciences*. New York: Cambridge University Press, 2004.

———. "Collective Memory, Group Minds, and the Extended Mind Thesis." *Cognitive Processing* 6 (2005): 227–36.

———. *The Politics of Truth and Reconciliation in South Africa: Legitimizing the Post-Apartheid State*. Cambridge: Cambridge University Press, 2001.

———, ed. *Human Rights, Culture and Context: Anthropological Perspectives*. London: Pluto, 1996.

———. *Human Rights in Global Perspective: Anthropological Studies of Rights, Claims and Entitlements*. New York: Routledge, 2003.

Winant, Howard. *The New Politics of Race: Globalism, Difference, Justice*. Minneapolis: University of Minnesota Press, 2004.

Wiredu, Kwasi. *Cultural Particulars and Universals*. Indianapolis: Indiana University Press, 1996.

———. *Philosophy and an African Culture*. Cambridge: Cambridge University Press, 1980.

Wittgenstein, Ludwig. "Bemerkungen über Frazers *The Golden Bough*." *Synthese* 17 (1967): 233–53.

———. *Philosophical Investigations*. Oxford: Blackwell, 2002.

Wood, Allen. *Unsettling Obligations: Essays on Reason, Reality, and the Ethics of Belief.* Stanford: CSLI, 2002.

Wood, Peter. *Diversity: The Invention of a Concept.* San Francisco: Encounter, 2002.

Woolf, Virginia. *The Death of the Moth and Other Essays.* New York: Harcourt, 1974.

Wright, Crispin. "Relativism and Classical Logic." *Logic, Thought and Language,* edited by Anthony O'Hear, 95–118. Cambridge: Cambridge University Press, 2002.

Wright, Richard. *Black Power: A Record of Reactions in a Land of Pathos.* New York: Harper, 1995.

Wyschogrod, Edith. *An Ethics of Remembering: History, Heterology, and the Nameless Others.* Chicago: University of Chicago Press, 1998.

——. "Representation, Narrative, and the Historian's Promise." *Ethics of History,* ed. David Carr, Thomas R. Flynn, and Rudolf A. Makkreel, 28–44. Evanston: Northwestern University Press, 2004.

Ya'icob, Zera. "God, Faith, and the Nature of Knowledge." *African Philosophy: An Anthology,* ed. Emmanuel C. Eze, 457–61. Oxford: Blackwell, 1998.

Youe, Chris. "Moving Forward, Staying Still: African Scholarship in the Anti-Colonial Age." *H-Net Book Review,* January 2007.

Young, Iris Marion. *Inclusion and Democracy.* New York: Oxford University Press, 2002.

Zuberi, Tukufi. *Thicker Than Blood: How Racial Statistics Lie.* Minneapolis: University of Minnesota Press, 2003.

Index

EMMANUEL EZE

was an associate professor of philosophy

at DePaul University.

Library of Congress Cataloging-in-Publication Data

Eze, Emmanuel Chukwudi.
On reason : rationality in a world of cultural conflict
and racism / Emmanuel Chukwudi Eze.
p. cm.
Includes bibliographical references and index.
ISBN-13: 978-0-8223-4178-9 (cloth : alk. paper)
ISBN-13: 978-0-8223-4195-6 (pbk. : alk. paper)
1. Reason. 2. Culture conflict. 3. Multiculturalism.
4. Ethnicity. 5. Philosophy, African. I. Title.
BC177.E94 2008
128'.33—dc22   2007044868